SCRAPBOOK OF THE AMERICAN WEST

ERNEST L. REEDSTROM'S

SCRAPBOOK

OF THE

AMERICAN WEST

The CAXTON PRINTERS, Ltd.

Caldwell, Idaho

1991

Edited by Gib Crontz & Francis Katz

Reedstrom, Ernest Lisle.
    Scrapbook of the American West / by Ernest Lisle Reedstrom.
        p.   cm.
    Includes bibliographical references and index.
    ISBN 0-87004-303-X : $17.95
    1. West (U.S.)--Civilization--Miscellanea.   2. Material culture--West (U.S.)--Miscellanea.
    I. Title.
    F591.R4176   1990
    978′, 02--dc20   90-43034
                                                                                                                CIP

Cover and book design by Teresa Sales.

Lithographed and bound in the United States of America by
The CAXTON PRINTERS, Ltd.
Caldwell, Idaho
141636

To Gib Crontz

CONTENTS

ILLUSTRATIONS

# ACKNOWLEDGEMENTS

When I finish a book I always leave the acknowledgements for the end. It's almost like saying goodbye to old friends, shaking hands with them for the last time. I don't want to think that way. I have great hopes of recalling each and every one back to work on another book, when the next one presents itself on the horizon.

This goodbye is especially sad, as I lost my best friend, neighbor, and editor, Gilbert Crontz, while working on this book. Gibby was most knowledgeable in weapons—both antique and single shot. He loaded his own shells and taught me many things . . . reloading, as well as basic English. While proofreading a manuscript, Gib checked every fact and questioned anything that might be flawed. It was a great pleasure to work with him, and without his re-tracing words and sentences, double checking my findings, and rewording, this book could not have been written. To Gibby, wherever you are, pard, I thank you. Your friendly voice in conversations is deeply missed, as is your presence, noted by your chair, sitting empty in my studio. God willing, pard, we'll meet on some distant frontier and reminisce of those better days. To you, Gilbert Crontz, a man who cannot be replaced in my estimation, I dedicate this book.

To my wife Shirley, who thoughtfully took over all of the household responsibilities, including cutting the grass, planting and canning, and relieving me of all of those many duties so I could continue work uninterrupted, A special thank you. Without your help, I could never have completed the manuscript on time.

My appreciation to my daughter Karen Reedstrom for her editorial comments, to Rebecca M. Crabb of Buckley Farm Homestead in Lowell, Indiana, to buckskinner Don Good and to military artists Phil Rodeghiero and Jim Nemeth, I thank you.

Photographs sometimes take the place of models,

and I thank the Arizona Historical Society; Smithsonian Institute; Newberry Library (Chicago); Nebraska State Historical Society; National Archives in Washington; artist Ron Bork; Joe Gish Collection of McAllen, Texas; Gordon Swope, Lincoln, Nebraska; Richard Ignarski of Albuquerque, New Mexico; Editor Phil Spangenberger of *Guns and Ammo*, Los Angeles, California; The Union Pacific Railroad Museum Collection; and, historian and author, Carl Breihan.

Jim and Karen Boeke of the River Junction Trade Company, McGregor, Iowa, provided special realism with their reproductions of unavailable clothing, holsters, saddles and outfit. These creative, enthusiastic geniuses will make the special pieces to "spec" in the outside chance that their catalog does not contain what is needed. Thanks!

Another outstanding source of authentic Americana is George A. Willhauck, Military and Americana Materials in North Hampton, New Hampshire. His catalogs arrive once a month, and almost always lists some piece—Civil War candle holders, badges, documents—you name it—that was unobtainable through normal channels.

The Red River Frontier Outfitters makes frontier clothing and military uniforms used by Hollywood film makers, and provide great descriptions as well as actual articles. They operate from Tunjunga, California. The owners are Phil Spangenberger and Clarence Streese.

A special thanks to Bob Schmidt, who operates the White Buffalo Leather Shop in Corvallis, Montana, for his permission to show his fine saddlery, especially the historically accurate models dating from the 1820s.

Costumes for re-enactments of battles are a specialty of Burgess & Company in Meriden, Connecticut. His military uniforms are historically accurate, and his help was greatly appreciated.

The proprietor of Old West Gun Leathers is Rod Castle, Eugene, Oregon, an excellent researcher and careful craftsman. Thank you, Rod, for your help in finding holsters and other outfits that look and feel like they were used in the old West.

Joe Covais is a historical tailor who operates in Charleston, Illinois, from an interesting shop. He works his magic from original articles. He uses cloth of the same weight and pattern as the original and copies the original stitching, even hand picking.

Fast-draw artist, author and historian George E. Virgines supplied a number of photos from his collection, and Jerry Rakusan, editor of *Guns Magazine*, has permitted me to use a number of articles and photographs that I had written in the past, published in the magazine. And, a thank you to *Guns and Ammo* Magazine and Peterson Publishing for their photo fillers.

Dotty and Al Massena, Victor Studios of Merrillville, Indiana, did some fantastic work on the black and white photos reproduced in this volume. Dotty's special technique for fading out a crack in a glass plate or retouching is something to witness. She has brought back the original look to old photos. Husband Al, has done top work in photographing special shots with models—without making them look posed. My great thanks to these two talented people.

William Graf and wife Mary have supplied out-of-print books that I have needed for more than fifteen years from their book shop in Iowa City, Iowa. The Grafs are energetic and nonstop searchers for the hard to find. They have managed to fill my every request, and they continue to amaze me with their ability.

And, my many thanks to Debbie Higgins, who types my manuscripts with accuracy and speed. Debbie, a graduate of the University of Illinois's Circle Campus with a Major in Spanish and Minor in History, has her own word processing business, Type Tech.

For technical assistance, I am indebted to Alan Feldstein for his critical views in weapons and military accouterments. Lastly, to Bob Craig who has acted as model, technical guide in military uniforms, and associate editor for this volume, I send a special thank you.

E. Lisle Reedstrom

INTRODUCTION

America and defeat cannot be made
to rhyme.

Eric A. Johnston
America Unlimited [1944]

I truly believe the subject matter of this book typifies the significance of that quote! America, by never believing in defeat, was made a great and glorious country by the very people depicted in the book, both the good and the bad, and by their indomitable spirit exemplified by their unique ingenuity.

This "sketchbook" is truly encyclopedic, and perhaps this word would have been a better choice for a title to at least indicate the scope and totality justified by the text. It is more like a "What You've Always Wanted To Know About _____ But Were Afraid To Ask!" book, and I, for one, am glad Lisle Reedstrom has the knowledge and skill to carry it off successfully.

For years now I've had to go from one source book to another in an effort to justify something I had written, wanted to write, or to footnote an observation by yet another writer. That exhausting procedure can now be alleviated, much to my relief, because there is no need to search beyond a single volume. Oft' times I am faced with the problem of having to identify a specific mode of transportation, or clothing or weapon used in a specific period. Lisle has now made it possible for me to have this information at my fingertips, not scattered throughout a library.

There are many authorities on specific subjects, a few who can boast of being an authority on some subjects, but not very many can state categorical authoritativeness on many subjects; Lisle Reedstrom can, as my telephone bills to him attest. He is always the first person I call when stuck on a simple technicality concerning things military in general and that which is western in particular. I know

people to whom I could turn when information was needed on western transportation, and even a specialist on just wagons. The same applies to almost all of the categories covered in this book. Apparently this is an age of historical specialization, so you medical doctors best move over. What a relief to have just one authoritative source!

One has only to turn to the military tactical manuals and other technical publications for horses, tactics, guidons and scouting. And there are various editions of each intending to up-date each as the years pass, and the technology of war becomes more sophisticated. Though removing arrows may be the least subject written upon, the major source is still the Surgeon General's *Report #3*, and it is very difficult to find, and expensive when you do find it. The balance of the subjects, except Gripes perhaps, must be found in obscure and long out-dated manuals published by the U. S. Government over the years. To have a synthesis of all this material in one reference is like having Federal budget explained on one page.

So, as best as I can determine, this will be the only single up-dated source for informative material of this nature and scope I know to exist. And that which I have just outlined is but one category in the book!

Lisle wrote and illustrated *Bugles, Banners and War Bonnets*, a definitive book on the Indian wars and the Little Big Horn in general. It won the third place Spur Award given by the Western Writers of America as the best non-fiction book for that year. It deserved that reward; but to have written it, the sum total of this author's memory bank data had to be brought to the fore. It was no accident such a book was written, no, indeed! It actually represented years of research, accumulation of information, countless illustrations, much trial and error and many successes, and most of all, a strong willingness to share this knowledge that made this particular book possible. His research prior to the standard this book has become, resulted in dozens of articles for as many different publications that are as varied as they are in number. Included are *Guns Magazine*, *True Frontier*, *Western Horseman* and *Guns And Ammo* plus many more. The current book he is working to illustrate, Greg Urwin's *The Illustrated Story Of The U.S. Cavalry*, will become, again, one of those "cannot do without" standards because of the fantastic illustrations he will have created for the book, accurate to the smallest detail. In my opinion they are far superior to those which have for years accompanied the publications of *The Company Of Military Historians*.

Unlike many art historians of today, and that really is Lisle's best description, Lisle has breathed the history about which he has written and illustrated. To me, that is as important as having the knowledge gained from secondary sources. Bob Utley, my favorite historian, once said to me that it is impossible to write about a subject until you have seen, walked and breathed the history, touching it, too, if possible. I could not agree more. This concept requires energy, patience, time and above all, money. Lisle has given generously of all in order to fulfill his destiny, that of a premier art historian. We are all richer for his many sacrifices, and only another writer can really appreciate the sacrifices which must be made. The only return that can be counted upon is the compliments paid by students and scholars.

Yes, America and defeat cannot be made to rhyme, and Lisle Reedstrom has illustrated most graphically this inexpungable, unconquerable grit and stamina, and has made it more believable. What he has written about is our true heritage.

John M. Carroll
Bryan, Texas

SCRAPBOOK OF THE AMERICAN WEST

CHAPTER I
THE INDIANS

The few white explorers and trappers that roamed the West before 1800 referred to the native Americans as "The Indians." It sounds as if the Indians were a homogeneous people, and nothing could be further from the truth. The Indians—even the name is misleading—were as diverse as the lands they inhabited. The area—roughly west of the Mississippi and Missouri Rivers to the Pacific and south to the central portion of Mexico—was a trackless wilderness to the white man in the early 1800s. The Indians, however, had it neatly divided and marked by signposts and boundaries. Only the white man couldn't read the tribal maps.

Trappers and traders estimated the total Indian population in the western area at about a million. But Indians didn't like to be counted, and white men were seldom allowed in the camps. Indian parents were especially careful about letting their children be seen and some tribes thought it immoral for white men to observe their women. So the estimates were a best guess and could have been far off the mark.

There were at least six hundred distinct societies among the Indians—six hundred nations—with a number of subsocieties within. Different tribes had specific racial characteristics as would be expected of peoples arriving from different parts of the globe. Some tribes came across the land bridge from Russia, some were distinctly Oriental, others came from Island cultures. The Eskimos of the northern lands were from the Incas to the south physically different in appearance and from the eastern Indians with their Scandinavian mixtures. Not only did they look different, but their languages were traceable to different root stocks.

In the early 1820s, there were at least 250 different languages and dialects, more than all of the languages found in Europe and Asia combined. Studies of these tongues revealed fifty-eight ancestral parent families or root stocks. The ethnologists were able to divide the Indians into seven cultural areas, including the Eastern Woodlands, Southeastern Woodlands, Plains, Plateaus, Southwesterns, Californias and Northwestern Coastals. Each group within the cultural area had its own version of language, its own characteristic dress, its own particular kind of dwelling, and its own rituals. Until the white man began to crowd the Indians, the tribes had their own hunting areas and sacred lands for burial and worship. Battles, when they occurred, were over cultural differences—some of the tribes were quite warlike, others were very peaceful. But as the lands began to shrink from the movements of whites, the Indians found peace more difficult.

The concept of individual ownership, especially of land, was foreign to most Indian cultures. Most tribes were at least semi-nomadic, hunted instead of farmed, and they roamed within an ill-defined area. For these tribes, the idea of soil having a specific worth was not something natural to them. While some Indians farmed—the Zuni and Pueblo, for instance—and understood the value of the soil, most of the western Indians did not.

As the lands and the number of buffalo began to shrink, Indians began to have an idea that the land was worth something to the white man. They noticed that white men would pay for parcels of land instead of fighting for it. So they sold land for guns and blankets—without really understanding what they

1

were selling—and were forced farther and farther west. As the tribes crowded into smaller areas, conflicts became more common and more bloody. This movement not only increased warring between the tribes, it also spread smallpox and other white man's disease. The Indian population began to shrink.

Piegan dandy

While cowboy and Indian thrillers depict Indians as wild, murderous savages, in truth they lived according to a specific moral code. Interest in spirits was aimed at keeping evil spirits away more than an interest in an afterlife, at least among early Indians. The tribes worshipped many gods, although many tribes had a special god that they called something like Great Spirit. If one tribe's Great Spirit was stronger than another tribe's Great Spirit on any given day, victory over the rival was likely. But the Great Spirits had their good days and bad days. The

white man's myth that Indians believed in a very Christian-like Happy Hunting Ground where the noble red man went as a reward, was wishful thinking, at least until white beliefs were known to the Indians.

The source of the belief that Indians worshipped a single Great Spirit came from a late attempt to unite the western tribes through a religion called Ghost Dance that emerged briefly about 1889. A Paiute Indian named Wovoka, adopted as a boy by a white settler named David Wilson, had a vision of being lifted to the sky by the Great Spirit. The young man reported that all of the old time Indians lived a happy life in this new land. A new dance, taught to Wovoka by the Great Spirit, was to unite the tribes in peace. The message was that Indians should stop fighting each other and live a good life so that all dead Indians and buffalo would come back to life, and no one would be sick or old or hungry. The Ghost Dance, seen when Wovoka was delirious with fever, was used by some Indian leaders as a rallying point to carry on war against the white man.

Indians governed their tribes with a variety of rudimentary forms of government. Usually the responsible males met in some kind of council, often

Mandan

planning for war or for moving the tribe to a new hunting area. The men would speak, one by one, airing any grievances or offering plans. Often members of friendly tribes were invited to attend the councils.

As the 1800s wore on, councils became frequent, as the tribes tried to find ways to prevent more white encroachment onto their lands. As treaty after treaty was made and broken, the tribal councils became more and more indignant. War parties were planned and battles carried out.

If the battles were not necessarily immediate, several weeks might be set aside for preparation. Before a war party left the main camp, tribes devoted themselves to a round of merrymaking. They gambled, raced horses, and held athletic contests. Feasting was endless during the days before the war party set out, and great bonfires were lighted for dancing and chanting of their war rituals. Their faces

Old man

and bodies were painted in different designs, and their hair was dressed with beads and feathers. Each warrior created his own dance, but the pulsing, rushing rhythm of the drums and chanting formed the different steps and patterns into a churning frenzy. As the frenzy reached an emotional peak, and the warriors prepared to burst from camp and fight their enemies, the women gathered and began to weep and wail with the sound of keening, as they begged their war-gods to bring their braves victory

and to sustain their lives. Then, with a shout, the men mounted their horses, using only braided horsehair lassos wrapped around the animals' lower jaws and secured with two half-hitch knots. Most of the Indians used no saddles and no other protection. Instead, the men leaned to one side or the other of the horse, using their mounts as a kind of shield to ward off enemy fire.

While in an emotional frenzy, painted and riding like banshees, the Indian war party was a frightening thing to see. When attacking a wagon train or such, the Indian raiders would ride in a tightening circle, fast as the very wind, howling and yelling. At first, the warriors would keep some distance, usually outside the easy firing range for the settlers. Then, as the settlers were worn down and thoroughly fearful, some of the braves became more daring and rode closer to the white party, firing somewhat erratically at the wagon train to confuse and possibly stampede the animals. When this strategy worked, a handful of the warriors separated from the main raiding party to round up the herd and drive it to the Indian camp. The rest of the raiders continued to terrorize the settlers, preventing any of them from escaping to regain their cattle and spare horses.

Before the tribes gained muskets, the white settlers had the upper hand during an attack. The Indian weapons—bow and arrow, spear, lance, tomahawk—while handled expertly and often in a deadly

Indian warrior charging an enemy.

Sioux

fashion, were effective only at a short range. Even the most expert of the Indian archers did not understand how to compensate for wind, motion or distance, and their arrows often were wasted.

To compensate for the difficulties with the manual weapons, many tribes of the Plains developed attacking strategies that substituted brilliance for firepower. When attacking a wagon train, the tribes surrounded the circled wagons, drawing the settlers fire at various points around the circumference and keeping just out of range until the settlers had to reload muskets or were simply out of ammunition. Then the Indians would rush the settlers, destroying the train and possibly carrying off women and children as slaves for the tribe.

Indians would attack at any point where the settlers could be overcome by force of numbers. In open range battle, the Indian was almost always mounted and was virtually always a dazzling horseman. The speed and skill of riding the Indian ponies was astounding, and the ferocity with which the

Indians attacked reminded the settlers of wild buffalo. Each charge was often closer than the last, bringing with it a rain of arrows. After each charge, the Indian would retire quickly, frustrating the settler who was unable to get off a good shot.

The early battles with the Indian tribes featured arrows, hatchets, and knives; by the early 1800s, trade guns were being distributed to the Indians as a matter of public policy. These weapons changed the kind of fighting between settler and Indian. There were three names that came under the heading of 'trade guns' that were either sold or traded to the American Indians: the "Hudson's Bay fusil," the "Mackinaw gun," and the "Northwest gun." In order for the "Noble Red Warrior of the Prairies" to compete successfully in the contest for survival, the white man's 'thunder stick' was in great demand. By 1800, the Hudson Bay Company designed a lightweight weapon of from five to six pounds, short barreled, and constructed in a simple fashion. All were smoothbore, shooting a one ounce ball or about a .66 diameter. There were some of a smaller caliber. Of course, many other weapons came from different manufacturers in the United States and from Europe.

The design of the weapon, especially its trigger guard, was made primarily for the Northern portion of the United States, because of cold weather. The enlarged iron trigger guard permitted a gloved

Cheyenne

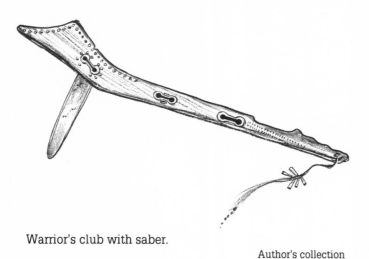

Warrior's club with saber.

Author's collection

4

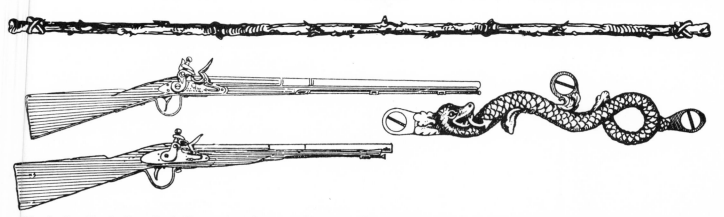

The Indian Trade Gun. Both illustrations here are flintlocks. On the right is the famous brass side plate in the form of a twisted sea serpent or dragon. When trading pelts for weapons, Indians always watched for this design.

Courtesy *Firearms, Traps & Tools of the Mountain Men,* C.P. Russell

finger to enter the opening and depress the trigger for ignition.

Indian trade guns were commonly used from 1775 to 1875, and one of these weapons would bring a price of twenty winter-killed beaver skins. These weapons were popular with many Indian tribes because they were ideally suited to their way of life. It was light enough to be carried on horseback, easy to load, and deadly enough to knock down almost any huge animal. When running buffalo on horseback, Indian hunters would pour black powder down the barrel by hand and, from a cache of lead balls in their cheeks, spit the ball from their mouths down on top of the powder. This was copied from the white hunters.

The western plains were a supermarket to the Indians. Everything was in abundance. They only took what they needed, and consumed what they took. The Indian was as shrewd as the animal he was hunting. The white man's "thunder stick" changed the Indian's way of hunting. The 'approach' was no longer needed. At 300 to 400 yards, an Indian could down a bull with hardly any effort at all. However, in the early days, a brave could send a single arrow completely through a running buffalo.

Painting by E.L. Reedstrom
Courtesy of the Gib Crontz Collection

Absaroka

circumstances, there was a great likelihood that the explosion would cause the light iron cylinder to rip open at a point just below the ball. As a result of such an accident, it was not at all uncommon for the hunter to lose an eye or a hand. However, not all trade guns were booby-traps, for even superior weapons might be expected to blow up under careless handling by the Indians.

The trade gun sported a brass side plate in form of a twisted sea serpent or dragon, and when trading, many tribes often watched for this design. Experts today speculate that this was a form of superstition. While percussion caps were not readily available to the Indian, flintlocks were always useful in far away camps and could continually be relied upon for hunting or warfare.

The bursting of the fusils can be easily understood since they rode horseback at breakneck speed and exercised little care in the seating of the musket ball upon the power charge. Often, while pointing the weapon, the ball would roll away from the powder charge and lodge somewhere in the barrel far from its proper place. When the rifle was fired under such

Brule Sioux

Absaroka

Why would the government permit the distribution of quality, if plain, muskets to the Indians who were attacking their constituency? This seemingly suicidal action began as part of a policy first described by Thomas Jefferson in 1803—that certain Indians be removed from their lands to permit expansion of white settlements. At this early time, the Indians to be moved were eastern tribes, and they were to be transported to "permanent lands" west of the Missouri and Arkansas rivers. President James Monroe endorsed the plan, and it was carried out by later presidents. The cost of agreement by the

Indians was frequently that they be given rifles and ammunition so that they could hunt buffalo.

Because the principle of death was not understood in the same way by Indians as by whites, Indians had no fear of meeting death in battle or otherwise. Early tribes believed that life continued after death, exactly as it had been before death occurred. While this existence was expected, it was seen as no better—no "Happy Hunting Ground"—and anything befalling the body in this life would continue to plague the person afterward as well. Thus, mutilation of the body of an enemy would continue to bother that enemy into eternity—although there was no clear concept of eternity, either. Indians were sent to their resting place with tools needed to earn a living and weapons to protect him. Burial grounds varied, but it was usually taboo to touch anything in the burial grounds. To do so would bring down wrath, either from the departed himself, or some greater spirit.

Arapahoe

Fool Bull, a well-respected medicine man in the Sioux, opposed the white man's laws and treaties until his own death.

Art by E.L. Reedstrom

Indian tribes continued to be removed from their lands with promises of money, guns, weapons, and other assistances. Most of these promises were kept in a cursory fashion until the Civil War drained the treasury. Tribes who had begun to depend heavily on government rations were unprepared or unwilling to fend for themselves that first winter of the Civil War, and the discontent grew and spread from tribe to tribe.

As winter came closer, the chiefs who had signed treaties that made the Indians virtual wards of the state grumbled and demanded immediate delivery of the promised powder, lead, rifles, blankets, and cattle. When the deliveries were not forthcoming, the tribes took matters into their own hands—along with rifles and other assorted weapons.

As the Civil War deepened, troops posted on the Plains were moved to the eastern battle sites. As the soldiers left the plains for the battles that would decide whether the Union would survive or split, the angry Indians became bolder and bolder.

The Homestead Act of 1862 and the building of a railroad from East to West brought more and more settlers to the western lands, and the Indians were again moved into less desirable areas. During the

1860s, the Sioux, headed by Red Cloud and other strong chiefs who had remained independent of the debilitating effects of what amounted to welfare, protected Sioux territories against white encroachment. Many of these warriors had survived the battles in Minnesota, (the original homeland of the Sioux) and had moved to the Dakotas during relocation.

Then, in the early 1870s, gold fever ran like a plague through the area. The outpouring of miners and prospectors was too much for the tribes to easily keep from their borders, and battles increased. General George Crook ordered the Sioux onto a reservation promising that the reservation would be respected, and no whites would be allowed to pass onto the land. Chief Sitting Bull and the younger chief called Crazy Horse refused to corral their people into a reservation. Sitting Bull is said to have shouted, astride his horse and brandishing his weapon "We are an island of The People in a lake of white men. If the pony soldiers want war, we will give them war like they have never seen." The result was called Custer's Last Stand. Sitting Bull then moved his band into Canada, then returned to the Standing Rock Reservation in South Dakota. Later, at the end of the century in 1890, a final Sioux uprising occurred as the white miners and prospectors came closer and closer to the Indians' last domain.

Sitting Bull was shot during an attempt by whites to arrest him, and Big Foot, then chief of a group of Sioux, led the warriors to battle at Wounded Knee. The Sioux were massacred.

While the Sioux were attempting to keep their lands in the northern part of the Great Plains, the Southern Plains were also a site of battle. The Sand Creek Massacre of 1864 consolidated tribes including the Arapaho, Cheyenne, Comanche, and Kiowa to punish the white troops for killing warriors, old men, women, and children. After that push by the army, Indian raids became more common and more frightening. In 1874, General Philip Sheridan led a campaign against the Southwestern tribes. The General who had burned Atlanta now subdued the Indian tribes after fourteen bloody battles called the Red River War.

A typical early Sioux Indian 'war shirt,' circa 1880. When most Indians arrived on the designated reservations, they made changes on their garments. Shown here is a war shirt with beaded strips across the front showing the American flag; in this way, the Indian expressed his sincerity to the U.S. government.

Private collection

Battle after battle occurred during these years, all over the West. The Walker War and Black Hawk War between the Utes and Mormon settlers, the Cayuse War in Oregon, the Modoc War in Tule Lake, California, the Nez Perce War in Montana, and the Apache struggles in the Southwest nearly eliminated many of the tribes. The few that did survive either took up the white man's ways or retired to the poverty of the reservation.

The west was safe for homesteading and development by the white man. The Indians were now peaceful. Or dead.

Hairstyles of the Western American Indian

Little has been written on the late nineteenth century American Indian's hairstyles, citing the limited amount of sources available. The subject is not as common as Indian lore, trade or peace pipes, or already documented Indian every-day wear.

Braided or loose hair styles were most common with our Western American Indians simply because it was part of an every day costume. Any special adornment of feathers, beads, scalp locks, or bird heads had a special meaning to the individual, and he or she would dress with it, usually for tribal meetings or great occasions.

Spotted Eagle—Sioux.

Art by E.L. Reedstrom

Feathers displayed by warriors revealed their bravery in battle. Shown here:
1. Killed an enemy
2. Cut enemy throat
3. Cut throat and scalped enemy
4. Many wounds

Art by E.L. Reedstrom

The early Arapaho tribesmen claim that their men parted their hair on each side while leaving the hair over the forehead standing upright. Over the temples it was cut into a zig-zag pattern. The hair fell down in front of the ears and was either braided or tied together. This was similar to the style of the Crows.

The Crow men were very handsome. Many early travelers were impressed by seeing a finely dressed Crow Indian in elegant costume with long glossy hair. In an ingenious way, the Crows added strands of hair to lengthen their own locks until it dragged to the ground. The scalp lock was a pompadour swept upward and stiffened. Ornaments were attached to this in loud colors beckoning the enemy to lift it. This same pompadour was sufficiently common to be

glossy, manageable, and soft. As long hair was mostly the custom, many younger women allowed the hair to hang far down the back, often reaching the hips. Another favorite style was to gather the hair into a thick mass resembling a 'beaver tail' and let fall down to the rear of the head. This style was generally adorned with ornaments and sacred wrappings.

Although combs were non-existent, plains Indians brushed their hair with the rough side of a buffalo tongue or with a porcupine tail mounted on a branch of a tree and bound with rawhide; or as among the Omaha, a brush of stiff grass at one end, woven about a wooden or bone handle. A common feminine style was to part the hair in the middle, from the forehead to the nape of the neck, then paint the parting line red. Blackfoot girls used two braids, letting each braid hang down loose behind their ears, tying it with a forehead band.

Any Indian with a rank in a tribal society wrapped his braided hair in animal skins of his choosing. The bright red felt fabrics that emigrants brought across the prairies caught the Indian's eye, and other colored silks or brightly colored fabrics were fashionable.

After the Indians settled down on the white man's agencies, he was ordered to wear a 'Citizen's dress.' The Department of Indian Affairs insisted that the Indian must cut his hair short and give up wearing braids. No Indian could be employed by an agent until he had his hair cut. Many agency Indians resented this, and when the government saw this, the order was not enforced. As the Indian took pride in his hair, it would pain him and humble him in the eyes of the white man if he had to cut it. To the white man, long hair was the symbol of old Indian ways. Another requirement was for the Indian to wear a beard. Since Indians pulled out facial hairs, the required beard was a sorry, straggling affair.

Many army scouts were able to smell an Indian a mile away. The reason for this was simple. The Indian prepared many formulas to stiffen the hair, and animal and human urine were among the added solutions to the sticky salve which dried like iron. When the warrior was caught down wind, any scout who knew the odor could give warning, even though the Indian or Indians were well out of sight.

Low Dog—Sioux.

Art by E.L. Reedstrom
Courtesy of *Old Army Press*

used as a tribal mark, as shown in Dakota pictographs. In earlier times, the Crow men divided their hair roughly into two parts and let it fall loosely down their backs and the sides of their faces. They were also conspicuous for the use of artificial adornments to the hair in the back.

The Sioux men wore such ornaments as earrings of dentalium shells, necklaces of bear claws, gorgets of mussel shell carved in button-like form, beaded chokers and quilled braid wrappings. They also fastened a trail of silver trade discs attached to a long leather band to their hair. Each of these fashionable attachments were to enhance the individual's dress. Other ornaments were worn in a manner to signify tribal status. Younger, unmarried men wore a band of quilling surmounted by two feathers from which hung a lock of horse hair tied to their scalp locks, reaching below the shoulder blades.

Young Indian women took pride in good care of their hair. Since their hair was always glossy black, and seldom turned grey, no special dyes were used to tint the hair.

Bear fat was the principal dressing. It kept the hair

The Indian Blanket

The blanket was the all purpose garment. It served as identification, as a way of signaling, and as a way of telling many things such as status or mood of the wearer.

For instance, bachelors in many tribes advertised the fact of their bachelorhood by wearing their blanket to cover their right shoulder, low in back and over the left hip. The corners met in the front middle, where it was secured by a casual forefinger and thumb, exposing the heart—to the cold and the warmth of attention.

A young married man draped his blanket around his shoulders and clutched it at the chest. As he aged, the blanket dipped to the waist, bunched or tucked into loose folds. The hunter or warrior wrapped the blanket tightly around his waist, tying it into a knot over his right hip. This kept the blanket in place, and allowed him to mount and dismount his horse easily without having to use his hands to keep track of a blanket.

In addition to everyday ways of wearing the blanket, many tribes had a more formal way of dressing—for meetings and tribal councils. At these occasions, blankets were partly folded around the rib cage, with the end carried over the forearm.

When the Indian addressed a large council, he would wear his blanket tightly around his chest, under his arms. The left hand held the end of the blanket, and the left arm was covered by the loosely draping blanket.

When the Indian meditated, either on a solemn occasion or to escape the everyday pressures of family and in-laws all living in the same area, he would throw the blanket over his head, exposing only his nose and eyes. This was a signal that conversation was unwelcome, and this was respected by tribal members. If the blanket was hanging loosely over the head and body, the Indian was signaling that he was angry and wanted to be left alone.

Tracking Moccasins

No two tribes cut and sewed their moccasins alike; toe and heel shapes were different. Some moccasins had an animal tail or a heavy long fringe attached at the heel, which was said to obliterate or wipe out the tracks as the wearer walked. However, the trail impressions showed the slithering marks of heavy fringe or loose trinkets that hung from the moccasins.

When a young brave was being taught how to identify an enemy's tracks, whether it was an Indian's or a white man's, his sharp eyes searched for every available sign. When the impressions showed that the toes of each track pointed inward it was probably made by an Indian. White men walked with their toes pointed outward and often a heavy man's foot-prints showed either a left or right foot track to form a similar pattern—that is pointing forward, whereas the opposite foot might point further outward.

An expert tracker could tell by studying tracks whether the enemy was running or walking by observing the impression of the ball of the foot; the runners were deeper than a normal walk. If the pursued was trying to throw his pursuer off the trail by walking backward, his steps would be shorter and

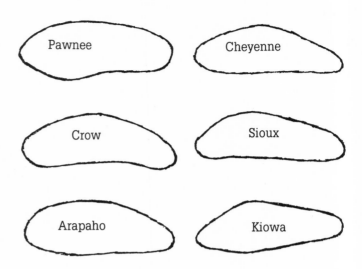

Moccasin soles and their shapes.

irregular in spacing. Heel marks would be deeper and besides there wouldn't be any scuffing at the toe. If walking forward in the snow, the toe impression would show snow being pushed down instead of broken "surface snow" being pushed up when walking backwards.

Snowshoes

The early use of snowshoes can be traced back to 4000 B.C., in Central Asia where evidence suggests that this device served as a foot-extender for easier travel over the snow. Had it not been for this simple early device made out of branches and bark, aboriginal people could not have expanded over the Northern hemisphere and survived. These northward migrations began somewhere from a central point in Asia into what are now known as Scandinavia, Siberia, and the Americas. This quest was not only for territorial rights, but for food and skins—and the lust for adventure. With these early snowshoes, explorers could travel over the heaviest of snows with ease, where it would be impossible for a human to walk without them.

As years drifted by, different innovations were introduced by various tribes. It was found that the branches and bark did not last very long, leaving a stranded hunter or venturer immobile. To rectify this, warm animal skins from a fresh kill, stripped and wrapped around a bent birch limb in cross sections, and frozen, was a much sturdier contrivance. But, when warm weather thawed the ice, the snowshoe with its animal skin strips thawed as well. Another solution was sought.

The most effective snow shoe came about when oil and the secretion from the Lac insect, better known as "shellac" (or closely related to it) was used to coat the animals' strips in order to saturate and harden the strips. The user of the snowshoe coated these strips

Snowshoes, as illustrated here, were generally handmade by both Indians and the white man. They also could be purchased from white traders or at any Hudson Bay trader's store. There were a number of these stores located throughout the Northwest. It wasn't uncommon to see Indian ponies traveling on short oval-type snowshoes to keep their hooves from sinking into huge snow banks.

Author's Collection

often to insure protecting against any deterioration. This process, or one similar to it, is still practiced today with a stronger hardening compound in the shellac (or a liquid plastic) saturating the leather crosshatch thongs.

The great innovations in snowshoe designs would have to be attributed to the Indians as they tended to move into the forested temperate zone where snowshoes were an absolute necessity for getting around

during the winter. Eskimos, living in the polar regions, did not find snowshoes essential for they traveled mostly over windpacked snow of the tundra and over sea ice. Snowshoes are not too often seen among Eskimo hunting bands. Indians of the American and Canadian west coast and the Algonquin Indians of the Ottawa and St. Lawrence River Valley areas brought the snowshoe to the highest peak of perfection. Beginning with a bearpaw design, they fabricated hundreds of patterns suited to all possible conditions. Even before the Spaniards introduced the horse in America, the Plains Indians used the snowshoe to hunt buffalo. It can safely be said that one common cultural characteristic of all the Indian tribes in any region where snow covered the ground was the snowshoe.[1]

Around the 1600s, when the French began to colonize the St. Lawrence River area, they probably were the first white people to use the snowshoe. As the French mingled freely with the Indians, they quickly learned how to make the best snowshoe during the winter months and the best canoe in summer.

The famous 1758 Battle on Snowshoes near Lake George in the Adirondacks led military leaders to realize how important snowshoes were in fighting a mock battle during winter. From that time on, the English colonies (later to become the United States), made snowshoes a part of their basic military equipment. During the great Northwest invasion of fur trappers and hunters, the snowshoe was found to be indispensable. During these times, both Indians and white men usually made their own snowshoes according to the patterns made by the Indians long before the bearded trappers and hunters came to North America.

The art of manufacturing snowshoes by small Indian groups of today is still practiced. And, surprisingly, it is found that a number of snowshoe clubs have carried on this tradition as a sport such as the various ski tournaments that occur each year. Snowshoes have not been completely displaced, especially in Canada's Province of Quebec where the use of snowshoes is firmly rooted in tradition.

The Bow and Arrow

Of all weapons that stand out over thousands of years of history, the bow and arrow deserves a comfortable spot as 'King of the Hill.' Even though todays' gun powder has pushed this primitive weapon aside, few people realize how effective the bow and arrow can be. Its history is dignified and heroic, as no single implement was standard equipment for hunting and warfare for so long. In our own plains and uncivilized west, the bow and arrow of the Indian warrior stood up effectively against the blackpowder weapons of the 'Great White Migration.' Eventually, the improvement of gunpowder and repeating firearms sounded "taps" for the bow as a military weapon. As excellent as it was for its primitive needs, it was without any further improvement, thus making the gun the weapon of the future.

The power of one arrow shot from an Indian warrior was so mighty it went through the largest and fattest war horse and imbedded itself in the ground beyond. Many ranks of Americans fell under a hail of arrows because they shot a volley too hastily and the Indians charged them before they could reload their weapons. Mexicans, who were constantly fighting the Apaches, learned to wrap blankets around their middle torso in many folds to keep arrows from making deadly wounds.

In making a good bow, a careful selection of timber had to be found. A favorite was the 'bois d'arc.' Others were ironwood, white elm, hickory, ask, and mulberry. The wood had to be straight grain and free from any knots. The heart of a tree was never used. Usually the wood was worked to a specific size while green and endless hours were consumed in the process of seasoning. After working the wood to a proper finish, it was rubbed with animal fat or brains to make it pliable. After more seasoning, the wood was rubbed by hand to a polish. Hot glue was spread on the fresh or wet sinew taken from the back of an animal and was wrapped around the wood. Later, a second application of glue was applied and rubbed to a smoothness. In the drying period, the sinew shrank tightly to the wood making a strong bow.

Highly prized bows were made by fitting together pieces of horn with glue and wrapping them tightly with sinew or strips of deer gut. The only problem

occurred during wet weather when the bow might become useless if the moist fittings gave way. Sinew-backed bows were carried among the Blackfeet, Sioux, Ute, Crow, Cree, Cheyenne, and Hidatsa, but never among the Southeast tribes.

The bowstring was made of twisted sinew and very strong. The tendons came from either buffalo or deer and were shredded into fine threads, then soaked in glue. While still damp, the tendons were twisted into a round even cord that was ten times stronger than a cotton cord of equal size. Just as water damage made percussion caps incapable of flashing for the white man, wet seasons rendered the bow string ineffective. Both races were handicapped by wet weather and partly for this reason there were fewer battles during damp or rainy weather. However, the Indians overcame this disadvantage and carried the bow string under their armpit to keep it dry.

Arrow shafts were made from tough, hard wood, usually mature ash or dogwood. It is believed that some Indians placed the blade of the hunting arrow in the same plane with the notch for the string. This way the head could pass between the ribs of an animal, which are vertical. For the same reason, the blade of the war arrow was placed at a right angle with the notch, since human ribs are horizontal. This is highly controversial, as it only takes a twist of the wrist to shoot an arrow from a horizontal position of the bow or a vertical position. There again, the spinning of the arrow in flight does not guarantee that the blade will enter the rib cage either horizontally or vertically.

Arrowheads were shaped for particular uses. Hunting arrows had long tapering blades with rear shoulders sloping backwards, fastened firmly to the shaft so it could be withdrawn easily from the wound. The war arrow was short, and sharp-bladed, with rear shoulders sloped forward forming barbs. Blade attachment to the shaft was slight, as it was intended that the blade would remain in the wound and eventually kill the victim, if it hadn't already done so. If not drawn out immediately, the sinew that fastened the blade to the shaft would loosen from the warmth of the blood and separate while the shaft

was being removed. Fifty percent of these wounds were fatal either because of an infection or a poisoned tip. Comanches dipped their arrow heads into dead skunks or rattlesnake venom.

It is not known why some arrow shafts were grooved from feather to head. A popular theory is that they permitted blood from the victim to escape so as to weaken him, or that these grooves symbolized lightning striking making the missile surely fatal. A more practical explanation is that the grooving kept the shaft from warping.

The flight and accuracy of an arrow depended greatly on its feathers. Turkey feathers were highly prized, as well as those from the owl and buzzard.

Feathers from these birds were not injured when dampened with blood; however, the feathers of the hawk and eagle were damaged. Arrows were precious possessions and every effort was made to preserve and retrieve them. Most tribes identified their arrows by bands of colors near the feathered end. Individual warriors or hunters had their own color combination or personal crest.

The bow and arrow is now used by todays hunters for sport only. However, for thousands of years this simple, taut-stringed implement used effectively turned armies about, fed wilderness families, and revamped history.

During a hunt, Indians kept track of their cohorts by watching the movements of the bow and arrow. The angle of the bow represented an animal or a human. If the bow was held vertically, it meant the arrow was for an animal because of the rib cage being vertical. The bow was tilted on a horizontal plane for a man whose rib cage was somewhat horizontal. With this observation, the Indians knew whether they were hunting or soon to do battle with their white enemy.

Art by E.L. Reedstrom

Painted Ponies

Painted Indian ponies of the Crow, Kiowa, Apache, Nez Perce, Comanche, Sioux, or Pawnee, were generally a basic standard, except that paint colors varied. On the field of battle between tribes, each warrior could read the colorful symbols of his enemy, telling heroic deeds about the capture of many horses and battle scars. These symbols were painted on both sides of his horse telling the same story on each side. It was with much pride and honor that a warrior displayed many courageous acts in symbols on his horse, which could be read by any Indian warrior.

Each brave had special family markings as well as his own heroic deeds—reserved for him alone—and, only upon preparations for a battle, did his wife or mother decorate his horse according to his past battle history. After the brave cleansed himself in a ceremonial sweat bath, he painted himself with the same colored symbols that appeared on his horse.

In order to please the gods or great spirit who was suppose to look over the warrior, the women prepared each symbol accordingly with her creative talent and artistic ability. Some of the favorite sacred symbols are shown in the illustration.

Battle scars were the highest honor an Indian horse could receive. Indians painted the scars in red, then circled each. The "upside-down" red handprint was bestowed on the right shoulder of the pony, only if the animal took his master through battle and safely returned him home. Personal battle awards were presented to the horse in the warrior's own fashion with lucky amulets woven in its bridle or braided coup feathers adorning the horse's forelock and tail. Colorful symbols were painted on the body artistically showing enemies taken hostage, killed, or ponies stolen.

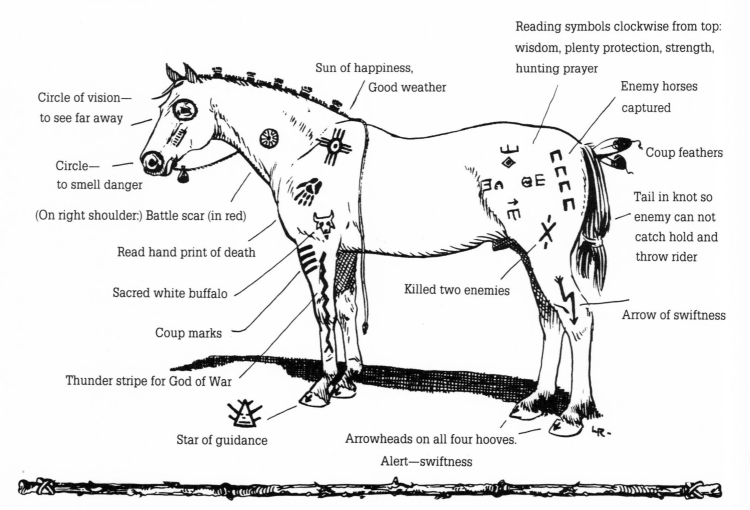

Circle of vision— to see far away

Circle— to smell danger

(On right shoulder:) Battle scar (in red)

Read hand print of death

Sacred white buffalo

Coup marks

Thunder stripe for God of War

Star of guidance

Sun of happiness, Good weather

Reading symbols clockwise from top: wisdom, plenty protection, strength, hunting prayer

Enemy horses captured

Coup feathers

Tail in knot so enemy can not catch hold and throw rider

Killed two enemies

Arrow of swiftness

Arrowheads on all four hooves. Alert—swiftness

Sign Language

Each Indian nation spoke a different language, and this diversity has given rise to much discussion among philologists. It must be conceded that the Indian nations had a very ancient history for although they lived in comparatively close proximity to each other, they spoke wholly different tongues. To communicate between tribes required something more than a verbal language.

Sign language was nearly universal among all Indian nations and was handed down from a remote period. Through this silent means of communication, a member of any tribe located in Texas could converse with a member of another tribe from the far north or along the St. Lawrence River.

Immediately upon meeting, conversation began by one of these mysterious mediums: usually the first step was by the movements of the horse or smoke signals, when a truce was declared; next, a friendly conversation was held by the more comprehensive means of signs by the hands. So well were the signs understood by all that no practice was necessary between the parties. It was important to follow closely the thread of conversation, for the wrong interpretation of a single sign was sufficient to break the whole chain of thought. Another peculiarity was the rapidity with which Indians could communicate with each other by it. The Sioux could express a great deal more in a shorter time with signs than by word of mouth.

Hand sign language was literally an expressive form of hand and finger manipulations; each movement or motion meant a word or several words. Sometimes it also established a full sentence. If an Indian wanted to say that you spoke in lies, with one finger he touched his tongue, then held up two fingers and pointed to you meaning you were double tongue or untruthful. If he wanted to give the distance of two or three days journey, with both hands he twirled his fingers, like that of a wheel in motion. By dropping his head to one side as if asleep, and showing a number of fingers as there were nights, he revealed the many days to travel at that particular place. In referring to the past, he stretched his right arm in front of him, with the index finger pointed outward, then drawing his arm toward him

White Eagle shows the sign of "man astride horse." When verbal communications were difficult between officer and Indian, sign language was easier to understand, especially after several weeks in the field with the scouts.

Author's collection

with a rolling or screwing motion, referring to many days back. If he meant a future time, his hand, with the index finger extended at his back, moving it forward in a screw motion, meant sometime in the future. By showing a man on horseback, he made the motion by placing his first and second fingers over his left or right hand, palm open and pointed forward with a rocking motion like bouncing. A large quantity of anything was shown by a sign of his hands shaped like a funnel, moving them in an upward fashion from the ground to a point several feet from the ground, forming the letter "A." Having nothing, he produced his upward palm, and like brushing something away from it with his forearm, showed that his palm was empty. Expressing a full meal, thumb and forefinger of the right hand over his stomach and then moving his hand to his mouth, indicated a full and tasty meal. These signs were understood by all Indians, traders, and mountain men, as an international language of communications.

Signaling

The white settlers saw the puffs of smoke from one Indian camp, and called them "smoke signals." There were numerous other kinds of Indian messages utilized across the plains: blanket waving, arm gestures, the noise that only an Indian could make in imitation of a bird, whistles, reflecting mirrors, or riding patterns. These signals were interpreted by friendly tribes and bridged the gap between languages.

Smoke signals were made by collecting smoke from a small smoky fire under a wet or dampened blanket and puffing the smoke patterns skyward by flipping the blanket upward to release the captured smoke. The fire, no bigger than a dinner plate, was covered by the blanket formed into a miniature tepee. The fire was made from green materials so that there was no danger of catching the blanket on fire. These signals could be seen for many miles across the plains. They followed a sort of Morse code that was fairly universally understood by most of the tribes in an area. Sometimes the settlers began to understand the code as well, as a close watch on signals was maintained.

At a closer range, blanket waving served as a means of communicating coming action: three waves in a rotating fashion usually meant for the other tribes to begin an attack. Directions to attack were communicated by arm signals and sometimes by the way in which firearms were held.

A mirror was a great prize to the Indian, as it provided a way to signal scouts or other tribes at great distance, without the need to build a fire. A long flash of light, followed by two short flashes meant "soldiers are coming," or "strangers are coming." Other signals were used to ask questions, given directions, or to make requests. Signals were rarely repeated, certainly not more than twice.

A skilled Indian could build a small fire in a matter of ten to fifteen minutes, and begin to create huge puffs of smoke for signaling his comrades of impending danger.

Art by E.L. Reedstrom

Scalping

There has been little written on Indian scalping their victims, and much has been misunderstood. During the early colonial period, the custom of scalping was confined to a limited area and was unknown in the Plains area until much later. Beginning with our colonial and more recent governments, it was the bounty system that actually stimulated the practice of scalping. A fresh scalp would bring the victor anywhere from one hundred pounds of sterling—equivalent to five hundred dollars—to forty pounds sterling for a male scalp over twelve years of age. For a female or child's scalp, twenty pounds sterling was given by the government.

The Indian had definite reasons which motivated his actions in battle, and like anyone else, he had to establish his position in society for bravery and its value in impressing other fellow warriors. At any rate, scalping was passed down in family tradition as a regulation or part of the Indian society which was never questioned. Some historians believe that the number of scalps obtained greatly aided the young warrior in boosting his standing in the village. It may have indeed been, but there were other "coups" or acts of bravery.

There were various conditions in removing a scalp. Some Indians believed that the scalp must be from an enemy or it would bring disgrace to the warrior. But there were times when the enemy might include anyone. During the Revolutionary War, the enemy could either be an American soldier or a British infantryman. It depended upon whether the source of payment came from the United States or Britain.

Common belief was that the art of scalping was a monopoly of the Indian, but the white mountain men of the 1830s also practiced it. For many tribes, scalping was not a method of killing an enemy. However, a scalp might be taken unintentionally from an unconscious victim taken for dead, as there had been numerous accounts of such happenings.

After a battle, when war trophies were brought back to the village, the scalp was dried, curiously ornamented, and displayed as a trophy in many forms. The most common way was to stretch it on a small hoop and attach it to a two foot long stick. This was generally used in the scalp dance. Smaller patches of hair generally ornamented different parts of clothing in the form of fringes on sleeves of garments. Other such trophies were suspended from bridles and used in parades. The skin side of the scalp was sometimes painted entirely red or one half red and one half black. On the other side, the hair was usual braided. Scalps were also suspended from poles that branched out of the tepee and were decorated with long and colorful strips of cloth or

Human scalp mounted on hoop with trade bead decoration. 1860–1885 Period.

Courtesy of Arnold Marcus Chernoff

silk. Sacred medicine bundles also contained painted scalps that were purified and prayed over. In most cases, the scalp was treated with the greatest of respect.

Indians had different methods of scalping their victims. One tribe would cut a diamond-shaped piece from the scalp lock, another tribe would cut a square patch, others a round patch. If a scalped corpse was found by a detachment of cavalrymen, the Indian scouts were quickly summoned to identify the missing portion of hair. Just by the shape of the missing scalp, the Indian scouts knew which tribe committed the act.

When the United States government offered bounties for various Indian tribes, it wasn't long before schemers began to concoct an imitation scalp either from a dog or a horse's tail or mane. After a flood of these phony scalps, loyal Indians were summoned to inspect these so-called-scalps before the bounty money was paid out. The Indians noted that it was most common for an Indian's scalp to be loaded with nits (the egg of a louse or other parasite). Thus, the presence of nits on the hair was considered proof that the scalp-lock was taken from an Indian.

Indian/Military Conflicts

Date	Place	Troops Engaged
1866.		
Feb 16	Near Jordan Creek, Oreg	C, 2 batln, 14 inf.
Feb 23	Jordan Creek, Oreg	Detachs C and D, 2 batln, 14 inf.
Mar 22	Round Valley, or Cottonwood Springs, Ariz	Detach F, 1 batln, 14 inf.
May 27	South Canyon of Owyhee River, Idaho	A and C, 2 batln, 14 inf.
May 31	Camp Wallen, Ariz	Detach G, 1 cav.
July 17	Canyon in Stein's Mtn., Oreg	Detach C, 2 batln, 14 inf.
Do	Reno Creek, Dak	D,E and F, 2 batln, 18 inf.
July 18, 20, 22	On Snake Creek, near Malheur River, Oreg	Detach I, 1 cav.
July 20	Crazy Woman's Fork, Dak	Detach G, 2 batln, 18 inf.
July 29	East of Ownes Lake, Cal	Detach D, 1 cav.
Do	Near Camp Cady, Cal	Detach D, 9 inf.
July 31	Near Ft. Rice, Dak	Detachs B, E, F, G, and H, 3 batln, 13 inf.
Aug 9	Near Ft Phil Kearney, Dak	Detach H, 2 batln, 18 inf.
Aug 13	Grape Vine Spring, Skull Valley , Ariz	B, 1 batln, 24 inf.
Aug 17	West Fork of Salt River, Ariz	Do
Aug 26	Near South Fork, Owyhee River, Idaho	M.1 cav.
Aug 28	Near Harney Lake, Oreg	Detach I.1 cav.
Sept. 10-16	Ft Phil Kearny, Dak	A,C, E, and H, 2 batln, 18 inf.
Sept. 13-16	Between Pino Creek and Ft Phil Kearny Dak	C.2 batln, 18 inf.
Sept 14	Near Camp Watson, Oreg	Detach I, 1 cav.
Sept. 20	Near Ft C S Smith, Mont	D and G, 2 batln, 18 inf.
Sept. 21	Little Horn or Tongue River, Dak	D and G, 2 btln, 18 inf.
Sept 28	Dunder and Blitzen Creek, Oreg	Detach M, 1 cav.
Do	La Bonte Creek, Mont	E, 2 cav.
Sept 29	Ft Phil Kearny, Dak	A, C, E and H, 27 inf.
Oct. 3	Cedar Valley, Ariz	Detachs C and E, 1 cav; detachs B, D and F, 14 inf.
Do	Purgatory River, near Trinidad, Colo	G, 3 cav.
Do	Long Valley, Nev	Detach A, 1 cav.
Oct 6	Near Ft. Phil Kearny, Dak	Detachs A, C, E and H, 27 inf.
Oct 14	Harney Lake Valley, Oreg	Detach I, 1 cav.
Oct 17	Hartsville, Tenn	B, 5 cav.
Oct 19	Pryer's Gap, near Ft C F Smith, Mont	Detachs A,C, E and H, 27 inf.
Oct 23	North Fork of Platte River, near Ft Sedgwick, Colo	Detach M, 2 cav.
Oct 26	Near Lake Albert, Oreg	Detach A, 1 cav.
Oct 30	Malheur country, Oreg	Detach A, 1 cav.

Date	Place	Troops Engaged

1866.

Oct 31	Trout Creek Canyon, Oreg	Detach H, 1 cav; Detach C 23 inf.
Nov. 17	Sierra Ancho, Ariz	E, 1 cav.
Nov 18	BlackJack, near Mitchellville, Tenn	M. 5 cav.
Do	John Day's River and Strawberry Valley, Oreg	Detach I, 1 cav.
Dec. 3	Near Camp Watson, Oreg	Do
Dec 5	Surprise Valley, Cal	Detach A, 1 cav.
Dec 6	Goose Creek, Dak	C, 2 cav.; detachs A, C, E and H, 27 inf.
Dec 9	Near Camp Wallen, Ariz	Attack on wagon train.
Dec 11	Grief Hill, Ariz	Detach C, 14 inf.
Dec. 14	Mule Pass, Pinal Mountains, near Camp Wallen, Ariz	Detach G, 1 cav: detach F, 32 inf.
Dec 21	Pino Creek, near Ft Phil Kearny, Dak	C, 2 cav; A,C,E and H, 27 inf.
Dec 24	Mud Creek, near Ft Clark, Tex	Detach C, 4 cav.
Dec 24-25	Ft Buford, Dak	C, 31 inf.
Dec 26	Owyhee Creek, Idaho	Detach F, 1 cav.

1867

Jan 1	Near Ft Stanton, N Mex	Detach H, 3 cav.
Jan 6	Crooked River, Oreg	Indian scouts.
Jan 8	Owyhee River, Idaho	Detach M, 1 cav; Indian scouts.
Jan 9	Malheur River, Oreg	F, 1 cav.
Jan 18	Eden Valley, Nev	Detach A, 8 cav.
Jan 19	Nueces River, Tex	Detach C, 4 cav.
Jan 29	Between Owyhee River and Stein's Mountains, Oreg	M, 1 cav.
Do	Near Camp McDowell, Ariz	F, 1 cav.
Feb 7	Vicksburg Mines, Nev	B, 1 cav.
Feb 15	Black Slate Mountains, Nev	Detach A, 8 cav.
Feb 16	Surprise Valley, Cal	Detach A, 1 cav., detach C, 9 inf.
Do	Near Warm Springs, Idaho	M, 1 cav.
Feb 23	Meadow Valley, Ariz	E, 1 cav.
Feb 27	Near Ft Reno, Dak	Detachs B and I, 27 inf.
Mar 2	Date Creek, Ariz	Attack on wagon train
Mar 11	Arab Canyon, Coso Mountains, Cal	Detach D, 1 cav.
March 12	Pecos River, Tex	Detach C, 4 cav.
Mar 28	Murderer's Creek, Oreg	Detach F, 8 cav.
Apr 10	Black Mountains, Ariz	Detachs B and I,8 cav.
Apr 16	Do	Do.
Apr 18	Rio Verde, near Black Mountains, Ariz	Do
Apr 19	Cimarron Crossing, Kans	Detachs B and C, 7 cav.
Apr 23	Tonto Valley, Ariz	Detach E, 1 cav; Indian scouts.
Apr 24	Near Ft Mojave, Ariz	Detachs B and K, 8 cav; detach E, 14 inf.
Apr 26	Near Ft Reno, Dak	Detach I, 27 inf.
Apr 27	Silvie's Creek, near Lake Harney, Oreg	Detach F, 8 cav.
Do	Near Ft Reno, Dak	Detachs D and I, 27 inf.
May 1	La Prelle Creek, Dak	Detach E, 2 cav.
May 5	Near Camp Watson, Oreg	Detach I, 1 cav.
May 6	Mazatzal Mountains, Ariz	Detachs D, 14 inf, and A, 32 inf.
Do	Dour Peaks, Mazatzal Mountains, Ariz	Detach D, 14 inf.
May 23	Near Bridger's ferry, Dak	E, 2 cav.
Do	Big Timbers, Kans	Detach E, 3 inf.
May 27	Pond Creek Station, Kans	I, 7 cav.
May 30	Near Ft Reno, Dak	Detach F, 27 inf.
Do	Near Beale Station, Ariz	Detach K, 8 cav.
Do	Beale Station, Ariz	Detach E, 14 inf.
May 31	Bluff Ranch, near Ft Aubrey, Kans	Detach I, 37 inf.
June 2	Fairview, Colo	G, 4 inf.
June 5	Cimarron Crossing, Kans	Detach I, 37 inf.

Date	Place	Troops Engaged

1867

Date	Place	Troops Engaged
June 8	Chalk Bluffs, Kans	Detach F, 7 cav.
June 11	Near Big Timbers, Kans	Detachs I, 7 cav, and E, 3 inf.
June 12	Near Ft Dodge, Kans	B, 7 cav.
Do	near Ft Phil Kearny, Dak	D, 2 cav.
June 14	Near Grinnell Springs, Kans	Detach H, 37 inf.
Do	Hualapai Valley, north of Peacock Springs, Ariz	I, 8 cav.
June 15	Big Timbers, Kans	Detach E, 3 inf.
June 16	Gallinas Mountains, N. Mex	Detach H, 3 cav.
June 17	Cimarron Crossing, Kans	Detach I, 37 inf.
June 18	Near Ft Phil Kearny, Dak	D, 2 cav.
June 19	Near Stein's Mountain, Oreg	Detach Indian scouts.
June 20	Foot of Black Hills, on U P R R, Nebr	C, Pawnee scouts.
June 21	Near Ft Wallace, Kans	Detachs G and I, 7 cav, and of D, 37 inf.
Do	Near Calabasas, Ariz	Detachs G, 1 cav, and of E, 32 inf.
Do	Near Calabasas, Ariz	Detachs G, 1 cav, and of E, 32 inf.
June 22	Goose Creek Station, Colo	Detach D, 37 inf.
Do	Monument Station, Kans	Detach F, 7 cav.
June 24	North Fork of Republican River, Kans	A,E,H,K, and M, 7 cav.
Do	Do	Detach A, 7 cav.
June 26	Wilson's Creek, Kans	Detach K, 38 inf.
Do	South Fork of Republican River, Kans	Detach D, 7 cav.
Do	Near Ft Wallace, Kans	G and detach I, 7 cav.
Do	Near Ft Wallace, Kans	G and detach I, 7 cav.
June 26-28	Monument Station, Kans	F, 7 cav.
June 30	Near Ft Phil Kearny, Dak	C, 18 inf.
July 1	Near Goose Creek, Colo	Detachs I, 7 cav, and of E, 3 inf.
July 3	Bad Lands, Dak	Detach A, 4 inf.
July 7	Beale's Springs, Ariz	Detach K, 8 cav.
July 8	Near Malheur River, Oreg	I, 1 cav.
July 9	Near Truxton Springs, Ariz	B and I, 8 cav.
Do	Near Ft Stevenson, Dak	C and detachs D and F, 10 inf.
Do	Near Ft Sumner, N Mex	Detachs G and I, 3 cav.
July 11	Bluff Ranch, Kans	Detach I, 37 inf.
July 13	South Fork Malheur River, Oreg	Detach K, 23 inf; Snake Indians.
July 15	Ft Aubrey, Kans	Detach I, 37 inf.
July 17	Downer's Station, Kans	Detachs H and K, 7 cav.
July 19	Malheur country, Oreg	I, 1 cav.
July 21	Buffalo Springs, Tex	Detachs A and E, 6 cav.
Do	Cimarron Crossing, Kans	Detach I, 37 inf.
July 22	Beaver Creek, Kans	Detach M, 2 cav.
July 27	Between Camps C F Smith and Harney, Oreg	F and M, 1 cav; Indian scouts.
July 29	Near Ft Hays, Kans	Detach G, 38 inf.
Do	Willow Grove, or Warm Creek, Ariz	Detach K, 8 cav.
Aug 1	Near Ft C F Smith, Mont	Detachs D,E,G,H, and I, 27 inf.
Do	Willow Creek, Ariz	Detach H, 14 inf.
Aug 2	Near Ft Phil Kearny, Dak	A,C, and F, 27 inf.
Do	Saline River, Kans	F, 10 cav.
Aug 8	Ft Stevenson, Dak	Detachs H and I, 31 inf.
Aug 11-14	Owyhee River, Oreg	A and detach E, 23 inf.
Aug 13	O'Connor's Springs, near Crazy Woman's Fork, Dak	B and detach A, 27 inf.
Aug 14	Near Ft Reno, Dak	Detach G, 18 inf.
Do	Chalk Springs, Dak	Detach E, 27 inf.
Aug 15	Ft Aubrey, Kans	Detach I, 37 inf.
Aug 16	Near Ft Reno, Dak	Cattle herders.
Aug 17	Near Plum Creek, Nebr	Pawnee scouts.
Aug 21-22	Prairie Dog Creek, Kans	F, 10 cav.

Date	Place	Troops Engaged

1867

Aug 22	Mountain pass, near Ft Chadbourne, Tex	Detachs D,G, and H, 4 cav.
Do	Surprise Valley, Cal	Boise Indian scouts.
Aug 23	Near North Concho River, Tex	Detach A, 4 cav.
Aug 30	Near Ft Belknap, Tex	F, 6 cav.
Sept 6	Near Silver River, Oreg	A, 1 cav.
Sept 8	Do	Do
Sept 10	Live Oak Creek, Tex	Detach K, 4 cav.
Sept 16	Near Ft Inge, Tex	Do.
Do	Saline River, Lans	Detach G, 10 cav.
Sept 19	Walker's Creek, 35 miles west of Ft Harker, Kans	Detach K, 5 inf.
Sept 20	Near Devil's River, Tex	Detach C, 4 cav.
Sept 22	Pawnee Fork Bluff, Kans	Detach A, 3 inf.
Sept 23	Arkansas River, 9 miles west of Cimarron Crossing, Kans	K, 5 inf.
Sept 24	Nine Mile Ridge, Kans	Do
Sept. 25	Bluff Ranch, Kans	Do
Sept 26-28	Infernal Caverns, near Pitt River, Cal	H, 1 cav; D, 23 inf, and Boise Indian scouts.
Sept 29	Pretty Encampment, near Ft Garland, Colo	Detach G, 37 inf.
Oct 1	Howard's Well, Tex	Detach D, 9 cav.
Oct 4	Near Camp Logan, Oreg	Detach E, 8 cav.
Oct 6	Trout Creek, Ariz	L, 8 cav.
Oct 10	Near Camp Lincoln, Ariz	Detachs C and G, 14 inf.
Do	Ft Stevenson, Dak	Detach H, 31 inf.
Oct 17	Deep Creek, Tex	Detachs F,I,K, and L, 6 cav.
Oct 18	Sierra Diablo, N Mex	D and K, 3 cav.
Oct 20	Crazy Woman's Fork, Dak	
Oct 25	Truxton Springs, Ariz	L, 8 cav.
Oct 26	Shell Creek, Dak	D, 2 cav.
Oct 26	Near Camp Winfield Scott, Nev	L, 1 cav; A, 8 cav.
Nov 3	Willow Grove, Ariz	Detachs E, 1 cav, and of L, 8 cav.
Nov 4	Goose Creek, Dak	Detachs D,E,G,H, and I, 27 inf.
Nov 5	Near Camp Bowie, Ariz	Lieut J C Carroll, 32 inf, and 1 citizen.
Nov 6	Near Ft Buford, Dak	Detach C, 31 inf.
Nov 7	Toll Gate, Ariz	L, 8 cav.
Nov 8	Near Willows, Ariz	Detachs E, 1 cav, and of L, 8 cav.
Nov 13	Aqua Frio Springs, near Camp Lincoln, Ariz	Detach C, 14 inf.
Do	Crazy Woman's Fork of Powder River, Mont	Detach recruits of 27 inf.
Nov. 14-15	Near Tonto Creek, Ariz	Detach Indian scouts.
Nov 17	Near Ft Sumner, N Mex	Detach E, 37 inf.
Do	Willow Grove, Ariz	Detach K, 8 cav.
Nov 20	Near Ft Selden, N Mex	K, 3 cav.
Nov 29	Shell Creek, Dak	D, 2 cav.
Do	Near Willows, Ariz	Detachs E, 1 cav and of L, 8 cav.
Dec 5	Eagle Springs, Tex	Detach F, 9 cav.
Dec 12	Owyhee River, Ore	Indian scouts.
Dec. 14	Near Ft Phil Kearny, Dak	
Dec 19	San Pedro River, near Camp Wallen, Ariz	Detach G, 1 cav.
Dec 26	Near Ft Lancaster, Tex	Detach K, 9 cav.

1868

Jan	Ft Quitman, Tex	Detach E, 9 cav.
Jan 4	Near Owyhee River, Oreg	Detach M, 1 cav; Indian scouts.
Jan 14	Difficult Canyon, Ariz	K, 8 cav.
Do	Beale's Spring, Ariz	Do
Feb 16	Near Kenny's ranch, Malheur River, Oreg	D, 8 cav.

Date	Place	Troops Engaged

1868

Date	Place	Troops Engaged
Mar 6	Paint Creek, Tex	F,I, and K, 6 cav.
Mar 10	Head of Colorado River, Tex	Detach D, 4 cav.
Mar 11	Near Tularosa, N Mex	
Mar 14	Dunder and Blitzen Creek, Oreg	H, 1 cav; C, 8 cav; D, 23 inf.
Mar 18	Near Ft Fetterman, Dak	Detach K, 18 inf.
Mar 20	Horseshoe and Twin Springs ranches, Dak	Do
Mar 21	Near Camp Willow Grove, Ariz	Detach E, 14 inf.
Mar 25	Cottonwood Springs, Ariz	Detach B, 14 inf.
Mar 26	Owyhee River, Oreg	Detach D, 8 cav.
Apr 1	Pinal Mountains, Ariz	G, 1 cav.
Apr 3	Rock Creek, Wyo	
Apr 5	Malheur River, Oreg	F, 1 cav; C, 8 cav; Indian scouts.
Apr 15	Ft C F Smith, Mont	Detach D, 27 inf.
Apr 17	Camp Three Forks, Owyhee, Idaho	E, 23 inf.
Do	Nesmith's Mills, near Tulerosa, N Mex	Detach H, 3 cav and citizens.
Apr 21	Near Camp Grant, Ariz	I, 8 cav.
Do	Upper Yellowstone River, Mont	
Apr 22	Near Ft McPherson, Nebr	
Apr 22-24	Do	Detachs B and C, 2 cav.
Apr 23	Near Camp Harney, Oreg	Detach scouts.
Do	Near Ft Ellis, Mont	
Apr 29	Camp Winfield Scott, Paradise Valley, Nev	Detach A, 8 cav.
Do	South of Otseos Lodge, Warner Mountains, Oreg	Detach D, 23 inf.
May 1	Near Camp Crittenden, Ariz	C, 1 cav.
Do	San Pedro River, Ariz	E, 1 cav.
Do	Gila River, near Camp Grant, Ariz	I, 8 cav.
Do	Hoag's Bluff, Warner Valley, Oreg	Detach G, 8 cav, and C, 9 inf.
May 13	Near Ft Buford, Dak	
May 15	Between Fts Stevenson and Totten, Dak	
May 17	Attack on Camp Cooke, Mont.	B and H, 13 inf.
May 18	Rio Salinas, Ariz	B and L, 8 cav.
May 19	Mouth of Musselshell River, Mont	E and detachs B and H, 13 inf.
May 24	Do	Detachs B, F, and H, 13 inf.
Do	Near Yellowstone River, Mont	Detach F, 13 inf, and citizens.
May 29	Camp Lyon, near Owyhee River, Idaho	Detach M, 1 cav, and Indian scouts.
May 30	Tonto Basin, San Carlos Trail, Ariz	B and L, 8 cav.
May 31	Castle Rock, near North Fork of Malheur River, Oreg	Detach E, 1 cav.
June 8-13	Apache Springs, N. Mex	Detachs G and I, 3 cav.
June 9	Snake Canyon, Idaho	Detach H, 23 inf, and Indian scouts.
June 13	Twenty-five Yard Creek, Mont	Detach F, 13 inf.
June 16	Toddy Mountain, Ariz	Detach E, 1 cav.
June 24	Near Battle Creek, Idaho	A, 23 inf.
July 4	Near Ft Phil Kearny, Dak	I, 27 inf.
July 5	Do	Detach A, 27 inf.
July 8	Between Verde and Salt rivers, Ariz	Detach E, 1 cav, and I, 8 cav.
July 17	Stein's Mountain, Oreg	C, 23 inf, and Indian scouts.
July 18	Near Ft Phil Kearny, Dak	Detach A, 2 cav, and B and F, 27 inf.
July 22	Near Camp Crittenden, Ariz	Detach K, 1 cav.
July 25	Big Salmon River, Idaho	Detach H, 23 inf, and Indian scouts.
July 26	Juniper Canyon, Idaho	Detach E, 23 inf.
July 28	Near Old Camp Sully, Dak	Detachs B,C, and E, 32 inf.
July 30	Tonto Valley, near Camp Reno, Ariz.	Detach A, 32 inf.
Do	On Republican River, Nebr (on line of U P R R)	Detach Indian scouts.
Aug 2	Cimaroon River, Kans	K, 7 cav.
Aug 8-Sept 5	Juniper Mountains, Idaho	Detach A, 23 inf; Indian scouts.
Aug 13	Walnut Grove, Ariz	L, 8 cav.

Date	Place	Troops Engaged

1868

Do	Saline River, Kans	Detachs H and M, 7 cav.
Aug 20	Ft Buford, Dak	B,C,E, and G, 31 inf.
Aug 22	Santa Maria River, Ariz	B, 8 cav.
Aug 23	Near Ft Totten, Dak	Detachs A,D, and K, 32 inf.
Aug 27	Hatchet Mountain, N Mex	F, 38 inf.
Aug 28	Near Platte River, Nebr	Pawnee scouts, A.
Aug 30	Republican River, Nebr	A and B, Pawnee scouts.
Sept 2	Little Coon Creek, Kans	Detach B, 7 cav, and A and F, 3 inf.
Sept 4-6	Tonto Creek, Ariz	E, 1 cav; I, 8 cav; Indian scouts.
Sept 9	Tonto Plateau, Ariz	Detach B, 8 cav.
Sept 10	Rule Creek, or Purgatory River, Colo	L, 7 cav.
Do	Near Lower Aqua Frio, Ariz	Detach B, 8 cav.
Sept 11	Rio Verde, Ariz	Do
Sept 11-15	Sandy Hills, on the Cimarron and Canadian rivers, Ind. Ter	A,B,C,D,E,F,G,I, and K, 7 cav; F, 3 inf.
Sept 12	Near Fort Reynolds, Colo	Escort.
Sept 13	Dragoon Fork, Verde River, Ariz	Detach B, 8 cav.
Sept 14	Horse Head Hills, Tex	Detachs C,F, and K, 9 cav.
Sept 15	Big Sandy Creek, Colo	I, 10 cav.
Sept 17-25	Arickaree Fork of Republican River, Kans	Indian scouts.
Sept 26	Near Ft Rice, Dak	Detachs A,B,I, and K, 22 inf.
Sept 30	Big Bend, Kans	D, 3 inf.
Oct 1	Attack on Fort Zarah, Kans	Do
Do	Between Fts Larned and Dodge, Kans	E, 3 inf.
Oct 3	Miembres Mountains, N. Mex	Detach E, 3 cav.
Do	Cow Creek, Kans	Detach D, 3 inf.
Oct 9	Salt River and Cherry Creek, Ariz	E, 1 cav; I, 8 cav; F, 14 inf; A, 32 inf; Indian scouts.
Oct 12	Big Bend of Arkansas River, Kans	H,K, and M, 7 cav.
Oct 13-30	White Woman's Fork, near Republican River, Kans	H, 2 cav.
Oct 14	Prairie Dog Creek, Kans	K, 5 cav.
Oct 18	Beaver Creek, Kans	H and I, 10 cav.
Oct 19	Dragoon Fork of Verde River, Ariz	B, 8 cav.
Oct 21	Between Fts Whipple and Verde, Ariz	Detachs L, 8 cav, and G, 14 inf.
Oct 25-26	Beaver Creek and Prairie Dog Creek, Kans	A,B,F,H,I,L, and M, 5 cav, and scouts.
Oct 26	Near Ft Dodge, Kans	E, 3 inf.
Nov 2	Between Wickenberg and Prescott, Ariz	Detach H, 14 inf.
Nov 3	Big Coon Creek, Kans	Detach recruits, 7 cav.
Nov 7-15	Willow Grove, Ariz	Detachs E and K, 8 cav.
Nov 9-11	Tonto Plateau, near Squaw Peak, Ariz	Detachs B and L, 8 cav.
Nov 18	Near Ft Hays, Kans	Indian scouts.
Nov 19	Near Ft Dodge, Kans	Detach A, 10 cav; A and H, 3 inf; detach E, 5 inf.
Nov 20	Mulberry Creek, Kans	Indian scouts.
Nov 23	Bill Williams Mountains, Ariz	B, 8 cav.
Nov 25-Dec 2	Scout from Camp McDowell, Ariz	E, 1 cav; I, 8 cav; A, 32 inf.
Nov 27	Black Kettle's Village, on Washita River, Ind T	A,B,C,D,E,F,G,H,I,K, and M, 7 cav.
Dec 10	Walker Springs, Ariz	E and K, 8 cav.
Dec 11	Willow Grove, Ariz	K, 8 cav.
Dec 13	Walker Springs, Ariz	E and K, 8 cav.
Dec 25	Wichita Mountains, North Fork of Red River, Ind T	A,C,D,F,G, and I, 3 cav; F and I, 37 inf.

1869

Jan 8-15	Scout in Bill Williams Mountains, Ariz	B and L, 8 cav.
Jan 13	Mount Turnbull, Ariz	Detachs G, 1 cav, and F and G, 32 inf.
Jan 25	Kirkland's Creek, Juniper Mountains, Ariz	E and K, 8 cav.
Jan 29	Mulberry Creek, Kans	Detachs C,G,H, and K, 9 cav.
Feb 4	Arivaipa Mountains, Ariz	Detachs G and K, 1 cav; Indian scouts.

Date	Place	Troops Engaged
1869		
Feb 5	Black Mesa, Ariz	Detach L, 8 cav.
Feb 27	Near Camp Grant, Ariz	Detach B, 14 inf.
Mar 3	Oak Grove, Ariz	Detach F, 32 inf.
Mar 13	Near Ft Harker, Kans	A,B,C,D,E,F,G,H,I,K, and M, 7 cav.
Do	Shields River, Mont	Detachs D,F, and G, 13 inf.
Mar 16	Near Ft Randall, Dak	Detachs C and F, 22 inf.
Mar 17-30	Scouts from Camp Goodwin, Ariz	Detachs B,F, and G, 32 inf.
Mar 22	Near Ft Fred Steele, Wyo	Detachs A,B,F,H, and K, 30 inf.
Mar 23	Near Camp Grant, Ariz	Detach #, 32 inf.
Mar 26	San Francisco Mountains, N. Mex	Detach C, 38 inf.
Apr 6	Near La Bonte Creek, Wyo	Detach A, 4 inf.
Apr 7	Musselshell River, Mont	Detachs D,F, and G, 13 inf.
Apr 14	Cienega, Ariz	Detach E, 32 inf.
Apr 16	Near Ft Wallace, Kans	Officer and escort.
Apr 20	Near Camp Crittenden, Ariz	Detach H, 32 inf.
Apr 22	Sangre Canyon, N Mex	A,F, and H, 3 cav; I, 37 inf.
Apr 29	Mount Turnbull, Ariz	Detachs C, G, and K, 1 cav; B, 4 inf; detach I, 32 inf; Indian scouts.
May 2-9	Scout in the Chino Valley, Ariz	Detach L, 8 cav.
May 6	Grief Hill, near Camp Verde, Ariz	Detachs B, 8 cav, and C, 14 inf.
May 7	San Augustine Pass, N Mex	Detach K, 3 cav.
Do	Paint Creek, near Double Mountain, Tex	Detachs E and F, 35 inf; Indian scouts.
May 10	Ft Hays, Kans	Detachs E and G, 5 inf.
May 11	Near Ft Lowell, Ariz	Detach G, 1 cav.
May 13	Beaver creek, or Elephant Rock, Kans	A,B,F,H,I,L, and M, 5 cav.
May 16	Spring Creek, Nebr	Do
May 18-26	Black Range Mountains, near Ft Bayard, N Mex	Detach B, 3 cav.
May 21	Near Ft Fred Steele, Wyo	Detachs B and H, 4 inf.
May 22-28	Near Mineral Springs, Ariz	K, 1 cav; detach I, 32 inf; Indian scouts.
May 30–June 3	Near Camp Toll Gate, Ariz	Detachs E, F, and K, 8 cav.
May 31	Buffalo Creek, Kans	Detach G, 7 cav.
June 1	Camp on Solomon River, Kans	Do
June 3-4	Rio Pinto, Pinal Mountains, Ariz	E, 1 cav; C, 8 cav; detach F, 14 inf.
June 7	Johnson's River and Pecos River, Tex	Detachs G,L, and M, 9 cav.
June 11	Salmon River, Kans	K, 1 art.
June 16	Near Tollgate, Ariz	Detachs E and F, 8 cav.
June 19	Ft Wallace, Kans	Detachs B,C, and D, 5 inf.
Do	Near Sheridan, Kans	Detach E, 7 cav.
June 19–July 5	Red Rock country, Ariz	L, 8 cav.
June 26	Santa Maria River, near Tollgate, Ariz	F, 8 cav.
June 27	Great Mouth Canyon, Ariz	K, 8 cav.
June 30	Burro Mountains, N Mex	G, 1 cav.
July 3	Hell Canyon, Ariz	L, 8 cav.
July 5	Frenchman's Fork, Colo	A,E, and M, 5 cav; Pawnee scouts.
July 6	Haw-qua-hallawater, Ariz	Detachs E, 1 cav, and C, 8 cav.
July 8	Near Republican River, Kans	Detach M, 5 cav.
Do	Republican River, Kans	
July 11	Summit Springs, Colo	Detachs A,C,D,E,G,H, and M, 5 cav; Indian scouts.
July 13–Aug 19	Scout from Camp Grant, White Mountains, Ariz	Detachs K and L, 1 cav; detachs B,F, and I, 32 inf.
July 22-23	North Platte, Nebr	K, 2 cav.
Aug 3	Ft Stevenson, Dak	E and F, 22 inf; Indian scouts.
Aug 15	Near San Augustine Pass, N Mex	F and H, 3 cav.
Aug 19	Eagle Creek, Mont	Detach B, 13 inf.
Aug 25	Santa Maria River, Ariz	B, 8 cav.
Do	Tonto Station, near Tollgate, Ariz	E,F, and K, 8 cav.

Date	Place	Troops Engaged

1869

Date	Place	Troops Engaged
Aug 26	Tonto Plateau, near Tollgate, Ariz	Do
Sept 5	Scout from Camp Date Creek, Ariz	B, 8 cav; detach F, 12 inf.
Sept 12	Laramie Peak, Wyo	Detachs D and G, 4 inf.
Sept 14	Popo Agie, Wyo	D, 2 cav.
Do	Little Wind River, Wyo	D, 2 cav.
Do	Little Wind River, Wyo	K, 7 inf (1 man).
Sept 15	Near Whiskey Gap, Wyo	Detachs B, 4 inf, and B,D,F, and I, 7 inf.
Sept 16	Salt Fork of Brazos River, Tex	B,E,F, and M, 9 cav.
Sept 20-21	Brazos River, Tex	Detachs B and E, 9 cav.
Sept 23	Red Creek, Ariz	D and L, 8 cav.
Sept. 26	Prairie Dog Creek, Kans	D,C, and M, 2 cav; B,E,F,L, and M, 5 cav; Pawnee scouts.
Sept 29-Oct 6	Miembres Mountains, N Mex	Detach B, 3 cav, and A and C, 38 inf.
Oct 5	Dragoon Springs, Ariz	Detach D, 21 inf.
Oct 8	Chiricahua Pass, Ariz	G, 1 cav.
Oct 12	Red Rock, Ariz	L, 8 cav.
Oct 29	Chiricahua Mountains, Ariz	G, 1 cav; G, 8 cav.
Oct 28-29	Headwaters of Brazos River, Tex	Detachs D and F, 4 cav; B,E,F,GL, and M, 9 cav; Indian scouts.
Oct 31	Chiricahua Mountains, Ariz	G, 1 cav; G, 8 cav.
Nov 6	Garde, Ariz	K, 8 cav.
Do	Between Fts Fetterman and Laramie, Wyo	K, 2 cav.
Nov. 10	Tompkins Valley, Ariz	Detach L, 8 cav.
Nov 16-28	Guadalupe Mountain, N Mex	F, 3 cav.
Nov. 24	Headwaters of Llano River, Tex	Detachs F and M, 9 cav.
Dec 1	Near Horseshoe, Wyo	Detachs A,D,E,F,G, and K, 4 inf.
Dec. 9-10	Walnut Hill, Lee County, Ea	Detach K, 5 cav.
Dec 10	Mount Buford, or Chilson's Creek, Ariz	E, 1 cav; A, 8 cav.
Dec 25	Johnson's mail station, Tex	Detach R, 9 cav.
Dec 26	Sanguinara Canyon, Guadalupe Mountains, Tex	F, 3 cav.
Do	Ft. Wrangle, Alaska	I, 2 art.
Dec. 30	Delaware Creek, Guadalupe Mountains, Tex	F, 3 cav.

1870

Date	Place	Troops Engaged
Jan 3-Feb 6	Scout on Rio Grand and Pecos Rivers, Tex	G and tech L, 9 cav; detachs L and K, 24 inf.
Jan 6-Feb 10	Scouts in Guadalupe Mountains, Tex	Detachs H and I, 9 cav.
Jan 13-Feb 3	North of Gila River, Ariz	Detachs K and M, 1 cav.
Jan 16	Indian Village, Tex	G and detach L, 9 cav.
Jan 20	Delaware Creek, Guadalupe Mountains, Tex	Detachs C,D, 1, and K, 9 cav.
Jan 23	Piegan Camp, Marias River, Mont	F,G,H, and L, 2 cav; A,F,I, and K, 13 inf.
Jan 28	Dragoon Mountains, Ariz	G, 1 cav; detach G, 8 cav.
Mar 9	Reno Road, near Camp McDowell, Ariz	Detach 1, 8 cav.
Mar 15-16	Near Sol's Wash, Ariz	Detach H, 21 inf.
Apr 3	San Martine Springs, Tex	Detach H, 9 cav.
Do	North Hubbard Creek, Tex	Detach F, 4 cav.
Apr 6	Near Clear Creek, Tex	Detach M, 10 cav.
Apr 25	Crow Springs, Tex	Detachs C and K, 9 cav.
Apr 30	Pinal Mountains, near San Carlos, Ariz	Detach E, 1 cav; B, 3 cav; detach A, 21 inf.
May 4	Miner's Delight, near Twin Creek, Wyo	D, 2 cav.
May 14	Mount Adams, Tex	Detach M, 4 cav.
May 17	Spring Creek, or Little Blue, Neb	Detach C, 2 cav.
May 19-20	Kickapoo Springs, Tex	Detach F, 9 cav.
May 25	Tonto Valley, Ariz	E, 1 cav; E, 3 cav.
May 29	Bass Canyon, Tex	K, 9 cav.
May 29-June 26	Near Camp Apache, Ariz	Detach A, 3 cav.
May 30	Holiday Creek, Tex	Detachs C and D, 6 cav.
May 31	Carlyle Station, Kans	

Date	Place	Troops Engaged

1870

Date	Place	Troops Engaged
Do	Bear Creek, Kans	Detachs B and F, 3 inf.
June 1	Solomon River, Kans	Detach M, 7 cav.
June 2	Near Copper Canyon, Ariz	Detach C, 21 inf.
June 3	Near Ft Whipple, Ariz	Detach M, 3 cav.
June 5	Apache Mountains, Ariz	Detachs K, 1 cav, and B and F, 3 cav.
Do	Black Canyon, Ariz	Detach M, 3 cav.
June 8	Red Willow Creek, Nebr	I, 5 cav.
June 9	Near Camp Supply, Ind T	A,F,H,I, and K, 10 cav; B,E, and F, 3 inf.
June 13	Ft Buford, Dak	C,E, and H, 13 inf.
Do	Grinnell, Kans	Detach M, 7 cav.
June 15	East branch of Rio Verde, Ariz	E, 3 cav.
June 18	North Platte, Nebr	E, 2 cav.
June 24	White Mountains, Ariz	Detachs A,C,L, and M, 3 cav.
June 25	Medicine Bow station, Wyo	Detach I, 2 cav.
June 27	Pine Grove Meadow, Wyo	Detach A, 2 cav.
June 27	Pine Grove Meadow, Wyo	Detach A, 2 cav.
Do	Calamus River, Nebr	Detach K, 2 cav.
July 12	Near North Fork, Little Wichita River, Tex	Detachs A,C,D,H,K, and L, 6 cav.
July 14	Near Mount Paso, Tex	Detach D and F, 4 cav.
July 25	Pinal Mountains, Ariz	F, 3 cav.
Aug 1	Skirmish Canyon, Apache Mountains, Ariz	K, 1 cav; F, 3 cav.
Aug 10	Stakes Plains, N Mex	D, 8 cav.
Aug 18	Mescal Ranch, Ariz	Detach D, 21 inf.
Aug 22	Near Camp McDowell, Ariz	Detach E, 1 cav.
Sept 30	Near Ft Concho, Tex	Detach E, 4 cav.
Oct 1	Yellowstone River, Dak	Indian scouts from Ft Buford.
Oct 5	Near Little Wichita River, Tex	M, 6 cav; Indian scouts.
Oct 6	Looking Glass or Shell Creek, Nebr	K, 2 cav.
Do	Pinaleno Mountains, Ariz	F, 3 cav.
Do	Near Little Wichita River, Tex	G, 6 cav.
Oct 16	Guadalupe Mountains, N Mex	B, 8 cav.
Oct 29	Pinal Mountains, Ariz	C, 1 cav.
Oct 31–Nov 22	Guadalupe Mountains, N Mex	Detach A, 8 cav.
Nov 14	Scout from Ft Richardson, Tex	Detach I, 6 cav.
Nov 18	Lowell Station, Kans	
Dec 14	Mount Turnbull, Ariz	F, 3 cav.

1871

Date	Place	Troops Engaged
Jan 1	Pinal Mountains, near Gila River, Ariz	Detachs G, 1 cav, and H, 3 cav.
Jan 7	Cienega, near Camp Verde, Ariz	Detachs A,E, and G, 3 cav.
Jan 9	East Fort River, near Mazatzal Mountains, Ariz	Do
Feb 12	Apache Pass, Chiricahua Mountains, Ariz	Detach C, 8 cav.
Feb 13	Sierra Galiuro, Ariz	F, 3 cav.
Mar 21	Peloncillo Mountains, Ariz	Detach K, 3 cav.
Mar 28	Gila River, near Gila Mountain, Ariz	Do
Apr 1–3	Camp Date Creek, Ariz	Detach B, 3 cav.
Apr 4	Sierra Ancho, Ariz	F, 3 cav.
Apr 11	Apache Mountains, Ariz	Do
Apr 12	Do	Do
Apr 16	Dragoon Mountains, Ariz	Detach K, 3 cav.
Apr 27	Ft Sill, Ind T	Detach E, 10 cav.
May 5	Whetstone Mountains, Ariz	Detach F, 3 cav.
May 12	Near Red River, Tex	Detach L, 10 cav.
May 17	Ft Sill, Ind T	B,D,E, and H, 10 cav.
May 20	Brazos and Big Wichita Divide, Tex	A, 4 cav.
May 21	Camp Melvin Station, Tex	Detach K, 25 inf.
May 24	Birdwood Creek, Nebr	Detachs G,H,I, and L, 5 cav.
May 28	Canadian Mountains, Tex	D, 8 cav.

Date	Place	Troops Engaged

1871

Date	Place	Troops Engaged
May 29	Kiowa Springs, N Mex	F, 8 cav.
June 1	Huachuca Mountains, Ariz	F, 3 cav.
June 8-9	East Fork River, Mazatsal Mountains, and Wild Rye Creek, Ariz	Detachs A,E, and G, 3 cav.
June 10	Huachuca Mountains, Ariz	F, 3 cav.
June 26	Camp Brown, Wyo	Detach B, 2 cav, and A, 13 inf.
June 30	Staked Plains, Tex	Detach I, 9 cav.
July 2	Ft Larned, Kans	C and E, 3 inf.
July 4	Bandera Pass, Tex	Detach M, 4 cav.
July 13	Cienega de los Pinos, Ariz	G, 21 inf.
July 15	Double Mountain, near Salt Fork of Brazos River, Tex	Detach G, 4 cav.
July 19	Bear Springs, near Camp Bowie, Ariz	Detach K, 3 cav.
July 22	Headwaters of Concho River, Tex	Detach F (1 man), 9 cav.
July 31	Near Ft McKavett, Tex	Detachs M, 9 cav, and A, 24 inf.
Aug 25	Arivaypa Canyon, Ariz	D,H, and detach F, 3 cav.
Sept 1	Near Ft McKavett, Tex	Detachs M, 9 cav, and E, 24 inf.
Sept 5	Chino Valley, Ariz	
Sept 19	Foster Springs, Ind T	Detach B, 10 cav.
Oct 11	Freshwater Fork of Brazos River, Tex	A,F,G,H, and K, 4 cav.
Oct 10	Do	Do
Oct 24	Horseshoe Canyon, Ariz	K, 3 cav.

1872

Date	Place	Troops Engaged
Feb 9	North Concho River, Tex	Detach B, 4 cav.
Mar 27-28	Near Ft Concho, Tex	Detach I, 4 cav.
Apr 17	Near Camp Apache, Ariz	Detach D, 21 inf.
Apr 20	Near Howard's Well, Tex	A and H, 9 cav.
April 25	Tierra Amarilla, N Mex	Detach K, 8 cav.
Do	Juniper Mountains, Ariz	Detach K, 5 cav.
Apr 26	South Fork of Loupe River, Nebr	B, 3 cav.
May 2	Near La Bonte Creek, Wyo	Detachs D,E,F, and G, 14 inf.
May 6	Scout from Camp Hualpai, Ariz	Detach K, 5 cav.
Do	Tierra Amarilla, N Mex	Detachs E and K, 8 cav.
May 12	Between Big and Little Wichita rivers, Tex	Detach C, 4 cav.
May 19	Scout from Camp Hualpai, Ariz	Detach K, 5 cav.
May 20	On La Pendencia, Tex	Detach C, 9 cav; detach K, 24 inf; Indian scouts.
May 22	Between Fts Dodge, Kans, and Supply, Ind T	Detach E, 6 cav.
May 23	Sycamore Canyon, Ariz	Detach A, 2 cav.
May 24	Lost Creek, Tex	Detachs A and K, 4 cav.
June 10	Bill Williams Mountain, Ariz	Detach A, 1 cav.
June 14	Ponca Agency, Dak	Detachs B,D,G,H, and K, 22 inf.
June 15	Johnsons Station, Tex	Detach H, 11 inf.
July 1	Gardiner's ranch, Sonora Valley, Ariz	Detach F, 5 cav.
July 12	Deep River, Ind T	A and L, 10 cav.
July 13	Canyon of Whetstone Mountains, Ariz	Detach F, 5 cav.
July 22	Otter Creek, Ind T	A and L, 10 cav.
July 25	Moore's ranch, Sonora Valley, Ariz	Detach F, 5 cav.
July 26-Oct 15	Yellowstone expedition	A,B,C,F,H, and K, 8 knf; A,C, and F, 17 inf; D,F, and G, 22 inf; Indian scouts.
July 27	Mount Graham, Ariz	A, 8 cav.
July 28	Central Station, Tex	Detach K, 25 inf.
Aug 4	Near Priors Fork, Mont	F,G,H, and L, 2 cav; C,E,G, and I, 7 inf.
Aug 6	Chiricahua Mountains, Ariz	A, 8 cav.
Aug 15	Palo Duro Creek, N Mex	B, 8 cav.
Aug 26	Neat Mt McKeen, Dak	Detachs B and C, 6 inf; Indian scouts.
Aug 27	Davidsons Canyon, Ariz	Detach F, 5 cav.
Sept 8	Camp Date Creek, Ariz	E, 5 cav.

Date	Place	Troops Engaged

1872

Date	Place	Troops Engaged
Sept 10-13	Between Beaver Creek and Sweet Water River, Wyo	B, 2 cav.
Sept 25	Muchos Canyon, Santo Maria River, Ariz	B, 2 cav.
Sept 29	North Fork of Red River, Tex	A,D,F,I, and L, 4 cav; Ton ka wa scouts.
Sept 30	Squaw Peak, Ariz	Detach A, 1 cav.
Do	Near Camp Crittendon, Ariz	Detach F, 5 cav.
Oct 2	Ft McKeen, Dak	B and C, 6 inf; Indian scouts.
Oct 14	Do	B and C, 6 inf; H, 17 inf; Indian scouts.
Oct 25-Nov 3	Santa Maria Mountains and Sycamore Creek, Ariz	B,C, and K, 5 cav.
Nov 3	Attack on Ft McKeen, Dak	B and C, 6 inf; H, 17 inf; Indian scouts.
Nov 25	Red Rocks or Hell Canyon, Ariz	C, 5 cav; Piute scouts.
Nov 26	Red Rock Country, Ariz	B, 5 cav.
Nov 29	Near Lost River, Oreg	B, 1 cav.
Dec 7-8	Red Rock Country, Ariz	K, 5 cav; detach G, 23 inf; Indian scouts.
Dec 11	Bad Rock Mountain, north of Old Camp Reno, Ariz	Detachs L and M, 1 cav; detach I, 23 inf; Indian scouts.
Dec 13	Mazatzal Mountains, north of Old Camp Reno, Ariz	Do
Dec 14	Indian Run, Ariz	E, 5 cav.
Dec 21	Land's Ranch or Tule Lake, Cal	G, 1 cav.
Dec 28	Salt River Canyon, Ariz	G,L, and M, 5 cav; Indian scouts.
Do	Red Rock Springs and Red Rock Valley, Ariz	Detach H, 5 cav.
Dec. 30	Mouth of Baby Canyon, Ariz.	Detach E, 5 cav.

1873

Date	Place	Troops Engaged
Jan 2	Clear Creek Canyon, Ariz	Detach K, 5 cav; 1 man, G, 23 inf; Indian scouts.
Jan 12	Tule Lake, Cal	G, 1 cav.
Jan 16	Superstition Mountain, Ariz	B,C,G,H,L, and M, 5 cav.
Jan 17	Modoc Caves in Lava Beds, near Tule Lake, Cal	B,F, and G, 1 cav; B and C and detach F, 21 inf.
Jan 19	East Fork, Verde River, Ariz	Detach E, 5 cav.
Jan 20	Lower Miembres, N Mex	I, 8 cav.
Jan 22	Tonto Creek, Ariz	K, 5 cav.
Feb 6	Hell Canyon, Ariz	Detach A, 1 cav.
Feb 20	Near Fosil Creek, Ariz	I, 1 cav.
Feb 26	Angostura, N. Mex	L, 8 cav.
Mar 19	Mazatzal Mountains, Ariz	K, 5 cav.
Mar 25	Near Turret Mountains, Ariz	Detach A, 5 cav.
Mar 27	Turret Mountains, Ariz	Detach A, 5 cav; detach I, 23 inf; Indian scouts.
Apr 11-20	Lava Beds, Cal	B,F,G,H, and K, 1 cav; A,E, K, and M, 4 art; E and G, 12 inf, B,C,I, and detach F, 21 inf; Indian scouts.
Apr 22	Diamond Butte, Ariz	Detachs L and M, 1 cav; detach I, 23 inf; Indian scouts.
Apr 25	Near Canyon Creek, Ariz	Do.
Apr 26	Lava Beds, Cal	A and K, 4 art; E, 12 inf.
Apr 27	Eagle Springs, Tex	Detach B, 25 inf.
May 6	Santa Maria River, Ariz	A, 1 cav.
May 7	Lava Beds, Cal	B, 21 inf.
Do	Ft A. Lincoln, Dak	B and C, 6 inf; H, 7 inf; Indian scouts.
May 10	Lake Soras, Cal	B and G, 1 cav; B, 4 art; Indian scouts.
May 17	Near Butte Creek, Oreg	Do
May 18	Near Remolina, Mexico	A,B,C,E,I, and M, 4 cav; Indian scouts.
May 29	Tularosa River, N Mex	Detach D, 8 cav.
May 30	Langells' Valley, Cal	B and G, 1 cav; B, 4 art; Indian scouts.
June 1	Willow Creek, Cal	F, 1 cav.
June 15-17	Ft A. Lincoln, Dak	B and C, 6 inf; C, 8 inf; H, 17 inf; Indian scouts.

Date	Place	Troops Engaged

1873

Date	Place	Troops Engaged
June 16	Forks of Tonto Creek, Ariz	Detach C, 5 cav; Indian scouts.
July 13	Canada de Alamosa, N Mex	C, 8 cav.
July 14	Lipan Creek, Tex	L, 4 cav.
Aug 4	Tongue River, Mont	A and B, 7 cav.
Aug 11	Yellowstone River, near Big Horn, Mont	A,B,E,F,G,K.L. and M, 7 cav; Indian scouts.
Aug 31	Near Pease River, Tex	E and I, 10 cav.
Sept 20	Near Ft Fetterman, Wyo	K, 2 cav.
Sept 23	Hardscrabble Creek, or Mescal Range, Ariz	Detach K, 5 cav; Indian scouts.
Sept 20	Sierra Ancho, Ariz	Detachs F,I, and L, 5 cav; detach H, 23 inf; Indian scouts.
Oct 1	Central Station, Tex	Detach K, 25 inf.
Do	Guadalupe Mountains, N Mex	C, 8 cav.
Oct 28-30	Mazatzal Mountains, Sycamore Springs, or Sunflower Valley, Ariz	H, 23 inf; Indian scouts.
Oct 30	Pajarito Springs, N Mex	D, 8 cav.
Nov 25	Near Ehrenberg, Ariz	Detach G, 5 cav; Indian scouts.
Dec 4	East Fork River, Ariz	K, 5 cav; Indian scouts.
Dec 5	Elm Creek, Tex	Detachs D, 10 cav.
Dec 8-Jan 20, '74	Scout from San Carlos, Ariz	Detach C, 5 cav; Indian scouts.
Dec 10	Kickapoo Springs, Tex	Detachs A,B,C, and I, 4 cav; Indian scouts.
Dec 23	Cave Creek, Ariz	K, 5 cav; Indian scouts.
Dec 31	Sunflower Valley, near Old Camp Reno, Ariz	B, 5 cav; Indian scouts.

1874

Date	Place	Troops Engaged
Jan 4	Wild Rye Creek, Ariz	Do
Jan 8	Pleasant Valley headwaters of Cherry Creek, Ariz	Do
Jan 10	Canyon Creek, Ariz	K, 5 cav; Indian scouts.
Feb 2	Home Creek, Tex	Detach A, 10 cav.
Feb 5	Double Mountains, Tex	G and detach D, 10 cav; F and detachs A and G, 11 inf; Indian scouts.
Feb 9	Cottonwood Creek, near Laramie Peak, Wyo	Detachs K, 2 cav, and A, 14 inf.
Feb 20-Apr 21	Scout in Bill Williams's Mountains, Ariz	Detach G, 5 cav.
Mar 8	Pinal Mountains, Ariz	Detachs B,F,H,I,L, and M, 5 cav; Indian scouts.
Mar 15	Do	H and detach F and M, 5 cav.
Mar 25-26	Superstition Mountains, Ariz	Detach K, 5 cav.
Apr 2	Pinal Creek, Ariz	Detachs F,L, and M, 5 cav; Indian scouts.
Apr 3-14	Pinal Mountains, Ariz	Detachs B, H, and I, 5 cav; Indian scouts.
Apr 4	Grand Canyon of the Colorado, near the, Ariz	Detach G, 5 cav.
Apr 11	Bull Bear Creek, Ind T	Detach G, 6 cav.
Apr 23	Near Ft A. Lincoln, Dak	A,B,E,F,G, and L, 7 cav.
Apr 28	Arivaypa Mountains, Ariz	Detach K, 5 cav.
May 2	Between Red River and Big Wichita River, Tex	Detach K, 10 cav.
May 9	Tonto Creek, Ariz	Detach K, 5 cav; Indian scouts.
May 17-18	Four Peaks, Mazatzal Mountains, Ariz	Detachs E and K, 5 cav.
May 18	Carrizo Mountains, Tex	Detach B, 25 inf.
May 21-June 6	Near Diamond Butte, Ariz	Detach K, 5 cav.
May 27	Sierra Ancho, Ariz	Detach A, 5 cav; Indian scouts.
June 5	Do	Detach I, 5 cav.
June 8	Pleasant Valley, Ariz	B, 5 cav; Indian scouts.
June 19	Buffalo Creek, Ind T	Detachs K, 6 cav, and D, 3 inf.
June 21	Do	Detachs G, 6 cav, and A, 3 inf.
June 24	Bear Creek Redoubt, Kans	Do
July 2	Castle Dome Mountains, Ariz	G, 5 cav.
July 4	Near Bad Water Branch of Wind River, or Snake Mountains, or Owl Mountains, Wyo	B, 2 cav; Indian scouts.
July 8-13	Crow Agency, Mont	Detach A, 7 inf.
July 13	30 miles west of Camp Date Creek, Ariz	G, 5 cav.

Date	Place	Troops Engaged

1874

Date	Place	Troops Engaged
July 19	Rattlesnake Hills, Wyo	B, 2 cav; Indian scouts.
Aug 15	Near San Carlos, Ariz	Indian scouts.
Aug 18	Black Mesa, Ariz	Do
Aug 19	Adobe Walls, Tex	Detach 6 cav; Indian scouts.
Aug 20	Chicken Creek, Tex	Do
Aug 22	North end of Sierra Ancho, Ariz	Indian scouts.
Aug 22-23	Wichita Agency, Ind T	C,E,H, and L, 10 cav; I, 25 inf.
Aug 30	Mulberry Creek, or Salt Fork of Red River, Tex	A,D,F,G,H,I,L, and M, 6 cav; C,D,E, and I, 5 inf.
Sept 7	Elm Fork of Red River, Ind T	Indian scouts.
Sept 8	Wichita River, Tex	Do
Sept 9	Dry Fork of Wichita River, Tex	Detach H and I, 6 cav; I, 5 inf.
Do	Sweetwater Creek, Tex	Detach H, 6 cav.
Sept 9-12	Near Canadian River, Tex	Detach I, 6 cav.
Sept 11-12	Near Wichita River, Tex	Detach H, 6 cav.
Do	McClellan Creek, near Wichita River, Tex	Detach I and M, 6 cav.
Sept 12	Between Sweetwater and Dry Fork of Wichita River, Rex	C,K, and L, 8 cav.
Sept 17	Headwaters of Cave Creek, Ariz	Detach K, 5 cav; Indian scouts.
Sept 26-28	On Red River, near Tute and Palo Duro canyons, Tex	A,D,E,F,H,I,K, and L, 4 cav.
Oct 4	Near Fort Sill, Ind T	K, 9 cav.
Oct 9	Salt Fork of Red River, Tex	A,E,F,H, and I, 11 inf; Indian scouts.
Oct 13	Near Gageby Creek, Ind T	H,K, and L, 8 cav; Indian scouts.
Oct 17	Near Washita River, Ind T	I, 6 cav.
Oct 21-Nov. 8	Expedition from Ft Sill, Ind T	I, 6 cav.
Oct 23	Old Pueblo Fork of Little Colorado River, Ariz	Detach I, 5 cav; Indian scouts.
Oct 29	Cave Creek, Ariz	Detach K, 5 cav.
Nov 1	Sunset Pass, Little Colorado River, Ariz	Detachs A and K, 5 cav.
Nov 3	Laguna Curato, Tex	A,D,E,F,H,I,K, and L, 4 cav.
Nov 6	McClellan Creek, Tex	H, 8 cav.
Do	Near Laguna Tahoka, Tex	A, 4 cav.
Nov 8	Near McClellan Creek, Tex	Detachs D, 6 cav, and D, 5 inf.
Nov 10	Near Ft Dodge, Kans	Detach B, 6 cav.
Nov 25	Snow Lake, or Jarvis Pass, Ariz	Detachs A and K, 5 cav.
Nov 28	Near Muster Creek, Tex	C,H,K, and L, 8 cav.
Dec 1	Canyon Creek, Tonto Basin, Ariz	Detach B, 5 cav; Indian scouts.
Dec 2	Gageby Creek, Ind T	Detach I, 6 cav.
Dec 8	Muchaquay Valley, Staked Plains, Tex	I, 4 cav.
Dec 12	Standing Rock Agency, Dak	F and L, 7 cav.
Dec 20	Kingfisher Creek on North Fork of Canadian River, Ind T	D, and detach M, 10 cav, and Indian scouts.

1875

Date	Place	Troops Engaged
Jan 2-Feb 23	Scout from Camp Apache, Ariz	Detachs B and I, 5 cav; Indian scouts.
Jan 3-6	Hackberry Creek, Kans	Detachs F, 5 inf, and K, 19 inf.
Jan 26	Solis Ranch, near Ringgold Barracks, Tex	Detach G, 9 cav.
Jan 27	Near Ringgold Barracks, Tex	B and G, 9 cav.
Jan 29	Sierra Ancho, Ariz	Detach K, 5 cav.
Apr 6	Near Cheyenne Agency, Ind T	M, 6 cav; D and M, 10 cav, and detach H, 5 inf.
Apr 23	North Fork of Sappa Creek, Kans	Detachs H. 6 cav. amd L. 19 inf.
Apr 25	Eagle Nest, crossing of Pecos River, Tex	Seminole negro scouts.
Apr 30	La Luz Canyon N Mex	D, 8 cav.
May 5	Battle Point, Tex	Detachs A,F,G,I, and L, 10 cav; Indian scouts.
June 1	Near Ft Verde, Ariz	Indian scouts.
June 3	Hackberry Creek, Ind T	Detach A, 4 cav.
June 9-15	Tonto Basin, Ariz	Indian scouts.
June 27-July 8	Do	Detachs A and B, 8 inf; Indian scouts.
June 29	Near Reynolds's ranch, Tex	A, 4 cav.

Date	Place	Troops Engaged

1875

July 1	Little Popo Agie River, Wyo	Detach D, 2 cav.
July 6	Ponca Agency, Dak	Detach G, 1 inf.
July 7	Near Camp Lewis, Mont	Detachs G and K, 7 inf.
Aug 28-Sept 2	North Platte River north of Sidney, Nebr	Detach G, 3 cav.
Oct 27	Between Buffalo and Smoky Hill stations, Kans	Detach H, 5 cav.
Nov 2	Near Pecos River, Tex	G and L, 10 cav; Indian scouts.
Nov 20	Near Antelope Station, Nebr	Detach G, 3 cav.

1876

Jan 9	Camp Apache, Ariz	A and D, 6 cav; E and K, 8 inf; Indian scouts.
Jan 22	Cimarron River, 125 miles east of Camp Supply, Ind T	Detach G, 5 cav.
Feb 1	Near Chevelon's Fork, Ariz	Indian scouts.
Feb 18	Carrizo Mountains, Tex	Detach B, 25 inf.
Mar 5	Dry Forks of Powder River, Wyo	C and I, 4 inf.
Mar 17	Crazy Horse's Camp, on Little Powder River, Mont	A,B,E,I, and K, 2 cav; A,D,E,F, and M, 3 cav.
Mar 27-28	Tonto Basin, Ariz	Indian scouts.
Apr 10	San Jose Mountains, Ariz. near Sonora line	Detach H, 6 cav.
Apr 13	Near Ft Sill, Ind T	Detach I, 4 cav.
Apr 28	Grace Creek, Nebr	Detach A, 23 inf.
June 9	Tongue River, Wyo	D, 2 cav; A,B,C,D,E,F,G,I,L, and M, 3 cav; D and F, 4 inf; C,G, and H, 9 inf.
June 17	Rosebud River, Mont	A,B,D,E, and I, 2 cav; A,B,C,D,E,F,G,I,L, and M, 3 cav; D and F, 3 inf; C,G, and H, 9 inf.
June 22	Elkhorn River, Nebr	K, 2 cav.
June 25	Attack on Crazy Horse's and Sitting Bull's band of Sioux Indians at Little Big Horn River, Mont	C,D,F,I, and L, 7 cav; Indian scouts.
June 25-26	Little Big Horn River, Mont	A,B,D,G,H,K, and M, 7 cav; Indian scouts.
July 7	Head of Tongue River, Mont	Detachs A,B,D, and I, 2 cav.
July 17	Near Hat, or Indian Creek, Wyo	A,B,D,G,I,K, and M, 5 cav.
July 17-19	Near Hat Creek, Wyo	Detach K, 3 cav.
July 29	Mouth of Powder River, Mont	E,F,G,H,I, and K, 22 inf.
July 30	Near Saragossa, Mexico	Detach B, 10 cav; Indian scouts.
Aug 1	Red Canyon, Mont	K, 4 inf.
Aug 15	Red Rock country, Ariz	Detach E, 6 cav; Indian scouts.
Aug 23	Near mouth of Yellowstone River, Mont. (attack on steamers Josephine and Benton)	G, 6 inf.
Sept 9	Slim Buttes (surprise of American Horse, Dak)	A,B,D,E, and I, 2 cav; A,B,C,D,E,F,G,I,L, and M, 3 cav; A,B,C,D,E,F,G,I,K, and M, 5 cav; D,F, and G, 4 inf; C,G, and H, 9 inf; B,C,F, and I, 14 inf.
Sept 14	Owl Creek, Belle Fourche River, Dak	Detachs A,B,C,D,E,F,G,I, and K, 5 cav.
Sept 15	Florida Mountains, N Mex	F, 9 cav.
Sept 18	Caves east of Verde, Ariz	Indian scouts.
Oct 4	Tonto Basin, Ariz	Detach E, 6 cav; Indian scouts.
Oct 11	Spring Creek, Mont	C, 17 inf; G,H, and K, 22 inf.
Oct 14	Chugwater, or Richard Creek, Wyo	Detach K, 2 cav.
Oct 15-16	Clear Creek, Mont	C and G, 17 inf; G,H, and detachs I and K, 22 inf.
Oct 21	Big Dry River, or Cedar Creek, Mont	5 inf.
Oct 23	Chadron Creek, near Camp Robinson, Nebr	B,D,E,F,I, and M, 4 cav; H and L, 5 cav; Indian scouts.
Oct 27	Surrender of Sioux Indians at Big Dry River, Mont	5 inf.
Nov 25-26	Bates Creek, near North Fork of Powder River, Wyo	K, 2 cav; H and K, 3 cav; B,D,E,F,I, and M, 4 cav; H and L, 5 cav; Indian scouts.
Dec 7	Bark Creek, Mont	G,H, and I, 5 inf.

Date	Place	Troops Engaged

1876
Dec 18 . . . . Near head of Red Water Creek, Dak . . . . Do

1877
Jan 8 . . . . Wolf Mountains, Mont . . . . A,C,D,E,K, and detachs B and H, 5 inf; E and F, 22 inf.

Jan 9-Feb 5 . . . . Scout in Tonto Basin, Ariz . . . . Detach E, 6 cav; Indian scouts.

Jan 9 . . . . Leitendorf range of mountains, N Mex . . . . Detachs H and L, 6 cav; Indian scouts.

Jan 12 . . . . Near Elkhorn Creek, Wyo . . . . Detach A, 3 cav.

Jan 23 . . . . Florida Mountains N Mex . . . . Detach C, 9 cav.

Jan 28 . . . . Sierra Boca Grande, Mexico . . . . Do

Feb 23 . . . . Hay Creek, near Deadwood, Dak . . . . C, 3 cav.

Apr 1 . . . . Rio Grande, near Devil's River, Tex . . . . Seminole negro scouts.

May 4 . . . . Lake Quemada, Tex . . . . G, 10 cav; Indian scouts.

May 7 . . . . Little Muddy Creek, Mont . . . . F,GH, and L, 2 cav; B and H, 5 inf; E,F,G, and H, 22 inf.

May 20 . . . . Near Camp Bowie, Ariz . . . . H and L, 6 cav.

June 17 . . . . White Bird Canyon, Idaho . . . . F and H, 1 cav.

July 1 . . . . Clearwater River, Idaho . . . . E and L, 1 cav.

July 3 . . . . Near Craig's Mountain, Idaho . . . . Detach L, 1 cav.

July 3-5 . . . . Cottonwood Ranch, on Clearwater River, Idaho . . E,F, and L, 1 cav, and citizens.

July 11-12 . . . . South Fork of Clearwater, Idaho . . . . B,E,F,H, and L, 1 cav; B,C,D,E,H, and I, 21 inf; A,D,E, and G, 4 art.

July 17 . . . . Weippe, Oro Fino Creek, Idaho . . . . Detachs B,E,H, and L, 1 cav; Indian scouts.

July 21 . . . . Belle Fourche, Dak . . . . Detachs A,D,E,F, and G, 3 cav.

Aug 9-10 . . . . Big Hole Basin, Mont . . . . L, 2 cav; A,D,F,G,I,K, and detachs B and E, 7 inf.

Aug 20 . . . . Camas Meadows, Idaho . . . . B,C,I, and K, 1 cav; L, 2 cav; detach E, 4 art; H, 8 inf.

Aug 29 . . . . Near Black Rock, Ariz . . . . Detach F, 6 cav.

Sept 8-10 . . . . Near San Francisco River and Mogollon Mountains, N Mex . . . . Detachs B and M, 6 cav; Indian scouts.

Sept 13 . . . . Canyon Creek, Mont . . . . K and detachs C and I, 1 cav; F,G,H,I,L, and M, 7 cav; detach E, 4 art.

Sept 23 . . . . Cow Island, Mont . . . . Detach B, 7 inf.

Sept 29 . . . . Near Saragossa, Mexico . . . . Detachs A and F, 8 cav; detach C, 10 cav; Indian scouts.

Sept 30 . . . . Snake or Eagle Creek, near Bear Paw Mountains, Mont . . . . F,G, and H, 2 cav; A,D, and K, 7 cav; B,F,G,I,K, and detach D, 5 inf; Indian scouts.

Nov 1 . . . . Big Bend of Rio Grande, Tex . . . . Seminole negro scouts.

Nov 29-30 . . . . Sierra del Carmen, Mexico . . . . A and K, 8 cav; C, 10 cav; Indian scouts.

Dec. 13 . . . . Ralston Flat, N Mex . . . . Detachs C,G,H, and L, 6 cav; Indian scouts.

Dec 18 . . . . Las Animas Mountains, N Mex . . . . Do

1878
Jan 7 . . . . Near Tonto Creek, Ariz . . . . Detach A, 6 cav and B, 8 inf; Indian scouts.

Jan 16 . . . . Ross Fork Agency, Idaho . . . . B,F, and I, 5 cav; C,D,E, and G, 14 inf.

Feb 5 . . . . Headwaters of Sunday Creek, Mont . . . . Indian scouts.

Feb 23 . . . . Near Ft Keogh, Mont . . . . Do

Apr 5 . . . . Mogollon Mountains, Ariz . . . . Detach A, 6 cav and B, 8 inf; Indian scouts.

May 20 . . . . Smith's mills, near Wickenburg, Ariz . . . . Detach I, 6 cav.

Do . . . . Head of White's Gulch, Mont . . . . Detachs D and E, 7 inf.

June 23 . . . . Silver River, Oreg . . . . A,F,G, and L, 1 cav.

June 28 . . . . Ft Sill, Ind T . . . . Guard.

July 8 . . . . Birch Creek, Oreg . . . . A,E,F,G,H,K, and L, 1 cav.

Do . . . . Upper Columbia River . . . . 10 men of ord dept; 10 men of 21 inf.

July 12 . . . . Ladd's Canyon, Oreg . . . . C, 12 inf.

July 13 . . . . Umatilla Agency, Oreg . . . . K, 1 cav; D and G, 4 art; B,D,E,G,H,I, and K, 21 inf.

July 20 . . . . North Fork of John Day's River, Oreg . . . . A,E,F,G, and H, 1 cav.

July 21 . . . . Middle Fork of Clearwater River, Mont . . . . Detachs B,H, and I, 3 inf.

Date	Place	Troops Engaged
1878		
July 26	Baker City, Oreg	C and detach K, 2 inf.
July 29	Sacramento Mountains, N Mex	Navaho Indian scouts.
Aug 5	Dog Canyon, N Mex	F and H, 9 cav; Indian scouts.
Aug 9	Bennett creek, Idaho	Detach K, 12 inf.
Aug 27	Henry's Lake, Idaho	K, 2 cav.
Aug 29-30	Index Peak, Wyo	Detach 5 inf; Indian scouts.
Sept 4	Clark's Fork, Mont	A,C,F,GI, and K, 5 inf; Indian scouts.
Sept 12	Near Big Wind or Snake River, Wyo	Detach G, 5 cav; Indian scouts.
Sept 13	Near Turkey Springs, Ind T	G and H, 4 cav.
Sept 14	Red Hill, Ind T	Do
Sept 17	Bear Creek, N Mex	Indian scouts.
Sept 18	Near Bear or Bluff Creek, Kans	I, 4 cav.
Sept 21-22	Sand Creek, Kans	F,G,H, and I, 4 cav; A, 16 inf; detach F, 19 inf.
Sept 27	Punished Woman's Fork, Kans	Detachs B,F,G,H, and I, 4 cav; detachs D,F, and G, 19 inf.
1879		
Jan 9-22	Ft Robinson, Nebr (revolt of Cheyennes)	A,C,E,F,H, and L, 3 cav.
Jan 15	Cormedos Mountains, N Mex	A, 9 cav.
Jan 20	Near Bluff Station, Wyo	B and D, 3 cav.
Mar 8	Ojo Caliente, N Mex	I, 9 cav.
Mar 25	Box Elder Creek, Mont	E and I, 2 cav; Indian scouts.
Apr 5	Mizpah Creek, Mont	Detachs E, 2 cav, and Signal Corps.
Apr 10	Near Ft Keogh, Mont	Detach B, 2 cav; Indian scouts.
Apr 17	Near Careless Creek Musselshell River, Mont	Detach K, 3 inf; detachs E and D, 7 inf; Indian scouts.
Apr 22	Countryman's ranch, Mont	Indian scouts.
Apr 30	Ojo Caliente, N Mex	Do
May 29	Black Range, Miembres Mountains, N Mex	Detachs C and I, 9 cav.
June 25	Tonto Basin, Ariz	Indian scouts.
June 29	Alkali Creek, Mont	Crow Indian scouts.
July 17	Sioux expedition, Milk River, Mont	A,B,C,E,G,I, and M, 2 cav; ;A,B,C,G,H,I, and K, 5 inf; C and K, 6 inf; Indian scouts.
July 19	Near Camp Loder, Mont	Detach I, 7 inf.
July 25	Near Salt Lake or Sulphur, Tex	Detachs H, 10 cav, and H, 25 inf.
July 29	Big Creek, Idaho	C and detach K, 2 inf.
Aug 14	Near Poplar Creek, on Missouri River, Mont	I, 2 cav; A,B,C,G,H,I, and K, 5 inf.
Aug 19	Big Creek, Idaho	Indian scouts.
Aug 20	Salmon River, Idaho	Indian scouts.
Do	Big Creek, Idaho	C and detach K, 2 inf.
Sept 4	Ojo Caliente, N Mex	Detach E, 9 cav.
Sept 16	Van Horn Mountains, Tex	Detach H, 10 cav.
Sept 18	Las Animas River, N Mex	A,B,C, and G, 9 cav; Indian scouts.
Sept 19	Miembres Mountains, N Mex	Navaho Indian scouts.
Sept 21	Big Meadow, Idaho	Indian scouts.
Sept 22	Near Middle Fork, Salmon River, Idaho	Do
Sept 26-27	Black Mountains, N Mex	Do
Sept 28	Near Ojo Caliente, N Mex	E, 9 cav.
Sept 29-Oct 25	White River, Ute expedition, Milk Creek, Colo	E, 3 cav; D and F, 5 cav.
Sept 29-Oct 1	Cuchillo Negro River, Miembres Mountains, N Mex	Detach A, 6 cav; detachs B,C,G, and L, 9 cav; Indian scouts.
Sept 30	Near Canada de Alamosa, N Mex	Detach E, 9 cav.
Oct 1, 6	Chamberlain Basin, Idaho	Indian scouts.
Oct 2-4	Milk Creek, Colo	E, 3 cav; D and F, 5 cav; D, 9 cav.
Oct 5	Do	E, 3 cav; A,B,D,F,I, and M, 5 cav; D, 9 cav; B,C,E,F, and I, 4 inf.
Oct 10	White River, Colo	E, 3 cav; A,B,D,F,H,I, and M, 5 cav; D, 9 cav; B,C,E,F, and I, 4 inf.

Date	Place	Troops Engaged

1879

Oct 20	Rifle Creek, near White River, Colo	Detach H, 5 cav; Indian scouts.
Oct 27	San Guzman Mountains, near Corralitos, Mexico	B,C,F,H, and M, 9 cav; Indian scouts.

1880

Jan 12	Rio Puerco, N Mex	B,C,F,H, and M, 9 cav; Indian scouts.
Jan 17	San Mateo Mountains, N Mex	Do
Jan 30	Cabello Mountains, N Mex	Detachs B and M, 9 cav.
Feb 3	San Andreas Mountains, N Mex	B,C,F,H, and M, 9 cav; Indian scouts.
Feb 7	Near Pumpkin Creek, Mont	Detach B, 2 cav; Indian scouts.
Feb 28	Sacramento Mountains, N Mex	A, 9 cav.
Mar 8	Porcupine Creek, Mont	I and K, 5 inf.
Do	Rosebud Creek, Mont	Detach E, 5 inf; Indian scouts.
Apr 1	O'Fallon's Creek, Mont	Detachs C and E, 2 cav.
Apr 3	Near Pecos Fall, Tex	F and L, 10 cav.
Apr 5	Miembrillo Canyon, San Andreas Mountains, N Mex	A, 9 cav.
Apr 6-9	Do	A,D,F, and G, 9 cav.
Apr 7	San Andreas Mountains, N Mex	Detachs D and E, 6 cav; Indian scouts.
Apr 9	San Andreas Springs, San Andreas Mountains, N Mex	L, 6 cav; Indian scouts.
Do	Shake Hand Springs, Tex	K, 10 cav.
Apr 16	Camp near South Fork, N. Mex	Detach G, 9 cav; G, 15 in.
Do	Mescalero Agency, N Mex	H and L, 9 cav; D,E,F,K, and L. 10 cav.
Apr 17	Near Dog Canyon, N Mex	H and L, 9 cav; Indian scouts.
Apr 20	Sacramento Mountains, N Mex	Detach L, 10 cav.
May 7	Ash Creek Valley, Ariz	Detach E, 6 cav; Indian scouts.
May 14	Old Fort Tulerosa, N Mex	Detachs E, I, and K, 9 cav.
May 24	Headwaters of Polomas River, N Mex	Indian scouts.
June 5	Cook's Canyon, N Mex	A,D,K, and L, 9 cav.
June 11-12	Ojo Viejo, Tex	Pueblo scouts.
July 30	Rock Bridge or Eagle Pass, Tex	C and G, 10 cav; Indian scouts.
Aug 3	Alamo Springs, Tex	Detachs B,C,G, and H, 10 cav, and scouts.
Aug 4	Guadalupe Mountains, Tex	F, 10 cav.
Do	Near Rattlesnake Springs, Tex	Detachs H, 10 cav, and H, 24 inf.
Do	Rattlesnake Canyon, Tex	B,C,G, and H, 10 cav.
Aug 17	Little Missouri River, Mont	Detach F, 7 cav.
Sept 1	Aqua Chiquita, Sacramento Mountains, N Mex	Detachs G, 9 cav, and C, 15 inf.
Sept 7	Near Ft Cummings, N Mex	A, 4 cav.
Oct 28	Ojo Caliente, Tex	Detachs B and K, 10 cav.
Nov 7	Mouth of Musselshell River, Mont	Detach M, 2 cav; Indian scouts.
Dec. 2	Camp near South Fork in White Mountains, N Mex	C, 15 inf.

1881

Jan 24	Near Poplar River, Mont	F, 7 cav; A,B,C,F, and G, 5 inf; detachs A, 7 inf, and F, 11 inf.
Jan 24	Near Canada Alamosa, N Mex.	
Feb 5	Candelaria Mountains, Mexico	Detach K, 9 cav; Indian scouts.
Apr 29	Ft Cummings, near Mexican line, N Mex	Do
May 3	Sierra del Burro, Mexico	Seminole negro scouts.
July 17	Alamo Canyon, N Mex	Detach L, 9 cav; Indian scouts.
July 19	Arena Blanca, N Mex	Do
July 25	White Sands, N Mex	Do
July 26	San Andreas Mountains, N Mex	Do
Aug 3	Monica Springs, N Mex	Do
Aug 12	Carrizo Canyon, N Mex	Detach K, 9 cav.
Aug 16	Rio Cuchillo Negro, N Mex	L, 9 cav.

Date	Place	Troops Engaged

1881

Do	Near San Mateo Mountains, Black Range, N Mex	Detachs B and H, 9 cav; Indian scouts.
Aug 19	McEwer's ranch in Guerillo Canyon, N Mex	Detachs B and H, 9 cav.
Aug 30	Cibicu Creek, Ariz	D and E, 6 cav; Indian scouts.
Aug 31	Near Ft Apache, Ariz	D and E, 6 cav; D, 12 inf; Indian scouts.
Sept 30	San Carlos, Ariz	A,B,C, and E, 6 cav.
Oct 2	Cedar Springs, Ariz	G, 1 cav; A and F, 6 cav; Indian scouts.
Oct 4	South Pass of Dragoon Mountains, Ariz	G and I, 1 cav: A and F, 6 cav; F and H, 8 cav, and Indian scouts.
Oct 8	Near Milk River, Mont	H and L, 2 cav.
Nov. 3	Canyon Creek, Ariz	Indian scouts.

1882

Apr 20	Near Ft Thomas, Ariz	B, 6 cav.
Apr 23	Near Steins' Pass, Ariz	Detach M, 4 cav; Indian scouts.
Do	Horseshoe Canyon, N Mex	C,F,G,H, and M, 4 cav; Indian scouts.
Apr 28	Hatchett Mountain, near Mexican line, N Mex	G and M, 6 cav; Indian scouts.
Apr 29	Shoshone Agency, near Ft Washakie, Wyo	Detachs H and K, 3 cav; Indian scouts.
June 1	Canyon near Cloverdale, N Mex	A, 6 cav; Indian scouts.
July 9	Medicine Lodge, Mont	L, 2 cav.
July 17	Big Dry Wash, or Chevelon's Fork, Ariz	D,E, and I, 3 cav; E,I, and K, 6 cav; Indian scouts.
July 23	Agency at Ft Stanton, N Mex	Indian police.
Aug 13	Near Ft Apache, Ariz	Indian scouts.
Nov 8	Near Tullock's Fork, Mont	Do

1883

Apr 14	Beaver Creek, or Sweetgrass Hills, Mont	Detach H, 2 cav.
Apr 19	Wild Horse Lake, near British line, Mont	Detach L, 2 cav.
May 15	Babispe River, in Sierra Madre, Mexico	Indian scouts, A,B,C,D,E,F, and G.

1884

July 15	Wormington Canyon, Colo	B and F, 6 cav.

1885

May 22	Devil's Creek, Mogollon Mountains, N Mex	A and K, 4 cav; Indian scouts.
June 8	Guadalupe Canyon, Sonora, Mexico	Detachs C,D, and G, 4 cav.
June 21	Opunto, Sonora, Mexico	Indian scouts.
June 23	Babispe Mountains, Mexico (Sonora.)	Do
July 28	Sierra Madre, Sonora, Mexico	Detachs G,H, and K, Indian scouts.
Aug 7	Do	Detachs G,H,I, and K; Indian scouts.
Sept 22	Torres Mountains, Mexico	Do
Oct 10	Near Lang's ranch, N Mex	Detach F, 4 cav.
Nov 8	Florida Mountains, N Mex	Detach A, 6 cav; Indian scouts.
Dec 9	Lillie's ranch, on Clear Creek, N Mex	C, 8 cav.
Dec 19	Little Dry Creek, or White Horse, N Mex	Do

1886

Jan 10-11	Near Aros River, Sonora, Mexico	Indian scouts; A,B, and C.
May 3	Near Penito Mountains, Sonora, Mexico	K, 10 cav.
May 15	Pinto, or Santa Cruz Mountains, Mexico	D, 4 cav.
June 6	Near Buena Vista, Patagonia Mountains, Mexico	B, 4 cav.
July 13	Yaqui River, Mexico	Detachs D and K, 8 inf; Indian scouts.
Oct 18	Black River Mountains, Ariz	H, 10 cav.

1887

June 11	Rincon Mountains, Ariz	Detachs E and L, 10 cav.
Nov 5	Crow Agency, Mont	A,B,D,E,G, and K, 1 cav; A, 7 cav; H, 9 cav; B and E, 3 inf; D,G, and I, 5 inf; C, 7 inf.

Date	Place	Troops Engaged
1888		
June 16	Pompey's Pillar, on Yellowstone River, Mont	Indian scouts.
July 28	Near San Carlos Agency, Ariz	Do
1889		
May 11	Cedar Springs, Ariz	Detachs C and G, 10 cav; detachs B,C,E, and K, 24 inf.
June 2	North bank of Missouri River, 15 miles from mouth of Little Missouri River, N Dak	K, 8 cav.
1890		
Mar 7	Near mouth of Cherry Creek, Salt River, Ariz	Detach L, 4 cav and K, 10 cav; Indian scouts.
Sept 13	Tongue River Agency, Mont	E and G, 1 cav.
Dec 15	Grand River, near Standing Rock, N Dak	E and G, 8 cav; Indian police.
Dec 28	Near Porcupine Creek, S Dak	A,B,I, and K, 7 cav; detach E, 1 art.
Dec 29	Pine Ridge Agency, S Dak	2 inf.
Do	Wounded Knee Creek, S Dak	A,B,C,D,E,G,I, and K, 7 cav; D,E,I, and K, 9 cav; E, 1 art; Indian scouts.
Dec. 30	Near Pine Ridge Agency, S Dak	D, 9 cav.
Do	Do	E,I, and K, 9 cav.
Do	Drexel or Catholic Mission, near White Clay Creek, S Dak	A,B,C,D,E,G,I, and K, 7 cav; D,E,I, and K, 9 cav; E, 1 art; Indian scouts.
1891		
Jan 1	Near mouth of Little Grass Creek, S Dak	A,F,H,I, and K, 6 cav.
Jan 7	Near Pine Ridge Agency, S Dak	Detach Indian scouts.
Jan 9	Near Ft Buford, N Dak	Detach E, 8 cav.
Dec 21-22	Retamal, Tex	Detach C, 3 cav and E, 18 inf.
Dec 29	Charco Renondo, Tex	Detach C, 3 cav.
Dec 30	Rancho Rendado Zapata, Tex	A and G, 3 cav.
1892		
Jan 24	Rancho Grominito, Tex	Detach C, 3 cav.
Feb 6-15	Near Grande, Tex	Do
Feb 18	Northeast of Palito Blanco, Tex	D, 3 cav.
Dec 24	El Alazan, near Roma, Tex	K, 3 cav; Indian scouts.
1893		
Jan 21	Near Baluarte Ranche, Tex (Julian Guerras Pastune)	Detachs D and K, 3 cav.
Jan 22	Las Tajitos ranch, near Brownsville, Tex	Do
Feb 23	Las Mulas ranch, Starr County, Tex. (30 miles north of Ft Ringgold)	Seminole scouts.
1896		
May 8	Guadalupe Canyon, Ariz	Detach E, 7 cav; Indian scouts.
May 16	In mountains near Lang's ranch, Ariz	Detachs C,E, and I, 7 cav, Indian scouts.

Source:
Heitman, Francis B. *Historical Register and Dictionary of the USA*. Washington, D.C.: Government Printing Office, 1903. Volumes I and II.

The Ghost Dance

The greatest of the Western Indian prophets was Wovoka, a Paiute from Nevada. When he announced his revelation from God in 1886, he was still comparatively young, being only thirty years of age. He claimed that he had seen God in a trance and that God had told him to tell the Indians to be good, to love one another, to work hard, and to have peace with the whites. He also claimed that he had been given knowledge of a five day dance which was to be repeated at regular intervals. Furthermore, Wovoka contended that he had been given control of the elements. A little later he announced that power had been given him to rule the West, even as President Benjamin Harrison ruled the East and God ruled Heaven. Wovoka never claimed that he himself was divine, but only that he was a prophet. Also he disclaimed responsibility for the "ghost shirt" which later became important. Although he undoubtedly practiced a certain amount of trickery and sleight of hand, he was probably sincere in his beliefs.

The doctrines preached by Wovoka spread like wildfire over the western plains, with each tribe changing and modifying them in accordance with its own mythology, beliefs, and hopes. Assiniboin, Gros Ventre, Cheyenne, Arikara, Mandan, Shoshoni, Arapaho, and Sioux were soon numbered among the believers, while the doctrines spread even to the Navaho and Pueblo of the Far Southwest. Everywhere the belief developed that in the near future all Indians, both living and dead, would be resurrected on a regenerated earth, with plenty of game and no sickness or death. The usual date set for the fulfillment of the prophecy was the spring of 1891. Fundamentally these Indian beliefs contained no menace toward the whites, for few of the Native Americans thought that the coming regeneration was to be obtained by a war against the whites. Rather they felt that the absence of war, lying, and killing would hasten the day when divine providence would intervene on their behalf.

The one tribe to embrace a hostile interpretation of the new beliefs was the Sioux—probably because of the unusually bad conditions under which they were living. They had recently lost the larger proportion of their land, and the remainder was barren and desolate. A cattle disease in 1888 and crop failures in 1889 and 1890 brought them to the verge of starvation. Epidemics of measles, grippe, and whooping cough took their toll. Fraud and mismanagement by their agents left them without relief. Consequently it was but little wonder that they adopted the messianic idea more seriously and vigorously than some of the other tribes.

The Sioux heard their first rumors of the new doctrines in the winter of 1888–89. A delegation was sent to visit the messiah in 1889 and was convinced of the truth of his message. When it returned in 1890, some 60,000 Sioux were soon interested in the beliefs the delegation reported. Somewhere in the relating of the message a new element was injected—the ghost shirt. This was a hunting shirt constructed on the pattern of the garments made by the Indians before the coming of the whites. Preferably it was of leather, but since leather was scarce, cloth was frequently used (often white muslin). The shirt was to be worn in all religious ceremonies and was believed to be bullet-proof. It probably represented symbolically the old customs to which the Indians were to return—a sort of parallel to the later Irish Gaelic renaissance.

The central ceremony of the new belief was the ghost dance. Men and women were both included

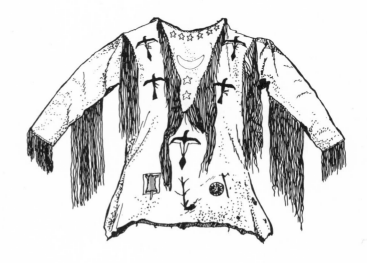

Arapaho Ghost Shirt, circa 1890s.

Art by E.L. Reedstrom

and both wore the ghost shirt. Those who were selected to take part in the dance had to fast for twenty-four hours. Then at sunrise, each went through the rite of "purification." This was done by the believer going into what was called a "sweat-lodge," a sort of willow tent covered with blankets and having hot rocks for the floor. The participant entered and poured water on the hot stones; the steam gave him an exaggerated Turkish bath. He stayed in the "sweat-lodge" for an hour until he was ritually perfectly clean and pure.

Next, the dancer painted his face dark blue with a red cross on each cheek. He then went to the chief or medicine man who painted two light blue crescents on his forehead and robed the dancer in the ghost shirt. No one but a great medicine man could perform this ceremony.

At high noon, the dancers all formed a circle joining hands (this is the only dance where the natives held hands). At a signal, everyone looked at the ground and began to circle around singing a weird and mournful dirge which, translated, was:

"Father, father, we want to see you. Father, father, we want buffalo. Father, father, we want our lands."

Sometimes the dancers would throw dust on themselves, followed by more dancing and wailing. This would go on about an hour when the medicine man would emerge from his tepee. They then broke the circle, threw up their heads and looked at the sun which appeared to be whirling around them. During this part of the dance, it was not infrequent for some of the dancers to faint. After the dance ended, everyone would sit down. One after another would relate his or her experiences and sensations during the dance. Visions and trances were not unusual.

The effectiveness of the ghost dance was heightened by several coincident factors. Ceremonial bathing in the sweat lodge preceded the dance. Fasting was used, and made each person more susceptible to religious experiences. The dance in itself was strenuous, particularly since it was given three times a day. More important, however, were the activities of the medicine men, who consciously tried to produce hypnotism. Whenever a dancer gave signs of being unusually excited the medicine man would approach and whirl a feather or handkerchief before his eyes. This motion was sufficient in many cases (particularly adolescent girls) to produce a dead swoon.

The ghost dance religion would probably have died a natural death if left to itself, since such was actually the case in other parts of the country, but the Sioux agents brought trouble by becoming alarmed and forbidding the dance. The result was that it became even more popular, being practiced at night in remote and inaccessible places. Rumors reached the Indians that white troops were on the way, and they worked themselves into a frenzy. Even Sitting Bull, the most important leader of the Sioux, joined the movement. By this time the agents were completely frightened and asked for aid from the Army.

With the appearance of the troops, about 700 warriors ran away from the reservation, being probably more frightened than hostile. A detachment of forty-three Indian police was sent to arrest Sitting Bull and bring him to the agency. By this time he was an old man, and had no idea of resisting white authority, but there were others who taunted him for his humility and so he gave the order for hostilities. In the resulting fight, Sitting Bull and some of his followers were killed, while the remainder were overpowered and captured (December 15, 1890).

Then followed a short and misdirected effort to force the Indians to submit. A "battle" at Wounded Knee Creek (December 29) resulted in the killing of 60 soldiers and 200 Indians of both sexes; in the pursuit following the engagement men, women, and children were massacred indiscriminately. This incident made the remainder of the Indians, who numbered possibly 4,000, thoroughly hostile. Various skirmishes took place, and the Nebraska militia was called out. By this time it was obvious even to the Indians that they had no chance of coping with the overwhelming number of white soldiers, and so on January 16, 1891, they surrendered to General Miles.

The Indians' Beef Issue

By the late 1890s, hostilities with the Plains Indians were about over, and most of the warlike bands had been settled on reservations. Many tribes such as the Sioux, Kiowa, Cheyenne, Comanche, and Arapaho, depended on the buffalo for its meat and the warmth of its heavy hide. When the U.S. government made certain to reduce the buffalo population to near extinction, it wasn't long before the hostile tribes finally surrendered.

The next step was to feed the Indians. Government beef was herded to a reservation and corralled. Saturday was usually chosen as "issue day," although some reservations gave out rations at intervals of two weeks. On larger reservations, they were given out only every four weeks. This was for the convenience of the Indians who lived several days journey from the Agency. The domestic issue, in addition to beef, consisted of such provisions as salt bacon, green coffee, sugar, navy beans, rice, hardtack, flour, baking power, and yellow laundry soap.

On Fridays, the Indians came from miles around by horse and wagon to pitch camp near the Agency, and early Saturday morning they would all gather at the corral, where about twenty head of cattle were weighed in, in lots of six to eight head. This lot was often driven into another enclosure within the corral where the head clerk or Tally-man would have the job of shooting each animal in the back of the head with a large bore repeating rifle. After all the cattle were killed, the Indian men would rush in to cut away the tongues, which was saved for their traditional feast and dance.

Indians being issued annuities at Ft. Berthold, Dakota Territory, circa 1889.

When the clerk and interpreter called out the name of each family or band to claim their beef, members from that family would drag the carcass to a chosen spot in the corral and begin the task of butchering. Generally the Indian men skinned the animal and the women and children all joined in to cut the beef into equal shares. Some bands preferred to cut the beef into halves, quarter, and sometimes half-quarters. Ribs were chopped away and thrown into piles. Entrails were cut out, washed, and cleaned carefully, then put separately. In fact, by the time all the butchering was done, there wasn't any sign of an animal left.

In Oklahoma, Kiowa Indians made "issue day" a close imitation to a buffalo hunt. A number of steers were weighed, branded (in case they should escape) ID for Indian Department, and let out of the corral and onto the prairie. The head Indian men, young and old, would strike after the cattle on horseback, much like the olden days, and run the animals to complete exhaustion—then they were shot. Kiowa women would follow closely with wagons and butcher the cattle where they had fallen. It was this sort of custom the Kiowas preserved, and they managed to recapture some of the excitement that came from the old days of hunting buffalo. Government beef issues were made for many years until various annuity payments were made in silver. Then from 1910 until 1926, purchase orders or checks were used instead of silver. The Indian was now walking the path of the white man, but his strong traditional heritage kept him from living like one.

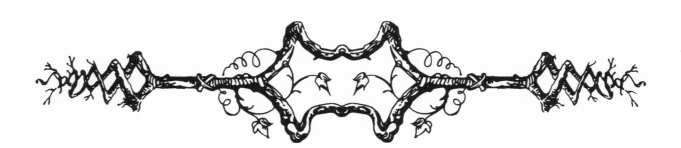

CHAPTER II

THE MEN OF THE MOUNTAINS

They lived on the fringe of the major groups of people settling the West, these mountain men did, and they wore fringes, too. In fact, there were several fringelike characteristics about these fiercely independent men who settled—or at least impinged on—the mountains, foothills, and rivers. The deeply-tanned skin took on a tattered appearance between seasons, and their long hair—blonde, brown, black, or gray—hung in fringes to their shoulders. They refused to settle in the growing towns, preferring the areas two or three days ride or paddle away from the settlers.

The mountain men were usually voyageurs or trappers, although some were simply hermits. Later, some shepherds followed the way of the mountain. Prospectors were taken with the solitude after gold played out in the Dakotas and other parts of the west, and took up mountain ways, building cabins or lean-tos against the snow cover. More than a few used the mountain and its secret face, to elude eastern laws and past indiscretions.

Mountain men, whether trappers, traders, or simply people who wanted to be alone, had one characteristic in common if they survived the first year. The language and friendship of the Indian was

John D. Baird, author and historian on mountain men, poses for the author in buckskinner's garb with his authentic 'Hawken Big 50.'

Author's Collection

absolutely essential if a lone white man was to survive in the Indian's forest or plains. These men learned to converse fluently enough to convince the tribes that they mean no harm and that they would be of value. Most of the trappers had Indian wives, which cemented the bond between the wild and free white man and his Indian soul brother.

What would the mountain men look like to an Easterner who chanced upon him in St. Louis, the "gateway to the West?" He might be short or tall, lean or stout. His voice could have the sound of Quebec, or Glasgow, or Warsaw, or a faint southern drawl. Sometimes, there would be a hint of the soft Quaker speech. Usually, the trapper or trader wore buckskins decorated in the style of his closest Indian tribe or that of his Indian wife. There would be the dark spots of animal blood, and following the personage, a waft of burned pine cones from his campfires. A beaver fur cap or wide-brimmed hat sat on top, and bullet pouch and power horn were slung around the man's neck on leather thongs. A second bag containing anything needed except articles connected with his gun was either around his neck or strung onto his strong leather belt, along with a knife in a leather scabbard and a long-barreled flintlock pistol. Clutched in one hand was usually a .50 caliber Hawken half-stock flintlock rifle. When he walked along the streets of St. Louis, the trapper adopted a slight crouch in his walk, and left an impression of several extra eyes on his head, looking out in all directions.

The mountain man arrived in the metropolis bearing the article of commerce that raised the most commotion during the 1830–1850 era. Fur was the topic of conversation everywhere among the two thousand regular residents, and even more among the large floating population of French-Canadian voyageurs, merchants from "back east," Spanish soldiers, immigrants, farmers, Indians with buffalo hides to sell, and others connected loosely to the gateway city. Beaver was the prime commodity, thanks to the raging fashion that required fine gentlemen to wear the glossy top hat made from the shy little animal.

The easterner would most likely see the trapper in

Two other styles of dress that a mountainee man might have worn.

Author's Collection

summer—not only was that the only time to travel through the network of rivers and streams down the Mississippi to St. Louis, but trapping was no good in the warm summer months, anyhow. Skins taken after March had no gloss and were thin and skimpy. So the trapper worked two seasons, late fall to early winter and late winter to early spring. During the dead of winter he retired to a snug cabin or base camp of some kind, repairing traps, mending ropes, and waterproofing his canoe with resin. After the howling storms and deep snows were over, he finished his second season and headed for St. Louis or some rendezvous point to sell his pelts and trade for necessaries. Some trappers spent time in the metropolis, trading or acquiring goods, or sampling wares not available in the mountains.

Some trappers carried on a dual existence, with a residence in the mountains or plains and another in town. Some even had wives in both, and this practice, while frowned upon by the church and possibly the female participants if they knew of it, was generally condoned by the general populace.

As soon as the breeze turned cool and the colors of autumn lit the landscape, the trapper donned buckskins and replaced his boots with moccasins. His paddle touched the river and he migrated upriver toward the beaver-laden streams.[1]

Beaver lived along the waterways, especially those rimmed with cottonwood, birch, willow, and aspen. These trees, especially their tender shoots, provided the beaver with their favorite fare. Beaver lodges were tunneled back into the bank, with entrances located slightly below the water level of the stream. For the trappers, knowledge of the beaver's habits

They were called the 'fringe people' by most Indians who knew them because of their fringed buckskins.

Art by E.L. Reedstrom

was a key to success. The animals kept several entrances to the main lodge, and traps set at the various different entrances prevented the beaver from escaping. Missing one of the entrances meant an empty trap.

One trapper alone could handle a string of about fifty traps—more if he could transport them into the beaver area. If the site was on a marsh, lake, or river, the trapper could carry in as many as a hundred traps and inspect them daily. If the site was not easily accessible by water or by horse and wagon, most trappers could carry only fifty traps in back packs. Sometimes, small parties of trappers worked together to increase the area they could trap over.

When setting the traps, each trapper carried four to six traps at a time to the beaver lodges. Each trap was set in about four inches of water near the entrances to the lodge. Traps were baited with a secretion of beaver scent gland, called castorium, directly on a leaf above the trap. The beaver, thinking a mate was near, stood to inspect the bait and walked right into the trap. The beaver was usually caught by the foot, and drowned in the water before he could escape.

At dawn, the trappers "ran the traps" or inspected the lines, removing the beaver and skinning them at the site. Back at camp the beaver skin was stretched on a frame, scraped, and dried. After the pelt was dry, it was folded, fur side in, for packing. The fur was not the only part saved; the tail was considered a delicacy, and the castor glands were carefully preserved for use as bait.

Fur dealers would buy only trapped furs. The presence of shot in pelts ruined them for the even expanse of fur needed for the toppers. Steel traps did not injure the pelt and good trappers were expert in setting their traps and running their lines to insure top quality fur.

Good trappers could earn several thousand dollars in a three months' season. A rule of thumb was seven dollars a day for a five weeks' trip, but this required a combination of good weather, good trapping grounds, good traps, good judgment—and a lot of luck. In the early 1870s, good trapping grounds were easily found. Later, however, the beaver moved farther and farther into the mountains, until their numbers were reduced so much that trapping became extremely difficult.

Trappers spent their time between seasons gambling, drinking, feasting, and swapping stories with the occasional visitors in camp. The stories, as tall tales will, grew even taller as they traveled around the circuit of camps. Often the original teller could not recognize the size of the grizzly, the wealth of beaver, or the size and ferocity of the attacking Indians. The fierceness of the winter increased proportionally to the passage of time, and the tales became classics as time wore on.

Some of the favorite stories described the exploits of the trappers at Indian fighting. While most trappers were friendly with some Indians, frequently the tribes hostile to his friends took special umbrage with the mountain man as a kind of representative of the tribe with which he was allied. Often the alliance was forged by a marriage of sorts to an Indian girl, and the trapper became embroiled in the inter-tribal battles between the nations. The trapper knew that he must be aware of the style of the warring Indians, and he usually added some refinements of his own. Trappers became expert in reading the signs of tribes that were not his allies, and knew how to move through hostile territory without being detected. The mountain man became expert at following trails and sensing danger. If he was caught off guard and could not slip away unseen, he had to plan a sudden decisive move that would catch the Indian equally off his guard and permit him to escape. On those occasions when combat was absolutely necessary, the trapper waged the bloodiest of battles. If his tactics failed and he fell into the hands of hostile tribes, he would be treated no better than his allies: there would be no mercy. Many of the tribes thought that eating some portion of their enemy captured the courage of their foe, or that some special kind of torture made them braver and stronger. Being captured was especially brutal and made fighting fiercely a reasonable alternative.

Still and all, many mountain men lived to a ripe old age, so their skills must have been great. Among the survivors, arrow wounds were common. Those who lived long knew how to extract the arrow head, an

releasing the shaft. Usually the time available was about a half hour. Most experienced mountain men had their own extraction methods, often depending on a special pincer plier which was used to bend or crush the barbed point so the head could be withdrawn without too much pain to the victim. (How much pain was "too much" was indescribable. The victim was usually filled with whiskey if it was available. Otherwise, a bite stick could be used to help the victim bear the pain. Sometimes the bite stick was bitten in two by the patient.) Seven out of ten victims of an Indian arrowhead are estimated to have perished. Some tribes poisoned their arrowheads with snake venom or other natural poisons. Avoiding the Indians' rain of arrows was definitely in the trapper's best interest.

The dress of the trapper had to fit into the surroundings if the mountain man was to be inconspicuous. As tribes of Indians moved about more after the white man broke treaties, the number of hostile Indians increased, and the trapper was under greater threat. Dressing like an Indian had some advantages, since it was harder for a tribe to be sure whether he was a scout or a lone man. It also had its perils—hostile tribes would try to eliminate a scout to prevent a battle unless they were looking for a fight.

The skins used in making buckskin clothing were trapped by the man himself. A breech clout was worn under leggings, which were trousers without a seat. The outside seams were fringed with long strips that may have been used as water drains, keeping rain water away from the main part of the garment. A coat or pullover, fashioned from buckskin covered the upper part of the body, and fringes were used on the shoulders, chest, sleeves, and sometimes around the pockets. On those occasions when buttons were used, they were either made from twisted leather thongs or from a slice of deer horn. Sometimes a storm cape was added, attached to the shoulders like an oversized version of Sherlock Holmes' overcoat, also hung with fringe. Feet were covered with moccasins made with a tough rawhide sole, and often first wrapped with a bit of blanket. A heavy blanket or buffalo robe wrapped the trapper when

This blanket-cut pullover with hood attached was generally worn as a wind-breaker in spring or fall. It is of a latter day fashion and was easily purchased from the Hudson Bay traders who always kept this style in stock.

Art by E.L. Reedstrom

ingenious weapon that caused the death of many trappers. The arrow came from nowhere, out of the wilderness, and usually knocked the wind from the victim and made it hard to breathe. The arrow lodged in a fleshy part of the body or in bone; the problem was to withdraw the arrow before the warmth of the body dissolved the connecting sinew and glue,

wind and snow threatened to stop him with the cold.

The mountain men had developed a way to make hats, adapting some of the techniques used on Fleet Street, the London home of hattiers and clothiers. They would dig a hole, sized and shaped to fit the head, and place a soaked piece of rawhide over the top, with grass or scrap buckskin tamped down in the hole to form a crown shape. The outside of the buckskin circle lay flat on the ground surrounding the crown form and was shaped with the hands to lie flat to form the brim. When the hat form was dry and firm, it was heated over a campfire to totally dry the skin and to smoke the surface to waterproof the hat. Strings and straps decorated the chapeau. For winter wear, a similar hat was formed from fur, often wolf, with the head of the animal on the front of the cap.

Trappers with Indian women as wives or companions often wore the bead patterns of her tribe on their buckskins. This beading, sewn in place, was made from a variety of materials, such as porcupine quill, feathers, stones, and other decorations. Sometimes the trapper contrived these decorations himself to attract a particular Indian woman, who often favored the white trapper as a mate, perceiving that she might get better treatment from the trapper than she would from a brave.

Mixing with the various people in the West, the trapper developed a language distinctive to his own trade. The words derived from the Missouri backwoods, from Indian languages and dialects, Cajun jargon, a little French and Spanish, and their own experience. A dead man was a "gone beaver" or he had "gone under"; if death was violent, he was "rubbed out." Fancy clothes, especially women's, were "fafarrow" or "foofaraw." Tobacco was "kinikinik," liquor was "Taos lightning" or "Picketwire firewater," and a rifle was a "smoke pole," "Ol' Betsey" or "Long Tom." A prime beaver pelt was a "plew," and a buffalo skull was a "kyack."

The choice and care of a gun was often the difference between survival and extinction. Many weapons were used by the trappers, but gradually the Hawken gun shop in St. Louis developed the favorite of many of the mountain men. The Hawken rifle was sturdy, simple, and dependable, and pos-

sessed accuracy and enough power to drop a buffalo in its tracks or stop a grizzly. The Kentucky rifle, an early favorite, proved to be too fragile for the rough life of the trapper, and not powerful enough to fell large game. If it fell from the saddle, the stock usually cracked, and the mechanism within the plate lock fouled from the fall. Gunsmiths weren't around every corner, and the Kentucky rifle lost favor in the west.

English sporting rifles were touted in the St. Louis area, but were generally too expensive. Another rifle, made in 1800 by Harper's Ferry, proved too heavy for a saddle gun. The percussion ignition system slowly improved, and the Hawken shop had plenty of time to adapt it, as it became a favorite over the flint ignition. Several years of input from the trappers helped Hawken to perfect his gun.

While most of the trappers were solitary men, their one companion on the trail and running their lines was a pack animal, often a mule selected for surefootedness, or a sturdy Indian pony. Some trappers claimed that their animals could sense unfriendly Indians, and pointed them out with their ears. Trappers often talked to their animals, and sometimes it seemed as though the animal understood. While some men mistreated their pack animals, most understood and respected these animals upon which they depended so heavily.

From the early 1800s on, these solitary men and their few companions opened the west. On the trail of beaver, gold, land, or other riches, they avoided the cities and moved farther and farther away from civilization, which pursued them like shadows. Trappers, Indians and fur buyers brought the source and supply of beaver pelts together at various places in the west and southwest. Taos, New Mexico, and Bent's Fort on the Arkansas River were two popular gatherings, referred to as Rendezvous. Caravans up from St. Louis brought new traps, guns, powder and ball, as well as coffee, tobacco, needles and thread, and beads. Other trinkets were offered for the trapper to use to entice the Indian girls. Choice pelts were brought for sale, and trappers traded, met their old cronies, and generally enjoyed a carnival atmosphere for a week or so. Rendezvous continued until 1840, then the scarcity of beaver and the lack of interest on

the part of buyers began to signal an end to the era of the mountain men. Some continued to trap, but the best creeks no longer sheltered the beaver lodges, and the trappers had to go higher and higher into the mountains to find the beaver. And the beaver top hat lost its gloss. So the mountain man became a simple hermit, or bought farms in Oregon or Missouri and tried to adapt to more ordered ways. Others served as guides or interpreters, or simply disappeared into the hills, never to be heard from again.

The Beaver Hat

The beaver hat had its origin in Europe sometime in the 1760s, and gained in popularity during the 1790s, when they really were "all the rage." Any properly dressed gentlemen of fashion wore the beaver chapeau. Styles changed somewhat during the approximately seventy years of their sway, to include a tapered beaver hat with a tall crown to the Lincolnesque stovepipe. Tradition required that the stylish man wear a gray beaver hat, usually with a low crown, during the day and a tall, slender, black beaver dress hat during the evening.

The Hudson Bay Company supplied beaver pelts to the European continent, including enough for the British to manufacture 600,000 hats, and they begged for more. In New York, the price of a beaver hat was ten dollars (at a time when a pound of sirloin steak cost nine and a half cents) and haberdashers had no trouble selling out. The hats were waterproof and easy to care for, as a brushing in the direction of the hair would retrieve the glossy luster of the pelt immediately.

Eventually, the silk hat's price dropped, and the fabric was improved, and the silk topper became fashionable. Whether the improvement to the top hat, or the shortage of beaver pelts brought about by overtrapping spelled the death knell for the beaver topper can only be speculated. By 1840, the wealth from beaver trapping was gone, and the trappers went on to other means of gaining a living.

Beaver hats of all sizes and shapes were the fashion of the early 1800s.

Author's Collection

The Attire of Mountain Men

This illustration shows an early mountain man's attire. The reason for long fringes hanging from shoulders and sleeves was to bind the clothing seams tight without the aid of thread or sinew. Should the buckskinner need to bind or tie anything together, the fringes were immediately available for that use also. Historians claim that the fringes also acted as a 'rain gutter,' so rain would drain off the buckskin and down the fringe and it wouldn't swell the seams.

Kit Carson's old friend was Tom Tobin. His full-length coat with fur collar shows a considerable amount of artistic embellishment. His trousers were also decked with colorful beadwork.

Kit Carson's grandson wore this coonskin cap and original buckskin outfit which was copied after the old buckskinner's styles and patterns.

The styles of the latter-day mountain men adopted skins other than beaver to trim a man's outfit. As the beaver trade began to thin out, fox, marten and otter began to appear on collars, sleeves, hems, gloves and boots, including women's apparel.

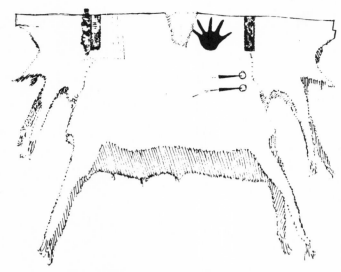

A man's shirt of the poncho type. This specimen is made of two deerskins. There are bands of quillwork over each shoulder, fringed on one side with crow feathers. On the opposite side of the fold is a transverse band of quillwork.

Latter-period style (1850–60s) adopted by scouts and plainsmen. The fringe is shorter and acts only to adorn the jacket in style. The wide-fringed collar reveals a large fall-back shirt collar, similar to a navy shirt. Mixed with these buckskinned jackets and pullover were commonly found woolen, cotton, and canvas windbreakers bearing the identical designs the mountain men fabricated. As the frontier began to settle, eastern manufacturers found a market for these jackets in the sporting field. The fringe always accompanied these jackets in some sort of style, but hardly anyone knew why it was there. At one time, included only from necessity, the long-hanging fringe finally served its wearer for style alone.

The Hudson Bay "Point Blanket"

In the minutes of a meeting of the London Committee of the Hudson's Bay Company, December 22, 1779, the earliest mention of "Point" Blankets is documented. There is little doubt that they were an article of trade before this date. The "Points," which were clearly visible on one section of the blanket, were known to every Indian as the price to be paid for the blanket. To illustrate this: two and a half "Points" equalled two and a half beaver or "plews," three "Points" equal three beaver, etc.

"Point" blankets were easily recognized by two distinguishing features. The blankets were generally a solid color with a three to four inch wide stripe or bar of a darker color, usually black, at either end. Part way up one side were the point marks. These narrow stripes about five inches long were woven into the blanket and placed so that they were perpendicular to the edge of the blanket. There were as few as two or as many as six point marks depending on the size of the blanket. In-between sizes were indicated by a half-length point mark. The buckskinners looked for a sturdy blanket to rely on while they were out in the mountains, and they found it in the "Point" blanket. For bedding, the 100 percent woolen material was warm and for a greatcoat, durable.

Colored blankets were introduced to catch the eye of the Indians, who insisted on the brightest colors as they were very choosy. French-Canadian "Voyageurs" adopted much of the Indian tribal dress, fashioning a "Point" blanket-type coat, or Capote as it was later called, similar to those they had seen in Indian villages. From that time, the blanket coat became almost universal with the early fur traders. At one time it was possible to determine the area the "Voyageur" came from by the color of his blanket coat. Those from Montreal wore blue coats, those from Quebec preferred red, from Three Rivers, white, etc.

The original mackinaw coats were made from Hudson's Bay "Point" blankets. During the War of 1812, Captain Charles Roberts, commanding the British troops who ultimately captured Mackinaw,

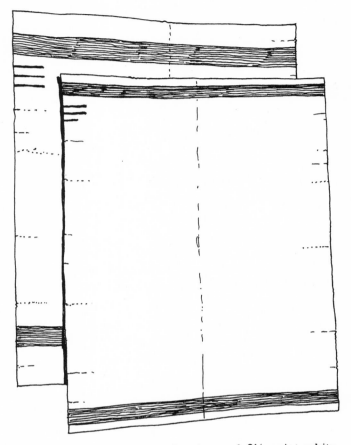

Early nineteenth century 3-point and 2½-point white Hudson Bay Company blankets.

Art by E.L. Reedstrom

was unable to obtain greatcoats for his troops, and seized a large number of "Point" blankets to make coats from.

By the early 1800s, point blankets were fairly standardized, being made in white and a few solid colors with appropriate point marks and a broad dark stripe near each end. A summary of specifications issued by the U.S. Office of Indian Trade in 1808 for blankets shipped to the post at Mackinaw:

3 point: 6'x5'2", wt. 4 lbs., stripe 2½" wide
2½ point: 5'4"x4'3", wt. 3 1/16 lbs., stripe 2½" wide
2 point: 4'6"x4', wt. 2¾ lbs., strip 1½" wide
1½ point: 4'x3', wt. 1 11/16 lbs., stripe 1½" wide
1 point: 3'8"x2'10", wt. 1½ lbs., stripe 1" wide

In addition to the solid colors, the "chief's blanket," with a set of multi-colored stripes at each end, was developed and became much more popular in the latter nineteenth century.

In 1834, a common blanket cost $4.25 or one good beaver plew or buffalo robe. By 1843, Sibille and Adams, traders on the White River in Nebraska, were getting five buffalo robes for their three point blanket.

Sources:
The Museum of Fur Trade, Vol. 12 (Bulletin) Spring 1976—No. 1
Charles Early & Marriott (Whitney) Limited, Oxfordshire, England (Letter)
Pearce Woolen Mills, Inc., Woolrich, Pennsylvania (Letter)

Mountain Man's Jargon

Tall, sinewy, and bony, the mountain man cares nothing of appearance. His wide brimmed hat is black and shining with grease. His hunting shirt is bedaubed until it had the appearance of polished leather. The scattered fringes down the outside of the leg, which ornaments his outfit, have pretty well thinned out to supply "whangs" for mending moccasins or pack-saddles. His possibles bag hangs from drooped shoulders and thrust into a bright colored sash folded over several times about the waist is his trusty Bowie knife, razor sharp, and carried in an Indian beaded sheath. As he approaches a friend, he shifts his large caliber half-stock rifle from one arm to the other and raises his right arm, his palm to the sky, and bellows in a graveled voice . . . "It's good fer these sore eyes to see'd an ol' beaver like ye'self . . . aire' ye got eny 'bacca in yer possibles?"

The jargon of a mountainee comes slow and is only half way understood, if you haven't had any experience in listening to their conversations. Most of these men were uneducated, used poor grammar and mispronounced many words . . . in which, after studying their language, this author believes that they made up their own words to shorten sentences. Sometimes one word may have several meanings, but by putting it in the right context the meaning was understood.

From several well-authenticated books mentioned in the reference department, you will find a host of terms that were used over one hundred and fifty years ago:

Apishamores—A saddle blanket made of buffalo calf skin.

Bacca—Meaning tobacco for short.

Blew-about—To exaggerate.

Booshway—Leader of a trapping party, or one who is in charge at a trading post, who has the authority to purchase peltries. (French) bourgeois (bur'zhwa) meaning "tradesman".

Bootle—The prize, or stolen items.

Boudins—(Boo-dins) sausages; buffalo intestines stuffed with meat. French; Boudin (boo-dan)

Buffler'—Short for buffalo.

Bull Boat—Buffalo hides were stretched over a circular willow frame and lashed together with thongs. These boats were smoked over small embers and then greased with bear fat.

Cache—To hide, a hiding place. From the French, 'cacher (ka-shay).

Captain—A leader, one who heads a large party. The word general shortened to "Cap'n."

Caravan—A group of pack mules or horses bringing in goods from the cities to the mountains. Or, carrying furs back out of the mountains to the cities.

Castor or Castorum—A sticky yellow substance taken from the glands of beavers, used to bait beaver traps.

Chawing—Meaning chewing tobacco. Later references "looking for conversation" or "jawing."

Coffee Cooler—A lazy person, avoids work. Takes breaks at his leisure.

This "Coon" or this Child—Referring to one's self.

Cordelle—French word for "tow rope." Voyagers had to tow their craft up river or 'cordelle.'

Coup—(Koo) French for blow or strike. Or taking a scalp during warfare.

Coureurs des Bois—(Rangers in the wood) Independent French Traders.

"Edge a Knife"—To sharpen it.

These "Diggins"—This area, this ground.

Made 'dog' of—Made a feast of.

Engagé—(On ga shay), a hired trapper. French meaning "enlisted."

Keep Your "Eyes Skinned"—To keep a sharp eye out, or watch closely.

Express—A fast messenger, a runner, to go from one camp to another carrying documents or important messages.

Flash in the Pan—Men who talked big but did little.

Fly-Blowed Buffler Meat—Rancid meat.

Fixins—Guns, traps, powder, blankets, and grub.

Foofaraw—Trade items such as beads, mirrors, ribbons, and bright trinkets. A French word for "fanfaron" which meaning 'braggin' or showing off.

Free-Trapper—One who traps for himself and is not hired out by anyone.

Fusees—Light guns in weight (fusils).

Glad Hand—Warm welcome.

Give Us Yer' Paw—A strong handshake.

Goats—Refers to Antelope.

Gone Beaver—Gone hunting.

Greasers—Spaniards, Mexicans, from their greasy appearance.

"Hep-a"—A call to a mule.

Hoodoo—A crazy place.

Hivernan—(Ee ver nan) a trapper who has spent a winter in the mountains. French (hiver), (ee-vair) 'winter.'

This "Hos"—Meaning this person. (This coon-this child.)

Jawbone credit—No signature, verbal agreement.

Kinnik-kinnik—Indian tobacco. The inner bark of the red willow which is used as a substitute for tobacco, which has an aromatic and very pungent flavor, and gives the smoker a highly narcotic effect.

Levé—(Lay-way) French word for "wake up." It was the alarm or call to break camp.

Lift Hair—Scalping someone.

Make Meat—Lay in a store of provisions.

Mangeur de Lard—(Ma zhur de lar) French for pork eater. Also, meant "greenhorns" who liked bacon instead of buffalo meat.

Medicine—A substance obtained from a gland in the scrotum of the beaver, and used to attract that animal into a trap. Modern beaver trappers still use this musk gland in fixing bait.

Mountanee Man—Mountain man.

Nor-west—North West.

No-siree-e—No.

Palabra—To answer or not say a word . . . or repeat.

On the Prairie—An Indian term for 'free gift.'

Parflesh—Buffalo 'sole' hides.

Partisan—Leader of a trapping party.

Thrown 'Plumb Center'—Bulls-eye.

Plew—(Ploo) A first class beaver pelt, used as a unit of exchange. Three to five pelts were worth six to ten dollars.

Possibles—Miscellaneous items that a trapper carried in his shoulder bag or 'possibles bag,' such as flint and steel, needles, thread, pipe, and tobacco, etc.

Pow-wow—Parley with Indians.

Prairie Queens—Hired women, pleasure women.

Punk—Tinder, a pithy substance found in dead trees. Pulling a handful of dry grass, which they screw up into a nest, they place the lighted punk in this, and closing the grass over it, wave it into the air to ignite.

Get in a "Racket"—Squabble, fight, or argument.

Raise—To 'raise beaver' meant to lift a trap from a stream and take the beaver from it.

Rendezvous—(Ran-da-voo) Each year the mountain men, Indians, and traders from the East would gather with their pelts and swap stories, feast, drink, and trade pelts for trinkets. Also, mountain men who worked for trading companies would turn their pelts over according to contract, and receive their pay. Games and much fun occurred here but it only lasted barely a decade. By 1840, with the near extinction of the beaver, it was all over.

Rubbed out—Killed, died, 'gone under.'

"Shoot sharps the word"—Good luck.

Small Fire—There's a difference between an Indian fire and a white man's fire. The former places the ends of the logs to burn gradually; the latter makes

such a gunfire so hot that he cannot approach it to warm himself.

Terra Firma—The ground.

Three Horn Drink—Large cup of rum or whiskey.

"Throw'd the Meat Cold"—The way mountain men indulged their appetites.

Thrown cold—Dropped dead.

Travies—Travois.

Two Shoot Gun Rifle—Double barrel (shotgun).

Up to Bear—A phrase meaning that the mountain man had learned the ways of the animal and could trap it with no difficult.

"Up the Green River"—Knives used by hunters and buffalo skinners. Thrusting the knife deep into animal or human flesh—up to where the indentures of the words 'Green River' read on the blade.

Voyageur—(Vwa ya zhu) French word for "traveler." Also to denote the French Creole boatman on the Missouri River.

Wah-keitcha—French engage. French Canadians (wah-keitcha or bad medicine) to the Indians.

War Sack—To store one's personals.

Whangs—Fringes from their buckskinned jackets used for mending moccasins or pack-saddles.

Wheel Trail—Wagon trail.

Whiskey-soak—Drunk; also, Locoed 'whiskey-soak,' crazy drunk.

Wipe Out—Kill.

Wiping Stick—Ramrod, or hickory wiping stick.

(Expressions)

"Scared hell West and cooked"—Took off frightened.

"Painter meat can't shine with this"—Painter meaning Panther; delicious flavor of a good cut of tender loin.

"Tickled a niggur's hump ribs"—Made someone laugh.

"Fired' be dogged"—An expression used when enraged.

"They're no account any ways you lays your sight"—No matter what you think.

"This beaver feels like chawin'"—Wants to chew tobacco or much later, chawin' meant talking.

"I never 'et dead meat—and wouldn't ask no one to do it neither, but, meat fair killed is meat anyway. So boy, put yer' knife in this ol' niggur's lights—and hep' yerself."

Source:
Firearms, Traps and Tools of the Mountain Man, Carl P. Russell, Alfred A. Knopf.
I Hear America Talking, S.B. Flexner, Van Nostrand Reinhold Co. 1976
Life in the Far West, Geo. F. Ruxton, University of Oklahoma Press, 1951

Buckskinner's Tools

Several interesting tools accompanied the mountain man including implements carried in his "possibles" bag and others worn on his belt or attached to parts of harness.

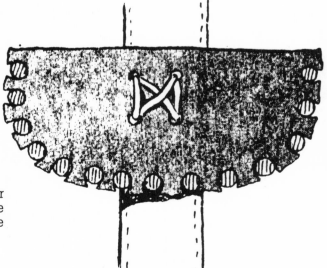

A leather percussion-cap holder. This cap holder was attached to the hunting pouch strap. The leather had to be tough and thick; usually moose hide was used when it was available.

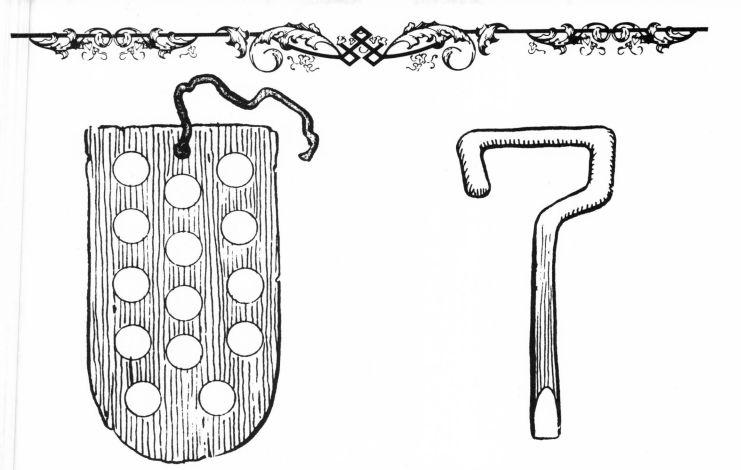

A half-inch thick block of wood, drilled with holes to hold a specific caliber of ball ready to be pushed out for a quick load. It was made in many shapes and any amount of holes for lead-patched balls.

An early forged-steel screwdriver that generally found its way into the possibles bag. These rather primitive tools were surprisingly efficient, and often were worth their weight in gold to the buckskinner.

When a mountain man found that his trusty rifle was either badly cracked or broken, he would mend the part with a wet rawhide patch. When it dried, it shrank to a strong and usually satisfactory repair.

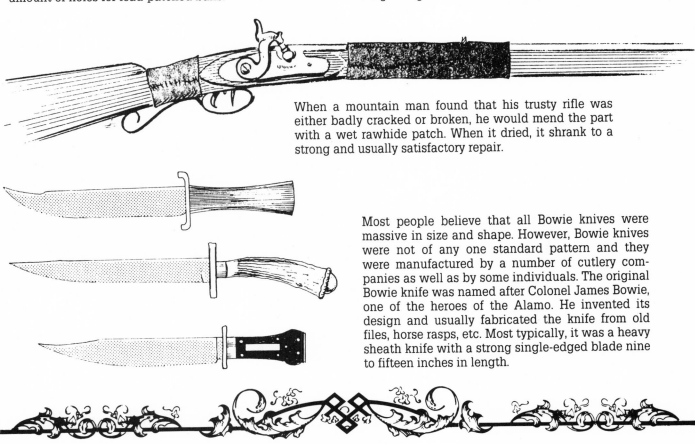

Most people believe that all Bowie knives were massive in size and shape. However, Bowie knives were not of any one standard pattern and they were manufactured by a number of cutlery companies as well as by some individuals. The original Bowie knife was named after Colonel James Bowie, one of the heroes of the Alamo. He invented its design and usually fabricated the knife from old files, horse rasps, etc. Most typically, it was a heavy sheath knife with a strong single-edged blade nine to fifteen inches in length.

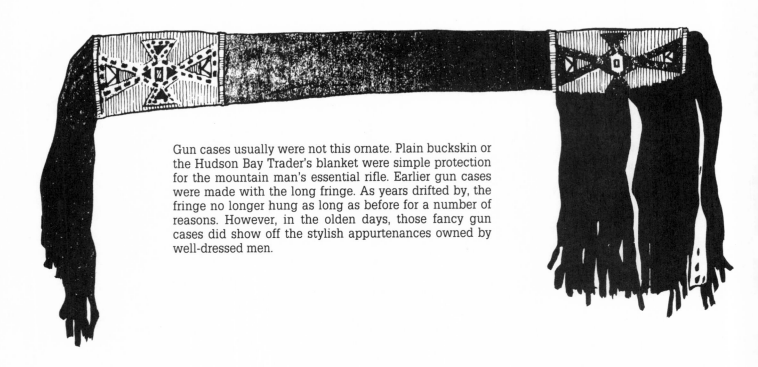

Gun cases usually were not this ornate. Plain buckskin or the Hudson Bay Trader's blanket were simple protection for the mountain man's essential rifle. Earlier gun cases were made with the long fringe. As years drifted by, the fringe no longer hung as long as before for a number of reasons. However, in the olden days, those fancy gun cases did show off the stylish appurtenances owned by well-dressed men.

Most knife sheaths carried by mountain men were decorative in style and very colorful. The sheaths illustrated here are from the Crow Indians. A very common knife sheath style was worn with a belt through the triangular opening. They were made of rawhide, either laced shut along the sides or riveted. Beads, brass tacks, and red wool edging were common decorations.

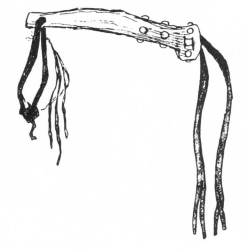

Most riders carried a "quirt" for whipping a mount ever forward. This example shows a handle of elk horn decorated with brass tacks. Thongs are for the wrist.

Throwing the Knife and Tomahawk

by Don Good as explained to E. Lisle Reedstrom

The Tomahawk

Before beginning to throw the tomahawk, the handle must be properly measured so that it fits the arm length of the individual. As the length of everyone's arm is different, you can't just pick up and throw a tomahawk and expect to hit anything with it. First you must fit the head correctly so that it is tightly secured to the handle. The handle must be cut off to the proper length. To cut the handle off to the proper length, you place the head of the tomahawk on a flat surface, like a table top, make a fist and double up your hand. Lay your arm down next to the handle at the elbow. The handle should come 1/2 inch above the closed fist. There should be 1/4 to 3/8 inch of the handle sticking up above the head of the tomahawk. This will properly adjust the weight and balance of the tomahawk for each individual's arm length. Small tomahawks are fitted and thrown the same way as the large ones.

Weight of the head is not a factor because you will choose the handle that fits that particular head. If you measure the handle properly, the balance will be correct for the head. The blade should be sharp so that it will bite into whatever type of wood it is thrown at.

Anyone who sells buckskinner's supplies will have both heads and handles. There are several different styles: Hudson's Bay, French-style, Squaw hawk, Bleeding Heart hawk, etc. A French-style, hand-forged tomahawk will cost about $22.00.

To begin throwing, select a tree stump or something very solid with nothing behind it which could be damaged, since you're going to miss the stump more often than you will hit it when you start out. The target is usually set up with a slight backwards angle so that the weight of the tomahawk and knife will not knock it over. Chest level is the normal height for the stump.

Put your back to the stump, walk off seven normal paces, and mark the spot. Throwing from this point will cause the tomahawk to turn once in the air before hitting the stump. Place the tomahawk handle in the center of the right hand with the thumb on the left side of the tomahawk (if you are right handed). Hold the handle very loosely and close to the end. Try a throw. Probably when you begin you will throw slowly and the tomahawk won't stick. It's like throwing a baseball. Step forward with the left foot and

release the tomahawk as you are looking at what you want to hit. Open your hand as if the handle suddenly became "hot."

The normal throw is overhand, but the tomahawk can be thrown side-arm. It can also be thrown by turning the head backwards. This will cause the tomahawk to make one-and-a-half turns, so that when it hits the stump, the handle will be turned up rather than down. If you want the tomahawk to make one-and-a-half turns you should step off nine paces rather than seven. If you want double turns (two revolutions of the tomahawk head before hitting the stump) you would walk back thirteen steps. For three complete revolutions you walk back nineteen steps, and twenty-five steps for four complete revolutions. Contests require longer distances, and you have to know how many steps back exactly so that the tomahawk will hit the stump and stick.

When you have had enough practice to hit your target consistently and make the tomahawk bite into the stump, but you are still throwing it all over the stump, you are not aiming correctly. You want to try to consistently hit the center of the stump. You must

Don Good, Buckskinner

Author's Collection

look exactly at the spot you want to hit. When you start hitting consistently into a small area, six to eight inches in diameter, and you notice that you are six inches off from the center of the stump, you need to move over six inches in the opposite direction you are off. If you are six inches off to the left, you move six inches to the right. If you are throwing high you move back the amount of distance you are high. Then you start consistently hitting the center of the stump. In contests the stump will be divided into sections, quarters for instance. You have to be able to pick your target and hit that section the center of the stump, no matter what section you are looking at. If you throw into the wrong area you lose points.

Tomahawk throwing is very much like throwing a baseball. It's a very easy motion. You want to throw hard at all times. Some contests have a very hard stump or a very soft stump, and if you don't put enough force behind your throw on a hard stump you won't stick it.

The tomahawk will bounce back from the stump if improperly thrown. You must be sure to have proper clearance, for yourself as well as anyone who might be watching. Anyone else around should be well behind or twenty-five to thirty feet off on either side. Never let anyone behind the tomahawk stump. No matter how professional you are, the tomahawk will sometimes bounce or you will occasionally miss. Rope off the area so that people can't get too close. Children are often curious and try to sneak up behind to see what you are doing. You have to keep your eyes open at all times. The tomahawk is not a toy, but a dangerous weapon.

The tomahawk is usually kept either at the back of the belt, sharp edge down, with the blade in a sheath or on the left side in the front. Some people will pull it out with the left hand and transfer it to the right in contests. It depends on the individual.

The Knife

It is best to use a professional-style throwing knife or the old Bowie-style knife. They are well-balanced with a large, heavy blade. The knife should be blade heavy, but overall weight and width do vary. Today's

Don Good, Buckskinner

Author's Collection

Bowie-style has a nine inch blade, about an inch and a half wide. Some people make their own throwing knives, but they are not always weighted properly. The knife should be sharp over its whole length so that it will go into the stump and stick solidly. If it's sharp and well-kept, it can also be used as a camp tool. The knife should be able to take a lot of abuse.

Never throw a knife by the blade, especially a sharp one. Let the handle slide out of your hand while opening your hand as if the handle suddenly became hot. Allow the knife to do the work.

Walk off six paces for the knife and turn. You may have to adjust your spot a few inches, but normally for throwing a knife with a single turn six steps is the correct distance. If you want a double turn on the knife you would step back eleven paces. For either the tomahawk or the knife if you want to make a double turn you double the distance and subtract one step.

Hold the knife on the very end of the handle with the thumb along the side and the center of the corner of the handle in the center of the palm of the hand. When the knife is released you would actually be holding it with only two fingers.

Sometimes if you are not looking exactly where you want to put the knife you will accidentally put the knife through your tomahawk handle. It is easier to throw the knife if you throw the tomahawk first and

then immediately take a short step and throw the knife. With practice you will know what length of step to take. When you find yourself hitting your tomahawk handle, you should begin taking a small step to one side or the other because you are throwing with such accuracy that in order to miss the tomahawk handle and head, you must take a step one way or the other to compensate. Using a playing card or other targets gives you something to throw at.

When doing a show, some experts will be talking with the crowd, then turn suddenly and throw the tomahawk, splitting a playing card or small, pencil-sized stick in half. Usually they will then immediately throw the knife, sticking it into another playing card or alongside of the tomahawk. This should not be tried by an amateur. This should only be done after you have a lot of experience and you know where you will throw the tomahawk at all times.

The Legend of the Hawken Rifle

As sturdy, simple, and dependable as the mountain men that it served, the Hawken rifle's accuracy and power was equal to the mighty buffalo and wily grizzly. Unlike the more elegant Kentucky rifle, the Hawken could withstand a drop from the saddle without cracking the stock or fouling the mechanism.

Jake Hawken, the elder of the Hawken brothers, was born in Hagerstown, Maryland, in 1786. He and his brother, Sam, born in 1792, learned the gunsmithing trade under the watchful eye of their father, Christian. Their father was a perfectionist and made sure the boys learned the trade well. The "C. Hawken" flintlock, a typical Pennsylvania rifle with a full stock, was the weapon on which the boys trained.

At the age of twenty-one, Jake felt that his years of learning should be put to the test. He had already been recognized at home as an excellent gunsmith and sharp businessman. This, however, was not enough for the ambitious young man. The call of the wild frontier had whispered in his ear for quite some time, so, in 1807, Jake headed west to St. Louis. There he met the challenge to succeed.

He found the road to success to be more difficult than imagined. The French settlement had begun the inevitable change that accompanies rapid growth. It was becoming the hub of a quickly growing fur trade industry. The town had its share of gun-toting desperadoes and a vast mixture of people. He soon learned to fend for himself in this new world. Jake mixed in with the two thousand plus residents as well as the greater number of drifters who constantly came through town. The beaver pelt and its availability was discussed by Eastern merchants, emigrant farmers, Indians, French-Canadian voyageurs, and Spaniards as well. The beaver pelt was in great demand, as it was used exclusively for gentlemen's top hats, which were in high fashion at the time. Eastern gents paid expensive prices for 100% beaver hats.

To meet the endless demand for pelts, the Missouri Fur Trading Company offered attractive contracts to anyone who would endure the life of a trapper. They advertised in newspapers as well as upon posters all throughout St. Louis. Upon entering into this type of contract, a more than adequate grub-stake was given

A late period Hawken rifle. Brass tacks reflect Indian treatment, and believed to be the work of the owner to cover up cracked wrist.

Smithsonian Institution

to each man. Any fur brought to the company was paid for upon receipt of goods. The best pelts guaranteed a bonus. This type of business arrangement attracted vagabond trappers from Kentucky, Tennessee, and other bordering states.

Jake adapted to this harsh, frenzied new life. He found work in this type of environment. Recognizing the need for a good source of weapons and service of them, he saved his money in hopes of opening his own gun shop. He used his excellent mechanical abilities and business sense to open such a shop in 1815. His small shop at 214 North Main Street, was strategically located for maximum visibility as fur traders came into town laden with pelts. He worked long hours alone in his shop.

Trappers and mountain men kept him busy. His shop became a regular stop as word of his excellence in the trade spread. He sold, repaired, and improved his weapons. The Hawken rifle gradually evolved: a tough, dependable muzzle-loader, tough enough to handle the rigors of mountain life. Jake's business was booming. As he began to realize his success, the Missouri Fur Company approached him with yet another tribute to his work and the reliability of the weapon. In the winter of 1821, the Hawken gun shop was commissioned to supply a sizable lot of percussion ignition rifles.

In 1822, Jake's brother, Sam, joined him in St. Louis, Sam's wife had recently passed away and so he left Xenia, Ohio to visit his big brother in St. Louis. Jake was overjoyed to see his little brother for many reasons. They both enjoyed each other's company in this new land far away from the home they shared in their childhood. Sam was proud of his brother's success in the gunsmith trade and surprised at the tremendous amount of work that met him at the door each day. He lengthened his "stay" in St. Louis to help with the overload of work in the shop. Sam realized that after the death of his beloved wife, Xenia, Ohio held nothing but painful memories. He grew accustomed to St. Louis and the hustle of this growing metropolis.

Sam made it his new home, taking interest in community affairs. Even politics drew his attention. He was fundamental in the establishment of "The Union Fire Company, Number 2." The 1838–39 St. Louis directory listed Samuel Hawken as the "First Engineer" of the Fire Company Station House. The two brothers entered into a partnership in the rapidly growing gun shop. Sam's "visit" lasted the rest of his lifetime.

Business continued to grow. As early as 1832, the brothers employed a handful of gunsmiths. They still had problems meeting the great demand for their quality firearms. The additional help had to work around the clock in a futile attempt to fill orders. The partnership was a great success. The rifles manufactured between 1822 and 1849 were marked in capital letters "J & S HAWKEN—ST. LOUIS" and were solid proof of the smooth running partnership.

Before 1836, the men moved their gun shop to Number 21, Laurel Street to accommodate the extra help and large inventory of lock plates, barrels, stocks, and finished goods.

Mountain men made the shop their first stop, trading guns and yarns, filling their horns with black powder and stocking up on percussion caps or flints. They also made their ideas for improvements known to the two brothers. With Sam's help, these were implemented as quickly as possible. Some of these vastly changed and specialized weapons became known as the "Hawken Rocky Mountain Rifle." Mountain men were very attached to their sturdy "Hawken" with its total reliability under adverse conditions. Upon making ready for a trapping expedition, one mountain man proudly announced that he was going "out in the pinyor with his big St. Louis gun—a Jake Hawken she is," and headed towards the wilderness.

Famous "buckskinners" of the period traveled great distances in order to obtain a legendary "Hawken" rifle. Mariano Modena, Joe Meek, Bill Williams, and many others journeyed to St. Louis and ordered rifles, stocked up on black powder and lead balls. The shop became somewhat of a social gathering place for these gruff men. They told stories of their harrowing experiences in the wilderness with hair-raising detail.

Jake and Sam listened to the specialized needs of their customers in the production of firearms. They

also kept abreast of new developments in the gun market from other areas of the country. Percussion rifles made their appearance in the late 1830s and thus, the great debate over weapon superiority between the flintlock and percussion weapons began. Hawken flintlocks were manufactured in great quantity. Quality flintlocks were generally preferred by the mountain men deep in the wilderness, as the weapon was still useful, even if fired with a makeshift flint.

Percussion caps were greatly affected by the weather and easily lost, rendering the weapon useless. Nevertheless, the stubborn mountain men gradually accepted the new-fangled weapon. It is difficult to say when the change to percussion weapons actually began or ended, but its firing method proved superior. The percussion firing system was well established by 1840, but no accurate records indicate when the two brothers began their production.

Records do indicate, however, the evolution of the half-stock rifle. Between 1835 and 1845 a large proportion of rifles sold were full stock. Because of the severe conditions under which they were used, vast numbers of breakages occurred in the long wooden forearm. After this time period, Jake revised the weapon. The widely acclaimed half-stock, ribbed model rifle made their mark in history. The Hawken brothers also manufactured belt and saddle pistols, both percussion and flint until the middle 1850s. All of these weapons, pistol and Mountain Rifle had "J & S HAWKEN" and "S. HAWKEN—ST. LOUIS" stamped on the lockplate.

Along with the percussion firing system and half-stock improvements, came the patented hooked breech system of loading. The brothers quickly adapted their line to the new loading system. Certain modifications of the stock were necessary. The long full stock was shortened. It was replaced by a metal rib complete with thimbles to accommodate the ramrod. Lengthening of the tang occurred. This enabled it to be tied to the long trigger bar with two screws that passed through the wrist area, strengthening this chronically weak area on the rifle.

With the high production level and constant changes, the brothers adopted an early form of the production line assembly of weapons. It was found that if the same gunsmith did a few installations repeatedly, a good quality weapon would be produced with precious time saved. Because of this method of production, great numbers of weapons were mass-produced with no discernible difference.

Virtually all Hawken rifles weighed ten and one-half pounds. This was true should it be a full or half-stock. Most lock plates were handmade in the Hawken shop and bore the Hawken stamp upon them. In the early days, it was necessary to find a supplier of ready-made locks. R. Ashmore, an English maker, was such a supplier. Outside sources of quality lockplates enabled swift production. Some rifles have, however, shown up with the name "Mejer" stamped on the plate. Adolphus Mejer was listed in the St. Louis Business Directory as a local dealer in pistols and rifles.

Exceptions did occur to the standard product. Weight exceptions were few, but worth noting. A few twelve to fifteen pound rifles were produced, special-ordered for those customers interested in tremendous shocking power and long range accuracy. For the most part, Hawken weapons were identical, due to the revolutionary method of assembly.

Personally, Jake and Sam were doing well. Despite their busy schedules, they somehow found time to socialize with local people. One day, Jake met a pretty young woman. They found a lot in common and continued to see each other. Eventually Catherine Allison and Jacob Hawken were married, giving Jake a different perspective on life. They also had a son named Christopher. They enjoyed a happy life for all too short a time, when disaster struck. With the constant influx of emigrants came many illnesses to which the American people had no immunity. Cholera made its appearance in St. Louis and brought death to the city. Catherine became ill and died in 1832, leaving Jacob crushed. His new found love had ended tragically with his life never to be the same. The epidemic was rather short-lived, but had made its mark on the Hawken family.

Despite personal happiness or tragedy, business still continued. With an ache in his heart for

Catherine, Jacob found his work consoling in a lonely sort of way. He returned to it half-hearted, as his business needed him badly.

The Hawken reputation for quality weapons was widespread, reaching throughout the country. Sam Hawken was surprised to find a letter addressed to him marked "confidential." Its writer, the famous Samuel Colt, had written requesting advice on an important matter. Colt was seriously thinking of establishing an armory in St. Louis. If built, this would change St. Louis and the lives of Jake and Sam greatly. He had enclosed a type of financial statement complete with gross sales for the year 1846-1847.

Sam's brother, J.B. Colt, wrote another letter on June 10, 1847 to a local businessman in St. Louis, James Lucas. Colt was seeking financial support for his endeavor. Lucas was not in favor of this idea and the project was dropped. Jake had no real opinion on the new armory, as he was still mourning his wife, some ten years later. Business still held its importance to him, but he generally tacked problems with less zeal as when his beloved was alive.

In the cold winter of 1848, cholera struck again in epidemic proportions. European ships brimming with emigrants came to port and infected much of St. Louis. A few deaths occurred in December, 1848. In the month of January, 1848, eight more people succumbed to the dreaded disease. Accurate records of the spread of this epidemic were kept. The disease spread rapidly due to the close proximity of homes and boarding houses in the city. It was almost impossible to live in such close quarters and not be infected. Warmer weather found the disease running rampant. People were panicked. Hardest hit were the poorer, unhealthy portions of the city such as St. Charles Street, Washington Avenue, and west Eighth Street.

It was during this time, that Jacob Hawken, crack gunsmith and revolutionary businessman, fell ill. On May 7, 1849, he became bed-ridden. Two short days later, he died, joining his beloved Catherine. The week of his death, one hundred eighty-one people passed away. His obituary was listed with many others in the *Missouri Republican* newspaper.

At half past seven o'clock, on the eighth instant, Jacob Hawken, Sen'r in the 63rd year of his age passed on. His friends and acquaintances are invited to attend his funeral this afternoon at three o'clock from the residence of his brother, Sam Hawken, 156 Sixth Street, between Morgan Street and Franklin Avenue.

His epitaph told of a courageous man who was gifted in many ways. His foresight was extraordinary in the early establishment of a source of quality firearms in a much needed area. He laid the foundation for good business and implemented one of the early assembly line production methods, insuring top of the line quality in his products. Many of the concepts he began became tradition to last for a hundred years of gun-making. He was to be missed by many.

His brother, Sam, was left with the responsibility of running the gun shop alone, as well as guardianship of his son, Christopher. He felt the burden of the shop and loss of his brother greatly. The epidemic's random killing of young and old was ruthless. Amidst the horror of this time, people began to pull together as only survivors of great tragedy can. Petty arguments and selfish needs were put aside as the diverse population united in an effort to heal themselves both physically and mentally.

The year of 1849 was indeed a most difficult one. Just nine days after Jacob's death, the community was faced again with another disaster. This time, the calamity was in the form of a devastating fire. The steamboat *White Cloud* was docked near the head of the landing in town. At 10:00 p.m. a fire broke out aboard this boat, and a strong northeast wind spread the flames to nearby steamboats. In less than one half-hour, the entire fleet was ablaze. The fire continued to spread into the city. Great numbers of buildings were burned to the ground. Large warehouses full of goods fed the fire. In an effort to stop the blaze, structures in the path of the flames were blasted.

The Hawken shop was a mere two blocks away from the raging fire. Miraculously, it escaped damage. Sam and a few gunsmiths had been ready with buckets of water and wet blankets.

With many of the flames finally extinguished, opportunists began looting. Shopkeepers raced to

the doors of the Hawken shop and armed themselves, relieving Sam of inventory in ammunition and guns.

The plague and fire of 1849 changed the physical makeup of the city. It also was a turning point for the direction of business in that area, as the fur trade was in its decline.

By the time the city recognized its full rebirth, the mountain men and trappers were gone. They had joined the Western Migration as guides, interpreters, emissaries, and messengers. A few even traveled to California in search of gold. Pioneers heading west often ended their journey near St. Louis because of the permanent Indian frontier along the bend of the mighty Mississippi from the 1820s through the 1840s. With Indians so close, confrontations once again became frequent. The Hawken gun shop was again pressed to fill orders for big rifles to be used on the frontier. Both white hunters as well as Indians sought after the big "St. Louie." This time, however, weapons and ammunition were purchased with customers never to return.

Local gun shops as well as imported Eastern weapons provided unwanted competition for Sam. It became impossible for him to produce the same quality as he had in past years. Consequently, the craftsmanship suffered. Construction variations occurred along with a distinctive change in style.

Sam changed the business name from "J & S Hawken" to "S. Hawken" after his brother's death. This new stamp was used until his retirement. In 1845, two gunsmiths working at the shop entered into a partnership with Sam. These gunsmiths, Christian Hoffman and Tristam Campbell, were brought into the partnership in order to sell items not made in the shop. They acted as a subsidiary to the Hawken Company. Cheap Eastern rifles as well as Allen pistols and Colt revolvers were added to the Hawken inventory. Also included in the business was Sam's son, William S. Hawken.

The city of St. Louis was continuously changing. Proof of its growth into a great commercial center was found not only in the vast numbers of people, but also in the presence of air pollution. Smoke and gas poured from factory stacks throughout the city. Because of this environment, Sam's health began to

deteriorate. He decided to travel to a less populated and cleaner area. He left for Denver on April 20, 1859 with William in charge of business.

Sam reached Denver on June 30, 1859. He wasn't quite sure what to do with himself. Gold mining interested him and he tried it for a short time. Old habits die hard and he found himself tinkering with guns once again. He stopped tinkering in January, 1860, and opened his own gun shop. Sam Hawken once again was prepared to manufacture his new style of rifles made "to order." The *Rocky Mountain News* advertised the new business with great fanfare. At his new shop, he hung a large rifle from a pole that was easily seen for blocks within the city.

The brisk mountain air had restored Sam's health to its fullness. Denver was good to Sam, but he missed the fast-paced, challenging lifestyle to which he had become accustomed. His son joined him in Denver after a brief service in the Mexican War. William had served in the Texas Rangers under General Henderson at the Battle of Monterey. At this battle forty-three men were armed with Hawken muzzle loaders against some six hundred to two thousand Mexicans. They succeeded in holding a bridge over San Juan Creek with weapons performing admirably. At the conclusion of the battle, only nine Texas Rangers were still standing. Young William Hawken was severely wounded, but had survived. He was mustered out of service and went north to find his father and new business doing well.

After a brief visit, Sam spoke of his burning desire to return to St. Louis. His son agreed to stay in Denver and keep the new business running. Sam returned to St. Louis in 1861, with William in charge back in Denver. Upon his return to St. Louis, Sam retired completely. The St. Louis directory revised its listing with: "William E. Watt—successor the W.E. Hawken-Rifle and Shot Gun Manufacturer, 21 Washington Avenue, Hawken rifles always on hand." Mr. Watt held a majority in the shop and joined forces with John Philip Gemmer, an old employee of the shop.

Gemmer was born in 1835 in Germany, but settled in Boonville, Missouri. He learned the trade from a gunsmith named John Sites. After learning the trade, he continued to St. Louis, made his acquaintance

with the Hawkens, gained employment with them, and eventually took control of the shop in 1862.

He paid tribute to the legendary brothers by allowing the Hawken name to remain outside of the shop as late as 1875. Out of that same respect, he kept the Hawken stamp on many rifles he produced. His name did appear on many double-barrel shotguns as well as on shotgun rifle combinations. He had learned good business sense from Jake and Sam and "his" shop prospered. His services were gratefully used when the War between the States began. His rank was of Corporal and he served as a top notch gunsmith in the Government arsenal in St. Louis. He, like his predecessors, kept abreast of the constant changes and needs of the industry. The new carbine was making its mark on the market. He was responsible for improvements in the Spencer carbine. The old reliable Hawken was still in demand, but the market gave way once again to progress with the modern breech loaders.

His abilities as a superb gunsmith allowed him to improve the Hawken lines with increased Spencer firepower. Many of these improvements were implemented with the use of government machinery. One of these "Spencer-Hawken" weapons lies in a collection today in Arizona stamped: J.P. Hawken, St. Louis. Until breech loaders had evolved completely, they could not replace the Hawken with its ballistic performance.

Gun enthusiasts and historians can visit the Missouri Historical Museum in St. Louis and view examples of the evolution of the Hawken rifle lines. Gemmer's ingenious influence is displayed in many weapons. One such gun is a trapdoor Springfield. It was completely rebuilt with the exception of the lock and breech mechanisms. A modified Hawken hammer was used to strike a firing pin instead of a percussion cap. The breech remained the same, chambered for the 45/70 government cartridge. The barrel underwent changes as it was octagonal with an underrib and guides for the cleaning rod.

The traditional Hawken half-stock is most evident with its scroll guard of iron and set trigger. In the many revisions/improvements, he always kept the traditional Hawken lines intact.

America was undergoing yet another change in the 1870s. The frontier was diminishing with vast open areas being closed in by the ever-growing population. The Industrial Age was beginning with handcrafted items of less importance, because of their proportionately high cost. Mass production by machines kept prices at a minimum, but with a degree of quality loss in the process. Gemmer struggled to keep his prices competitive, but was soon convinced that he could not compete. He worked feverishly with antiquated tools completing beautiful, but more expensive pieces by hand. He was forced to give in to large business. His customers consisted of "gun-cranks" who constantly sought to improve weapons of the period. During this time, Ol' Sam Hawken frequented the shop, reminiscing of the old days. He tried his hand at making one last "Rocky Mountain" gun. This piece is proudly displayed at the Jefferson Memorial Museum in St. Louis today.

Gemmer changed his business structure to that of a supplier of ammunition and custom gunsmith. He continued to make his own guns completed with stamped nameplate of "J.P. Gemmer." Traditional Hawken weaponry was stamped "Hawken." He finally entered into a well-earned retirement in 1915. When he retired, the doors of one of the oldest and most famous firearms businesses in America were closed forever.

Sam lived with his daughter, Mrs. Fred Colburn, in the country. In total his gunsmithing days totalled over seventy years. He lived in close proximity to St. Louis, enabling him to make frequent trips to the area which gave him the best days of his life. Sam lived a full life and passed away on May 19, 1884, at the age of ninety two. He was buried at Bellefontaine cemetery in his beloved St. Louis. He joined his legendary brother in a better place.

It is interesting to note that upon J.P. Gemmer's death in 1919, he was buried close to his dear friend Sam Hawken at Bellefontaine cemetery as well.

Over the years, the Hawken rifle remained the most desirable firearm to those men responsible for taming the great wilderness during the early and mid-1800s. The Hawken rifle stood the test of time. It is with no wonder that this weapon became as

legendary as its makers. Jake and Sam had courage in standing by an ideal in the gunsmith business. They were able to adapt within themselves to their changing environment as was the weapon they produced, changing history and the lives of those they touched.

The Rendezvous

During the fall of 1823, a Virginia gentleman named William Ashley took the crucial step of pushing the American fur trade into the heart of the Rockies and beyond, expanding geographical knowledge of an unknown territory.

Ashley had once been a judge and a munitions maker in the War of 1812, and was elected lieutenant governor of Missouri when that state entered the Union. Thus, holding this office he found it easy to enter the speculative field of the fur trade, which was just coming into being. Together with a former partner, Andrew Henry, who had more experience in the fur trade than Ashley, they proceeded to organize their own outfit, which later became known as the Rocky Mountain Fur Company.

In the *Missouri Gazette and Public Advertiser*, Ashley inserted an ad in the help wanted section soliciting the services of "enterprising young men willing to go into the wilderness and hunt for furs." Ashley recruited a large number of men with his ad, adventurers such as Ted Smith, Jim Bridges, Hugh Glass, James Clyman, Tom Fitzpatrick, and many, many more.

In the Spring of 1823, Ashley led these men out of St. Louis with plans to follow the Missouri north to the Yellowstone country, where all would scatter in

At a rendezvous, furs were traded for beads, weapons, trinkets and any other necessities for use in the mountains. Here two buckskinners dicker over a trade musket and a twist of tobacco.
Courtesy Fort Tassinong Muzzleloaders

every direction and set about trapping for furs. In order for Ashley to keep in contact with his trappers, he explained that he would meet them in July, 1825, at Henry's Fork on the Green River with a caravan load of supplies from St. Louis. Here they would all be paid for their services of the previous months and reoutfitted for the entire next year. For the next few weeks, the trappers would lounge around, gamble, swap stories of their adventures, and do a great deal of drinking. Ashley even invited Indians to come in and swap furs for trinkets, weapons, or gun power, and partake in the numerous games and enormous feasts. Nearly every year the rendezvous site was changed and Ashley's fur company remained free to search out new beaver country.

One of the most often played games was "Ferret Legging." A ferret, an animal of the weasel family, was used in hunting rabbits and rats and kept on a leather leash by many mountain men. The game was to tie both bottom pant legs and drop one ferret down each leg, just to see how long a man could stand the scratching and biting these animals would do trying to escape. Betting was high, but just watching a tough mountain man's face screw-up in various contorted expressions was the funniest part of the contest. The man who withstood the commotion and didn't drop his breeches first, won the sport.

It was at one of these gatherings that the giant Montana "Puffball" resembling a ball of dough, or when dried, powder, was introduced. Some specimens of "Calvatea" ballooned to more than three feet in diameter. It was found that the dry interior served as tinder to build a flame from the spark of flints and steel.[2]

These mountain men who marked the first trails through the Rockies flourished only briefly. By 1840, the fur bearing animals were largely trapped out and the popular summer fairs or "rendezvous" which everyone had looked forward to ceased to exist.

CHAPTER III

WILD ANIMALS

The Beaver

The beaver was found throughout this entire country in all the rivers in which they could live. This exception is made because some of the rivers were so filled with alkaline matter and other impurities that no animal life could exist in them. The quest for these animals is responsible for most of the early discoveries in the west. It was the beaver that gave rise to the formation of the various fur companies. In the market, beaver skins brought in twenty dollars each in gold.

This animal is worthy of note because of its remarkable intelligence and curious habits. They assembled on the banks of clear-flowing streams on which was situated a growth of cottonwood timber,

and with their sharp cutting teeth—two of which are in the upper and two in the lower jaw—could cut down a tree a foot and a half in diameter in a short time, taking out chips (four or five inches in length and two or three inches in width) with their teeth. The result of their labor was equal to the work of the best woodsman with a sharp axe. They always felled the tree in the direction of the stream, so that as much of it would fall into the water as possible. They could cut down the entire forest along the river bank in a short time.

When the trees were felled, beaver colonies quickly cut them into lengths sufficient for use in building dams across the river. Then with tails and paws the

Beaver

beaver moved the logs into the stream, placing them in position much the same way as an engineer would in building a dam that was expected to sustain the pressure of a large body of water. Beaver dams were built in crescent shape, the crescent being up the stream, and were built in the fall of the year. These animals built dams that were sometimes twenty feet in height, forming a pond above the dam twenty feet deep, and from ten to a hundred feet wide, the dams being so securely constructed that they withstood the severe freshets of spring. In the pond above the dam, they stored cottonwood on which they partly subsisted during the winter.

Their habitations were in the ground or bank, near the river, and were built a sufficient distance to protect them from encroachment either by water or their natural enemies (the principal of which was man). The mouth of the tunnel leading to the beaver's home was deep down in the water of the pond above the dam. It was then dug upward above the level of the water, when it made a sharp turn downward, going below the water level. Again it made a turn upward, going above the surface until it reached the bank where it had its home. Its habitation was the most ingenious in construction that can be imagined. The beds were located on the sides so that one or two beavers could lie comfortably. The animal required a bed of considerable length for a full-grown beaver, tail and all, was from four to five feet in length. Its tail was from one foot to eighteen inches long, and was unlike the tail of another animal (being stiff) so that it required a special place for its reception to enable its owner to lie comfortably.

The beaver's tail, next to its cutting teeth, was its greatest tool. It was used for transporting logs, dirt, and heavy substances, also as a hoe, trowel, and broom.

The beaver was the most affectionate of animals, as well as one of the most knowing. Being fond of playing with their young in the water, it was interesting to watch them unobserved. They indulged in all sorts of antics with their young, turning somersaults, swimming with great rapidity, jumping out of the water and then diving head first, cutting such capers as only a beaver can. Trappers in olden days used to lie for hours watching them in their sportive moods, and then shoot them at a favorable opportunity.

The manner of trapping the beaver was by means of an ordinary trap, patterned like the modern steel rat-trap, only stronger and without teeth in its jaws. A heavy chain was attached to it, fastened to a stone, a tree, or a stick firmly driven into the ground. The trapper entered the stream some distance above where he intended to place his trap, and waded to the spot he had selected for it. He thus prevented these intelligent animals from scenting his trail. After setting his trap at the bottom of the pond, he placed near it a stick of sufficient length to reach above the surface of the water. On the exposed end of this stick was tied dried castor of the beaver; this had a strong musky smell, resembling that of the musk deer. As soon as the beaver appeared above the water and scented the castor it immediately swam to the stick. He then followed it with his nose to the bottom and was caught in the trap by one leg. The smell of the castor seemed to cause this wily animal to lose all sense of its surroundings. If the beaver did not drown, it would sometimes gnaw its foot off to escape.

The foot of the beaver was webbed and was used for swimming. They also had nails with which they scratched the earth in a similar manner of the mole or badger. Their meat was juicy and resembled fresh pork. They were exceedingly wild, and their sense of smell was very acute. At the approach of danger they dove deep into the pond, rarely if ever entering the tunnel leading to their homes if there was the slightest chance of being observed. The beaver was as much at home on land as in the water, and when on the ground was in constant motion. However, it never strayed far from water.

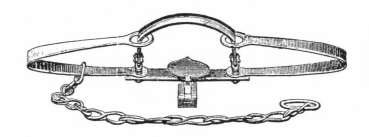

One Type of beaver trap

Bears

Although the bear family is at home in many parts of the world, there are but three varieties indigenous to our country: the black, the cinnamon, and the grizzly.

Of these, the black bear was the most common, and was smaller in size than the cinnamon or grizzly, usually weighing from two to four hundred pounds. Its coat was soft and the fur thick and long. It is clumsy in appearance, with a thick-set body, and short, stout legs. Though it is active and vigilant and had great strength, it could scarcely be called a ferocious animal, for it always avoided man. It changed its haunts with the seasons: in the spring living on roots and juicy plants found in the vicinity of streams, ponds, and lakes; during summer spending most of its time in the under-brush, feeding on berries, bugs, frogs, and such small animals as it could procure. In the fall it sought higher ground, and ate wild fruits, acorns, and nuts.

It was extremely fond of honey. In its rambles through the woods this excellent climber never passed a bee tree without robbing it of its store of sweets. Although living for the most part on vegetable food, the black bear was also carnivorous. It would not eat meat which was tainted, unless pressed by hunger. Notwithstanding its clumsy gait it could run rapidly, and when closely pursued would, whenever possible, take to a tree. The bear was a good swimmer, crossing rivers with ease. Cubs were dropped in the spring, and were as frolicsome as kittens in their play. By the time cold weather set in, the cubs had attained fully two-thirds of their growth, and when hibernating were fat and in good condition to remain in a torpid state until the return of spring.

When hibernating, these animals generally hid themselves in the hollow of an old tree, or in caves and crevices, where they remained undisturbed until spring. Sometimes the heavy snows and ice imprisoned them until long after the usual time for making their appearance.

Indians regarded the bear as a great prize: first, for its skin, which made a beautiful robe; next, for its claws and teeth, used as ornaments; next, for its meat, the red man's pork and a dainty dish; and last, though not least, was the fact that when an Indian had killed four bears it was considered equal to taking an enemy's scalp. This was considered by them equal to counting a coup.

The black bear was to a certain extent migratory in its habits, and before very severe winters set in, they sometimes moved southward in large numbers. It was sagacious in escaping the hunter, but when wounded would, like all the bear family, fight to the death. It was dexterous in the use of its forepaws, and when fighting it stood on its hind legs boxing after the manner of an athlete. With one blow of its sharp claws it could tear out the entrails of a dog. All the bear family have very strong jaws, with which they can crush any small animal.

The cinnamon bear resembled its cousin, the black bear in form and size, as well as in its habits. It was larger, however, and more fierce and dangerous when molested; like most of the bear family, it was comparatively harmless if let alone. The larger specimens of this animal measure from nose to tail over five and a half feet, and in height a little over three feet. It lived largely on berries, roots, and vegetable food, though it by no means disdained flesh when it could get it. It never voluntarily attacked man, but retired on seeing him. If cornered or wounded, it was about as ugly a customer and gritty a fighter as could be found.

Its hair was softer and thicker than that of the black bear; under it, the fur was finer in texture and considerably longer. Naturalists are generally agreed that the cinnamon is not a different specie of bear, but a distinct variety. The idea was once prevalent that it was a cross between the grizzly and the black bear, but has been rejected more recently. It was sometimes known as the silver-tip bear, on account of the silvery color of the hair at the extremity of its stunted tail. It has never been found near the sea-coast, or in any place far removed from the vicinity of the Rocky Mountains. It is a northern animal, not being found as far south as Texas. Its natural habitat was west and north of the Missouri River, in the direction of the cold and barren regions of the northwest and found in no other part of the world. Its existence was unknown to naturalists until the advent in that region of the fur trappers and hunters. They purchased a bear's skin from the Indians, which was of a pale reddish brown; this, the Indians said, was from an animal entirely distinct from the grizzly bear. This led to inquiry as to the different species or varieties of bears in that region. The Indians showed the different kinds of bear skins they had, and persisted in saying that there were three kinds of bears in their territory: the grizzly, the extremities of whose hair were of a white or frosty color; the black bear; and another bear, having white hairs in his light reddish-brown coat.

The cinnamon bear had long been known to the trappers and fur traders before white settlers entered that territory, and the skins of these animals, on account of the fineness of the fur, were much sought after and were more valuable than those of the black bear.

The grizzly bear was the largest and most formidable of any of the bear family in the West, sometimes attaining the length of nine feet and weighing ten to twelve hundred pounds. Specimens have been shown weighing as high as eighteen hundred, and even two thousand pounds. Its habitat were about the same as that of the cinnamon bear.

The coat of this animal was a dirty brown or a

The Grizzly Bear may be called the "King of American Wild Beasts."

grizzly gray, whence it derived its name. Its claws were long and large—seven or eight inches long and sharp and gouge-shaped—and were used with terrible effect in striking down or tearing its prey. They were also of great efficiency in digging for roots. With its sharp claws the grizzly would, at one blow, tear the entrails from a buffalo, ox, or horse. Like its cousins it was a great boxer, and used its forepaws with tremendous effect when in battle. In moving, it had a shambling, clumsy gait, its head constantly swaying from side to side. Its color ranged from brown to nearly black, and sometimes to almost white. It confined itself exclusively to the Rocky Mountain regions and the plains adjacent thereto; where the grizzly made its haunts, the black and the cinnamon bears were scarce. All other animals retreated from the presence of this ferocious beast.

Next to taking the scalp of an enemy, the Indians considered the killing of a grizzly bear their greatest feat. They greatly prized the long claws, the large, sharp teeth, and great warm coat. They wore the claws as ornaments around their necks, and were fond of boasting of their battles and hair-breadth escapes in killing this powerful beast. When the Indians knew that a grizzly bear was in their vicinity, the men mounted their best horses and, armed with their best arms, went in parties to give it battle.

Wolves

Regular visitors in every camp were wolves, both gray and coyote. The latter were skulking beast that sat at a safe distance from the camp, and uttered such unearthly howls that the noise of three or four often sounded like hundreds. Should there be from fifteen to twenty gathered about the camp, their howls prevented anyone from sleeping that night. They were cunning thieves and arrant cowards, and were despised by every person in that country. With the setting in of cold weather these famished animals became very bold, and coming into camp, would eat a pair of boots, the leather of a saddle, or anything they could find to appease their voracious appetites.

The large gray wolf was a more dangerous animal. He was a cunning, skulking thief, and approached the camp by stealth, carrying away whatever he could get hold of. In winter, when these animals suffered from hunger, they became very vicious, and a pack of them often attacked cattle and horses, killing and devouring them. At times old hunters and trappers shot one of the pack; then the rest, crazed by the smell of blood, proceeded to eat their companions alive.

The skins of both kinds of wolves were sent East and made into clothing, robes, mats, fur hats, or ornaments. If Easterners had known wolf habits, the skins probably would not have been popular. The dirty beasts crawled into the carcass of an animal which had been dead for a long time, and once inside of it, rolled over and over in the putrid mass, saturating their hair as much as possible with the filthy and rotten inside of a dead animal. It was not uncommon to locate the presence of these animals by their disgusting odor.

Wolf

The Buffalo

Years ago buffalo herds were numerous and large, and covered almost the entire country west of the Mississippi River to the eastern chain of the Rocky Mountains. To persons not accustomed to seeing them in herds, the surprising statements as to their numbers over 100 years ago may seem to be over-done; countless travelers remembered any statement that exaggerated the number of these huge beasts that roamed over the western country. Many people traveled for months at a time and never been out of sight of their countless numbers. The artillery at Fort Kearney actually fired into them to keep them out of the fort.

In Kansas, where the buffalo grass was plentiful, their numbers were incalculable. As far as the eye could reach in every direction was a solid moving mass of buffalo and the plains were literally black with them. Soon after the Union Pacific Railroad was opened, its trains were detained for hours while waiting for buffalo herds to cross the railroad tacks. At first, the engineers thought they could rush the trains through the herds with impunity, but they soon discovered that the only way was to let the animals take their own time in crossing.

They were not always assembled in close, compact herds, but were frequently scattered while feeding on the prairies, after the manner of domestic cattle. During the early 1840s, it would have been impossible to estimate their number even approximately, but there were millions of them. It is difficult to realize that they almost became extinct.

Formerly the buffalo ranged over the greater part of the American continent. They were migratory, and their wandering habits were well understood by the Indians. The Indians claimed to know of four kinds: the common buffalo found on the plains, mountain buffalo, wood buffalo, and beaver buffalo. The Indians' account of the many varieties of buffalo may be correct, as the different kinds of robes in their possession seemed to testify.

The new coat of the buffalo was dark brown in color. Later it grew paler, and when the hair was shed, the coat—especially of the young animals—became a dark brownish red. The cows had one calf at a birth, which was usually dropped during May or June. At birth the color of the calf was a bright yellow, with a pale red stripe covering its backbone; this stripe gradually changed to the natural color with age. The robe was at its best in the fall or winter when the buffalo had its full winter coat. Occasionally a buffalo robe was seen "in the silk". These robes were as beautiful as they were rare. The hair was fine and of a dark rich color, as glossy as the finest silk, and as soft as velvet. There was no shaggy mane on these robes for every part of the skin was covered with hair resembling the coat of the finest horse.

Buffalo

The buffalo supplied nearly all the food of the North American Indians especially for those living west of the Mississippi River and east of the Rocky Mountains. These great animals roamed as far north as the Saskatchewan River in Canada, and as far south as Mexico. Millions of them were slaughtered every year for the sustenance of the Indians occupying this vast territory. They supplied them not only with food, but furnished them with robes and hides for clothing and dwellings. Many of their tools were made from its hide, horns, and bones. The hide of the bulls was tanned and used for lodge covers. When dried in the sun—after the hair was taken off—the hide became as hard as flint; this was used for soles of moccasins, belts, and other purposes. It was also used to keep dampness and cold out of their beds, being laid on the ground and the rest of the bedding placed on top of it.

The rawhide was cut into strands and braided into ropes. The green hide was converted into kettles in which they boiled their meat. The tough, thick hide of the neck of the bull made battle shields that were shown to be unpenetrable by arrows and lances. The Indians, in short, allowed not a part of the buffalo to go to waste. The brains were used in tanning skins; the bones were boiled and the extract was used as a soup. The marrow was eaten and the entrails were also eaten either cooked or raw. There was no sweeter meat than that of a fine barren cow or young bull, the most desirable part being the muscle lying on both sides of the animal's withers. This was called the hump. The liver and tongue were of fine flavor. No one ever thought of telling the number of buffalo he had killed, unless able to produce the tongues; the number of these told their own story.

The Indians were not alone in pursuit of the buffalo. Wolves, both gray and coyote, frequently attacked the old bulls for their meat. A number of wolves would single out an old bull; one or two attacked him in the rear, and with their sharp teeth cut his hamstring, bringing him down on his haunches. This accomplished, they at once proceeded to eat their victim alive. When a pack of wolves attacked a buffalo, they set up a yell that was unearthly. Their noise did not seem to frighten these old monarchs, but they formed themselves in a circle, preparing for battle in which some were sure to be killed. When grazing along the foothills of the mountains and thus attacked, and one of their number lay prostrate surrounded by hungry wolves, a grizzly bear sometimes made his appearance and with one stroke of his paw cleared every wolf from their prey. Then they sat at a respectful distance from the carcass of the animal, licking their jaws, and whining like whipped dogs. Not until bruin had finished his meal and taken his departure would these skulking scavengers again attack the carcass.

These great animals were migratory, not from inclination, but from necessity. When the ground in the far north was covered with snow and ice, it was impossible for them to reach their food, and when the rivers were frozen over, they were compelled to eat snow to quench their thirst. It was distressing to see them on the ice of a frozen river endeavoring to get water. They slipped and fell in all manner of ways; sometimes they fell into an airhole in the ice, one after another falling or being pushed into the water and drowned.

The buffalo were peculiar in one respect: if they attempted to cross a road upon which was a moving wagon train, body of troops, or a railway train, they all invariably crossed in front, never breaking and crossing at the rear. When alarmed and running, their heads were always down, and they kept as close together as possible. While moving in this manner those in front were unable to stop even if they had the desire to do so because those in the rear forced them irresistibly on. Should a herd be suddenly frightened and start to run over a precipice, all of them rushed over before they could stop. The Indians, knowing that these animals were valuable to them, were careful not to kill more than were required for their needs.

Late in the summer and fall, abundant buffalo gnats annoyed these great animals beyond endurance. The buffalo gnat was a small black fly that looked like a black bead. It settled on the buffalo burying itself in the thick hair and hide—driving them almost frantic—sometimes eating great sores on them. Buffalo "wallows" were depressions in the land caused by the animals wallowing in the dirt, trying to free themselves from the countless gnats that were torturing them. When the first telegraph line was erected over the plains, the poles were

frequently thrown down from some unaccountable cause. It was subsequently discovered that this was done by the buffalo scratching themselves to allay the irritation caused by the gnats. An experiment was made of driving heavy spikes in the poles to keep the animals away, but this attracted them all the more.

Under ordinary circumstances buffalo were stupidly dull and inoffensive animals, spending their time in eating and sleeping, fighting gnats during the day, and seldom going far from water, which they required in large quantities.

When the buffalo shed their long hair—which turned to a dirty brown in the spring—they presented a singular appearance with the old loose hair hanging in patches and mats over their bodies.

It is the opinion of historians that if care had been taken in domesticating the buffalo, they could have become a valuable addition to our food supply, and furnished robes for use in the northern latitudes during the cold weather.

It was not uncommon along the borders of civilization to find domestic cattle running wild with buffalo herds. These cattle, after they had been with the buffalo for a short time, became much more ferocious and wild than the buffalo themselves.

One of the most useful products of the buffalo, along the woodless course of the overland wagon road was the buffalo "chip." This was the dried dung of the buffalo, and was composed of the woody fiber of the grass which the animals had eaten. After lying in the sun, these chips became dry and were the only article on this long road which could be collected and used for fuel. They made a hot fire, with only a small flame.

Without buffalo chips it is difficult to conceive how travelers and plainsmen could have secured fuel for cooking purposes, for there was absolutely no other fuel in that country. Perhaps fastidious people would revolt at having their meals cooked over such fire, with the wind blowing and covering the edibles with the ashes and dust from the burning embers. But hunger is the best sauce, and as a cook once said when some gentlemen who were on a hunting expedition asked what time dinner would be ready: "Dinner in this camp is always served promptly at six

o'clock, except on three occasions; when it is earlier, when it is later or when we don't dine at all." In early days it would have been the latter alternative to everybody on the plains but for buffalo chips.

The old bulls always formed a sort of fringe around the great brown surging herd and were usually scattered in groups or singly at a distance of from a hundred yards to a half a mile from the body of the herd. The old bulls were kept at a distance by the young bulls, after the latter had attained full growth and strength. Hence when buffalo were attacked by wolves, it was the old bulls on the outer edge that met the attack. Their ostracism resulted in forming a guard for the rest of the herd. When the herd was frightened or stampeded, however, the old bulls mingled with them in their flight. At times groups of these ex-monarchs abandoned the herd entirely, wandering away by themselves.

When young bulls attacked the old ones, they were no match for the latter in single combat. When a young bull attacked one of these sturdy old fellows and was defeated, other young bulls came to the assistance of the beaten animal and a desperate and ferocious combat was sure to take place. The fight sometimes lasted for hours, and in the furious encounter the young bulls were often disabled or mortally wounded. The old bulls were sometimes of enormous size and strength, and fought with great ferocity. It was only after the fiercest and most protracted encounter that they would relinquish leadership among the herd, leaving the places to their younger rivals. During these combats the young and old bulls fought until both fell exhausted. In this condition, with blood pouring from many wounds, tongues hanging from their mouths, panting and gasping for breath, they continued the battle. The ground fought over in these encounters showed the fierceness of the struggle, torn and covered with blood and tufts of hair. Sometimes one or two bulls might lie prostrate mortally wounded; at other times, suffering with a broken leg or having lost both eyes, they remained on the scene of carnage presenting a pitiable sight. In this condition they were frequently eaten alive by wolves, bears, and other carnivorous animals. It did not take long after blood had been drawn until the keen-scented scavengers made their

Although it is far from the ideal rest for shooting, sometimes frontier riflemen, like this buffalo hunter (portrayed by Phil Spangenberger) would use the saddle as a means of steadying a big rifle like the Sharps. In this situation, the horse had to be well-trained for there was no place to tie one's mount in open country like this. Shooting across the saddle was often the best way to shoot and keep the horse in check.

appearance in large numbers, particularly wolves. They quietly sat or stood in circles by daylight, around the scene of battle, and at the first opportunity one of the bolder or hungrier made a dash for its victim. If successful, it was but a short time before the carcass was literally covered by these snarling beasts. If the battles were at night—especially when the weather was sharp and cold—the wolves set up an unearthly howl. Soon there were countless numbers of them on the spot waiting an opportunity to appease their voracious appetites.

The killing of an old bull was a perilous undertaking even for armed men. When a number of old bulls discovered the hunter, they prepared for battle with their heads down, their eyes glowing like balls of fire. At the first shot they either ran away or charged the attacking party. A wounded buffalo bull was a very dangerous animal, using every effort in his power to reach his pursuers. With blood running from his nose, scarcely able to move, he would tear the ground with his sharp hooves, tail erect in the air, doing his utmost to induce the pursuer to come near enough for attack; until life had left him it was dangerous to go near the furious beast.

The excitement of the first buffalo hunt usually was a vivid and pleasing memory. To see the Indians on their fleet ponies, in swift pursuit of those shaggy-maned monarchs of the prairies, was a spectacle more thrilling than the fiercest bull fight in the enclosed amphitheaters of Spain. To participate in the hunt was still more thrilling, an experience never to be forgotten, and so fascinating that the more it was indulged in the keener grew the enjoyment, until finally it became a passion. The space for the hunt was as limitless as the prairies. In the eagerness of the chase every muscle quivered, every nerve was at its fullest tension, every faculty was keenly alert, and the excitement brought with it the glow of health and the vigor of youth. It was magnificent outdoor sport. The long rides, the exhilaration of the exercise, and deep draught of pure air, made this sport one of the most fascinating that could be experienced.

When on a buffalo chase only the best horses were used. It was necessary that the animal selected should have not only great courage and speed, but intelligence enough to carry its rider without guidance after the killing once began. When the shooting started the reins were dropped over the pommel of the saddle, and were not touched again by the rider until he was through firing. The horse was

expected to jump over a rock or hole of his own accord, avoiding all obstacles in the way.

After approaching the herd as closely as possible without being discovered, the hunting party dashed into it. The buffalo, now thoroughly alarmed, first stared wildly, then crowded together with heads down and tails up, rushed at a mad pace from their pursuers. Small herds joined the others in their flight until they formed an immense solid black mass fleeing across the prairie. In their flight, they raised great clouds of dust which could be seen for miles. This was exceedingly trying for both men and horses. The eyes, nose, and mouth of both soon became filled with dust and when dampened by the moist breath, formed a sticky mud that was not only disagreeable in itself, but created intense thirst.

Should the ground be soft or wet, both rider and horse were covered with the wet earth, which the buffalo, in their flight, threw back with great force from their sharp hoofs into the faces of horse and rider. It required a horse of courage to withstand the constant rain of clods of earth on breast, flanks, face, nostrils, and eyes.

When buffalo were frightened and started to run or stampede, they kept close together, forming a compact mass. Should one stumble or fall, many others stumbled over their prostrate comrade before it could rise. Often he could not get up at all. The hunter had to avoid groups of fallen and stumbling buffalo for should he get into them his horse might also fall, and both horse and rider could be severely injured if not trampled to death.

Buffalo hunting was a science that had to be learned. For those not accustomed to it, it was dangerous sport. The inexperienced hunter was always doing what he should not do, sometimes wounding his horse or that of a comrade, or wounding or killing himself or someone else. A man might be ever so good a hunter for other game, and yet be the very worst bungler in hunting buffalo.

In killing these animals the hunter rode boldly into the fleeing herd, his horse running only as fast as the buffalo. Then, selecting the animal desired, he fired directly behind the fore shoulder—the tenderest place—and a shot entering at this point was most likely to strike a vital part. This threw the buffalo

down, and after the hunter had exhausted his ammunition or shot a sufficient number, he returned and killed those he had already wounded and left lying on the prairie. When in the chase and shooting these animals, it was necessary at all times to have one or two buffalo between the rider and the animal selected to be shot, for if this precaution was not taken the wounded buffalo was liable to fall in front of the horse of the hunter, or strike the animal next to it a severe blow with its horns. It was useless to fire at the head of one of these huge beasts, for no ordinary bullet would penetrate its thick skull. Yet an experienced buffalo hunter could shoot a buffalo in the ear, killing it instantly. The animals selected to be killed were usually barren cows, young bulls, or heifers. The meat of the old bulls was strong in flavor and stringy, although it was used as food by the Indians.

Frequently distinguished visitors insisted on learning something of the life of this wild country. On several occasions, they were escorted on a general hunt for antelope, elk, deer, buffalo, and sometimes bears. When a herd of buffalo was discovered, a detail of eight or ten of the best troopers in the command were chosen for the chase, selecting those who were good shots and expert riders.

When any of the civilians cared to accompany the troopers on a buffalo hunt the first request made of them was to disarm themselves. This was sure to excite their indignation and was invariable followed by the question, "Why do you ask us to disarm? We can't kill buffalo without weapons." The invariable reply was that it was more important that they should not kill or wound themselves or any of the troops. Then starting for the chase, each civilian (or greenhorn) was directed to ride close to one of the troopers, always keeping the civilians on the right, as the firing was usually to the left with a carbine, and to the right with a pistol.

Fear seemed to take possession of anyone making his first attack on these animals. The experience of all plainsmen, mountaineers, and army officers, when initiating new men in the buffalo hunt, was that they became very nervous and excited when coming up with the herd, and were seized with what was known as "buck ague." When once seized with buck ague, inexperienced hunters trembled as though suffering

from a violent attack of chills and seemed to lose control of themselves, discharging their arms unconsciously in every direction.

During the chase the buffalo, when frightened and running at top speed, squeezed so close together that they sometimes crushed the legs of the hunter against his horse. On such occasions it was necessary that the experienced hunter exercise control over the novice and force him to ride as rapidly as the running buffalo. Should he attempt to stop his horse, he might be run down by those pressing relentlessly forward in his rear.

Often a hunter had been compelled to strike the back of a buffalo with his carbine to prevent the horse from being thrown. After all the ammunition had been expended or enough buffalo were killed, it was not uncommon for the hunters to find themselves in the center of a great herd of these animals a mile or more in diameter. The effort then was to withdraw. This was accomplished by slacking the pace of the horses until the herd ran past, for if the hunters attempted to stop at once, the buffalo, in their mad

rush might throw the horses down and trample everyone to death. It often required half an hour's run to get out of a great herd.

A report of the Department of the Interior, dated at Washington D.C., July 1, 1902, says: The number of buffalo running wild in United States, 30; in Canada, 570; in captivity in United States, 664; in Canada, 30; in Australia, 12; Belgium, France and Holland, 14; Germany, 46; Russia, 2, and in England, 26, and in captivity in other countries, 100, making a total of 1,494. In speaking of the great changes which have taken place in the fauna of America, the report says of the buffalo: "The fate of the bison, or American buffalo, is typical of them all. 'Whether we consider this noble animal,' says Audubon, 'as an object of the chase or as an article of food for man, it is decidedly the most important of all our American contemporary quadrupeds.'"

Source:
"The Buffalo in America" - Privately printed -N.Y., 1907 (E.L. Reedstrom collection).

Mountain Sheep

The mountain sheep was a peculiar animal, having the habits of the chamois, living only on the highest peaks of the mountains. The horns of the bucks were immense; it is claimed by some hunters that the buck—when pursued—jumped from a precipice, and landed on its horns instead of feet. This is hard to believe, for the females had no horns, and Nature does not provide such marked advantages for the male portion of any of the animal kingdom.

They did not in any way resemble domestic sheep, either in habits or appearances. The hair was a straight, thick, dirty gray, and was useless for any purposes of manufacture. In size they were larger than the common goat, which they somewhat resembled in appearances. They were exceedingly nimble and sure-footed, and jumped with great rapidity from crag to crag when pursued by the mountain lion and other carnivorous beasts.

The home of this animal seemed to be among barren rocks, where little vegetation grew. Yet when

secured by the hunter they were always fat and in good condition. There was no water where they roamed, but snow was perpetual in the valleys below them, and this supplied the necessary drink. They went in herds numbering from one to two hundred. Living as they did in such isolated places, it was exceedingly difficult to find or kill them.

Mountain Sheep

The Otter

Otter

The otter was perhaps the most valuable of all the fur-bearing animals of America because of the richness of its fur. This animal measured about two and one-half feet from its nose to the root of its tail. It lived almost exclusively on fish, but when hungry it ate frogs, snakes, and other small animals. It was admirably adapted by nature for pursuing and catching fish. Its body was lithe, and its toes so broadly webbed that it was able to propel itself with great speed through the water. The tail was long, and was used as a rudder to direct its movements in the water, while its short, powerful legs were so loosely jointed that the animal could turn them in almost any direction with ease. The hair on its body and limbs was of two kinds: a close, fine soft fur lying next to the skin protected the animal against heat and cold; the other was long, shining and coarse, permitting the animal to glide easily through the water. Its teeth

were very sharp and strong, and when diving for fish it rarely missed its prey. In color the otter varied somewhat, but was generally of a rich brown, intermixed with whitish gray.

The otter made its home along the banks of rivers and streams, generally in some natural crevice or deserted excavation. If these could not be found, it made a hole for itself. The entrance to the holes or burrows were always below the surface of the water. When alarmed, the mother otter with her young plunged into the stream, taking refuse amid the vegetation, or anything that afforded shelter. As they could not remain under water for a great length of time, they often came to the surface for air, would put their noses above the surface, fill their lungs, then disappear again.

The otter was a remarkable fighter and could defeat almost any animal of its size. In fighting a dog,

it required but a short time to cut the flesh of its opponent to shreds with its sharp teeth. They were prolific, and had from three to five young at a birth. The young made their appearance early in spring, about March or April. They were nursed by the mother, but were soon turned adrift to obtain their own living. They were extremely fond of play, both young and old went to an inclined bank of a river, sliding into the stream on their wet bodies. The trappers called these places "otter slides." At the bottom of the slides he placed his traps into which the otter plunged, becoming prisoners. Like the beaver, when caught in traps it would sometimes gnaw off its foot to regain its freedom.

The beaver and otter were the most sought after of all the animals by the different fur companies of the country. About the same means were employed in capturing them, and both were trapped at the same time. The otter did not go to the ponds like the beaver, but was found almost everywhere. The meat of the otter was never considered a palatable dish. As it lived largely on fish, its flesh had a strong, fishy flavor. These animals were prized only for their fine fur. In the early days the otter was found in great abundance, but in latter years became scarce.

Among the Indians otter pelts were much prized. They used them for making medicine bags, pouches, and articles of ornament. Having only limited means for capturing them, it was difficult for the red men to secure the wary animals at all. When they did, it was usually at an otter slide, where they waited for days at a time, patiently watching for an opportunity to shoot them. If they did not kill it instantly, the animal disappeared in the water, dragging itself off to its hole, where it died. After death the others dragged the remains into the stream to float away with the current.

The Prairie Dog

Prairie Dog Community

The little, reddish-brown marmot called the "prairie dog" by settlers, who thought that the high-pitched "yek" sounded vaguely like a small dog, is a defenseless little beast that eats plants, insects, grubworms, or whatever is at hand. A mound builder, his underground cities with connecting tunnels once housed about five billion of the little varmints, stretching from central Texas and western Arizona to northwestern Montana.

The little critter is usually pot-bellied from sitting for hours on end, upright, at the entrance to his personal tunnel, looking for danger.

Prairie dogs were not especially loved by the settlers. Not particularly prized as a food source (although they were eaten when they could be hunted and killed), the little creatures thought that planted crops were just another sign of divine intervention in their behalf, and nearly ate the settlers out of house and home. They managed to further infuriate farmers by obstructing irrigation ditches. The massive tunnels often were the cause of lame horses, as the tunnels collapsed under the weight of a horse, breaking legs all too frequently. Shotguns and dynamite didn't really put much of a dent in the population until the U.S. Biological Survey used poisoned grain and lethal gasses to bring the population under control.

CHAPTER IV

WAGONS WEST

The Conestoga Wagon

Conestoga, Lancaster County, Pennsylvania was little more than a wide spot in the road when it produced the first sturdy wagon that was to be called by its name. The first wagon rolled down Conestoga's streets sometime in the mid-1700s, built to carry up to ten tons of farm gear and produce. The wagon gained

Ruby Rivers and his family arrived in Carbon County, Wyoming, in 1883. This photograph was taken by F.M. Baker on flats between Elk Mountain Post Office and Mill Creek on the Overland Trail. Several women have cut off the bottom of their skirts a good twelve inches for ease in walking. They also sewed up pockets of lead shot within the hems to keep their skirts from flying over their heads during a good wind.

Courtesy Union Pacific Railroad Museum Collection

Ox Yoke

Bullwhacker

Animal feed box

Hand brak

Lazy board

The Conestoga wagon.   Art by E.L. Reedstrom

its fame as the main conveyance for easterners seeking to become westerners. The sturdy wagon with its flapping white dust-covers looked like a masted ship as it eased over the prairies, taking the name Prairie Schooner, after the name "Turnpike Schooner" lost real meaning.

The land ships were propelled by four to six horses, mules, oxen or, sometimes, cattle. The driver held the reins on the left side of the rear animal, passing wagons in front of him on the left side. This may have been the impetus for making this a nation of 'left of the road drivers' after the automobile became common.

The first of the wagons were painted like the Pennsylvania Dutch farmers painted their own, with a light blue wagon bed and red wheels and wagon tongue. The frame and flooring were generally oak. The wheels themselves were usually gumwood with hickory spokes, when possible. In time, the design changed somewhat, with the bed becoming flatter,

smaller and lighter than its eastern counterpart, as fitted the long trek over mountains deserts, and assorted other geographic ills.

The animals pulling the "camel of the prairies" were usually divided into three teams, referred to as the lead team, swing team and wheel team (reading from front to back). When the animals used were good, fresh horses, the conveyance would move up to twenty miles from sunrise to set. Cattle or oxen would make about six miles, if the terrain wasn't too difficult.

The Conestoga became forts, boats, and anything else needed at the moment. Perhaps the strangest use was that of court room and scaffold, when a member of the wagon train committed some atrocity. The wagon tongue was used, on occasion, in place of a tree when a hanging was unavoidable and the wagon train had seen nothing but sand and rock. The tongue was pointed skyward, and the condemned man launched from the drivers seat into eternity.

Dugouts and "Soddies"

The tenderfoot on the Plains tried to outwit Mother Nature, building a one-room dugout facing south, burrowing into a hillside or creek bank and roofing the ten by twelve foot space with willow, cedar, and sod chunks. The warm sun, thought the tenderfoot, would keep the dugout warm. Imagine his chagrin when the snow drifted in, entombing the occupant until spring or death, depending on his cache of supplies.

If the tenderfoot's supplies lasted, the dugout could be warm in the winter. Sometimes, however, keeping the dugout warm proved hazardous, too— many people died from carbon monoxide from faulty stoves and blocked chimneys. As there were no windows, ventilation depended on inexactness in construction and dumb luck.

A balance had to be achieved somehow. If the construction was sufficiently inexact to permit air to avoid carbon monoxide poisoning, it might leave enough space for rattlesnakes to take up residence. At best, dugouts were plagued with lice, fleas, centipedes, and rodents.

Another hazard was range cattle, who favored the lusher growth of grass on the roof. Cows loved to graze the roof, and frequently "dropped in." If the inhabitant of the dugout happened to be at home (and out of the path), the cow stayed for lunch, but the roof usually had to be replaced.

As the residents of the dugouts grew more sophisticated, they began to construct a half-dugout, about waist high, with sod walls and windows of oiled-paper or glass. A storm cellar was dug nearby to keep provisions, and to provide a safer place when tornadoes roared across the plains, taking everything in their wake.

Eventually, the tenderfoot learned how to exist with Nature, and became a successful homesteader, building a sod house with four walls, windows, and timbers to support the roof. The walls were made of the dense sod, which insulated the building against the elements. Then the homesteader could marry and raise his children, as well as grow crops to augment his hunting.

A sod house on the prairie.   Art by E.L. Reedstrom

A Pioneer Woman's Backyard Pharmacy

Willow—The inner bark was used to make tea for reducing fever.

Mint—Mint leaves made into tea soothes upset stomach.

Sassafras—The inner bark of the roots was boiled in water for a "spring tonic" and as a beverage with meals.

Catnip—The leaves were made into a tea and fed to babies with colic.

Wild Ginger—Mainly used as a flavoring.

Violets—A strong tea made with the leaves was used to wash sores. Now it is thought that it contains an antiseptic property.

Poke—Young shoots were eaten in the spring with relish after a long winter of no greens. The berry's juice was used for ink and dying yarn. Mature plants and berries are poisonous.

Elderberry—The mature stems were used as pea shooters, flutes, "spiles" for tapping maple trees. The inner bark was boiled with lard, rosin, and beeswax and used as a salve for sores, cuts, and burns. The berries were used in pies, jellies and wine.

Goldenrod—The flowers were used for dying yarn. The leaves were made into tea for nausea.

Dandelion—The leaves and small flower buds were a sought-after spring green. Dried and roasted roots made a coffee substitute. Also used as a remedy for dropsy.

Tansy—Tea made from the leaves was thought to cure fevers, colds, and stomachache. It was not used by expecting mothers.

Yarrow—Crushed leaves were used to stop bleeding of wounds and drunk as tea for "lung complaints."

Mullen—The tea made from this plant was a remedy for coughs, cramps, and general pain reliever.

Chicory—Young leaves were eaten as a spring green and the roots dried and roasted as a coffee substitute.

Jerusalem Artichoke—This native midwestern plant has quantities of edible tubers which are dug in late fall. They were cooked like potatoes and pickled.

Butterprint—The seed pods were used to put designs in butter and cookies.

Teasel—The seed heads were used to brush up the nap on woven wool material.

Horsetail—The stems were tied into bundles to scrub pans. Tea made from this plant was thought to be a diuretic and astringent.

Cattail—The "fluff" from this plant was used to stuff mattresses and pillows. Leaves were used to make chair seats; shoots, roots, and young flower buds are all edible.

Jewelweed—Fresh juice of this plant is rubbed on the skin to relieve poison ivy. Also, tea made from this plant was thought to help jaundice.

Cranes Bill—The powdered root was used to stop bleeding of wounds. Tea was taken for dysentery.

Red Raspberry—Leaves dried and made into tea were used for dysentery, ease childbirth pains and a wash for sores.

Wormwood—Tea made from this plant was thought to expel worms.

Milkweed—Milkweed down makes excellent fill for comforters, and pillows. Young shoots, flowers, and small seed pods were boiled as a table vegetable. Dried root tea, a diuretic.

Sumach—The berries boiled in water and cooled make a refreshing drink similar to lemonade. It was also used as a gargle for sore throat.

Wild Cherry—The inner bark was used as a remedy for the ague, coughs, and a sedative.

Peppergrass—Also called "poor man's pepper." The seed used for seasoning.

Rose Hips—Tea made from these berries was used as a treatment for scurvy.

Beebalm Horsement—This plant was taken as tea for nausea and used as a wash for wounds and sores. Listerine mouth wash uses the same chemical found abundantly in this plant.

Source:
Use of Plants by Charlotte Erichsen (Brown); *Dandelion, Pokeweed and Goosefoot* by Elizabeth R. Schaeffer. Rebecca M. Crabb, Manager & Historian at the "Buckley Homested" in Lowell, Indiana. (Lake County Parks and Recreation Department).

Carriages and Vehicles of the late 1800s

LATE STYLES OF FASHIONABLE CARRIAGES AND SLEIGHS.

Jump Seat Phaeton. Tandem Dog-Cart. Goddard Buggy. Physicians' Rockaway.

Brougham. Dos-a-dos Wagon. Village Cart. Vis-a-vis Phaeton.

Canopy Top Phaeton. Victoria. Surrey Wagon. Four Passenger Wagon. T-Cart.

Top Surrey. Side-Bar Buggy. Corning Buggy. Concord Spring Buggy. Depot Wagon,

Square Body Sleigh. Shell Body Cutter. Pony Sleigh with Rumble. Victoria Shell Body Sleigh. Six-Passenger Shell Body Sleigh.

Russian Cabriolet Sleigh. Cabriolet Sleigh. Russian Vis-a-vis Sleigh. Victoria Sleigh. Leather Top Landau Sleigh.

Copenhagen Sleigh. Portland Cutter. Jump Seat Sleigh. Curricle Sleigh. Russian Sleigh. Albany Swell Cutter.

MODERN FASHIONABLE CARRIAGES AND VEHICLES IN GENERAL USE.

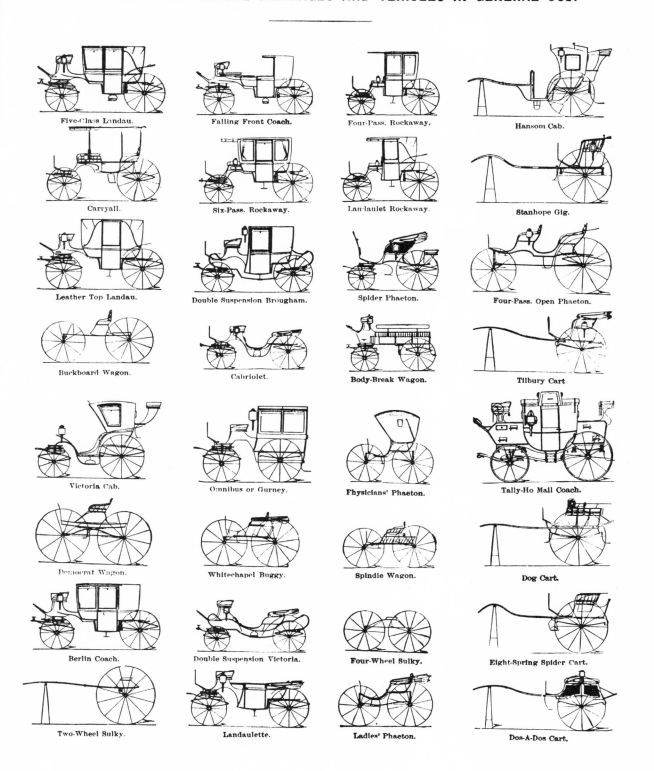

Five-Class Landau.   Falling Front Coach.   Four-Pass. Rockaway.   Hansom Cab.

Carryall.   Six-Pass. Rockaway.   Lan-laulet Rockaway.   Stanhope Gig.

Leather Top Landau.   Double Suspension Brougham.   Spider Phaeton.   Four-Pass. Open Phaeton.

Buckboard Wagon.   Cabriolet.   Body-Break Wagon.   Tilbury Cart

Victoria Cab.   Omnibus or Gurney.   Physicians' Phaeton.   Tally-Ho Mail Coach.

Democrat Wagon.   Whitechapel Buggy.   Spindle Wagon.   Dog Cart.

Berlin Coach.   Double Suspension Victoria.   Four-Wheel Sulky.   Eight-Spring Spider Cart.

Two-Wheel Sulky.   Landaulette.   Ladies' Phaeton.   Dos-A-Dos Cart.

The Concord Stage

The stagecoaches that provided the most rapid transport available in the West until the completion of the railroad started out in Concord, New Hampshire. They were first built around 1813. These coaches had room inside for nine passengers on the upholstered benches, plus nine more on top of the coach. The riders on top of the coach really did ride "coach class" and usually these seats were taken by riders traveling short distances. Baggage rode on top of the coach—along with the second-class passengers—and the driver's box was shared with an express messenger who also "rode shotgun" as an additional guard in case of trouble.

Just below the driver's box was the "front boot" where currency, gold, and other precious cargo rode under the watchful eye of the express messenger.

Riding the stage was a little like riding an ocean-going vessel because of the brace suspension (two curved iron braces attached to the running gear attached to leather straps that served as springs). The body of the coach rode on these swaying straps. At top speed, the coach swayed like a ship, sometimes causing seasickness when the coach was crowded.

Still, riding the stage was luxurious for the time, as the coaches were lined with russet leather. Canvas curtains could be rolled up or let down depending on the weather. A team of four or six horses were used to pull the coach, and speeds of twenty-five miles an hour were not uncommon. These speeds, while difficult to handle when moving in the mountains and around hairpin turns, were necessary for coaches committed to carrying the mail and important documents with all due speed.

STAGE RIDERS

TAKE NOTE!

"Spit with the wind, not against it."

This was one of the rules of the road laid down by Wells-Fargo for riders of its cross-country stages, over a hundred years ago.

There were other rules, many of them as applicable today for auto and bus passengers as for those stage riders of another generation:

1. Abstinence from liquor is requested, but if you must drink, share the bottle. To do otherwise makes you appear selfish and unneighborly.

2. If ladies are present, gentlemen are urged to forego smoking cigars and pipes as the odor of same is repugnant to the Gentle Sex. Chewing tobacco is permitted but spit WITH the wind, not against it.

3. Gentlemen must refrain from the use of rough language in the presence of ladies and children.

4. Buffalo robes are provided for your comfort during cold weather. Hogging robes will not be tolerated and the offender will be made to ride with the driver.

5. Don't snore loudly while sleeping or use your fellow passenger's shoulder for a pillow; he or she may not understand and friction may result.

6. Firearms may be kept on your person for use in emergencies. Do not fire them for pleasure or shoot at wild animals as the sound riles the horses.

7. In the event of runaway horses, remain calm. Leaping from the coach in panic will leave you injured, at the mercy of the elements, hostile Indians, and hungry coyotes.

8. Forbidden topics of discussion are stagecoach robberies and Indian uprisings.

9. Gents guilty of unchivalrous behavior toward lady passengers will be put off the stage. It's a long walk back. A word to the wise is sufficient.

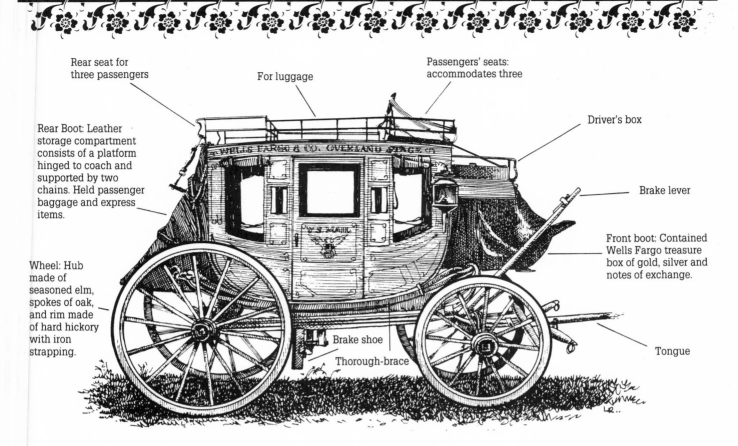

Rear seat for three passengers

For luggage

Passengers' seats: accommodates three

Driver's box

Rear Boot: Leather storage compartment consists of a platform hinged to coach and supported by two chains. Held passenger baggage and express items.

Brake lever

Front boot: Contained Wells Fargo treasure box of gold, silver and notes of exchange.

Wheel: Hub made of seasoned elm, spokes of oak, and rim made of hard hickory with iron strapping.

Brake shoe

Thorough-brace

Tongue

The Concord Stagecoach or "A Cradle on Wheels"

Pioneer Recipes

SOURDOUGH BISCUITS AND BREAD

The night before you make your sourdough biscuits, set aside a small piece of dough and place it in a jar, covering with either water or milk. The dough that the settlers used was made of flour, water and salt. They used whatever fats they had available. By morning the sourdough can be used as leavening. You merely add flour and water and whatever you think necessary. Then, proceed as with ordinary biscuits or bread.

* * * * *

APACHE BREAD

1 cup yellow corn meal
1 cup white corn meal
1 tsp. salt
½ tsp red pepper
1 cup boiling water
½ cup bacon drippings
Corn husks

Sift the yellow and white corn meal, salt and red pepper together. Add the boiling water and beat; then add the bacon drippings. Form mixture into small rolls (oblong) and wrap each roll in a corn husk, tying each with string to keep intact. Place on a pan and bake in a moderate oven (350° F.) about one hour.

* * * * *

HOE CAKES

Mix 2 cups cornmeal, 1 tsp. salt and 2 Tbs. lard. Add 1 cup hot water and stir well. Thin with 1 cup cold water to pouring consistency. Drop batter (as pancakes) on a hot, greased griddle. Turn to brown on both sides. Serve crisp and hot.

* * * * *

MILK TOAST SOUP
(Always Served as a Diet for the Sick)

Pour 1 cup hot milk over 2 slices of brown toast. Add a dash of salt and 1 tsp. butter to bowl. Serve hot.

* * * * *

RABBIT SAUSAGE PATTIES

Soak a dressed rabbit for twelve hours in a quart of water to which 1 tablespoon of salt has been added. Remove the meat from the bones and chop fine. Add

    1 onion chopped
    ½ cup bread crumbs
    3 Tbs. bacon or sausage fat

Salt, pepper, and poultry seasoning to taste. Mix thoroughly and make into patties. Cook slowly in a covered frying pan, browning on both sides.

* * * * *

BUFFALO HUMP AND ROAST BEAVER TAIL

These two dishes are off the present day menu. Both were a great delicacy among the pioneer, trapper, prospector and the early Indians. Buffalo hump roasted over the campfire tasted like very fat beef. The beaver tail was barbecued over the embers. Eaten only with salt, it resembled boiled perch or bone marrow. There was a disagreeable smell of oil about it. If this could be removed and beaver was available it might become a famous dish for the modern epicure.

* * * * *

FISH

During the pioneer's day, the streams of the West abounded with splendid fish. From the clear cool waters of brook and river the pioneer obtained a principal part of his food. He knew how to handle fish and how to cook it. The following hints will provide their worth today:

First, kill the fish immediately after it is caught.

Draw and remove the gills. With your thumbnail, remove the kidney, which lies along the spine at the back of the visceral cavity.

Do not wash your fish.

If the fish is to be held for several hours, wipe dry with a cloth, paper, or grass, if nothing else is handy. The bacteria which cause spoilage develop more rapidly in a moist surface. Dry grass is very good for packing in the creel, because it allows air to circulate freely around the fish and keeps them dry.

This is most desirable, especially with trout, which soften and deteriorate rapidly. Though this deterioration is retarded in the dry, rarefied air of the high altitudes, your catch will decompose rapidly in the more humid atmosphere encountered when you leave the mountains.

* * * * *

BROILED FISH

    Fish
    Salt and pepper
    Salad oil or melted fat
    Parsley

Sprinkle both sides of prepared fish with salt and pepper. Place fish on preheated, greased broiler about two inches from the heat. Brush with melted fat, and broil ten to fifteen minutes, or until slightly brown.

CHAPTER V

WESTERN WEAPONRY

Favorite Rifles of the West

The Kentucky rifle, both in flintlock and percussion, was a favorite firearm in our early colonies, from the Revolution up to the War of 1812. The first American traders, trappers, and explorers carried the Kentucky rifle across the Great Plains and into the Rocky Mountains. Their calibers varied from squirrel rifles of .28 caliber up to a .60 caliber for dropping large animals. The full-stock Kentucky rifle's effective range was approximately 400 yards, and at 300 yards its accuracy was fifty percent on human targets.

The major advantage of the Kentucky was its long barrel for it was a straight shooter that could be easily carried and would not consume too much precious powder and lead. Its disadvantages were the set triggers, intricate lock mechanism, and a weak wrist that when accidently dropped, often cracked or broke in two, rendering the rifle useless or dangerous to fire. Along with these drawbacks, it was also under-powered for killing grizzly, elk, and buffalo at long range.

Trying to satisfy the demands of the hunters and mountain men venturing deeper into the western wilderness, gunsmiths tried to solve these problems with modification suited to the new environment by shortening the barrel boring to a larger caliber,

strengthening the wrist of the stock and shortening it also. This half stock was called the "Plains rifle."

One of the most famous type of Plains rifle was made in the 1820s through the 1840s by Jake and Sam Hawkens of St. Louis. They were the first gunmakers to successfully set up shop at the "gateway to the West." The Hawken rifles were fired by the new "percussion system" of ignition, which actually took a little time in catching on. Most frontiersmen were fond of their flintlocks and were afraid of making a sudden change in ignition systems as percussion caps were not at all plentiful on the plains. A handful of flints lasted a long time.

The percussion system was a great innovation and a step forward from the flintlock. Even the best flintlocks, including Kentuckies, only fired about three quarters of the time as dampness caused fouling, hangfires, and misfires along with other problems. For a flintlock to "flash in the pan" without firing became so common that the expression was often used to describe a man who talked big but did little. The percussion system later paved the way for the metallic cartridge which made repeating rifles possible, but this was slow in developing.

The "Sharps" breech loader was a revolutionary weapon, ideal for western use because of its short

Side-hammer Sharps, best known buffalo rifle is granddaddy of all heavy, large caliber single-shots. An example of some of the calibers that were available: .40-90, .44-60, .44-77, .44-90, .44-100, .45-70, .45-90, .45-120, .50-90, .51-40.

Art by E.L. Reedstrom

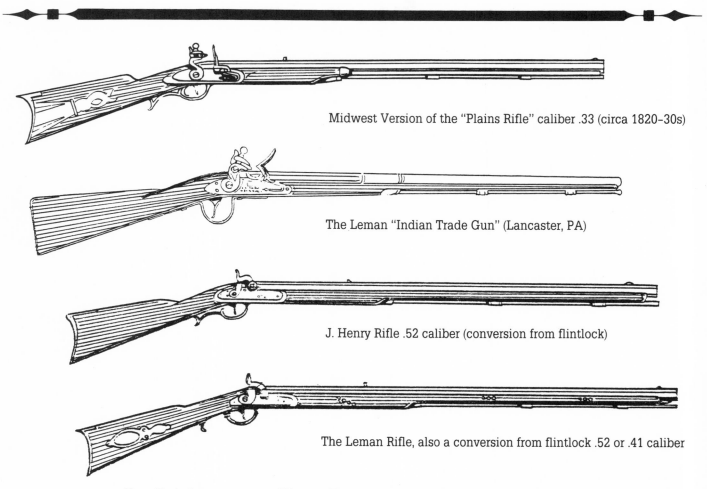

Midwest Version of the "Plains Rifle" caliber .33 (circa 1820–30s)

The Leman "Indian Trade Gun" (Lancaster, PA)

J. Henry Rifle .52 caliber (conversion from flintlock)

The Leman Rifle, also a conversion from flintlock .52 or .41 caliber

Above illustrations are courtesy of *Firearms, Traps and Tools of the Mountain Men,* C.P. Russell (Knoff Pub.), with changes

barrel. It handled a variety of calibers from .36 to .52, employing a linen or paper-wrapped cartridge. The trigger guard acted as a lever which lowered the breechblock exposing the chamber. When a paper or linen cartridge was inserted, the breechblock was closed, thus shearing off the end of the cartridge and exposing the powder. When the trigger was pulled, the hammer hit the percussion cap which exploded and the ignition of the powder fired the weapon. A skilled shooter could fire from four to five shots a minute. In 1850, the Sharps became the most popular weapon in the West.

When metallic rim-fire cartridges appeared on the scene later in 1850, they proved to be more effective than the old percussion system. The most glaring defect common to all percussion breech-loading firearms was the escaping gases at the breech causing loss of velocity and accuracy. The new metallic cartridge sealed the barrel against any blow-back and placed the primer directly in close proximity to the charge.

The new cartridge was made of a case of thin copper alloy, with primer, charge, and bullet contained all in one. By far, it was an improvement over the paper or linen wrapped cartridge fired by a percussion cap, but it too had many hang-ups, especially for heavy charges. This soft metal rim-fire cartridge had to be thin enough to be crushed under the hammer's blow in order to detonate the priming compound. Even when the rim metal was light enough to be crushed, the detonating compound was not always equally spread around in sufficient quantities to insure an explosion.

Defects were many with the rim-fire cartridge and they had to be remedied. The center-fire cartridge was then developed for large caliber weapons and came into general use shortly after the Civil War. This case was made of brass which was much heavier than that of the old rim-fires. The new cartridge carried a detonating compound in a small cup located in the center of its base where the firing pin was certain to fall. This new center-fire cartridge was

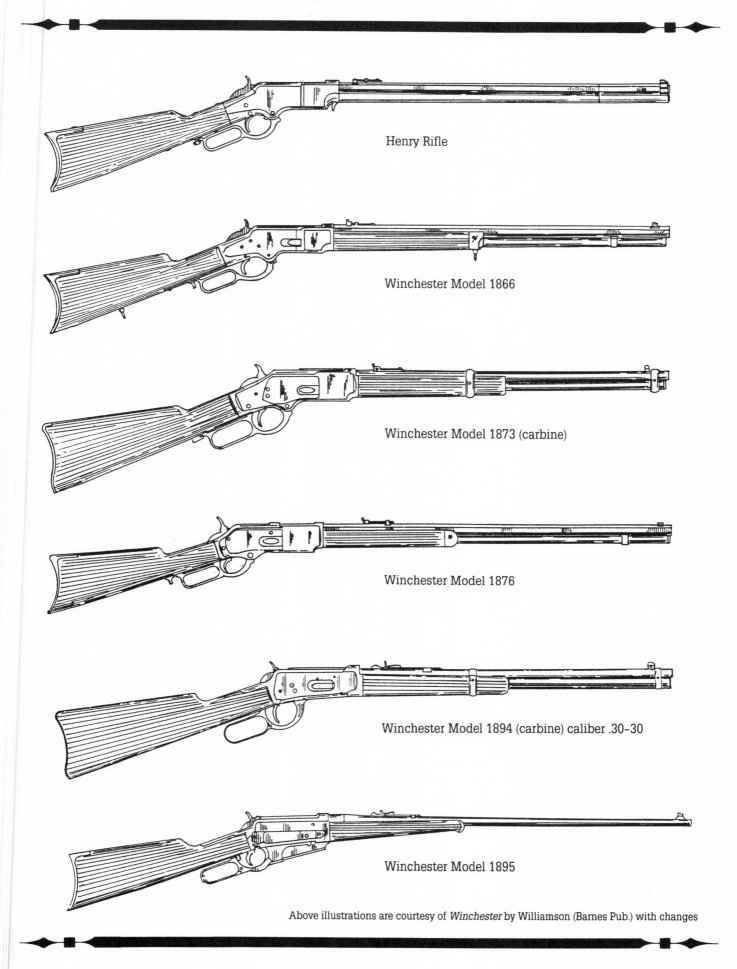

Henry Rifle

Winchester Model 1866

Winchester Model 1873 (carbine)

Winchester Model 1876

Winchester Model 1894 (carbine) caliber .30-30

Winchester Model 1895

Above illustrations are courtesy of *Winchester* by Williamson (Barnes Pub.) with changes

more expensive to produce than the rim-fire, but westerners wanted a heavier cartridge with an increased powder charge and were willing to pay for it.

The first successful breech-loading magazine rifle was the .56–.50 caliber seven-shot Spencer repeating army model, patented March 6, 1860. The breech-block was operated by the trigger guard acting as a lever, much the same as the Sharps rifle. It could be fired seven times in ten seconds or with reloading, fourteen times in one minute. This was by far the fastest firing weapon yet invented. The shells were magazined in a metal tube and housed in the rifle's butt. The shells were butted nose to base, and any quick jar such as dropping the rifle on its butt could set one or several shells off simultaneously. It was, however, adopted by the Army and mass produced for use in the Civil War. The .56–.50 caliber Spencer, used in so many Indian skirmishes, was soon referred to as the "Indian Model." The troops found its performance unlike any other weapon they had seen and nicknamed it "Load on Sunday—shoot all week."[1] As many of these weapons moved westward after the war, constant use of them provided an ideal testing ground for even more improved models. It has been said that the West helped develop these weapons as much as they helped develop the West.

The "Henry" rifle model 1860 was indeed a classic and a well-balanced weapon, firing a flat nose .44 caliber rim-fire bullet. It looked a great deal like the later lever action Winchester, with the exception that the receiver, at the breech was made of brass. It took fifteen shells in a tubular magazine located beneath a twenty-four inch barrel and weighed nine and a half pounds. It was the first rifle to load and fire a shell one at a time by one simple motion of the lever. This extracted the empty cartridge, cocked the hammer, and loaded another shell in the chamber all in one swift motion. It was able to deliver, with a single reloading, thirty shots a minute.[2] As we will see later in this chapter, the Henry rifle led the way to the rifle of the West, the "Winchester."

In 1866, one year after the Civil War ended, Oliver Winchester and B. Tyler Henry (a plant superintendent at Winchester) remedied some faults of their 1860 model. As popular as it was, its mechanism was complicated. Their first improvement was to incorporate a side-loading gate in its brass frame, doing away with loading into the tubular magazine. This gave it a less complicated action, but it still continued using the .44 rim-fire cartridge with twenty-eight grains of powder. This particular rifle was the Winchester Model 1866, known as the "Yellow Boy." It was sometimes referred to as a saddle carbine by frontiersmen, early cowboys, the general public, and Indians as well. Even with its own shortcomings it was in serious competition with the Spencer repeating rifle.

When Spencer's firm failed in 1869, Oliver Winchester purchased the plant hoping to land some big military orders, to no avail. It was probably a blessing in disguise, because Winchester worked harder on his new model for civilian use, which opened more doors to civilian contracts than he had anticipated. Winchester took great strides in perfecting his 1866 model and to correct its deficiencies. The result was his 1873 model, .44–40, a twelve shot, twenty inch barrel carbine, and the fifteen shot, twenty-four inch barrel rifle. Another advantage of the '73 Winchester rifle, was its caliber. Colt's Peacemaker revolver was chambered in 1878 for the .44 Winchester rifle cartridge. A man on the plains had only to carry one kind of ammunition for his rifle and pistol. The Winchester '73, with its Colt counterpart, is attributed to having killed more game and Indians than any other firearm in the West.

Other calibers were introduced by this now mighty Winchester firm as it progressed with its western trade. In 1875, Winchester offered its "One of One Thousand" rifles, a premium grade rifle, specially selected and finished with "1 of 1000" engraved on the barrel. It was only a moderately successful promotion, and Winchester gave it up after two or three years. The rifles sold for sixty dollars to one hundred dollars. The 1879, a .38–40 Model 73 was manufactured and then a .32 caliber (.32–20) and a .22 caliber rim-fire. The 1873 model was made until 1898, but the Winchester firm also made many other models during those years. The company produced "Centennial Model 1876," handling a .45–75–305 cartridge. The Northwest Canadian Mounted Police adopted this model in a carbine. The .50–110 Express Model 1886, was entered in the race with other gun manufacturers for a larger caliber in rifles needed for big game hunting in the West. It appeared too late for the buffalo, but arrived in time for elk and grizzly. In

1894 came the famous Model '94, and the next year was fitted with nickel steel barrels, making possible the use of smokeless powder. Durable, portable, economical, the Winchester .30-03 became the favorite all-purpose gun for ranchers and westerners in general.

The Remington rolling block .50 caliber was a favorite with western big game hunters. The rifle was manufactured by Remington from 1867 to 1890 in various calibers from .22 to .58 and was also known as the Remington Buffalo Gun and Remington Sporting Rifle No. 1. Buffalo hunters began demanding harder hitting, long-range weapons, and were not satisfied with their all purpose saddle gun, the '73 Winchester. Buffalo could be killed from horseback at short range, but this was too dangerous and time-consuming. Far more practical in the commercial hunter's view was the dismounted stationary method commonly employed using a big bore rifle with the barrel supported by a muzzle rest of some kind such as crossed sticks or a log. Commercial buffalo hunting was reaching its climax, and the larger firms clashed competitively. Remington's rolling block, single shot, chambered for a .44-90 cartridge with a heavy 400 grain bullet, was called by its makers, "The Buffalo Gun."

Eli Whitney, Jr., was another who offered stiff competition with his Laidley-Whitney .44, .45 and .50 caliber single shot breechloader. Another was the Ballard, with a variety of calibers from the .22 to .56, all single shot. The .45-70's were very popular with buffalo hunters. After the firm failed in 1875, Ballards were manufactured by John M. Marlin, under the name of Marlin-Ballard. The Marlin firm also produced the Model '81 in various calibers, beginning with the .45-70 model.

The Sharps' Buffalo rifle was a favorite with buffalo hunters. Sharps made a good name for itself during the Civil War and in the West long before Winchester and Remington came on the scene. To continue its popularity in the weapons race after the war, the company, in 1869, modified some 30,000 percussion carbines to take the new metallic cartridges. The result was the "Big Fifty," with calibers in .40-95 or .40-100.

About the same time Sharps brought out a sporting rifle to take .40-75 or .40-70 cartridges, and later was chambered for the .44-70 and .50-70 loads. In the .45 caliber firing a 440-grain bullet with a 120-grains of powder, the rifle had a shocking knock-down power to kill dependably at 1,000 yards. This .45/120/550 Sharps cartridge used a 3-1/4" brass case. The .44 caliber Sharps Creedmoor (Creedmore), a rifle with a kick like an Army mule, was also favored by buffalo hunters who swore by its devastating knock-down power. Sharps banked too confidently on the success of the single-shot weapon when repeating rifles were becoming popular. It wasn't long after the great buffalo herds were gone when the Sharps firm closed its doors.

The shotgun came West long before the Civil War. It was mostly a defensive weapon used on humans at

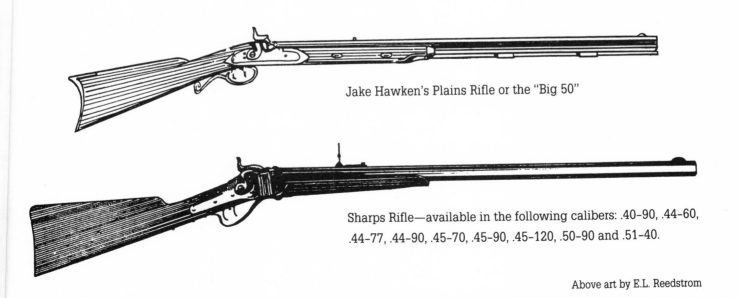

Jake Hawken's Plains Rifle or the "Big 50"

Sharps Rifle—available in the following calibers: .40-90, .44-60, .44-77, .44-90, .45-70, .45-90, .45-120, .50-90 and .51-40.

Above art by E.L. Reedstrom

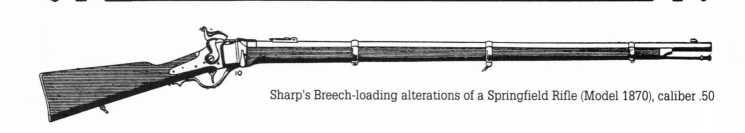

Sharp's Breech-loading alterations of a Springfield Rifle (Model 1870), caliber .50

U.S. Springfield Rifle (Model 1873), caliber .45-70

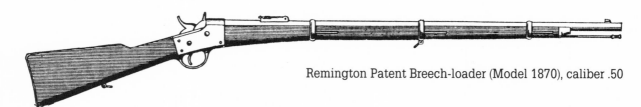

Remington Patent Breech-loader (Model 1870), caliber .50

Above illustrations courtesy of F. Bannerman Catalog with changes

close range. Whether a single or double barrel, many were carried by guards on overland stages, lookouts in gambling halls, prison guards, outlaws and lawmen. Some of these guns were altered by sawing off the stocks at the weapons wrist and shortening the barrels so they could be hidden beneath clothing. Wells Fargo guards carried English-made double barrel 10 gauge shotguns, with a barrel length of approximately twenty inches.

The double barrel shotgun played a part in many of the violent incidents recorded in Western history. Black Bart, the California bandit-poet, held up a score of Wells Fargo Stage coaches behind a threatening double barrel shotgun. A cut-down shotgun was carried concealed in a leather shoulder sling by "Doc" Holiday and was used by him in the OK Corral fight in Tombstone, Arizona.

The use of the shotgun was so wide and the makers so many, that we need only to mention the weapon as a type universally used during the entire period of Western history from the days of the '49ers up to the present. Most older double barreled guns were made with one barrel full choke and one barrel modified—full choke for long range, modified for a quick close shot.

10 gauge: manufactured for ducks and geese
12 gauge: manufactured for rabbit, squirrel, upland game
16 gauge: manufactured for small birds
20 gauge: manufactured for rabbits, quail, and pheasant

The Weapons Ignition System

Reliable accounts state that the flintlock, of Spanish origins, was invented early in the seventeenth century prior to 1630. The mechanism that ignited the charge was caused by flint striking against steel and causing a shower of sparks. The flintlock was invented simultaneously in Spain and Holland. It was used as late as the American Civil War, but its greatest popularity occurred in the years between 1670 and 1835.

Whenever a war between hostile countries would come about, the arms makers were always trying to produce a newer system and an easier, quicker method of loading a weapon. When the percussion cap ignition system was introduced, many patterns were patented and produced between 1812 through 1825. This ignition system was based on the principle of percussion, i.e., of an explosion caused by a blow. Specifically, it is the ignition system in which the priming charge is fired by a hammer blow on a percussion cap. The firearm is discharged by percussion of a hammer on fulminating powder contained in a cap or cartridge. The percussion lock superseded the flintlock in the mid nineteenth century. It's unusual to note that this system was hard for mountain men and Indians of the American west to accept, as they felt the flintlock was much more reliable and flints were easier to acquire than percussion caps.

A Frenchman by the name of Flobert came up with a copper bulleted breech cap for his rifles and pistols. This idea brought on the metal cartridge case. By 1835, A.M. Pottet invented a safer center-fire non-consuming cartridge case, and in 1855, a patent cartridge, chiefly for revolvers was patented by Messrs. Samuel Colt and William Eley. The paper cartouche which was used considerably during the Civil War, in both rifles and pistols, was short-lived as the cartridge copper case shell was much in demand. Generally copper was used as case metal in rim-fire cartridges and brass was used in center-fire cartridges.

FLINTLOCK
Side gooseneck

FLINTLOCK
Reinforced

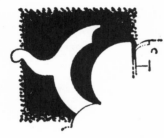

PERCUSSION
Shotgun

PERCUSSION
Circular

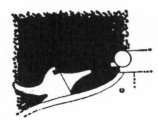

CARTRIDGE
Bisley

CARTRIDGE
Dual purpose

Ignition System

The 'Plow-handle'

A term most Westerners used to identify any handgun. The nickname derived from the unusual handle of an early Colt.

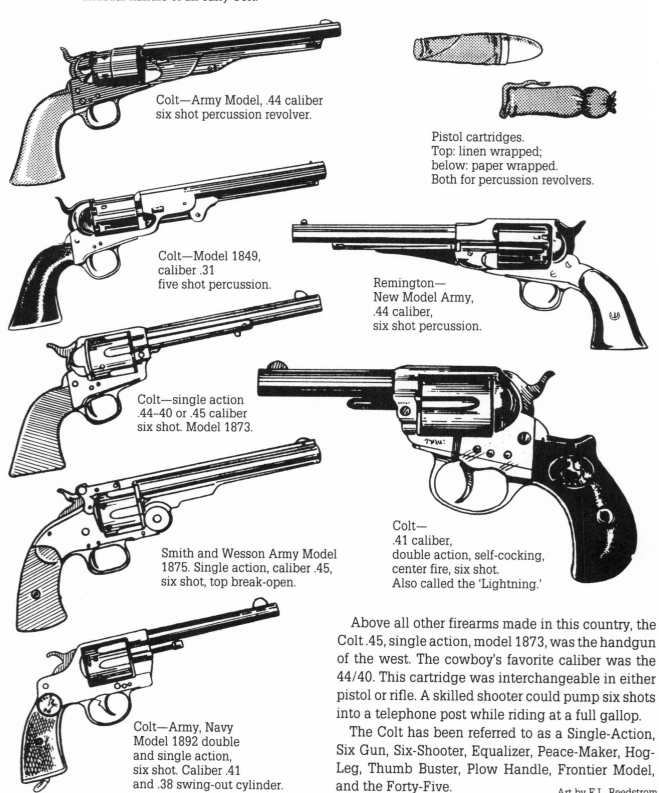

Colt—Army Model, .44 caliber six shot percussion revolver.

Pistol cartridges.
Top: linen wrapped;
below: paper wrapped.
Both for percussion revolvers.

Colt—Model 1849,
caliber .31
five shot percussion.

Remington—
New Model Army,
.44 caliber,
six shot percussion.

Colt—single action
.44–40 or .45 caliber
six shot. Model 1873.

Colt—
.41 caliber,
double action, self-cocking,
center fire, six shot.
Also called the 'Lightning.'

Smith and Wesson Army Model
1875. Single action, caliber .45,
six shot, top break-open.

Colt—Army, Navy
Model 1892 double
and single action,
six shot. Caliber .41
and .38 swing-out cylinder.

Above all other firearms made in this country, the Colt .45, single action, model 1873, was the handgun of the west. The cowboy's favorite caliber was the 44/40. This cartridge was interchangeable in either pistol or rifle. A skilled shooter could pump six shots into a telephone post while riding at a full gallop.

The Colt has been referred to as a Single-Action, Six Gun, Six-Shooter, Equalizer, Peace-Maker, Hog-Leg, Thumb Buster, Plow Handle, Frontier Model, and the Forty-Five.

Art by E.L. Reedstrom

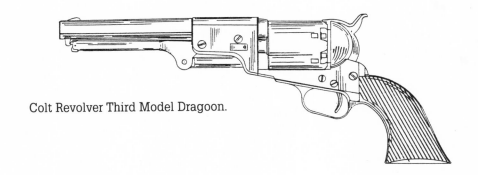

Colt Revolver Third Model Dragoon.

Flatau's Pistol Hanger

L.S. Flatau's Pistol and Carbine Holder was actually fashioned after a short-lived experimental Army Model 1874 holster. This holster had a swivel belt attachment that was patterned for the U.S. Cavalry. It didn't last long and was finally dropped after troopers found out the many faults it harbored.

The inventor Flatau had other ideas and adopted the same technique with various modifications. To keep the cost down, he dropped the leather covering that protected the pistol from all elements.

In the late 1870s, Flatau approached the Army Board through certain appointments by influential friends who sought to gain something out of it. Flatau had adapted the single action Army model pistol by adding an elongated stud coming out of the hammer pin on the left side. He then added a slotted plate, similar to a tuning fork, to a looped gun belt on the right side. After the stud was inserted in the plate, the pistol could be fired by swiveling it from the hip.

After a number of army field trials, the swivel gun/holster failed to gain acceptance. Reports showed that it was very dangerous and serious accidents could come from it. Mainly, the non-existence of any leather covering would allow damage to the weapon from the weather.

Flatau's swivel holster went public with some success. Lawmen and gunslingers found a need for it and perfected his invention. It was an easier way to carry and fire a pistol after much training. They could also be assured of getting a shot off quicker than their opponent. The success of the swivel holster was not long-lived because after a few years, the western frontier slowly died away and the need for Flatau's pistol hanger was gone.

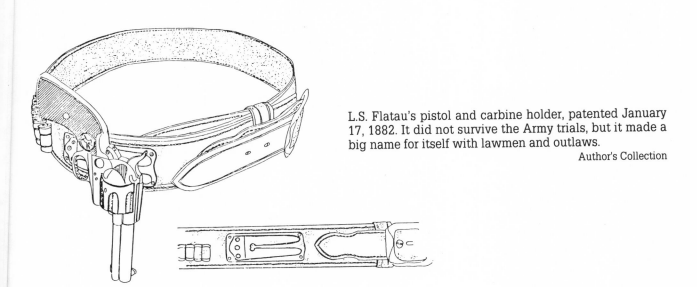

L.S. Flatau's pistol and carbine holder, patented January 17, 1882. It did not survive the Army trials, but it made a big name for itself with lawmen and outlaws.
Author's Collection

Curious Weapons

Oddball firearms seem to be limited only by the imagination of arms designers. There had been cane guns and umbrella guns, each holding a single shell. Pistols have been concealed into a glove. Belt buckle firearms shot as the wearer's arms were raised. A knuckleduster pistol was a combination of brass knuckles, a firearm at one end and a dagger at the other; this could be folded easily and pocketed. Other unusual guns were sleeve pistols, palm pistols resembling a woman's compact, purse pistols that fired peashaped bullets, huge horse pistols with a yawning one inch bore, pepperboxes with several barrels clustered around a common axis, single-shot pistols built into knife handles, door locks firing a cartridge through the keyhole discouraging night prowlers, a twenty shot pistol, and the famous "belly-gun" carried by most cardsharks (the two shot .41 caliber Derringer).

In their curious ways, all these weapons testify to man's remarkable ingenuity in settling matters promptly or for personal defense.

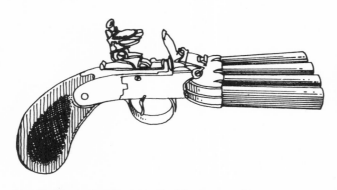

Duck's Foot pistol—so called because of its appearance; it was not a weapon to fool with for all of the barrels went off at once. It was used by guards against mobs, and probably was quite effective.

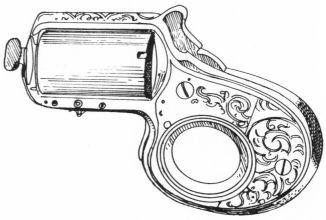

Knuckle-duster—this version, called "My Friend," had a pepper box design containing either five or seven shots. The great advantage of this gun was that if you missed your man with your bullet, you could run up and smack him several times in the face with your knuckle gun.

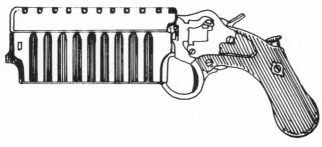

The Harmonica gun—an early attempt to produce a repeating pistol. It was used in various calibers. This model had ten chambers. Any of these multiple-barrel pistols can be put in the carrying position by pushing the barrel group with the hammer held slightly raised, until the hammer is in line with the last barrel, and then turning and pivoting the group. An ejector rod is screwed into the butt of each of these short-barreled pistols.

The Belt pistol—with its oval iron plate was seven inches long with an inch and a half pistol barrel. In this gun, a cord runs from the lock through a channel in the belt for a foot or more, before being carried up to the shoulder and down through a coat sleeve. A man ordered to put up his hands can grasp the weight and tighten the string as he raises his arms. Many times, a part of the man's garmet caught the sparks burning a wide area of clothing. Should the belt wear away or rot, it was obsolete and often neglected. Soon it was discarded.

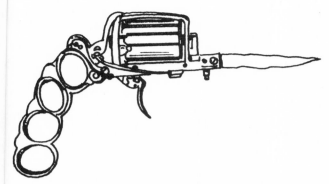

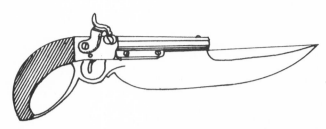

Dolne Apache pistol—this amazing weapon combined all the elements of fighting back. It had brass knuckles for a handle so you could hit your opponent, and if this didn't work, a knife was quickly available to slice him up. The gun is a six shot, double action, and fires a 7mm pin fire cartridge. It was used extensively in France and then introduced into the United States via San Francisco.

The "Cutless pistol" or Elgin pistols (another name was the "Pistol-Sword")—the idea here was to combine a pistol and a Bowie knife. These arms were used by the militia, privateersman, or other citizen martial bodies, besides our Navy for repelling boarders and the merchant marines trading in the Far East.

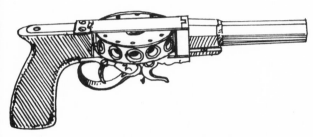

This "Monitor" or turret gun was only moderately successful. It was produced by John W. Cochran. This seven shot pistol was also called a "mousetrap gun" by the men of the period because of its similarity in shape to a then popular mousetrap. The underhammer lock was sturdy, simple but often useless when the percussion caps fell off underneath.

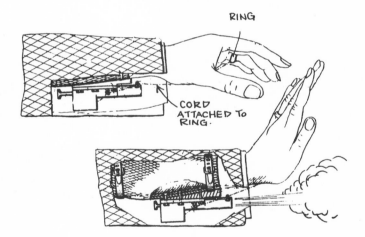

Sleeve pistol—an automatic concealed firearm for self-defense. A 130 caliber center fire cartridge pistol was fastened beneath the forearm by two straps. The barrel unscrews for loading the shell. The gun is cocked by pulling back a striker similar to the device commonly used on pen or pencil pistols. A wire cord is run from the striker release to a ring on the middle finger. When the hand is flipped upward and back, the pistol fires.

Art by E.L. Reedstrom

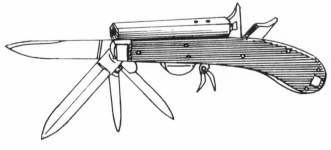

Knife pistols came in a wide variety of shapes, sizes, and calibers. Some even had an assortment of knives where you could choose any size blade depending upon the build of your opponent. They were a formidable weapon in the days when a single shot pistol missed and another form of weapons could be relied upon quickly.

The Road Agent Spin

Phil "Rawhide Rawlins" Spangenberger is a skillful gun handler. He has traveled the country as well as Europe demonstrating the art of western weaponry.

Courtesy of Phil Spangenberger

1A. Underhanded "Road Agent Spin." The revolver is held in the hand, butt forward, with the middle finger in the trigger guard and the thumb resting on top of the indention of the hammer.

2A. With a quick flick of the wrist, the gun is thrown (or twirled) forward, cocking the hammer with the thumb.

3A. Continuation of 2A., showing cocking motion.

4A. As the pistol reaches the forward position, the middle finger has pulled the trigger by sheer rolling movement of the gun against the finger. Also, the thumb has released the hammer, and the trigger being pulled will fire the revolver. This is the fastest of the "Road Agent Spins. (Photos 1 and 2 are full view of this stunt)

One Gun/Two Hand Switch Sequence

1B. Here is a trick used only to show the gun-fighter's dexterity. It would be difficult, if not nearly impossible to try, in a realistic situation. First, Phil draws the revolver.

3B. As soon as the arm is fired, the author spins it in his hand.

2B. He fires his Colt at the opponent (unseen) to his right.

5B. As the gun is switched into the left hand, it is cocked and brought around into position.

4B. Continuing spin, gun is pivoting on trigger finger, while author reaches for it with left hand.

6B. Gun is quickly fired at opponent (unseen) at left. This trick can be accomplished very quickly, but takes lots of practice. If done properly, it looks impressive.

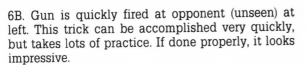

Holster Flip Draw

This is what I consider the most difficult trick (at least for me)! In this draw, the gun is laid in the holster upside down. The thumb hits the gun behind the front sight, flipping the gun in the air. As the pistol flips over into the "right side up" position, Phil reaches forward, catches the revolver, cocks it and fires it, all in an instant.

1C. Ready position.

2C. Hitting the barrel with the thumb, flipping the pistol.

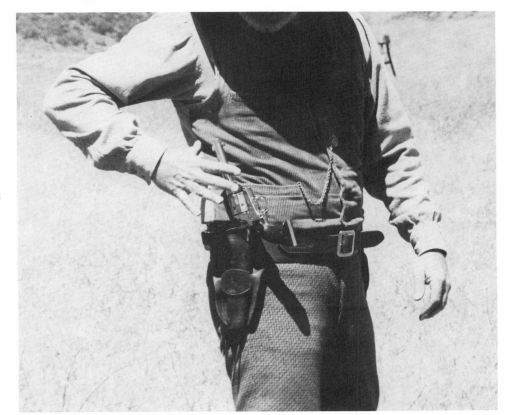

3C. Reaching for the Colt as it flips forward and over.

4C. Phil has caught the revolver, cocked and fired it.

Texas or Border Shift

This is a genuine old-time trick that's known to have happened in the Old West. Using the right hand as the strong, or shooting hand, Phil (after running out of ammo in the right hand Colt) lowers the blued revolver in order to flip it over to the left hand. As the gun flips to the left hand, Phil cocks left hand gun and quickly tosses it laterally to the right hand, where he catches it and fires it just before he catches the blued gun. A blued and nickeled revolver were used for this stunt, so that the reader can follow the action of each Colt.

1D. In order to throw the Colt into the air, it is lowered quickly, then flipped upward and leftward.

2D. Lowering the blued Colt for flip.

4D. Phil has transferred the nickeled Colt to his right hand as the blued revolver flips end over end, into position to be caught with left hand.

3D. Blued Colt is flipped upward and to the left hand. At the same time Phil is cocking the nickeled revolver.

5D. At the moment he catches the blued Colt, Spangenberger fires the nickeled Colt in his right hand . . . and the gunfight continued!

Over the Shoulder Toss

Performed just as a stunt to demonstrate the pistoleer's dexterity. The Colt is flipped rearward and upward in a single swing, arcing the gun up and over Phil's back. It flips end over end, into an aligned position, in front of him, where he reaches for it, catches it and cocks it firing it in a smooth motion.

1E. After a fancy spin to add to the showiness of the trick, Phil extends his arm to get the maximum arc to the throw.

3E. Colt is caught in mid air as it flips over Spangenberger's shoulder.

2E. Colt is flipped backward. Spangenberger does not let go of gun until it is in proper position for a good flipping arc.

5E. Gun flips forward as Phil reaches out and catches it in mid air.

4E. As Colt flips over shoulder, Phil looks up for it and begins to reach forward for gun.

6E. As he brings Colt into position, Phil cocks and fires it. This is a fancy trick that audiences enjoy. Sometimes he will throw the gun with the right hand, drop his right hand (as if he weren't going to do anything) then reach out and catch the Colt with his left hand.

Fast Draw and Some Disbeliefs

The myth of 'fast draw' has been dramatized considerably in cheap Hollywood westerns and serial movies since the invention of moving pictures. The 'white hat' hero stole the show with his two-gun, concho-studded belt and holsters, riding the range on a white stallion in pursuit of the outlaws in their black hats who stepped out of the bounds of the law. Under careful scrutiny, the legend of 'fast draw' appears to be more fiction than reality.

Just by close study of the early pattern holsters, one can see that it was impossible to draw a pistol from the hip with the swiftness fiction writers love to portray while building up their heroes. Modern improvements on both holsters and hand guns reveal the present day fast draw artist would be able to out draw the Western idols of yesterday quicker than the dropping of a coin. However, hitting the opponent with such a lighting move is a different story.

Both research and trials have been made by present day fast draw artists, and they have found that the tests far surpassed the 'old timers' draw.'

The percussion cap pistol, or Sam Colt's equalizer, of the 1850s was not designed for fast draw or quick shooting, and a quick-draw holster would have been pointless. The common army belt holster or 'scabbard' that was issued had a large flap to cover the handle of the pistol to protect the weapon from the weather. However, many officers and enlisted men cut off the top of these flaps so the handle of the gun was exposed for quicker use. This caught on with army personnel, civilians working the gold fields, and law enforcement agencies. The large flap was either in the way when drawing out the pistol or it was handy to stop up a hole in a shoe. The holster was being manufactured with open tops south of the border and was later classified as the 'Mexican' style. The holster snugly held the cap and ball revolver, but covered up the trigger guard.

These 'thumb-busters' were not suitable for fast draw because of their complicated mechanical design. Trigger springs and hammer main springs were weak and would break under any fancy fast draw methods. Fanning any of these cap and ball revolvers would be dangerous—one could lose several fingers in attempting this feat. When cartridges for single action Colts came into being, the possibility was there, but only to the professional who brought the gun to a gunsmith to have the piece tuned specifically for fanning. Only a few used this method with some accuracy at short distances.

Identifying a fast draw artist at his work in a shoot out could mean the gunman had a weapon up his sleeve or a belt buckle gun in order to hit his opponent at a short distance. Wild Bill Hickok never used holsters. His weapons were always butts forward (Army style), thrust into a wide silk waistband. The 'cross over draw' was just coming into style, and it may be that Hickok originated it. Hideaway guns were becoming a fad. They were found in the crowns of hats (single shot pistols), tucked into boots (single shot boot guns), strapped under the arm, or in hideaway pockets from which a man could shoot without taking the weapon out. From the late 1860s through the 1890s, many innovations and varieties of weapons appeared, some designed by the professional shootist, bounty-hunter, gambler, and law enforcement officer. Anyone who lived by the code of the gun needed an edge, to be one step ahead of his opponent. Here were a few tricks of the trade.

A sling of elastic material tied to a gun, allowing it to hang inside a loose sleeve, was a common trick. When someone got the drop on another so armed, all he had to do was throw his hands up briskly and a short-barrel revolver would spring into his palm.

The swivel holster or the L.S. Flatau Pistol Hanger, patented in 1882, was a cheap and efficient means of carrying firearms on the person. Its design provided a button which formed a part of the pin upon which the hammer of the gun was pivoted. Riveted to the waist belt was a metal plate with something like a tuning fork running horizontal to the belt. The pistol's button fell into place between this tuning fork and pushed backward until it fell into a slot to hold it secure. To fire the weapon, all the shooter had to do was pull back on the hammer while he leveled the gun, and fired. To remove the weapon he pulled up and pushed the gun forward. His pistol was now free of the belt attachment.

The technique of fast draw in sequence by former top-gun and expert George E. Virgines.

A. The hand is posed about five inches from contact with the gun.

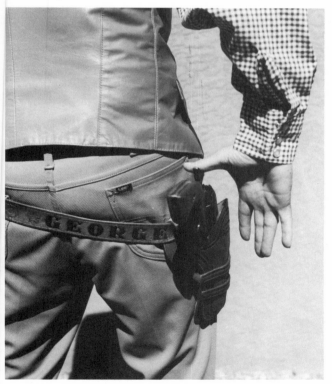

B. The thumb is the first initial contact with the hammer of the gun.

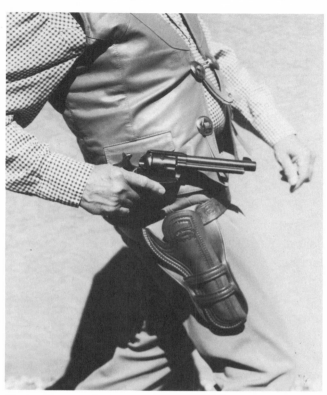

C. As the gun is drawn, hammer back, finger about to slip off the trigger guard, and ready to fire the gun.

D. The fast draw is completed, shot on target.

Courtesy George E. Virgines

John Wesley Hardin contrived a dual suspender holster rig for two pistols, butts facing each other. When he thought he needed his weapon, he slowly reached to his breast pocket as if to secure a cigar— and quickly revealed a single-shot firearm, much to his opponent's surprise.

Another clever devise was cutting down the pistol's barrel. These were called belly guns and could be withdrawn from any pocket without difficulty. Some gamblers even cut the forward trigger guard off (leaving part of it) so that portion wouldn't be in the way of a fast trigger finger.

The first shoulder holster came from an idea of a full belted pistol and holster slung across the shoulder and around the neck, with the pistol dangling beneath the man's arm pit.

To sum up, the quick-draw old timers mainly had something up their sleeves. They probably got the first shot off with these tricks of the trade, not from fumbling around trying to draw a revolver from a tightly-gripped holster at their side.

How did the present fast draw holster come about? Before the Spanish-American war and until World War I, when the Army switched from leather to the webbed belt system patented by Anson Mills, the Army fashioned a long leather thong at the bottom of holsters. This was tied to the soldier's leg to keep the holster from bouncing about. When movies came into being, the script writers though that the tying of a holster to the leg came from a method of quick draw—or rather they copied this method and used it to build movie heroes. At any rate, the fast draw Western rig changed considerably. It was designed for the prince of pistoleers and the viewers marveled at their deeds. It is now designed for quicker action for many fast draw gun club competitions and gun enthusiasts, but its prototype was born on a Hollywood movie set.

CHAPTER VI

THE GOLD FIELDS:

Gold Rush: 1849

Gold Fever broke out in California. The strike started early on the afternoon of January 24, 1848, with a seemingly trivial request for a burned-out tin plate. The request came from an Indian runner who wanted the plate for James Marshall, a lumberman who was working on an upper tributary of the American River, near Sutter's Coloma Mill. The two mill hands who were asked to get the tin plate and give it to the Indian—lumbermen named Brown and Bigler—fetched the plate for their boss and handed it to the runner. They went back to their work on the sawpit, forgetting all about the incident.

At quitting time, Jim Marshall showed up with a handful of gold-colored nuggets that hammered flat without breaking. He went back to his find, brought out more nuggets, and the local officials tested the samples. It was concluded that there was, indeed, a gold mine—and a rich one at that.

Sutter, the mill owner, negotiated a three year lease around the area from the local Indians before the word got out. He desperately tried to obtain title from the Military Governor. Unfortunately, his excitement got in the way, and his announcements about the find, coupled with loose lips in the Governor's office,

The prospector is rocking his 'Rocker' and panning a creek.
Art by E.L. Reedstrom

started a stampede to the gold fields that produced signs in most of the closed shop windows that read "Gone to the Diggins."

By mid-June, this gold fever had reached its peak, with three-quarters of the businesses closed in San Francisco. Soldiers deserted the Mexican War in great numbers; eventually two thousand men left the area's work to mine for gold.

As the word spread, the size of the strike inflated with it. Prospectors' tales of gold grew bigger with each telling. One such prospector, Sam Brannan, a Mormon with missionary zeal, galloped through town with a "Poke" full of nuggets, triggering a full blown avalanche of humanity down the hills and valleys, taking ordinary business with it like saplings in an earthquake.

How much gold was there? Despite the disap-pointment over exaggerated claims, the strike was significant. Before the close of 1848, five thousand men worked the mines, producing about 5 million dollars. The average daily yield of gold per man was about two ounces, selling for about twelve dollars per ounce.

What of the original finder of the rich diggins? Jim Marshall took to drinking. He sold autographed cards and drifted around. Sutter—the mill owner who gave his name to the gold fields—eventually learned that his land grant from Mexico was declared invalid by the U.S. Supreme Court. Sutter desperately tried to hold his claim together, but finally, gave up, a broken man, and moved to Pennsylvania. He died in 1880, just as Congress decided that they had treated him wrongly.

Black Hills

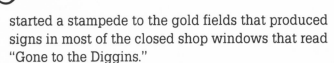

The Black Hills of Dakota remained unexploited by the scores of drifting prospectors who were always skirting the mining frontier. There were rumors that the dark, domed mountains possessed pockets of gold, giving way to serious talks among the miners in various camps to investigate and explore this mysterious area. Beside gold, an abundance of timber, game, and crystal clear water was available. However, it was also guarded by the fierce Sioux Indians as their religious sanctuary and private game reserve. Stories that circulated the mining camps claimed that few white men had penetrated these sacred mountains covered with dark green fir trees that appear black at a distance, giving the area its name, but no one ever returned from those hills and lived to tell of their experience.

For years frontier camps heard stories of Indians appearing at Fort Laramie with bags full of gold nuggets, squandering their new wealth on trinkets, whiskey, and guns. Post commanders tried desper-ately to keep this discovery secret lest their men would desert and make way for the hills in pursuit of its riches. But, as long as gold fields farther west remained to be exploited, the tales of gold in the Black Hills was not tested. Under the watchful eyes of the powerful warlike Sioux and guarded by Federal troops who pledged to keep out all intruders, the situation seemed to be under control. By 1874, however, western mines were passing into the hands of eastern capatalists, and thousands of self-seeking prospectors turned their attention to the Black Hills, certain that the mysterious forest-clad mountains would reveal their riches that had been denied the miners elsewhere.

Expeditions were formed. Prospectors planned to push their way past the soldiers guarding the promised land. Newspapers agreed that if such a stampede succeeded, it would overshadow the rush to Pike's Peak. Washington was aroused by these reports and the only way to stop the invasion was to disprove the rumors of gold in the Black Hills. They decided to make a full official investigation. Pur-suant to General Philip H. Sheridan, U.S. Army, an expedition was organized at Fort Abraham Lincoln, located near Bismarck, North Dakota, in June 1874, for the purpose of reconnoitering the route from that post to Bear Butte in the Black Hills and also explore the country south, southwest, and southeast. They planned to study the possibilities of establishing army posts to watch over the threatening Sioux Indians.

"Boy General" of the Civil War, Lieutenant Colonel George Armstrong Custer, was chosen to command the expeditionary force which consisted of ten troops of the Seventh Cavalry, two companies of Infantry, a detachment of Indian Scouts, an engineer officer, a stereoscopic photographer, a group of scientists along with interpreters, teamsters, and 1,000 men in all. One hundred and ten wagons, ambulances, and three Gatling guns (modified models of 1866, in both .50 and 1-inch calibers) broke a new trail toward the Black Hills.

As the command reached the interior of the Hills, smoke signals began to appear on the horizon and scattered Indians were seen at a distance, but there was no attempt at any hostility. The scientists gathered much valuable information as to geology, zoology, and paleontology in the area explored, but the presence of precious metals in large quantity was disappointing to the scientific party. However, the miners in the command reported to Custer that gold

was found "in the grass roots," creating newspapers to print-up headliners . . . , "GOLD! The Land of Promise—Stirring News from the Black Hills."

By a treaty of 1868, the Black Hills territory had been reserved for the Sioux Indians who, years earlier, and through warfare, defeated the Cheyennes who made their home there. By reporting of gold in paying quantities, the expedition only increased public pressure on the government to allow the area to be developed. After being moved around several times, the Sioux refused to abandon their sacred territory to the Army. A number of encounters began between the Indians, prospectors, and hunters. Due to this growing problem with the Indians, Custer and the Seventh Cavalry was ordered into the field. With the continued invasion of the white man into Sioux country, hostilities made it necessary for both the Sioux and Custer's famed Seventh Cavalry to meet headlong into the Army's first defeat at the Little Big Horn, on June 25, 1876.

Deadwood — A Town Too Tough To Die

Deadwood! The name had a ring to it that conjured up all of the wildness, the bright promise, and the wicked unreality best described in the *Penny Dreadfuls,* those little books sized just right for boys to secret inside their arithmetic books and savour instead of learning their times tables. In the mid-1870s, the town lived up to its name. A stage driver named it the "orneryest place this side of Hell." Deadwood suffered from rapid growth and high visibility—it looked something like a present day movie set, easy to disassemble and move, if the scene didn't seem to work out.

Deadwood was near the site where Custer's soldiers had located gold nuggets, triggering a stampede of gold-hungry prospectors and would-be prospectors from the California fields and the western territories, and from those tired of chasing Indians and interested in chasing wealth instead.

But in early 1876, the gold had not materialized. The Sioux, on whose land a small amount of gold had been found, were not particularly pleased about this latest treaty-bending exercise. It was a very fluid

situation—the kind that breeds heroics, not necessarily heroism.

So a lot of characters with heroic-sounding names began to appear. Although there were a great number of saloons in town, the favorite was Lewis and Mann's Number 10 Saloon. Some, Arapahoe Joe, Texas Jack Omohundro, and Captain Jack Crawford are simply names. Others were real, including Colorado Charlie Utter, whom we know as the owner of a sizeable camp at the edge of Deadwood. Kittie Arnold, known as the "Quartz Queen of the Hills," and Calamity Jane were members of the breed known as "soiled-doves with hearts of gold" and apparently did quite well for themselves, given a rising market and restricted supply.

The laws of supply and demand must have worked well in Calamity Jane's case. Described as having a, "figger like a busted bale of hay," Martha Jane Cannary gained the name Calamity Jane more for her inability to handle glassware than for any hair-raising escapades. She only wore the fancy buckskins with colorful Indian bead work and fringes

Deadwood City at its very beginning in 1876 with a population of about four thousand.

while performing for a short while with Buffalo Bill Cody's Wild West show. Generally, she wore male garb none too clean.

Other "long winded" characters came later, such as Potato Creek Johnny E. Perrett, a long-time prospector who could chew most of your ear off with hair-raising stories that you'd have to think twice about.

Wild Bill Hickok appeared in town early on August 1, 1876, looking to line his pockets in poker games. He had left his new wife, Agnes Lake Thatcher, an equestrienne and high wire artist, back East while he went to improve his finances—or so we suppose.

Hickok—born James Butler Hickok—triggered more legends than most. He was a "preacher's kid" and a more than normal hell-raiser who managed to

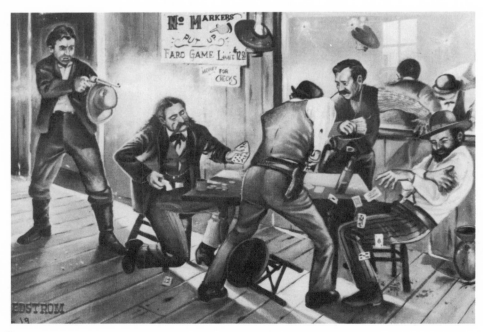

The Shooting of Wild Bill Hickok. On August 2, 1876, in Number 10 Saloon, Deadwood, South Dakota, Will Bill Hickok was playing poker with Charley Rich, Carl Mann, and Captain Massey. Jack McCall, the assassin, entered the saloon in a careless manner. He sauntered around the room and then stopped directly behind Bill. Swiftly McCall drew a 45 caliber Colt and fired. The bullet passed through Bill's head, and pierced Captain Massey's left arm. Bill's poker hand read "Aces and Eights," two pair, and since that day, it is better known as "Dead Man's Hand" in the West.

Painting by E.L. Reedstrom

"Calamity Jane" to her cohorts, but to family she was Martha Jane Canary. She always claimed a close relationship with Hickok, however, it was only casual. In this photo, she appears to be pregnant. Scene is in front of "Wild Bill's" grave, circa 1903.

Author's Collection

shed the nickname "Duckbill" for his somewhat prominent nose by getting it changed to Wild Bill during an early clash with outlaws. He seemed nervous when he appeared in town, having heard of some death threats. In fact, he asked a banker friend if he would lock him in the vault for the night, as he feared an attempt on his life.

Despite all of the things going for Wild Bill, the afternoon of August 2 was not headed right. He had been playing cards throughout the day, and had to borrow money because he was losing. In addition, Charley Rich, a buddy of Wild Bill's had usurped his place—with his back to the wall—just to plague Bill.

Across the street, Tim Brady and Johnny Varnes goaded "Broken Nose" Jack McCall into attacking Wild Bill for everyone thought that Wild Bill would become the new sheriff of Deadwood. The discussion escalated until almost four o'clock; the pair gave McCall twenty-five dollars as down payment on a two hundred dollar bounty they placed on Wild Bill. The drunken youngster crossed the street, entered the Number 10 Saloon, drew a .45 caliber Colt and fired. The bullet passed right through Bill's head, emerging below his right cheekbone and then pierced Captain Massey's left arm before it spent its course. Bill slid from the stool, his fingers clutching his best hand that afternoon—aces and eights, two pair—a hand that has been called the "dead man's

hand" ever since by players in the western country.

McCall was tried almost immediately for the crime, and then set free, probably with considerable pressure from many of the ne'er-do-wells in Deadwood who feared the possibility of law and order coming. However, Deadwood was still on Indian Territory at that time, and the nearest U.S. Marshall held that the trial was, therefore, invalid. About a year later, McCall was retried and hanged.

Justice to Broken Nose Jack didn't materially change the general atmosphere around Deadwood. The threat of Indian attacks lessened as the Sioux signed the treaty that exiled them to Canada and made their lands into the Dakota Territory. And the

.45 Caliber Colt, Serial #2079, used by Jack McCall to kill Hickok.

Courtesy Carl W. Breihan

town on Deadwood Gulch grew to a more-or-less stable population of about four thousand, with another two thousand people just drifting around the area. Prospectors added another four thousand, and the hills near town bristled with tents and all manner of shacks.

Safety from Indian attack—well, relative safety for there were still tales of scalps being taken by renegades—brought out another kind of culture. The gambling halls were open all day and the streets of Deadwood teamed with speculators of all kinds, tramps, card sharks, and just plain bums. There was a con man on every corner, and only experience and alertness kept the lucky prospector from losing his grubstake—and his socks!—to the old shell game in one guise or another.

From June of 1877 on, prospecting party after party outfitted from Deadwood and headed into the Black Hills and up into the Big Horn country. In less than three months, six hundred men and boys had left from Deadwood, searching for gold, fame, and fortune. One such party numbered one hundred and fifty, outfitted with high-priced provisions and equipment. But no word came of a strike to rival Sutter's Mill.

Deadwood was a "pricey" place to outfit. A three-cent stamp cost a quarter in Deadwood, and the prices for trail provisions and equipment were as high as the market would bear. Thousands who came to Deadwood to prospect never got near the reported goldfields—they ran through their stake gambling, drinking, just living—and then were too broke to go back home.

The opportunity to take advantage of the opportunists that came to Deadwood was just too tempting. There was a game on every corner, and living costs skyrocketed to at least twice that in Denver or Salt Lake. Still they came. The fever for gold burned, and in rode or walked the unlucky, the greedy, the man of small competence.

The prospecting parties poured out of Deadwood, up into the Powder River, Crazy Woman's Fork, Willow Creek. No news of any big strike came as the summer wore on, and the disgusted hangers-on who floated back to town talked more of renegade Indians than of gold nuggets. Parties panned their way up the east side of the Big Horn toward the Montana border and along the Wind River. They met the parties panning their way down from Rawlins, Green River, and Ogden—but no real amounts of gold appeared. All of the parties headed toward Deadwood in the meandering fashion of a mountain stream. The meandering streams, meanwhile, were being thoroughly picked over, with no big strikes appearing. Deadwood waited, shell games at the ready, to pick over the prospecting parties as completely as they had picked over the mountain streams. Winter approached.

A businessman of the time, concerned for the health of the town and seeing things a little more

A three family cabin set in the heart of the goldfields. Gold was so plentiful in areas that when the clothing got muddy while working a claim, the clothing would be carefully washed or rinsed in clear water. The dredges would then be panned out.

Author's Collection

long term than the others, wrote to the *Deadwood Times*: "There are thousands of men in the Hills who would be glad to work for their bread, or enough money to pay their way back home; but there is no employment for them. The placer claims are all taken by the first comers, and the quartz leads are not yet sufficiently developed to require many laborers. I never saw so many sick-looking men in my life as I have seen in Deadwood. They come here without a cent in their pockets, expecting to gobble up gold by the basketful, and they soon go away with a 'flea in their ear'. . . . They come here full of greedy expectations, but in twenty-four hours their gorgeous air castles have blown away into bubbles."

The local press (the two Deadwood papers and others in the nearby settlements) apparently tried to print the truth about conditions and didn't encourage the indiscriminate stampede that headed for Deadwood. The furor over gold may have been fanned by newspapers in Nebraska and Wyoming, but more likely by the stage companies that stood to gain as well, as high prices could surely be charged for equipment for prospecting. Cheyenne, Sidney, Sioux City, and Omaha each claimed to be the best outfitting point for the land of gold, and each city did all it could to keep the gold fires well fanned and burning brightly.

Of the local inhabitants, about two hundred were in business with capital in amounts from $500 to $10,000. Possibly five hundred more carried out legitimate mining operations in the local gulches and earned enough to be called miners. About six hundred more were employed as day laborers, earning amounts from meals to four dollars per day. All of the rest wandered around, cursing the luck that brought them to Deadwood or philosophically waiting from something to turn up. With more than half of the population unemployed and ill-housed, it is little wonder that Deadwood became famous as the site of shootouts between a succession of fastest guns of the West, filling up Boot Hill cemetery with the second fastest.

Still they came. Every stage arriving from Sidney, Cheyenne, and Fort Pierre was packed to the gills; prairie schooners sailed in from every direction; ox and mule carts bumped in over the mountain trails; and lone riders slumped into town. Sorriest of all were those who walked in, bloody toes leaving a trail through worn-out soles.

Local estimates noted two hundred arrivals on an average day during the middle of the summer of '77. At first, few left Deadwood, preferring to believe the stories of gold nuggets free in the streams, waiting to be picked up. Later in the fall departures quickened. More would have left if they had the means, and there was wistful comments about "God's Country," back in the States, anywhere outside Dakota Territory.

What of the riches of the Black Hills? Less gold was moving out of the area than had been the case in '76—and the truth crushed the expectations that had built Custer City. The whole country, from Custer to Deadwood, was producing not more than $3,000 per day, while the number of men competing for the gold had swelled to 40,000—meaning that a dime per man was being produced. Probably less than fifty claims were paying off. French Creek, the site that caused the furor which built Custer City in 1875, was nearly played out two years later. The few claims along this famed creek that were producing paid one dollar to five dollars per man, but only if worked with expensive pumping equipment. As the creeks dried up, not enough water was available for the kind of working that would pay off.

One old miner who had panned and prospected all over the west for forty years proclaimed that French Creek wasn't as "good as diggings in Cherry Creek above Denver—that wasn't worth workin'. French Creek is rim-rock and high bar on a deep flat gulch. It will pay for about fifteen miles, from grubstakes to wages."

As the air turned crisp, an air of excitement pervaded the area, as experienced miners watched for placer claim owners to sell—all of the claims on French and Spring Creeks were for sale. Along Rapid Creek, the biggest stream in the hills, and its tributaries Castle and North Rapid, bars of gold were paying from two dollars to ten dollars per day. Would the bed rock pay off? Were the stories of great gold veins true?

Claims were recorded, end on end, along Rapid Creek and Castle Creek, but only little pockets of gold had rewarded miners so far. Some experiments were being run—if any of the areas paid off big, the resulting stampede of suckers would cause all the claim owners to sell off and escape with their shirts and a little extra.

Deadwood Gulch had been paying off for about three miles of its length. Placer claims of three hundred feet in length had paid from $10.00 to $30,000. The quartz deposit ran flat a mile or so on each side of Deadwood creek, like a flat, flinty, white coal vein, with iron oxides and streaks of gold running through it. Several lodes facing the gulch were being worked. These lodes, with romantic sounding names like Woolsey, Hidden Treasure and Father de Smet, were producing ore paying from twenty dollars to forty dollars per ton. These extended shallowly away from the creek. Miners speculated about when the lode would run out. Low grade ore worth eight dollars to ten dollars per ton was coming from the fissures on the head of Bobtail Gulch and Gold Run.

Unlike the gold-containing areas in California and Colorado, or any other good gold country, the Black Hills geology is a fooler. Nothing is regular. The foldings that produced the weird beauty of the Black Hills twisted the gold veins so that pockets appeared—rich veins—and then disappeared. Nothing runs deep. Nothing is predictable. Placer claims pan out and then play out. There is enough to tease: the promise of glory, but without substance.

While hunger and want were clearly apparent, there was a hilarity born of desperation, the look-the-other-way desire to make the best of everything. Money wasn't flowing from the gold fields, but the Deadwood merchants were managing to get theirs. Those who owned city lots held out for high prices, $100 per frontage foot, for building spaces on the main streets. A little caboose located on a spur rented for $125 per month. A dollar in gold dust bought a good seat at the Gem Theater or the Bella Union, where stars were brought from Chicago at costs of ten dollars per week to entertain the elite of Deadwood. The Gem favored ballet, and featured lady waiters. The Melodeon offered a stage that would accommodate five or six entertainers and a long room where monte carlo, faro, roulette and ten dice tables provided a place for money to exchange hands rapidly.

Social life of the town was told in the pages of the local newspapers, a sheet of foolscap delivered anywhere in town for eighteen dollars worth of gold dust; no coonskins, scalps, or diluted bug juice, demanded the publisher.

A new bank opening in Deadwood provided a social event in the fall of 1877. The paper assured the populace that the new banking emporium opening would be "celebrated tonight, and George Shingle says he will have corps of waiters to supply the wants of gentlemen who desire anything in his line of refreshments, and we do not speak wide of the mark when we say that he can put them up right." An ad for Blooms, on Lee Street, noted that the store, "is in receipt of party vests, ties and gloves, which will be in demand for the opening."

Another item in the paper noted that the Toll Gate up on Bear Butte Rapid charged "packed pilgrims five cents to enter, loose pilgrims were free."

Morality was somewhat unconventional by Eastern standards. The paper noted that, "Mrs. Marquette, whose husband poisoned himself on Monday night, married again on Tuesday morning, before her dead husband was fairly cold. This is only proof of the businesslike character of the denizens of Deadwood."

Charity was urged: "Miners, men of wealth, you upon whom the Hills has seen fit to lavish her richest treasures, you to whom the earth has chose to empty her apron of gold—did it ever occur to your mind that thousands more deserving than you have been denied these gifts, and have been reduced to beggary, while they labored, struggled and endured, to procure them?" according to the paper's editor.

Like the geology of the area which held more promise than substances, the town also was impermanent. Buildings—especially stores and saloons—were built in sections that could be taken apart and moved to the next boom town at a moment's notice. Few men had families in Deadwood. Those who did kept rooms at the back of a store and took their meals out, for the most part. Houses were virtually unavailable, and the few that were offered were extremely expensive. Household goods were outrageously priced and groceries out of sight.

For the men who lived alone, costs of living were quite diverse. Meals could be bought for fifty cents or five dollars, as one preferred. Hotel fare was uncertain. Often flour ran out, and even when available at twenty dollars per hundred weight, the bakers' loaves were described as a marvel of littleness. When there was no bread, bacon was the staple, boiled, baked, or fried, served with a radish or onion on top to give it some flavor.

A few homesteaders, people who gave up the dream of gold, settled onto the fertile patches near the Spearfish River and set out gardens of fresh vegetables which provided the townspeople with a little variety, and the homesteaders with ready money.

Ramshackle buildings seemed to grow in volume out of the mud streets of Deadwood, like expanding balloons. Construction was feeble, with hardly any serious thought or planning used while erecting these shanties side-by-side. They were literally fire traps. Many times in the middle of the night a fire alarm was given for volunteers and a bucket brigade. The great fire of 1879 leveled much of Deadwood, including Saloon Number 10 where Wild Bill was killed. But it didn't take long before construction began over the still warm and smoldering coals. Deadwood was a town too tough to die.

Lack of a good base of supply plagued Deadwood and neighboring areas. Coal oil was sometimes as high as seven dollars to fifteen dollars per gallon, and matches often ran out. Hotels were dark early, stores closed as soon as darkness came, earlier in the fall. The theaters were sometimes lighted with a few tallow candles. Everything was in short supply, except whiskey.

Deadwood was a wide open town in those days. Courts were established some time in the '77-'79 era, but the police were often in league with the gamblers and criminals went unpunished, unless they tried to cheat the gambling houses. Saloon men defied the license laws and refused to pay the $100 license fee. Claim jumpers and land sharks stole what they were able and could feel safe from the law. Too much gold, yet not enough, too many to share in too little—such was Deadwood during the boom days of the Dakota Territory.

Somehow, Deadwood survived through the tumult of gold fever and outlaws, and many of the more colorful characters stuck around. Calamity Jane, just before she died a pauper in an unheated cabin near Deadwood, asked to be buried, "near Wild Bill—he was my barroom friend." She was buried in a nearby plot, and a statute of Bill was erected on his grave. Vandals destroyed it several times, and when the graves were moved to a new cemetery the statue was not replaced again.

Source:
Following the Guidon. Custer, Elizabeth. New York: Harper, 1890.
My Life on the Plains. Custer, George A. New York: Sheldon & Company, 1874
An Account of Deadwood and the Northern Black Hills in 1876. Bullock, Seth. Pierre, South Dakota: South Dakota Historical Collections, Vol. XXXI; 1962.
Wild Bill and Deadwood. Fielder, Mildred. Superior Publishing Company.
Pioneer Days in the Black Hills. McClintock, John S. ed. Edward L. Senn. Deadwood, South Dakota, 1939.
Black Hills *Daily Times*, September 4, 1877.
Black Hills *Daily Times*, September 21, 1877.
Chicago *Times*, June 9, 1877.

Gold Seeker's Equipment

Adventurers and gold seekers flocked into the Klondike country in the late 1890s, all with a hungry appetite to locate the golden pot at the end of the rainbow. Many experienced miners warned the enthusiastic prospectors that no man should attempt such a trip without stocking up with a year's supply of provisions, tools, underclothing, canvas, and at least $500 to $1000 in cash. At the beginning of the new strike, many rushed into the Klondike area without taking this good advice and large numbers were forced to turn back by the Northwest Mounted Police.

A simple practical list was drawn up by experienced miners who had already spent a decade in the Klondike region and reproduced in newspapers and magazines. The long list stated preferences as to quality and quantity of different foods that were essential for the duration of a year.

The food supply for one man varied from four and a half to five pounds and would bring the supply of food for the year to 1,600 pounds. The foods were to be high in carbohydrates and stimulants such as alcohol were to be left behind.

A pound of tea was equivalent to seven pounds of coffee, and three-fourths of an ounce of saccharin would be the same as twenty-five pounds of sugar. For the dreaded scurvy, citric acid was included.

A general outline below is as follows:

Knife, fork, spoon, cup and plate
1 can opener
Frying pan
Coffee and tea pot
9 soap cakes
1 can of mustard
1 tin of matches (for four men)
1 stove (for four men)
1 gold pan
150 pounds of bacon
400 pounds of flour
25 pounds of rolled oats
125 pounds of beans
10 pounds of coffee
25 pounds of sugar
25 pounds of dried potatoes
2 pounds of dried onions
15 pounds of salt
1 pound of pepper
75 pounds of dried fruits
8 pounds of baking powder
2 pounds of soda
1/2 pound of evaporated vinegar
12 ounces of compressed soup
1 set of granite buckets
1 large bucket
Scythe stone
Two picks and 1 shovel
1 whipsaw
2 axes for four men and 1 extra handle
6-8″ files and two taper files for party
Drawing knife, brace and bits, jack, plane and hammer
200 feet three-eighths inch rope
8 pounds of pitch and 5 pounds of oakum for four men
Nails, five pounds each of 6, 8, 10 and 12 penny
2 pairs shoes

1 pair gum boots
4 pairs blankets (for two men)
4 towels
2 pairs overalls
1 suit oil clothing
Tent, 10 x 12, for four
Canvas for wrapping
2 oil blankets to each boat
5 yards mosquito netting for each man
3 suits of heavy underwear
2 pairs heavy mackinaw trousers
1 heavy rubber-lined coat
1 dozen heavy wool socks
1/2 dozen heavy wool mittens
2 heavy overshirts

Two or three changes of light clothing and one heavy makinaw was important, and, a small variety of medicines for each man.

This prospector is panning a wash. It takes a little know-how and skill to pan a creekbed and some luck in finding a little color (gold). A man could pan from $2.00 to $20.00 a day. Higher stakes made millionaires out of them in a few short days. But, those were the exceptions.

Art by E.L. Reedstrom

The Burro, An American Workhorse

The burro, man's other beast of burden, is one of the world's oldest pack and riding animals. It is not certain that this strain extends as far back as the horse, and its appearance as a domestic animal is equally obscure. If it were not that the burrow came from Spain to Mexico and America's Southwest with the Spanish conquerors, both provincials might be backwards in their development. The burro has always been the poor man's all purpose work beast used either for harness or saddle. For four centuries throughout a land where water and feed were scarce commodities, the burro survived where less durable animals could not.

The Southwest's Spanish mule, a product of a mustang mare bred to a burro "jack," is an American improvement designed to beef up both size and strength to the burro's durable body. The result is a sturdy and active breed of small mules which takes the place of both horses and burros in many quarters. It was most likely that this Spanish stock set America's eastern states up in the mule business, although, some of this breeding did come up from the Southwest by way of Mexico.

The American West was fast being tamed and changed, and those who sought fortunes "looking for colors" in the mountain recesses preferred the sure-

Burros were not only pack animals for the prospectors in the wilderness, they were the night's sentry. Any odd noises would provoke their attention in that direction. When water was sought, the burro could scent it beneath the ground and commence to paw the ground above it.

Author's Collection

A typical old-fashioned prospector and burro are loaded down with boxed backs for a lengthy stay in the mountains (period unknown).

Author's Collection

footed burro as a reliant pack animal as well as a constant companion. Carrying the prospector's food and equipment, the small long-eared burro could withstand a little over 150 pounds of evenly distributed weight on his back. With pick, shovel, blanket, tent, rifle, canned goods, flour, pots and pans, and other accoutrements of a desert rat, the docile burro crept up the winding mountain trails with ease, where a horse would refuse to travel. The animal served as confidential adviser and friend as well as a beast of burden.

Where water was scarce, it was the burro that pawed at the desert's sandy floor locating a small pool of muddy water. At nights he served as camp sentinel, acknowledging any noise quickly, with ears erect and looking in the direction of the disturbance.

These animals have responded to certain danger by nudging a sleeping man with their nose to awaken him. When times were lean and the prospector had no grain for his animals, he let them run wild in the desert to forage for themselves. The burro would withstand the desert vegetation, but a horse in the same predicament would probably starve. The burro was just as much a part of the development of the West as the cowboy was to the cattle industry. Without this sturdy little animal, the prospector would probably be little known to our history books, and the growth and expansion of the American West would have taken a little longer.

Source:
Man on Horseback, Glen R. Vernam. Harper and Row, Publ., N.Y.

The Packsaddle

The packsaddle was probably derived from the Spanish or borrowed from Mexico. It used a simple method of two cross-trees to which a load was lashed. Horse, mule and burro were used to pack food, timber, water, equipment and ammunition for the army. The saddle, as illustrated here, varied. Usually a double rigged packsaddle was used for heavier loads. It had two cinches or belly bands as well as a breast collar and a breech or hip strap. This helped to keep the pack from sliding backward on the animal's back or forward.

A good packer would be certain to distribute the weight evenly on each side. A thick pad of felt or woolen blankets was beneath the packsaddles. A burro could withstand around 150 pounds on his back and a horse is comfortable with 75 to 90 pounds on each side. Anything over that, the animal would not move an inch. Usually they would drop to the ground and begin to roll about, trying to work the packs loose. During a good long hike, the packs are often checked and the cinches tightened. If a pack should roll to one side, it might cause some damage to the animal's back. When the packs are removed, the blankets are left on until the animal is cooled off; then, after the pads are removed, the backs are checked for any bruise caused by the weight of the packs. Saddle sores are easily developed and if not

properly attended to, can cause the horse or burro to become incapacitated for a considerable period of time.

Another form of packsaddle is the 'aparejo' (ah-par-ay'ho), a stuffed leather pad with a broad cincha. The diamond hitch, double and single, and the squaw hitch are used in securing the pack.

The 'sawbuck' saddle went everywhere the prospector ventured, carrying his bedroll, tent, grub, and tools.

Author's Collection

Throwing the Diamond Hitch

The head packer took his place on the left side of the pack horse, with the helper on the right side. Taking the last rope and cinch in the right hand, with the loose end in the left hand, he laid the loose end on top of a pack lengthwise with about eight feet behind the pack. He then passed the cinch under the horse to his helper, doubled the rope, and passed the doubled end over the pack to the helper, who hooded the looped end in a cinch hook, with the long end of the rope to the front. Then he pulled the cinch up snug by pulling on the long or front rope, and the helper pulled on the hind rope.

Reaching on top of the pack, he pushed the front rope under the hind rope for a space of about eighteen inches on top of the pack. Next he took hold of the rope lying lengthwise on top of the pack (but under the two ropes lying crossways of the pack) and pulled up a loop about eighteen inches long and laid it back towards the rear of the pack. He then took the front rope (as it hung on the left side of the pack) and passed it back of and around under and in front of the pack. The helper took hold of the loop, and drew the rope tight by standing in front of the pack.

When the helper had drawn the rope tight he passed it down in front of the pack on the right side, then under and up behind the pack. Then he took the loose end of rope and drew it tight and fastened it.

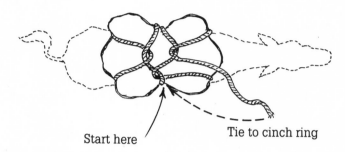

Start here　　　　　　Tie to cinch ring

The top of the diamond hitch.

Art by E.L. Reedstrom

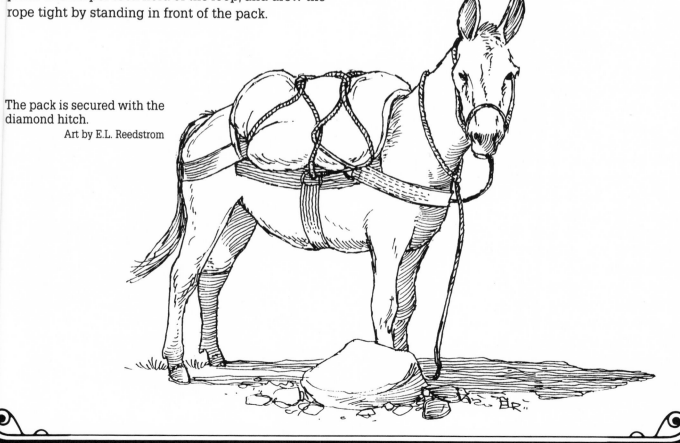

The pack is secured with the diamond hitch.

Art by E.L. Reedstrom

Glossary of Mining Words

Amalgamation—A process using mercury to collect fine gold and silver particles from crushed ore, whereas rock does not dissolve in quicksilver. Both minerals can later be separated by heat or pressure. If by heat, plenty of ventilation is needed as the fumes are deadly. By pressure, the mercury is dropped into a "Shammy-Skin" and literally squeezed out through the pores of the skin. (Drop-step amalgamation process is one method. This is done by coating copper plates with mercury.)

Assay—Test scientifically for values.

Bed Rock—Gold is heavier than iron, and always settles on the bottom of creek beds or "Bed-rock."

Blank—A panning with no values.

Bonanza—A rich vein of silver or gold.

"Burning Out a Pan"—Miners were neglectful. They would wash up in their gold pan, and forget to burn the pan out over a camp fire. If the soap or grease was not burned out, the pan could not be used to work gold.

A "Bust"—Bone broke, shut down, bankrupt.

Button—As "Gold Button"; when raw gold is melted down to the size of a small coin.

Capping (rock):Worthless material often covering ore (vein).

Claim—A parcel of land claimed by a settler or prospector and usually marked by building a stone pile and somewhere within, is a tobacco can with recorded papers, name, location and date of staking the claim.

Claim Jumping—Working the same claim that someone else has legally recorded and placed his monument.

Colors—Small particles of gold showing amid the residue in a prospector's pan after washing.

Country Rock—Common rock of no value, native to the area.

Coyoting, or Coyote Diggings—Small diggings made by miners to reach gold deposits resting on bed-rock without excavating all the overlying soil. The vertical shaft, with tunnels radiating like wheel spokes, was very similar to the holes dug buy coyotes.

Cradle—A rocker, used in washing gold from dirt and gravel.

Crevicing—Prying gold from cracks in rocks by using a knife.

Cross-cut—A tunnel crossing an ore vein. This was used to communicate between work gangs as well as ventilation.

Double Jack—Large hammer for striking drill used in two-man endeavor when boring hole for dynamite. "Single Jack"—one man endeavor.

Dynamite—Forty percent dynamite sticks were the most commonly used. These were primed with caps connected to wires and leading to a hand "pump" generator. Forty percent dynamite was very touchy. If ever hit with a hammer on a cement or rock foundation with enough pressure, it would go off. Dynàmite loses its effectiveness when the glycerin soaks through the paper enveloping the bulk within.

Float—Piece of loose ore unattached to any particular vein.

Fool's Gold or Iron Pyrites—To any "tenderfoot" this may be mistaken for gold. Although once gold has been seen with its metallic color, a person would be able to distinguish the two. Some areas where outcrops of "Fool's Gold" is found, a touch of your own saliva rubbed into the bright colors will produce a darker color.

Gallows Frame—A wooden or steel scaffold atop a mine shaft carrying the hoisting rope.

Grubstake—Staking a prospector with food and equipment in return for a share of the findings.

Hard Rock Ore—Ore that had to be removed by blasting, or vein-material with values that must be freed from the ore, usually by crushing.

High Grade—High in value.

High Grading—Valuable high-grade chunks of ore stolen from the mine by the miners.

Hungry—Barren of mineralization.

Hydraulic Miners—The simple flume and riffles method was used on a larger scale by hydraulic miners who worked the gravel into the flume by means of a powerful nozzle or "Gun." Water under high pressure was piped to this nozzle, then by means of a long lever, it was directed against the gravel banks carrying large quantities of the material into the flume to be processed as in common placer mining.

In Place—Ore attached to the vein.

Lode—Working below the ground on a rich vein or ore. The 'principle' vein was called the "Mother Lode." (Body of mineral)

Long Tom—This is an improvement on the cradle. It consists of two troughs or boxes. A "California Tom" is about twelve feet long, twenty inches wide at the upper end, and thirty inches wide at the mouth. It is supported on stones or logs and is worked by two to four men. The apparatus is used only where water is present, so that a constant flow is secured.

Low Grade—Low in value.

Mortar and Pestle—An iron vessel in which gold bearing rock is pounded into dust with a pestle and then hand-panned.

Mother Lode—Main body of ore in the mineralized belt.

Muck—Debris left in a mine or shaft after blasting hard rock. A "Mucker" is a miner who shovels this material into a chute or mining car.

Open Pit Mining—Working a rich out-crop in either gold or silver within an open pit.

Ore—Any material containing valuable metallic constituents for the sake of which it is mined or worked.

Pan—Gold pans came in different sizes, from a ten inch to an eighteen inch width. They looked similar to a frying pan, with the exception of a handle.

Pay-Dirt—Turning gold or silver into money.

"Peacock Gold"—Gold ore, so fine it floats on top of water, giving the effect of the colors of a peacock's hind tail.

Placer—Working above ground. Also, working an active streambed containing fine particles of gold or silver which is usually worked by washing-out with a miner's pan. (Another name is "Toplander.")

Pocket—Enriched area (usually small) occurring in veins or creek bottoms.

Pyrite (Iron Pyrite) or Fool's Gold—A bright heavy yellow mineral which is hard and brittle.

Quartz—Either a white or clear crystal line mineral, in which gold or silver veins were commonly found.

Quick-silver—Mercury.

Salting a Mine—Planting rich ore samples into mines already gone "bust," in order to attract unwary buyers. Also, gold watch shavings poured into 12 gauge shot-gun shells and fired into a wall of low grade ore.

Shaft—A vertical shaft or an inclined excavation, the main entrance to a mine leading to tunnels where ore was worked.

Single Jack—See "Double Jack."

Sluice—A long trough made of wood, for washing placer gold. By shoveling rock and dirt into a steady stream or water. Gold and other heavier particles rest at the bottom where corduroy and cleats caught the much sought after material.

Sort—Separate ore as to its value (low, medium and high grade).

Sourdough—Fermenting dough or batter, for the next day's bread. Also a term for an old experienced prospector.

Spitter—A long stick containing a match at the end to light a three or five minute fuse. This gives the miner enough time to crawl out of either an incline or vertical shaft. If in a vertical shaft, he had to climb a rope ladder, a chain ladder, a wooden ladder, and throw himself over the lip-opening of the mine, all to avoid getting hit with an explosion of rock and dirt.

Stamp Mill—A system that was powered by stream, water or electricity, in which the ore, both rock and gravel, was fed by shovel and pounded to a fine powder by huge iron stamps (sometimes iron balls).

Tailings—A pile of low grade ore heaped in front of a 'Dead-Mine'. These tailings brought enough gold (re-worked by prospectors), to keep them in beer, wine, and tobacco.

To Cobb—Knock section containing lesser value from each piece of ore leaving only that part having to extremely rich value.

To Gut—Take rich part of vein and leave only low grade.

Winch—Built on top of a vertical mine shaft where a bucket can be lowered and brought back up by a man maneuvering a hand crank coupled with a strong manila rope (1/2 inch thick).

CHAPTER VII

THE MILITARY IN THE WEST

Cavalry Life

Cavalry schedule for a long, hard, campaign: First call for "reveille" sounded at the crack of dawn. The men turned out promptly, struck their shelter halves and packed their saddles. Fifteen minutes later, "assembly" was sounded and the men fell in for roll call. After roll-call, the troops were marched to the horse pickets by their first sergeants, to water, groom and feed their horses. The men were then dismissed for breakfast.

In the field, rations were hardtack, bacon, and hot coffee. Half an hour before breaking camp, "boots and saddles" was sounded, followed fifteen minutes later by "stand to horse," when the roll was again called. First sergeants reported any absentees or sickness to troop commanders, who in turn reported to the adjutant. Troop commanders then ordered "prepare to mount" and moved out when the "advance" sounded.

After thirty minutes of marching, the troops were halted, the men dismounted to check packs and tighten girths. Short halts were usually made at the end of each hour, and horses were generally watered once during the day's march. Every so often a trot was ordered to give animal and man a different pace.

When a campsite was chosen, troopers unbridled, tied up horses, and wiped saddles and bridles. The animals were fed a little hay and their backs checked for sores from the saddle. After "stable call," the men were allowed to "mess." "Retreat" sounded at sundown and "extinguish lights" sounded at 8:30 p.m.

Source:
Reedstrom, E.L. *Bugles, Banners and War Bonnets.* Caxton Printers (1978)
Guns Magazine, July Issue, 1980, centerfold

Corps Colors

Corps Colors represented the different branches in the U.S. Army. Each branch adhered their organizational colors to various parts of their uniforms, such as: braiding around the caps, cuff edging, sleeve stripes, hat cords, and trousers side seams. This organization of colors held throughout our military history from the early 1840s on to our present status. The colors of each branch is as follows:

Early Dragoon .... Light orange yellow
Infantry .... Blue
Cavalry .... Yellow
Artillery .... Scarlet

Ordnance Corp .... Dark red	Engineer Corp .... Yellow
Hospital or Medical Corp .... Crimson	Signal Corp .... Orange
Quartermaster's	Indian
Assistant .. Pale yellow with white piping	Scouts ..... White cloth piped with scarlet
Commissariat .... Gray and white piping	(March 1891)

Bugles

The bugle call that woke the troopers was a call to the change taking place in the country. Bugle calls were based on a new system introduced during the 1840s, unified so that all bugle calls could be recognized from outfit to outfit. Since most buglers couldn't read notes, the calls were learned by note, and it took some time for the calls to be passed around all through the Territories.

Bugles have only five notes, so all of the calls are based on these five note and intonation. The calls—charge, a call heard at today's football games in response to first-downs; reveille, a call that originated during the Crusades; breakfast or chow, a call that sounds like the bugler is calling "soupy, soupy, soupy"; taps or extinguish lights; and retreat.

The 1874 *Army Manual* noted that trumpets or bugles would be used for giving commands whenever it could be "done to advantage" followed by oral commands given by the chiefs of subdivisions. The signals were given so that all movements to the left were on a descending chord. Changes of gait were on the same note. Bugle calls grew over the years, and it was noted that the horses often knew the bugle calls as well as the troopers did, responding directly and rapidly.

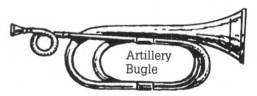

Artillery Bugle

Brass, key of "G" weight 5½ pounds (also nickel plated).

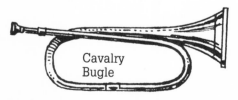

Cavalry Bugle

Brass, key of "F", weight 5½ pounds, reinforced bell.

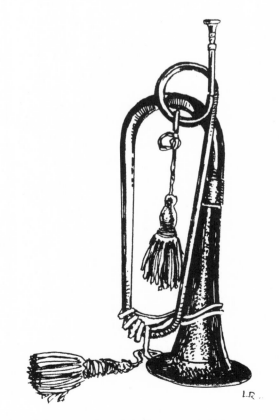

Branding and Punishment

By December, 1868, a private who deserted his post was tried before a General Court Martial, found guilty and sentenced to a dishonorable discharge. He was obliged to forfeit all pay and allowance due him except the just dues owed the laundress and sutler. He was to have his head completely shaved and his left hip branded with a hot iron bearing the letter "D" for deserter, two inches in length, and he was then drummed out of camp. Later, indelible ink that took many washings to erase was substituted for the branding iron. With this change, the letter "D" was reduced to one and a half inches in length.

Punishment was quite severe in the frontier army. Even though flogging was abolished in 1861 by an Act of Congress, veteran officers who believed in severe discipline usually believed in using the lash. From twenty to thirty lashes might be delivered on the raw flesh of a man's back with plaited leather thongs for stealing and up to one hundred lashes was the punishment for whiskey smuggling.

Men were also "spreadeagled" on the ground for two hours or more in the hot sun. Flies and buffalo gnats covered his hands and face, tormenting him horribly. "Bucked and gagged" was another favorite punishment, although not as severe a torture as the former. Another method, standing on the edge of a barrel for half a day, required the balance of a circus acrobat. One false move might find the soldier on the ground with a damaged knee or heaped inside the barrel wedged like a sardine.

Wearing a "wooden overcoat," was another method of punishing a man. The bottom of a barrel was knocked out and a hole cut at the top end large enough to slip over a man's head. The victim would be paraded around the post in this manner for the duration of the day.

"Knapsacking" or "knapsack drill' meant a soldier was paraded around carrying heavy rocks or stones in his backpack, marching to the beat of a drum under the watchful eye of a guardsman for several hours. Some underwent "isolation on a platform" or tied spread-eagled to a wagon wheel all night. Carrying a twenty-five pound log on one's shoulder for a half a day was for a lesser offense. Anyone carrying this weight believed the log grew in size and weight after a few hours.

Being strung up by the thumbs to an overhanging beam and standing flatfooted on the ground was another disciplinary measure. This punishment could be altered and the man strung up by his toes, if necessary.

Reporting without proper equipment or out of uniform were lesser offenses which were punished by double guard duty. "Drunk and Disorderly" brought a sentence of digging a hole ten feet square by ten feet deep under the watchful eye of a guard, restoring a man to sobriety by the time the hole was filled in. If found with a bottle, the unlucky solider was ordered to dig such a hole and bury the bottle.[1]

Bucked and gaged.

Art by E.L. Reedstrom

Fancy Gauntlets

During the Civil War, both cavalry officers and enlisted men wore white or fawn-colored buckskin gauntlets with large, flared cuffs, six inches or more long and often made with a wide opening at the sides to accommodate the uniform sleeve cuffs.

Not all cowboys, scouts, stage and train drivers adopted this army pattern for their work, but they did serve a purpose in protecting hands from the elements as well as preventing the cold winds from blowing up their sleeves. They also protected their wrists from rope and rein burns besides scratches from the prairie brush.

With an abundance of these gauntlets in army stockpiles, trading posts and Indian reservation storekeepers purchased great quantities of them, employing Indian women to decorate the stiff cuffs with designs using colorful glass trade beads, porcupine quills and, in some cases, fringes. Designs were of American flags, eagles, coats of arms and almost any imaginable emblem. Later, these gloves were manufactured by eastern factories and sold all over the western frontier. However, in place of the colorful beads and porcupine quills, these gauntlets exhibited threads from machines, embroidered in various designs. Leather workers stamped or hand-tooled cuffs with basket-weave and floral patterns into gloves too gaudy for the humble wearer.

Performers with the great Buffalo Bill touring show wore fanciful costumes and ornate gauntlets during their acts, and so it was thought by the audience that all of the westerners out on the frontier wore this sort of get-up. However, most cowboys claimed that these "bucket tops" could cause severe accidents while roping and working with animals, and that they were a catch-all for anything that dropped into them.

Source:
From the personal collection of J.M. Gish, McAllen, Texas.
From the personal collection of E.L. Reedstrom.
The Illustrated Catalogue of Arms and Military Goods, Schuyler, Hartley & Graham's (1864); Reprint by Norm Flayderman.

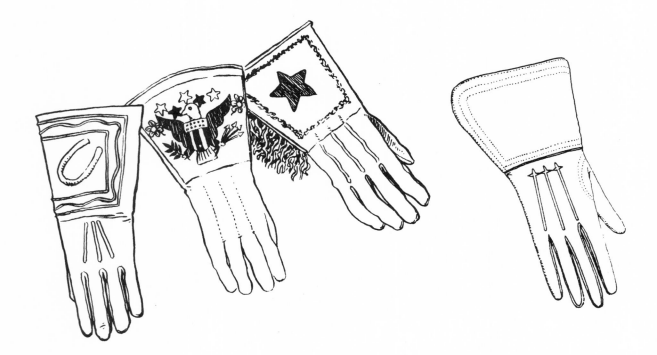

Deadly Arrows

An arrow launched from an Indian's bow has a softly swishing sound when passing its mark but a deadly effect when hitting its target. The velocity of an arrow can penetrate a tree exposing half of its shaft and if aimed at the fleshy parts of a buffalo, can pass through its entire body. The sound of passing arrows struck deadly fear into soldiers like the rattle of a diamond back ready to strike.

Out of ten individuals shot with arrows, seven were expected to die from the wound. Either shock or the venom-tainted steel point took its victim, as the arrow points were dipped into dead livers of animals or rattlesnake venom.

Even when the arrows were not tainted by poison, they produced much destruction when entering a human's body, either by severing an artery where much blood is produced within a short time or by blood poisoning. Unlike the hunting arrows that could be withdrawn from a wound with relative ease, war arrows could not because of their barbed points.

Wire loop for extracting arrow heads embedded in soft parts.

Wire twister recommended by surgeons; length is twelve inches.

Wire loop twisted once on itself for snaring impacted arrow heads.

Assortment of amputation tools used by military surgeons.
Courtesy Carl Rumps Collection

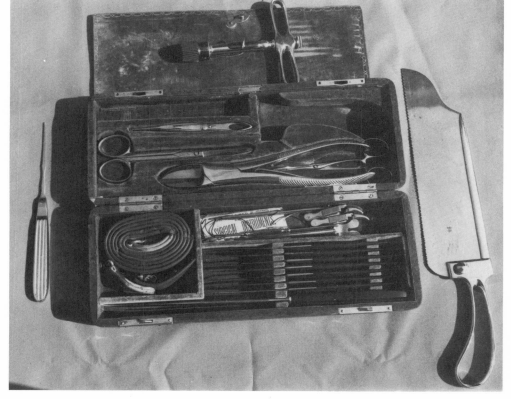

These points were usually glued to the end of the two-foot shaft and wrapped with animal sinew that would soften at body temperature so that the shaft would separate from the point, leaving the rather large foreign object in the body to inflame and infect, causing blood poisoning. This softening action often took less than half-an-hour, so that a man hit in the heat of battle was in very bad shape by the time a doctor arrived.

As many arrow wounds occurred during the Indian wars, army surgeons had already had experience in designing unusual tools to remove the arrow point without too much injury and pain to the victim. The early "duck-bill" forceps that crushed the arrow barbs so as to withdraw the point were effective. This instrument was used, with some modification, from the Dark Ages through the Indian wars with much success.

One surgeon remarked that it was exceptional to meet with a single wound. If one arrow found its mark, surely two or three others would follow.

Average Plains Indian arrows measured from twenty-four to twenty-nine inches in length. Turkey or eagle feathers were most common for the shaft, as blood from either animal or human would not harm them.

There is a distinguishable difference between a war arrow and a hunting arrow. Barbed arrows had to be cut or pushed through the body, whereas hunting arrows were much easier to extract. The steel point on the war arrow was horizontally attached to the shaft, against the vertical notch at the other end. This belief materialized over the many years of war with the white man (his ribs were horizontal) that the arrow had a better chance to enter the chest cavity. The arrow point on the hunting shaft was placed at the tip on a vertical plane, in line with the notch at the other end, as animal ribs are found to be vertical. The end feathers were placed at certain angles, controlling the flight of the arrow. There was hardly any rotary turn at all, and the arrow found its mark between the ribs of the animal or the man.

By removing an arrow impacted into bone, a slight gentle rocking of the shaft was necessary by the surgeon, then a well annealed iron wire was produced, two and a half feet in length, passed through a hole in the long suture-wire twister and fastened to the handle, exposing a loop at the end. This loop was then passed down the arrow shaft to snare the arrow point. The wire was taken up and compressed around the point and in one motion both foreign body and instrument were removed.

Of course the worst wound was in the abdomen, a fact well-known to the Indians. The Mexicans who fought these enemies of the border for many years knew the Indians were always aimed at the umbilicus, and they were always prepared to meet them in battle with a blanket around their middle and folded up many times. This helped to protect the abdomen against the flight of arrows.

Source:
War Dept., Surgeon General's Office; A Report of Surgical Cases Treated in the U.S.A. from 1865 to 1871. Circular No. 3.
Mystic Warriors of the Plains. T.E. Mails. Doubleday.

The Gatling Gun

Richard Jordan Gatling did not have the opportunity to see his "battery" gun in action during the Civil War. The late date of its introduction prevented the use of this weapon in a great number of campaigns where its effectiveness could have been appreciated. However, it was put to many practical tests by the officers of the U.S. Ordinance Corps.

At the very beginning, Gatling's gun was referred to as a "novel engine of war," and it did receive positive claims from military men who knew how well it could function in guarding bridges, fords, and roadways. It could be fired equally well day or night with hardly any recoil to destroy the accuracy of its aim once it was sighted on a target. One favorable comment came from Lt. Maclay, U.S. Ordinance: "The advantages claimed for this gun are: 1) there is no escape of gas at the breech; 2) there is no recoil which can destroy its accuracy; 3) it performs the operations of loading, firing, and extracting the case simply by revolving the crank; 4) accuracy; 5) rapidity of fire."

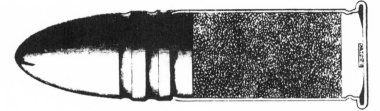

Gatling Gun, Model 1871, on an all metal carriage.
From *Army, Navy Journals*, 1871.

One inch cartridge for Model 1865 (actual size).
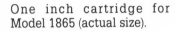

The report concludes "All parts of the gun work well."

The government decided to adopt the Gatling gun as part of its arsenal. An order for 100 weapons was issued to Talbot, Jones, and Company of Indianapolis, Indiana, dated August 24, 1866. Fifty .50 caliber guns were ordered by General A.B. Dyer; each weapon had six steel barrels, all rifled. The wooden field gun carriages were to be seasoned white oak, with all iron or steel parts blued. The only exception was the gun barrel; it was to be browned (a blue-black rusting process). Two sizes of Gatlings were manufactured by the Colt's Arms Company in Hartford, Connecticut: a one inch caliber capable of being fired 100 times a minute, and one of the .50 caliber, which could be fired two hundred times a minute. Both used copper-case prime cartridges and each had six steel rotating barrels.

The weight of the gun and its carriage was comparatively light, rendering it capable of being drawn by two horses, where four or six horses were required for the lighter field-piece. In addition, the Gatling had no recoil because both gun and carriage were of sufficient weight to overcome the recoil of each discharge. Thus no time was lost in sighting after the first fire. If an operator, other than the one who was cranking, moved a wheel forward or backward to give the gun a lateral pass while firing, the gun could sweep a sector of any circle within its range.

Some officers had objections to the Gatling gun, even though its firepower was that of two companies of infantry even though it took only four infantrymen to operate it.[2] Training of gun crews was often inadequate. During the late 1860s and early 1870s, target practice was infrequent because of objections to extra expenditures for ammunition. It was said that the weapon was clumsy and hard to conceal. The operators were exposed to enemy fire in a stationary position, and the weapon would lose its

At the Washington Trials of May 8, 1866, three Gatling guns are posed on the banks of the Potomac. The one inch guns and the .50 caliber have all passed severe tests.

Courtesy National Archives Records Group, Washington, D.C.

effectiveness if any of the men were wounded. Officers cautioned the operators to keep their heads down when firing because the gravity-fed ammunition case was above the men. A stray bullet might slam into the feed case rendering it useless or exploding several cartridges within it.

The men of the Seventh U.S. Cavalry had already found uses for the Gatling gun. One company, returning from the Hancock Expedition in 1867, ran into a large herd of buffalo while escorting a wagon train on the Smoky Hill route. When the buffalo threatened to stampede the wagon train, two companies of cavalry dismounted, knelt and fired volleys into the oncoming herd. this only frightened the animals and they headed straight for the train. Two Gatling guns then came into position and began firing. After a number of buffalo were killed, the rest of the herd broke around the wagon train. A detailed group of soldiers went forward to cut the hind quarters of the dead buffalo, loading them into the wagons for garrison consumption.

The mobility of these weapons had not been too highly criticized by other commands, but during the Little Big Horn Expedition, Custer refused three Gatling guns on the basis that they might hamper or slow down his command while traveling in difficult terrain.[3] The weight of each machine, not including the carriage and limber was 224 pounds. Total weight of carriage, omitting the gun was 202 pounds. The limber (empty) totaled 200 pounds. The smaller gun had a range of up to one mile, while the larger size had a range up to two miles. Accuracy was not an issue when considering the effectiveness of each range.

Even if Custer had accepted the guns, it is not likely that the odds would have been in favor of the gallant 7th Cavalry as they were outnumbered ten to one. As the Indians were everywhere, it would not have been long before they picked off the guns' operators and possibly gained another weapon for their own arsenals.

Anson Mills, Father of the Web Belt System

(Reprinted with permission from *Guns Magazine*)

Americans have long made heroes of their fighting men and named weapons after their inventors. Western towns were named for Indian fighters and explorers. Somehow, Anson Mills missed glory—and his memory and contributions deserve better.

Mills made it possible for the soldier to keep an adequate supply of ammunition on hand as weaponry made its rapid advances. Without such support systems, the better weapons couldn't have been used to advantage, and the edge in battle would have been lost. To paraphrase a cliche, for want of a belt, a gun could be lost.

Who was this unsung inventor who developed the piece of equipment sorely needed by Indian fighters and later, Doughboys who were the first Americans to fight on European soil? Anson Mills was born a Quaker in Thorntown, Indiana, on August 31, 1834. His father, James P. Mills had come to Indiana after the "big city," Philadelphia, began to crowd at his elbows. He began life over in the little Indiana community of plain people, teaching his children the peaceful, hardworking Quaker ways.

One of young Anson's first chores was to "hand-in" the warp during weaving. He stood under the loom, lifting the warp, thread by thread to the women who passed it through the reed and harness loom, making the grey and blue fabric from which the family clothing was cut. The wool had been hand-clipped from the sheep, carded and spun into yarn by other family members. Anson apparently remembered something of this early chore, because he was the first to conceive the weaving of his ammo belt in one piece.

Anson's boyhood was spent on the family farm, learning carpentry as he grew older as well as other practical skills. But the simplicity and peace of Quaker life was not enough to hold him, and he longed for a life in the Army. One can imagine that there must have been some chagrin at his ambitions, but on June 1, 1855, he was appointed to West Point, and entered his first year as an Army man.

His desire to succeed at West Point was not enough, and he was discharged sometime early in 1857. He had learned to survey at West Point and

Anson Mills, inventor of the military looped web belt.
Art by E.L. Reedstrom

went to Texas after his discharge, where he made the original plat for the city of El Paso and gave the town its name.

Rumblings of Civil War were heard on the Texas Plains. When the vote was called regarding whether Texas would stay in the Union or leave to join the Confederacy, Mills cast one of only two votes against secession. Outnumbered and out of step with local views, Mills headed for Washington to volunteer for the Union Army. In June of 1861, he received an antedated commission (dated May 14, 1861) as a first lieutenant in a newly organized regular infantry regiment. His first engagement was at the battle of Shiloh.

From Shiloh (April 6, 1862) until the end of the war, Mills was in the field in the West, under a number of top ranking officers. He fought at Murfreesboro,

Chicamauga, and in the Atlanta and Nashville campaigns.

In 1863, he was promoted to the rank of captain. By early 1865, he had moved on to fighting Indians on the Western frontier. Taking time out to marry Hannah Cassel, daughter of William C. Cassel of Zanesville, Ohio on October 13, 1868, Mills returned to the frontier to fight in the Rosebud campaign against the Sioux in 1876, after a transfer from infantry to cavalry in early 1871. His career continued to improve, with a promotion to major in 1878, lieutenant-colonel in 1890, and then to full colonel in 1892.

While learning to command was apparently of importance to Mills, a major interest was in improving the methods of carrying sufficient ammunition to prevent the horror of running out of cartridges when suddenly faced with the enemy. This problem, which had been getting more serious with each improvement in weaponry, was discussed with much heat in the *Army-Navy Journals* published beginning in 1862. The *Journals* carried many articles from enlisted men, and some of the descriptions of difficulty with equipment and uniforms were best described as boiling diatribes. One soldier alleged that the Department of the Army must have employed "three deformed" women to serve as models for the uniform. The problem of carrying enough ammunition without being overwhelmed by its weight was discussed many times, and the sloppy ammo box was roundly criticized. It became clear that much ammunition was wasted when it popped out of the box during the heat of battle.

As early as 1866, a leather belt was beginning to appear, used by civilian scouts and frontiersmen. The critics of the general army issue became interested in the belt design. Mills, inspired by the concept of an easy-to-carry belt that kept ammunition handy, devised his first version. The leather belt was crafted by the Fort Bridges' saddler, and featured fifty loops to hold the heavy metallic .50 caliber cartridges used by the soldiers.

Mills reported on the use of the belt in an 1866 issue of the *Army-Navy Journal*, describing the belt, and its comfort when worn around the soldier's waist. The unit appeared to hold enough cartridges

efficiently. Mills applied for and received the first of a series of U.S. patents for the ammunition belt.

The War Department was finally beginning to respond to the complaints of the military regarding ammunition transport, and began to look at other ways to handle cartridges. The old tin-lined leather boxes had been designed for paper cartridges, and while the Department wasn't totally sold on the concept of looped belts and the exposure that cartridges would get from inclement weather, they were ready to look at some changes. It should be noted that there was a large number of ammunition boxes, left from the Civil War, still in inventory. As expected, the Department would have preferred to be able to use the equipment already on hand. Explaining the large surplus to Congress during the economically depressed Reconstruction period probably represented some "downside risk" to somebody's career. Some things just don't change.

So, the military slowly developed their options and time passed. In 1872, the Ordnance was still considering options and time was still passing. The Department continued to experiment with modifications of the old style cartridge box.

The "Life Preserver" consisted of a number of old cap boxes strung around the waist.

They lined the boxes with sheepskin. They added wooden blocks drilled to hold the new cartridges. Paper boxes were tried, with different modes of packing the shells, along with canvas loops coated with shellac and sewn inside the boxes in double rows. Many of these innovations carried the names of the inventor: the Dwyer pouch, the McKeever box, the Hagner box. None were particularly successful.

To be honest, the frontier troops weren't completely satisfied with their new looped belts, either. The copper cartridges reacted with the acids left on the leather from tanning and produced a green

verdigris that caused the shells to stick in the belt, preventing quick easy loading. Sometimes this residue made the shell hard to eject from the weapon after firing as well. Some improvements were needed.

To remedy this, troops under General Nelson A. Miles covered the leather loops with canvas flaps attached to the belt. These belts were used for some time: a number are preserved in the Custer Battlefield Museum as trophies when they were taken from the battlefield.

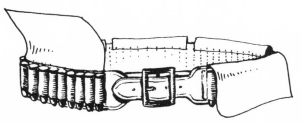

The "Fair Weather Christian Belt" with flaps covering cartridges in sections.

Ordnance was still considering options in the early 1870s although the number of modifications that anyone could think of for the ammunition boxes still sitting in inventory was dwindling. One more method of using the boxes was tried and was somewhat successful. A number of the boxes was attached to a belt and placed evenly around the body, distributing the weight more evenly and making it more comfortable. This concoction could carry forty rounds of ammunition weighing about five pounds. Military men knew that excess weight, even as important as ammunition, would be dropped by soldiers on a long march, even at the risk of punishment. The long march, and the chafing and aching caused by excess weight, made soldiers brave enough to drop the weights despite threats from their superiors. Forty rounds of ammo, at that time, were felt to be enough for almost any circumstance.

Another design that appears to have surfaced in 1874 combined a pouch suitable for carrying forty rounds of carbine shells, with two sets of double loops that would slide into the most efficient position. The front loops held twelve rifle shells and the

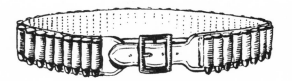

The "Prairie Belt"

back held an additional eight. A smaller pouch—one of those leftover Civil War cap boxes, actually—was to hold pistol ammo. The sliding loop system was designed by Colonel William B. Hazen of the 6th Infantry and named for him.

The Ordnance Board of 1874, like their previous numbers, was better at considering options than solving problems. Redesigned boxes—design after design—were submitted and rejected. Vests designed to hold cartridges were submitted and rejected. Mills submitted his latest design for looped belts at every equipment board organized to solve the ammunition supply problem between 1866 and 1876, and each design was rejected without a favorable comment from any board member. While the Board sat, commented, and rejected, the cavalry and infantry on active service against the Indians tossed the regulation boxes into any convenient ravine and fabricated a version of a looped belt. It was, after all, a matter of life and limb.

Years had rolled by since Mills' first design, and he continued to improve his designs and refine his materials. In his autobiography entitled *My Story*, he writes of his struggle and the patience of his wife, Hannah: "I purchased foot-powered lathes, drills, etc., to develop models of my various belts and equipment. I installed them in one of her best rooms in each succeeding one of perhaps twenty posts, soiling the carpets . . . with grease and shavings, which would have driven most wives mad."

A bit of a break occurred in 1876, when a team of Ordnance Inspectors actually visited the Indian Territory and fighters under the commands of Generals Terry and Crook. The Ordnance Team noted that the looped belts were being used exclusively, and that the general issue ammo boxes were disdained by the soldiers. The team reported that it was impossible to compel the soldier on the frontier to

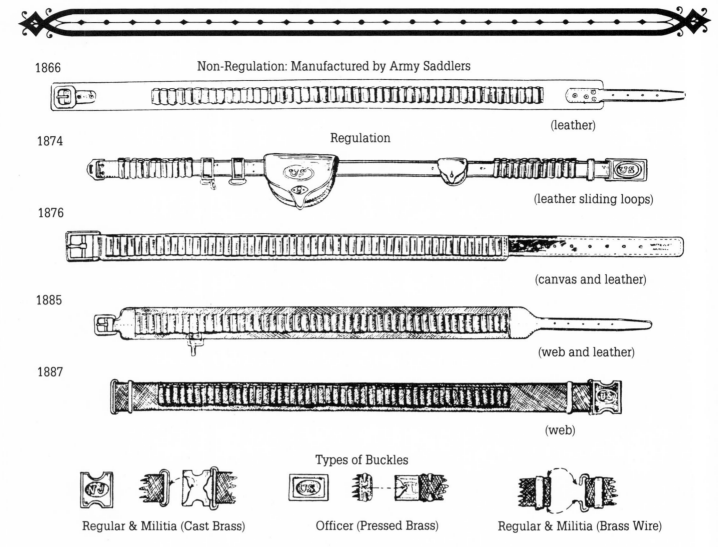

1866   Non-Regulation: Manufactured by Army Saddlers

(leather)

1874   Regulation

(leather sliding loops)

1876

(canvas and leather)

1885

(web and leather)

1887

(web)

Types of Buckles

Regular & Militia (Cast Brass)   Officer (Pressed Brass)   Regular & Militia (Brass Wire)

The Looped Cartridge Belt and Its Adaption by the U.S. Army

Courtesy Company of Military Historians

keep the regulation boxes after using the looped belts. The Ordnance Department looked foolish in the eyes of the soldiers, reported the team. The Board, not wishing to look foolish finally recommended that looped belts be manufactured and issued to replace the boxes. After approval by the Chief of Ordnance, thirty thousand sewn canvas belts were fabricated at Watervliet Arsenal.

Shortly after the first issue of these canvas belts, a more advanced model designed by Anson Mills was accepted by the Chief of Ordnance. The belt was a woven web design with space for fifty .47-70 cartridges, and was covered by a U.S. patent, and was to be made by Mills' own company. It was now 1878.

The next year saw more of the Mills' cartridge belts

manufactured. These belts—7509 of them—were made on hand looms at the time. While Mills probably did not personally "hand in" the warp, it is probable that the experience of the eight-year-old Mills must have had an impact on his methods. A means to mass-produce the web was soon to follow. In 1885, a gray, woven belt featuring either forty-five or fifty loops, fitted with a leather strap and buckle was adopted as the official cavalry belt. This, and earlier canvas types, were replaced by completely woven web models with fifty loops by the late 1880s.

Weaponry continued to develop, and the Spanish American War saw a move away from the .45-70 Springfield "charcoal burners" with their puff of smoke to mark the soldier's position to the enemy to

the U.S. Magazine Rifle Model 1892, Krag-Jorgensen. The .30 caliber bolt action rifle, complete with knife bayonet and top barrel covered with wood to serve as a hand guard, used smokeless powder and accommodated five smaller cartridges. This meant another change in the cartridge belt, and Mills' factory was expanded to produce a thousand belts a day to equip the soldiers.

Mills was appointed brigadier general in 1897, and retired from active duty to run the factory and continue improving the various items. The factory was expanded rapidly to meet the demands for the new belt, and the now full-time businessman Mills devoted his best energy to the best design possible.

Sometimes opportunities that seem golden are less so. The mercifully short war (April to August, 1898) was less than merciful to Mills. He reported that the rapid termination of the war "put us in a practically bankrupt condition, a hundred thousand belts on hand and no market for them and a large indebtedness." Some of the belts were sold to two Canadian regiments preparing to leave for the Boer War, and by June 1901, orders were received for equipping three thousand British troops as well. Rescued from economic ruin, Mills accepted a post as the American member of the International Boundary Commission, a group that settled cases between the United States and Mexico. In 1905, his fortune assured, Mills sold his interest in the manufacturing firm, while continuing to collect royalties for his many patents.

Although Mills was retired from active service, his every day involvement with manufacturing the belts, the U.S.—and time—marched on apace. The belt was again redesigned for use with the U.S. Springfield Magazine rifle Model 1903. The gun and belt accompanied the Doughboys into Flanders and beyond during their first engagement on European soil. Internationally known as the "Gun of Glory" it also saw service in World War II until it was replaced by the equally famous Garand M1 rifle. Now a single weapon replaced the combination of rifle and carbine, modeled after the German Mauser.

With the advent of the Springfield Model 1903, five-shot, clip-fed rifle, the cartridge belt once again underwent a total re-designing. The Model 1910 webbed cartridge belt for .30 caliber was referred to

as the Mills Infantry (dismounted) Belt, having ten pockets, two clips in each, totaling 100 rounds. Thomas C. Orndorff and Anson Mills invented and developed the first webbed cartridge belt with only nine pockets, each pocket contained four clips, totaling 180 cartridges. When filled, these belts averaged ten pounds in weight so it was necessary to attach shoulder straps to help support the added weight. However, the ten pocket was favored and soon adopted by Ordnance.

Mills also manufactured much of the marching equipment with no leather appearing in the entire outfit. Knapsack, haversack, and canteen covers were almost entirely of tightly woven waterproof webbing. This equipment was exclusively used in the Army, Navy and in British service. Buttons fashioned with the spread eagle design, of brass or dull finished bronze were earlier models. Accompanying this belt was the Model 1910 first aid packet, attached to the cartridge belt front. The Model 1905 bayonet with wood grips, was manufactured at the Springfield Armory and the Rock Island Arsenal. A bayonet scabbard was of olive drab webbing with a leather tip.

Anson Mills lived in Washington from 1894 until his death in November, 1924. The Indiana farm boy with the peaceful Quaker heritage, commented in later years about his accomplishments: "I only regret that they (his newly perfected equipment) were not designed for construction . . . but, rather for destruction."

Leather equipment throughout the world was to be replaced by Mills' web ammunition carriers and its accompanying web equipment, a new innovation in military turnover.

Source:
U.S. Muskets, Rifles and Carbines, Col. Gluckman
U.S. Firearms, Hicks
Ordnance Memoranda No. 11, No. 13 (1872)
Ordnance Memoranda No. 18, No. 19 (1874)
Ordnance Memoranda No. 29 (1874)
Ordnance Memoranda, Horse and Cavalry Accoutrements (1891)
My Story, Anton Mills (private printing)
Instructions for Assembling the Infantry Equipment, Model 1910
The McKeever Box in the Regular Army, Schornak (Vol. XV, No. 3 Fall, Journal of the Military Collectors and Historians)
The Book of Rifles, Smith
The Book of Pistols and Revolvers, Smith
Dictionary of American Biography, Vol VII, C. Scribners Sons
The National Cyclopedia of American Biography, Vol. X

The 1874 Manual of the Saber (Dismounted)

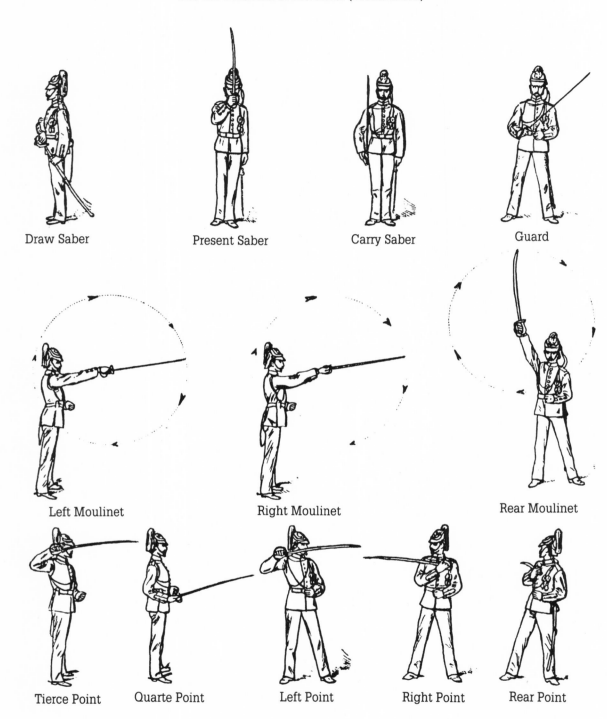

Draw Saber   Present Saber   Carry Saber   Guard

Left Moulinet   Right Moulinet   Rear Moulinet

Tierce Point   Quarte Point   Left Point   Right Point   Rear Point

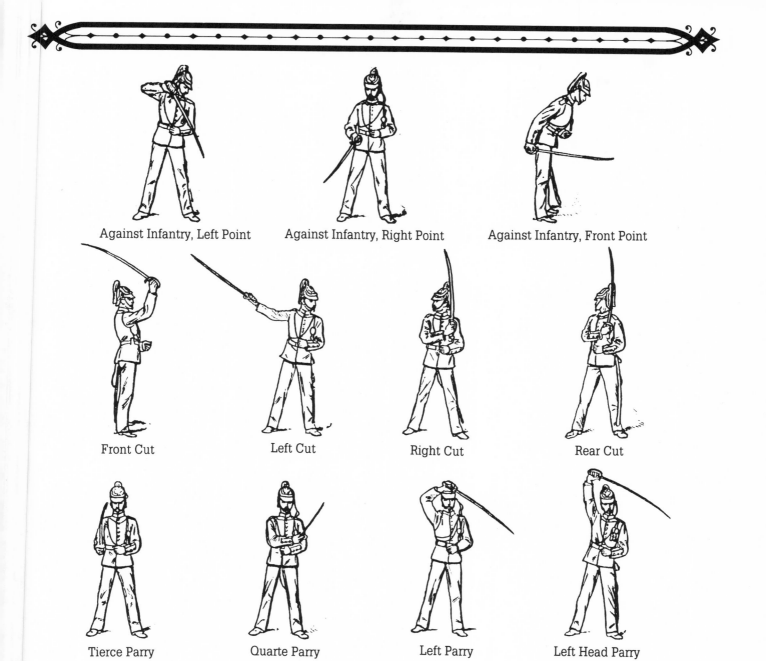

Against Infantry, Left Point   Against Infantry, Right Point   Against Infantry, Front Point

Front Cut   Left Cut   Right Cut   Rear Cut

Tierce Parry   Quarte Parry   Left Parry   Left Head Parry

Right Head Parry   Against Infantry, Left Parry   Against Infantry, Right Parry

U.S. Military Disassembly Tools

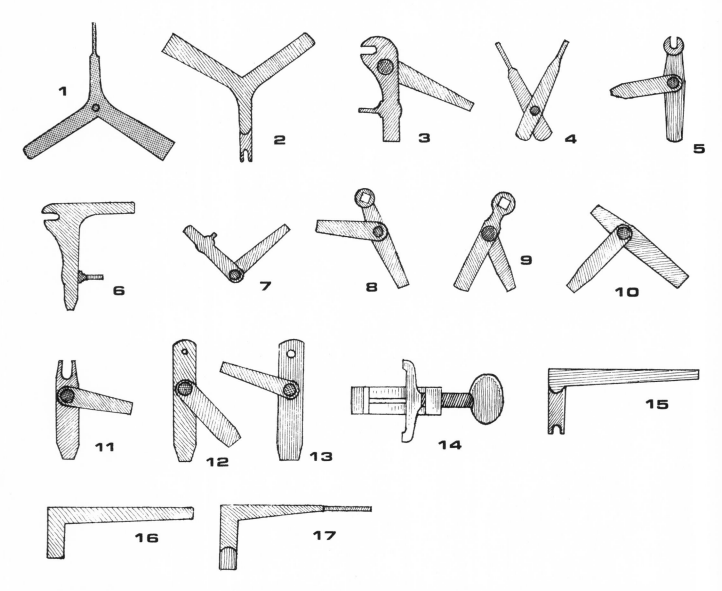

Since about 1835, the United States government issued very small, compact, disassembly tools with each weapon, most of which could be carried in a soldier's pocket, cartridge box, or stored in the butt of a rifle. These tools were a combination of nipple wrenches, screwdrivers, pin punches, and spring depressors. The tools were originally designed to be used with one particular weapon. One tool was almost universal in use. Excellent steel was used in the manufacturing of these tools—never iron—as strength was of the utmost importance. There are seventeen illustrations listed here which were most

common and useful to the solider in the field. There are many more variations that were issued. However, due to the limited amount of space, we have chosen the following with a description for each one.

There are some Army, Navy surplus stores that still have these later period tools available for only a few dollars each. As these tools have not caught the eye of collectors, many can still be purchased at gun shows and flea markets.

Sources:
The American Rifleman, March, 1963
Francis Bannerman catalogs.

1. Combination of two screwdrivers and a pin punch for a Hall flintlock Model 1837.

2. Essentially the same as No. 1, except the pin punch is replaced a nipple wrench.

3. Screwdriver, pin punch, and mainspring wrench for the Springfield breechloading rifle Model 1879.

4. Tumbler and band spring punch for .58 caliber rifled muskets and later the .50 and .45 caliber rifles.

5,8,9. Two screwdrivers and a nipple wrench. This was the main tool carried in the field during the Civil War for most muskets.

6. A variation of the Model 1879 tool, (similar to No. 3) only having better leverage.

7. Krag Jorgensen .30 caliber tool, with two screwdrivers and a pin punch.

10,12,13. Three bladed screwdrivers, issued in numerous variation to armorers since 1835, with a few still in service.

11. A rare Civil War musket tool which did not see as much service as the others, probably because of the poor metal which became brittle and chipped when pressure was applied.

14. Armorer's tool for disassembling locks, a spring vise which consisted of two jaws closed by a thumb screw. Used from the mid-1830s until about 1900 when the .45-70 rifle was dropped from service. This was not a soldier's issued item.

15. Screwdriver and nipple wrench for Colt's patent Model 1851 and 1860 revolvers.

16. Two bladed screwdriver for use with U.S. .38 caliber revolvers. Still used in government armories for other arms, as can No. 17.

17. Screwdriver and pin punch for .45 pistol Model 1911.

The Development of Infantry Accoutrements

(Reprinted with permission from *Guns Magazine*)

It is undoubtedly true that the best training for war is war. During the early battles of this country, young and ever-confident soldiers contributed much toward changes in their accoutrements (trappings or equipment) because of necessity. Cumbersome bullet pouches, heavy with lead ball, unevenly distributed on shoulder or waist belts made it difficult for the professional soldier to manipulate in the field of battle. There was nothing picturesque about the early American infantryman with the entanglement of leather straps and bullet pouches, as he accomplished more through threat then he achieved in actual battle.

During this arduous period, the antiquated Ordnance Department was bombarded with suggestions for new techniques and alterations from officers returning from the field. However, meager appropriations made it impossible to completely forget the serviceable equipment on hand. Until the supply was exhausted, the board of officers could not meet again and consider such changes. Only a severe changeover in weapons and cartridges would alter any modifications in accoutrements.

There were few professional soldiers among the vast growing ranks during the Revolution. Some had gained a little military training by drilling in militia

companies; some fought against Indians and French. Military experience was lacking. Men balked at discipline and resented commands; " . . . they regarded an officer no more than a broomstick, . . ." General Washington explained. Uniformed regiments were seldom found in the army; frontier buckskin hunting suits and everyday clothes were worn. Not until 1778, when a shipload of brown and blue uniform coats arrived from France, did the American soldiers dress alike. Crossed cartridge box and bayonet belts were generally accepted by 1774. Interesting to note, no particular cartridge box was standard issue, although in 1776 a standard box was attempted. At first cartridges were carried loose, much to the discomfort of the rifleman finding ball and loose powder at the bottom of the box from constant jarring. Wooden inserts made of maple or beech were added, bored with twenty to thirty holes and large enough to slip a single paper cartridge in and out. When filled, the box might weigh five or six pounds. Special troops and mounted men frequently carried cartridge boxes on the front of the waist belt, usually in a smaller variety. These boxes were nothing more than a large leather flap nailed on the back of a wooden block with wide shoulder straps added. Actually, the American troops were often equipped with cartridge boxes much worse than those described. A pick and brush (fastened together on one cord) were attached to the shoulder sling as an aid to keep the touch hole open and pan clean on the rifle. It is well to note that the powder horn and flask did not disappear entirely because of the cartridge box.

Shoulder belts were prevalent among American forces. A double frog attached to these belts carried a sword for the officer and a bayonet for the enlisted man; however, the soldier was not usually required to have both. (Less than half of the American soldiers were equipped with bayonets.) These belts were subject to variations. Since the tomahawk was a popular weapon in the wilderness, belts were crudely fashioned for them, but they were not a standard regulation. Incredible as it may seem, no flints were produced in America at this time; all flints found in this country were of the European style. On July 18, 1775, the Continental Congress recom-

mended the militia of various states be furnished twelve flints per company. Bullet molds were not usually considered as a part of the personal equipment of the soldier. Gang molds were preferred for military purposes, with as many as twelve bullets on one side and as many buckshot as possible on the other. One mold for every eighty muskets was recommended; however, it was common practice for the riflemen to obtain their own personal molds.

The first official U.S. military musket was the Charleville musket, a weapon of the French army. The Marquis de Lafayette arranged for the shipment of a large supply at the cost of five dollars apiece. There were seventeen different models from 1717 to 1777. The model used during the American Revolution was the model 1763, a .69 caliber rifle with a 44-inch barrel, weighing around ten pounds. After the Revolution, the Springfield Armory was established and manufacture of these smoothbores began in 1795. These were called U.S. Musket, Model 1795, which remained the standard weapon for years to come. The Brown Bess was principally the soldiers' infantry weapon until about 1778.

In 1812 the United States, for a second time, went to war with Great Britain. Nearly three years later, after suffering a series of bitter defeats, the U.S. managed to win. Uniformity began to show in the soldiers' accoutrements—especially in cartridge boxes. This box, made of leather, contained a wooden block bored with holes of a suitable diameter to contain the cartridges to be carried, and a huge leather flap tended to keep out the elements. This box held approximately twenty-six to twenty-nine paper cartridges. A similar box, although small, was contracted 1808 and saw much service in the militia. Embossed on the leather flap was an oval with the letters "US" on either side of an eagle bearing a shield, olive branch, and arrows. A wreath surrounding the oval also made up a border around the inside edges. Above the oval, a ribbon bearing the motto "E PLURIBUS UNUM" appeared. This box continued in service until the early 1840s , when the arrival of the Model 1842 percussion musket necessitated a reduction in overall dimensions. Among several principal weapons that served the American troops during the War of 1812 was the Springfield Model

1808. With a 44½–inch barrel and a .69 caliber bore, it ranked as the second official United States arm made at the Springfield Armory.

Since the foot soldier cannot be expected to carry additional tools to break down his weapon, he was issued a small, compact disassembly tool, which could be carried in a pocket, stored in the butt of the rifle, or carried in a separate pouch in the cartridge box. This became a standard issue about 1835, and consisted of one or more of four main parts—screwdrivers, spring depressors, pin punches, nipple wrench—principally designed to be used for one particular arm. With the advent of the single shot percussion pistol in 1842, the first military saddle holster appeared on the scene. Flintlock, percussion pistols, as well as Colt Dragoon revolvers were issued in pairs to mounted officers. Twin holsters carried the pistols fastened securely across the saddle pommel forward of the user's thighs. These box-like holsters were made of heavy black bridle leather with brass studs to fasten the huge top flaps. Some were fitted with a brass cup covering at the bottom, and an additional pocket under the flap to carry percussion caps and balls.

In January, 1846, President Polk ordered American troops into territory claimed by Mexico, and on April 25, American and Mexican soldiers exchanged fire and the seemingly inevitable territorial war with Mexico began. Despite the fact that the new percussion cap system was a tremendous advancement, the military was slow to accept it. There were several reasons for this. First, the military generally maintained a reactionary attitude toward the adoption of anything new. Secondly, the adversaries of the percussion system claimed that soldiers would be likely to drop or lose the caps and hence be defenseless in battle. It would make all military flintlocks obsolete and eventually thousand of arms would have to be converted. However, buyers of civilian arms were quick to recognize the advantage of the new percussion caps, even though the military did not.

In 1842, the U.S. Army had officially abandoned the flintlock, converting many of the Model 1831 muskets to percussion. The Mexicans were worse armed; they used the clumsy Brown Bess musket which Britain had used against the U.S. in 1776 and 1812, and had recently sold to Mexico. Relatively few regiments of U.S. Volunteers carried percussion rifles, which they performed creditably on occasion. The Jeff Davis Mississippi Rifles won such fame that their weapons were promptly christened "Mississippi Rifle." It was equipped with a bayonet—but still too slow to load and quick to foul. The U.S. percussion musket model 1842 (.69 caliber), was first issued at the front during the Mexican War, and it is claimed that some of the soldiers refused the new rifles, favoring their old flintlocks. With the advent of the new percussion musket, leather cartridge boxes took on another change in appearance. The U.S. Rifleman's outfit model 1841, patterned after the Kentucky riflemen's bag, was designed for the model 1841 Mississippi Rifle. Accompanying the pouch was a powder flask, stamped with an infantry bugle and labeled "Public Property." Cartridge boxes resulting from the changeover of firearms to percussion now contained two tin liners, each large enough to accommodate two packages of ten cartridges each—a total of forty rounds in the cartridge box. The huge leather flap was embellished with an oval brass plate and the letters "U.S." On the carrying strap or shoulder strap, in addition, was affixed a round brass plate, embossed with an eagle. A further reduction in caliber required boxes to become small, though the trappings of the boxes remained unchanged. After a few minor improvements, this box was later classified as the model 1855 cartridge box; for the percussion caps, a model 1855 cap pouch was introduced. This pouch had lamb's wool lining within and a vent clean-out tool (nipple pick).

The Civil War, in a sense, was the first modern war that used repeating rifles, metallic cartridges, and telescopic sights. Northern arms manufacturers such as Remington, Colt, and Henry turned out quantities of rifles, pistols, carbines, howitzers, and mortars. In the first days of the war, Yankee volunteers marched into battle carrying antiquated muskets and various types of European rifles. Except for arms made at the Tredegar plant in Richmond and another in Selma, Alabama, most Southern ordnance was purchased in Europe. The South never adopted a standard shoulder weapon although the British-made .577

Enfield muzzle-loading rifle was most prevalent among Southern troops. The United States Rifle-Musket 1861 was designed as the result of dissatisfaction with the Model 1855 tape lock musket, which in service was not satisfactory. The Maynard tape primer was unreliable for general service, and by recommendation of the Ordnance Board, the military returned to the ordinary percussion cap method of ignition. A patch box was recommended for this model, but due to the onset of the Civil War (production began about the same time) the patch box was eliminated to speed up production and reduce costs.

The infantry cartridge pouch of the Civil War was much the same in appearance as that of the Model 1855 box, with only a few modifications. This box was almost universally used by both Northern and Southern armies throughout the Civil War. Because of the wartime shortage of brass, the newly manufactured boxes were altered slightly by dropping the oval brass U.S. plate and substituting an embossed oval with U.S. on the flap. This box could be used with the shoulder sling or it could be suspended from the belt. Two separate tin inserts, each one with a lower division, open in front, and two upper divisions, contained a bundle of ten cartridges and the other four cartridges. Double flapped, with an implement-pocket sewn to the front of the box the complete box was made of black bridle leather, and to the accompanying shoulder sling was affixed a round brass plate with an eagle. The cap-pouch, made of black bridle leather and lined with sheepskin, was styled after the 1855 model. A steel wire cone-pick with a ring handle was carried.

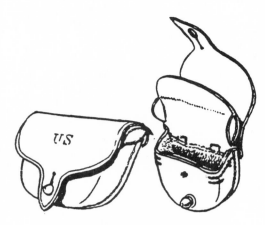

B. Model 1874 pistol cartridge pouch

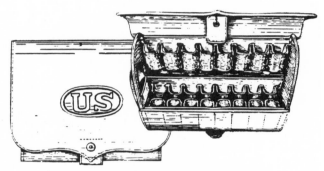

C. Model 1872 Infantry Box—Hagner #1

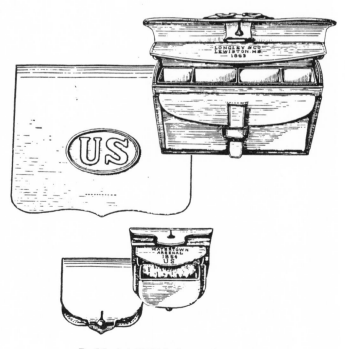

D. Model 1855 Infantry Box

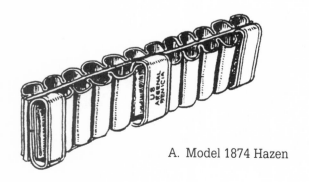

A. Model 1874 Hazen

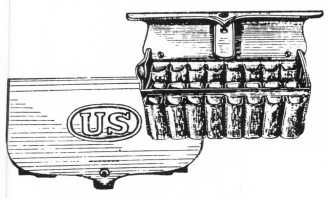

E. 1872 Infantry Box—Hagner #2

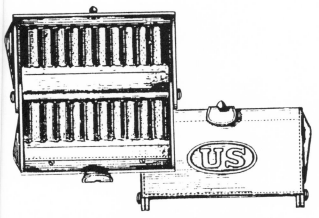

F. Dyer's pouch for cavalry—1874

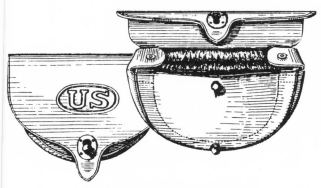

G. U.S. McKeever for .45-70 and .30-40s.

Most military muskets and rifles were equipped with either a socket or saber bayonet, depending on make or model. All U.S. regulation rifles and muskets except the Model 1841, 1855, and Remington 1863 rifle used the socket bayonet. Cavalrymen, during the Civil War, carried their percussion weapons butt forward on the right side; on their left hung the saber.

During conflict, the right hand could draw either saber or pistol, while the left hand controlled the reins of the horse. Infantry officers and Cavalry troops carried the oval-flap holster for percussion pistols. Included with his equipment, the infantryman carried a combination tool, open-end nipple wrench, and two screwdrivers. With the adoption of the Spencer rifle toward the end of the war years, the Blakeslee patent cartridge box was issued. Containing ten tinned tubes, each holding seven cartridges, it was most useful, and the quickest loading device ever seen.

Four years of war had tempered the army of the United States and ranked her a great military and fighting force. Admired by European military men, the campaigns were required study by foreign staff colleagues—but before the smoke of the last great battles had time to clear, old veterans picked up their arms once more to deal with a new and skillfully maneuvering foe, the American Indian. Throughout the Civil War, fighting on the frontier had never ceased; and after the end of the Confederacy, the military's task was doubled with the great migration to the West. Broken treaties, thievery by Indian agents, and whiskey-peddling, gun-selling traders added more kindling to the fire. Now, more than ever, tribes sought to bar the white man's path across the continent and fought a savage war for survival.

The army was dissatisfied with the Model 1870 and the performance of the .50-70 cartridge. In 1872 the Ordnance Board was satisfied with .45-70, a ballistic alteration over the old .50-70, and developed the new Springfield "trapdoor" Model 1873. Two models succeeded the Springfield Model '73 "trapdoor" in the .45-70 caliber—models of 1884 and 1889—until the adoption of the Krag in 1892. The infantry was furnished with two leather cartridge boxes; pattern 1872 Type 1, holding twenty-four cartridges and carrying a tool in a side compartment, and Type 2, pattern 1872, holding the same amount of shells but smaller in size. Both boxes were suspended from the belt with the aid of a "Brace Yoke," but this system was practiced only if both boxes were worn providing a total of forty-eight rounds of ammunition. Otherwise, a single cartridge box (No. 1) could be worn alone (during drills or

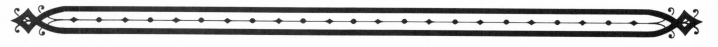

INDIAN WAR
1876

Much of the serviceable equipment left over from the Civil War was used extensively on campaigns in the West. Shown here are some of these left-overs with alterations made for the Cavalry from 1874–1877.

A. Springfield Carbine, Model 70. .50 caliber. Saw much action in the early 1870s. Soon a newer model, the 1873, was offered and served through the Custer fight.

B. Colt Single Action Army revolver. Issued to the cavalry in 1874.

C. Black leather saber belt, with rectangular brass plate bearing U.S. coat of arms and German silver wreath, as described in 1861 Ordnance manual.

D. The .45 caliber cartridges used in the guns of the era. The .45 Colt for the revolver, and the .45-70 for the carbine.

E. Dyer pattern cartridge pouch, issued in 1874. Carried on the belt, it held 40 cartridges. Wool lined.

F. Carbine sling of Civil War Patterns, 2½″ wide. Slung over the shoulder, and attached to ring on carbine swivel bar.

G. Pistol holster of Civil War pattern.

H. Issue pistol cartridge pouch, altered from a Civil War percussion cap box.

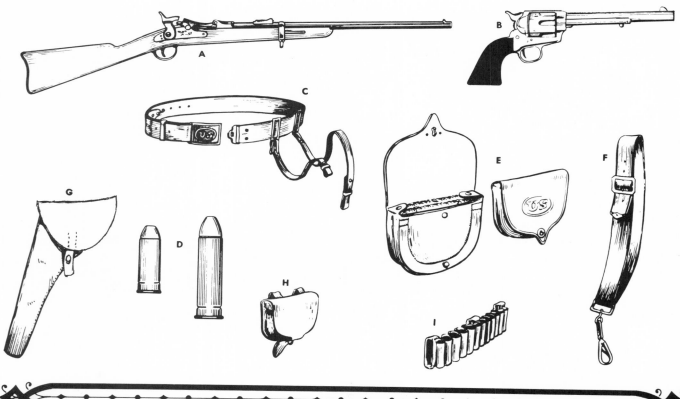

garrison duty), sufficiently supported by the waist belt and placed either in front or behind. On the front flap of both 1872 patterns was embossed the U.S. oval. The loops for holding the cartridges were constructed from cloth strips shellacked to some degrees of stiffness and sewn to the inside of the box in three rows (eight loops to a row).

Between 1866 and 1880, hundreds of cartridge boxes were submitted for trial by the army. A great many of them were used and adopted for issue on an experimental basis and then discarded. Few boxes that were used by the Army were made anywhere other than at the arsenals. (However, during the Civil War, it was necessary to contract them out.) The "Half Moon" Dwyer pattern cartridge pouch issued in 1874, held forty cartridges, and was lambs wool-lined, carried on the belt. Modified from the original pattern of the early 1870s, it was then carried on the shoulder sling by mounted companies, and although several other types of pouches were used, the Dwyer pattern seemed to be the favorite. On the front flap was the usual U.S. oval.

Keeping company with the Colt Model 1873 Army revolver was the black leather holster from the Civil War with its wide semi-circular flap. This holster was designed with a belt loop to accommodate the

regulation belt of 1.9 inches wide. A large loop on back of the same pattern holster was designed for looped cartridge belts, of the Mills patent, and was not accepted by the army until 1878. In 1881, a two-hole half flap holster was designed for the 1873 Colt and Smith and Wesson Schofield revolvers, and manufactured at Rock Island Arsenal. Most popular of cartridge boxes to come out of the transition period of the 1870s was the McKeever pattern. This box was to be in continuous service for some thirty-six years with the regular army, and can still be found in use by the guards as standard dress equipment at the Arlington National Cemetery. With the Springfield breech-loading rifles, the combination tool designated "Model 1879" was issued. It has a screwdriver, pin punch, mainspring cramp, and a secondary screwdriver riveted to the tool, and was made only at the Springfield Armory.

As early as 1876, the importance of the cartridge belt was realized. During the hardest of campaigns, the black leather cartridge boxes were too slow in supplying shells for the new breechloading rifles. The soldier on the Western frontier was quick to remedy this fault by copying the ammunition belts from the civilian scouts attached to the frontier posts. The scouts and frontiersmen devised a method of

This "Prairie Belt" was both leather and looped webbing. Some of the soldiers carried their ammunition upside down. They claimed it was easier to push a shell down and pull it out—much quicker then pulling up and then out.

Author's Collection

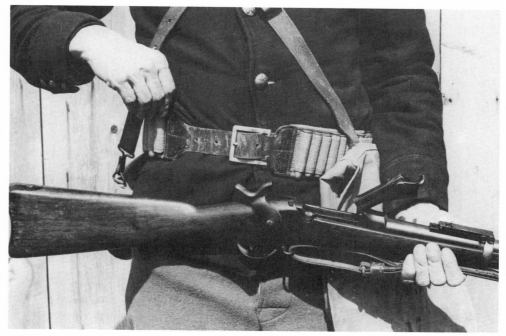

putting their cartridge within easy reach by fabricating homemade leather belts with loops to hold their revolver and rifle ammunition. Captain Anson Mills devised a method to manufacture a woven web ammunition carrier, which for a number of years was rejected by the Army. Finally, in 1878, after years of pleading, Mills succeeded in getting the Army to accept his newly-perfected woven belt which carried fifty .45–70 cartridges. The government arsenals did not produce these belts; instead they were purchased from contractors. Leather equipment throughout the world was to be replaced by web ammunition carriers and its accompanying web equipment, a new innovation in military technology.

In the 1880s web belts came into fashion, and these belts were used in the field during the Spanish-American War of 1898 and the subsequent Philippine Insurrection and still is in use today. The war between Spain and the United States was of short duration, mainly because the Spanish Army lacked discipline, training, and leadership. Although Spanish troops out-numbered U.S. troops in the field and were armed with excellent German-made Mauser rifles, the average Spanish soldier had never been properly trained in the use or care. Many Americans still carried the old-fashioned Springfield Model 1884 trapdoor rifle—a cumbersome weapon that fired black powder cartridges, belching a white cloud of smoke and giving away the position of a soldier. The forces of Regulars and Militia that stormed ashore in Cuba in 1898 were not trained for jungle fighting. There was a shortage of everything the men needed, including the accoutrements for the weapons. Still, U.S. training won the day.

The .45–70 Springfield "charcoal burners" were finally replaced by the U.S. Magazine Rifle Model 1892, Krag-Jorgensen, caliber .30, a bolt action, with a knife bayonet. It held five cartridges and was the first U. S. rifle with a wood handguard covering the top of the barrel. This was also the first rifle to use smokeless powder and a reduced caliber cartridge. The smaller cartridge allowed the doubling of the number of loops on a belt by establishing a second row superimposed on the first. A single row loop belt, depending on length, forty-five to fifty loops, for the .45–70 and .30 caliber were manufactured.

Bandoliers for both calibers and of similar patterns were produced in dark blue, gray, and tan—Kackee or Cook-ee called by some British units in North and South Africa (a Hindu word meaning dust color "Khaki"). The trend toward Khaki had led to the introduction of brown colored fatigue clothing and webbed equipment during the Spanish-American War. All web cartridge belts were not fixed with the brass U.S. (or Militia plate) belt buckle; they could be unfastened and worn without.

The first U.S. knife-type bayonet was used with the Krag rifle. Two other bayonets were used on the 1896 and 1898 models; they were called Bolo bayonets. One was shaped after the old Bowie. The Bowie and Bolo bayonets were experimental; used in the Philippines unsuccessfully, they were soon dropped.

The New York cavalrymen used a black leather

Jim Nemeth poses as an Indian War Soldier in the complete uniform of the 1880s.

SPANISH AMERICAN WAR
1898

The Spanish American War was the ideal sanctuary for fakers, bunco-artists, highwaymen, bank robbers and murderers. The Army enlisted anyone physically able to carry a rifle and never inquired into a man's background. The forces of Regulars and Militia who stormed ashore in Cuba in 1898 were not trained for jungle fighting. Many were overcome by the intense heat and others fell with malaria. Hospital tents swelled with feverish soldiers, greater in numbers than their wounded comrades who fell in battle. There was a shortage of everything the men needed, including accouterments, ammunition and weapons. At the beginning of the war, troops were armed with the antiquated pumpkin roller, the .45 caliber trap-door Springfield rifle. Each time a soldier fired his rifle, a cloud of white smoke would belch from the muzzle of the weapon, revealing his hiding place to enemy snipers. However, with the introduction of the .30/.40 Krag-Jorgensen rifle, which used smokeless-powder ammunition, our soldiers had a decided advantage over the enemy, and their capable marksmanship with these rifles proved to be both deadly and efficient.

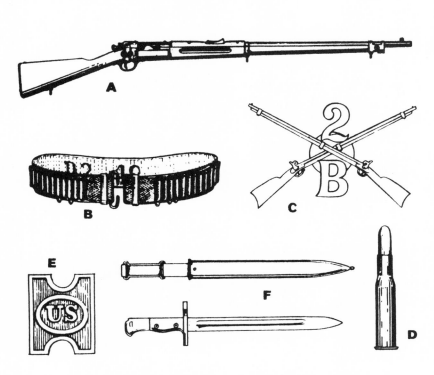

A. U.S. Rifle Model 1892, the Krag-Jorgensen. The first U.S. regulation rifle to use smokeless powder ammo in reduced caliber.

B. Mills cartridge belt, adopted in 1878 as an improvement over the old hand-sewn belts which were unsatisfactory.

C. Cartridge .30 caliber U.S. or .30–40 Krag, using a 220 grain patched bullet.

C. Dress chevron worn as cap ornament by enlisted infantrymen.

D. Cartridge, .30 caliber U.S. or .30–40 Krag, using a 220 grain patched bullet.

E. U.S. Army brass buckle for web loop cartridge belt.

F. Krag bayonet patterned after the Swiss Model 1889 knife bayonet. Shown with scabbard.

Art by E.L. Reedstrom

Sources: The Rough Riders, New American Library, by Teddy Roosevelt. San Juan Hill, Random House, by Will Henry (1962).

half-flap holster for the Colt .38 caliber, double-action revolver. Stamped "N.Y." within an oval, the holster was carried on the right side with the revolver butt forward, with a twelve-round leather cartridge pouch worn on the belt. It should be noted that the first successful webbed belt accepted by the army was the Mills Pattern of 1887, blue or gray color, featuring forty-five loops, single row, for the .45–70 cartridge, with the U.S. brass buckle and a steel bayonet scabbard attached to a swivel frog.

The combination tool for the .30 caliber Krag came with two screwdrivers and a pin punch, riveted together at the head end of each. This tool was issued with the rifle and carried in the butt stock on later models, stamped "U.S." on the pin punch blade.

The United States entered the First World War in the spring of 1917. During the gigantic troop movements, the Doughboys experienced a nightmare of tanks, automobiles, horses, artillery, supply wagons, and endless lines of troop movements. Added to their discomfort was the weather, for rain beat down on "tin hats" giving a man a pounding headache. Hobnailed boots weighing four pounds each worked blisters on tired feet. Olive-drab uniforms spattered with mud, and an entangled arrangement of heavy equipment on his back: that was the fighting infantryman.

The U.S. Magazine rifle Model 1903, caliber .30, was suitably used for both infantry and cavalry, eliminating the long standard combination of rifle and carbine. The basic design for this rifle was taken from the German Mauser. Internationally known as the "Gun of Glory," it saw service through World War I and World War II until it was replaced by the equally famous Garand M1 rifle. Both weapons were designed by the Springfield Armory. With the advent of the Springfield, Model 1903, five-shot clip-fed rifle, the cartridge belt once again underwent a total redesign. The Model 1910 webbed cartridge belt for .30 caliber was referred to as the Mills Infantry (dismounted) Belt, having ten pockets, two clips in each, totaling 100 rounds. Thomas C. Orndorff and Anson Mills invented and developed the first webbed cartridge belt with only nine pockets; each pocket contained four clips, totaling 180 cartridges.

When filled, these belts averaged ten pounds in weight, so it was necessary to attach shoulder straps to help support the added weight. However, the ten-pocket was favored and soon adopted by Ordnance. Mills also manufactured much of the marching equipment with no leather appearing in the entire outfit. Knapsack, haversack, and canteen were almost entirely made of tightly woven waterproof webbing. This equipment was used almost exclusively by the Army, Navy, and in the British service. Accompanying this belt was the Model 1910 first aid packet, hooked to cartridge belt front.

The Model 1905 bayonet with wood grips was manufactured as the Springfield Armory and the Rock Island Arsenal. A bayonet scabbard was of tan webbing with a leather tip.

It is not surprising that the interest created by the evolution of this country's fighting man, his tools of war, and how he used them can be traced from one battle to another; however, it is surprising how the infantry man survived these medieval-type clashes with antiquated weapons and equipment when our enemies were better equipped in most cases.

The fighting man today is better equipped and better trained than ever before. The war tools and weaponry of our contemporary armies now include a large degree of individual specialization. However, with all the bewildering array of complex and organized gadgets, the destiny of any future war will be decided the way it always has been, by the action of our combat infantrymen.

Source:
The Book of the Continental Solider, Peterson
The History of Weapons of the American Revolution, Neumann
Soldiers of the American Army, Kredel
Cadet Grey, Todd & Chapman
U.S. Ordnance Manuals, 1841, 1850, 1861
Civil War Collectors Encyclopedia, Lord
Guns Digest (1965) *U.S. Bayonets*, Yust
U.S. Muskets, Rifles and Carbines, Col. Gluckman
U.S. Firearms, Hicks
Ordnance Memoranda No. 11, No. 13 (1872)
Ordnance Memoranda No. 18, No. 19 (1874)
Ordnance Memoranda No. 29 (1874)
Ord. Memo., Horse and Cavalry Accoutrements (1891)
My Story, Anson Mills (history of the field woven belt)
Instructions for Assembling the Infantry Equipment Model 1910
"The McKeever Box in the Regular Army," Schornak (Vol. XV No. 3 Fall,
    Journal of the Military Collectors and Historians)
The Book of Rifles, Smith
The Book of Pistols and Revolvers, Smith

Order Arms

Carry Arms

Sling Carbine

Present Arms

Inspection Carbine

Support Arms

Right Shoulder Arms

Secure Arms

Reverse Arms

Parade Rest

Rest on Arms

Arms Port

Load

Ready

Aim

Fire Kneeling

The U.S. Heliograph

The Heliograph was an instrument used to send signals by reflecting sunlight with a mirror or mirrors. Heliographs were used by the armies of several countries during the late 1800s.

Heliograph equipment varied somewhat from country to country. The heliograph used by the U.S. Army had a mirror with a sighting rod (or else two mirrors) mounted on a tripod. A screen or shutter for interrupting the flashes was mounted on another tripod. If the sun was in front of the sender, its rays were reflected directly from a mirror to the receiving station. The sender used the sighting rod to line the flash up with the receiver. If the sun was behind the sender, its rays were reflected from one mirror to another, and from the second mirror to the receiver. The flash was lined up with the receiver by adjusting the two mirrors. Messages were sent as short and long flashes by opening and closing the shutter. The flashes represented the dots and dashes of the Morse code. The distance the heliograph signals could be

same time an experimental telephone line was being installed, the first heliograph was tested by the U.S. Signal Corps. Flashes were read over a thirty mile range. It was nearly ten years later that the heliograph was actually used in an important campaign, this one against the cunning Apache Indian.

In the spring of 1886, General Nelson A. Miles assumed command of troop movements in Arizona, pursuing the notorious Apache chief, Geronimo. The telegraph lines could not be protected against the wily Apaches, who chopped down the poles, and cut the copper wires, splicing them with thin strips of rawhide. General Miles formed a network of heliograph stations throughout the southern portions of New Mexico and Arizona, primarily to keep a watchful eye on the marauding Apaches. It took sixteen months to round up and capture the small party of Apaches and the heliograph of the Signal Corps played a small but important part in bringing about the final surrender of Geronimo and his band.

seen depended on the clearness of the sky, the length of uninterrupted sight, and the size of the mirrors used. Under ordinary conditions, a flash could be seen thirty miles or more with the naked eye and much farther with a telescope.

At Fort Whipple, Arizona Territory, in 1877, at the

Source:
Winners of the West, October 30, 1935.
"General Miles' Mirrors," B.J. Rolak; *Journal of Arizona History*.
Annual Report of the Chief of Signal Office of the Army to the Secretary of War for the year 1887; (Part 1, page 7).
The Heliograph in Miles' Campaign, Fuller.
Personal Recollections, Gen. N.A. Miles.

Accoutrements in 1876

Much of the serviceable equipment issued to the Seventh Cavalry at Fort Lincoln in 1876 came from great stockpiles of Civil War goods laying in the dark storage bins collecting dust and mildew. From these, only slight alterations were made for the cavalry by Ordnance; after extensive use in the field, newer ideas were proposed by officers. Only a small percentage of these ideas met with the approval of Ordnance. In 1872 and 1874, Ordnance gave careful attention to problems and experimental ideas and made recommendations for redesign of both cavalry and horse furniture, but could not afford to eliminate leftovers from the Civil War.

The Seventh Cavalry for its summer campaign was peopled with a strange mixture of New Jersey clerks, Minnesota farm boys, teachers and lawyers, toughs and drunkards. There were "snowbirds" who enlisted in the fall and deserted in the spring and tough old "regulars" with service stripes from elbow to cuff. The guard house was not unfamiliar to this roughshod, tobacco chewin' and free swinging lot who had little to do with their superiors. The army paid little enough for harsh and dangerous frontier duty with long hours on guard, monotonous army routine and digging ditches. Bedbugs, beans and bacon fat became daily jokes between duties, and iron-tipped arrows from the Sioux knew no rank.

Cavalry equipment seems excessive today. Curious oddities hung from the saddle and seemed to engulf the horse all around, except for the head and tail. Blanket, overcoat and shelter tent made up a good-sized roll behind the saddle. Tin cup, frying

pan, canteen and a haversack of hard tack clattered and bobbed on one side of the horse. In addition to this cumbersome load, lariats and iron picket pins hung on the opposite side to assure some balance.

The Springfield "trapdoor" 45/55 carbine was, ballistically, a great improvement over the old .50–.70. In 1873, some 1,942 carbines were manufactured, and in 1874, 10,873 were distributed to the cavalry with serial numbers up to 35,000. A drop in production of carbines came in 1875; only 7,211 were issued with serial numbers up to 60,000. Any number of these weapons may have found their way to the Seventh Cavalry, already preparing for the field. The instruction manual for the Model 1873 Springfield carbine literally advised the solider not to shoot too fast and to buy himself a pocket knife from a convenient Post Sutler, who offered a clasp knife of badly tempered iron at a then exorbitant price. It was suitable only for cutting plug tobacco.

The copper shell casings were too soft, and when fired would often expand in the chamber. The extractors, in withdrawing a jammed shell, could not help cutting through the rim or pulling off the head entirely. One can picture the Indians trying to pawn off these battle relics for muzzle-loaders after realizing this problem.

The first large revolver for self-exploding metallic cartridges was called the New Colt Model 1873 Army Metallic Cartridge Revolving Pistol. It was surely a treat to the cavalry man compared to his old percussion pistol. The six-shot cylinder was chambered for a .45 caliber metallic, self-primed, center-fire cartridge. A 250-grain lead bullet was backed by thirty grains of powder instead of the factory forty, and was made at government arsenals. An initial order for eight thousand pistols for cavalry use was placed by the government in 1873. The Colt was found to have fewer, simpler, and stronger parts, and was easier to dismantle for cleaning. Colt won over Smith & Wesson, whose only superiority was its speed of ejecting empty cartridges.

Supporting the necessary cartridge pouches for rifle and pistol was the black leather saber belt, with rectangular brass plate bearing U.S. coat of arms and German silver wreath, as described in 1861 Ordnance Manual. Many of the saber hangers or leather straps sewed to the belt were purposely cut off. Besides the rectangular brass plate, the oval U.S. Civil War buckle was also used. The Colt was accompanied by the black leather holster of the same pattern as the Civil War model, with its wide semi-circular flap. This holster was designed with a belt loop to accommodate the regulation belt of 1.9 inches wide. A new half-flap holster with the larger loop on the back was designed for looped cartridge belts, or Mills patent, and was not accepted by the army until 1878. However, it has been found that many soldiers had fashioned belts similar to the Mills patent earlier than 1876. A wide variety of non-regulation holsters were also worn by officers and troopers, along with many large flaps from the old pattern, found cut off.

The pistol cartridge pouch, as described in Ordnance Memoranda No. 13, 1872, "For the present, the Infantry cap pouch, to carry twelve pistol cartridges." These were altered from the old regulation percussion cap box. The "Half Moon" Dyer pattern carbine cartridge pouch, issued 1874, held forty cartridges, was wool-lined, and carried on the belt. It was modified from the original pattern of the early 1870s, which was then carried on the shoulder sling by mounted companies. Several other types of pouches were used, but the Dyer seemed to be the favorite. The carbine sling was 2½ inches wide, of thick buffalo hide, and also of Civil War vintage. It was slung over the shoulder and attached to a ring on the carbine swivel bar. The sling had a heavy two prong brass buckle and was issued up till 1885. The barrel of the carbine was slipped into the Civil War carbine socket, which, attached to the "D" ring on the right side of the saddle, served to steady the barrel.

The average weight of the soldier was around 140 pounds. Complete horse furniture and accoutrements, with the included 140 pounds of man totaled out at 240 pounds and 12½ ounces. This weight was borne by a horse at the commencement of a five day march. The tin utensils, the carbine and saber kept up a continual din, as the horse and trooper crept up the trail at a rate of three to four miles an hour. There was nothing picturesque about this field cavalry man in the mid-70s, as he accomplished more through threat than he achieved in battle.

Custer, A Legend

George Armstrong Custer was born on December 4, 1839, in New Rumley, Ohio, the son of Emanual H. Custer and Maria Ward Kirkpatrick Custer. "Auti" (a nickname the family gave him) had three brothers: Nevin, Thomas Ward, and Boston. Margaret Emma was his only sister. In his youth as well as in later life, Auti was athletic, loved horses and played mischievous jokes on his friends and family. His work in school was poor, but he always managed to get by and pass. Even as a boy, the only books he liked to read were stories about war and life in the military. His dreams were realized when he received an appointment to West Point Military Academy at the age of eighteen, achieved through his father's political pull in Washington, D.C.

Custer stood nearly six feet in height when he first attended West Point. He was broad shouldered, very active and weighed in the neighborhood of 150 pounds. He attended the Academy from July 1, 1857, to June 24, 1861, and was commissioned Second Lieutenant, Company G, 2nd U.S. Cavalry to rank from his date of graduation. Custer was just in time to participate in the first Battle of Bull Run, and he subsequently fought in nearly 100 engagements during the Civil War. In recognition of his cool daring, Custer was appointed to the staffs of McClellan and Pleasanton, and quickly rose to the rank of Brigadier General. He was the youngest General in the Army during the Civil War. The newspapers found that he made good copy and dubbed him the "Boy General." On February 9, 1864, Custer married Elizabeth Clift Bacon, the daughter of Daniel Stanton Bacon of Monroe, Michigan. Within two years, Custer now twenty-five years old, had earned his second star. On April 9, 1865, Custer received a battlefield flag of truce and upon further investigation, he found that Lee had surrendered. The surrender terms were signed at the McLean house at Appomattox, Virginia, and Custer was given the small table used for that purpose, in recognition of his accomplishments.

A year of idleness passed before he was again appointed to a field command. This time Custer was sent out to the West to organize the 7th Cavalry at Fort Riley, Kansas Territory. He assumed the rank of Lieutenant Colonel on July 28, 1866—the date the regiment was organized. George Custer was a man of immense strength and endurance, using neither tobacco or liquor. His advice to anyone regarding liquor was that he had quit drinking because he could not be a moderate drinker, and had given up the habit two years after leaving West Point. At this time, Custer entertained himself by reading and by

Lt. Col. George Armstrong Custer is the most written about cavalry officer in American History.

Art by E.L. Reedstrom

writing his war memoirs with the help of his wife, Libbie. He also engaged in the art of taxidermy, and practiced mounting his own trophies. His politics were simple. He was thought to be a Democrat, but even though he was considered possible political timber for the Presidency, the attractions of public office did not prove to engage his serious interest.

On June 25, 1876, Custer led five companies of the 7th cavalry into the midst of hostile Indians. The "Battle of the Little Big Horn" lasted only thirty five minutes, but resulted in the deaths of 265 solidiers and civilians—Custer's entire unit. George, Thomas Ward, and Boston Custer died within a few feet of each other. A year later Custer's remains were brought back east to be re-buried at West Point, in accordance with his wife's wishes. And finally, fifty-seven years later, Libbie Custer died and was buried at last beside her beloved husband.

The reader may be interested in a few more details regarding this unusual and controversial man, information derived from microfilm at the Custer Battlefield Museum in Montana. While at West Point, Custer was 5 feet, 10½ inches tall, but stood about 6 feet when fully adult. During the Civil War he weighed 160 lb., which rose to 170 in the 1870s. His eyes were blue, and his much-publicized hair was of a golden tint, including his mustache, and though usually depicted as long and flowing, actually was sometimes cropped short. He had broad shoulders, wore a size 38 jacket, size 9C boots, and a 7¼ hat. Finally, Custer's physical actions were described as graceful, and he was considered an excellent dancer.

Source:
Microfilm, Reel 4 (Libbie Custer); Custer Battlefield
Reedstrom, E.L. *Bugles, Banners & War Bonnets.* Caxton Printers (1978)

Custer's Carbines Jam at the Little Big Horn

(Reprinted with permission from *Guns Magazine*)

If Lt. Col. George Armstrong Custer had had his wish, he may have chosen the Spencer seven shot carbine over the Springfield trapdoor. The Spencer might have been better odds against the Indians.

Painting by E.L. Reedstrom

When Lt. Col. George Armstrong Custer rode towards the Little Big Horn River with his gallant 7th Regimental Cavalry trotting behind him, he probably felt very much assured that the campaign would go quickly and successfully. After all, he had the best crack troopers one could expect and in addition, brand new weapons furnished by Army Ordnance, the .45 caliber Colt revolver and the highly tested Model 1873, .45/55 Springfield carbine.

On the afternoon of June 25, 1876, the young commander, while leading a cavalry attack against an Indian encampment, was among the first to fall. Sporadic pistol and carbine fire was exchanged against the charging savages as they raced across the Little Big Horn River on foot and on horseback. The troopers halted, regrouped, and after picking up their wounded leader and comrades, retreated to the highest knoll. Here they battled for the most of forty minutes under the hail of bullets and arrows. After the company commanders saw that they were out-numbered and help was nowhere in sight, they shouted orders for each man to 'Save the last bullet for himself.'

Almost immediately, the news wire service received the grim report. The United Sates, already busy enjoying and celebrating its Centennial, was shocked in reading of Custer's defeat. Ever since the news release, the battle of Little Big Horn has become one of the most controversial engagements in American history. The battle, shrouded in mystery, has created an American legend of near epic proportions.

Since that unforgettable day, historians have been trying to lay the blame somewhere and on someone. Major Reno was denounced for showing cowardice in the face of the savages. Benteen was discredited for not bringing up the much sought after ammunition that Custer desperately needed. Custer, himself, was dubbed a 'Glory Hunter.'

But, there's another side of the story of the mysterious events that took place at the Little Big Horn, that was taken up within certain military circles. That was the Springfield carbines' performance in the hands of the troopers. It is best to begin with an official report submitted by Major Marcus A. Reno to the Chief of Ordnance, several weeks after the Battle of the Little Big Horn.

Head Qrs 7th Cavalry
Camp on Yellowstone
July 11, 1876

Genl. S.V. Benet
Chf. Ord. U.S.A.

I have the honor to report that in the engagement of the 25 & 26 June 1876 between the 7th Cav'y & the hostile Sioux that out of 380 carbines in my command six were rendered unserviceable in the following manner, (there were more rendered unserviceable by being struck by bullets) failure of the breech-block to close, leaving a space between the head of the cartridge & the end of the block, & when the piece was discharged,—the block thrown open, the head of the cartridge was pulled off & the cylinder remained in the chamber, whence with the means at hand it was impossible to extract it. I believe this is a radical defect, & in the hands of hastily organized troops would lead to the most disastrous results. The effect results in my opinion in two ways—in the manufacture of the gun the breech block is in many instances so made that it does not fit snug up to the head of the cartridge, after the cartridge is sent home, & it has always been a question in my mind whether the manner in which it revolves into its place does not render a close contact almost impossible to be made—another reason is that the dust, always an element to be considered in the battlefield, prevents the proper closing of the breech-block, & the same result is produced—There may be a want of uniformity in the flange of the head of the cartridge, which would also render the action of the extractor null, in near the dead bodies.[4]

Very Resp'y
M.A. Reno
Maj. 7th Cav'y
Comd'g Regt.

After examining most of the reports from the officers of Custer's command stating that the Springfield was not at all up to expectations, we finally arrive at the following conclusions.

Recognizing that the new .45/55 caliber Springfield carbine, model 1873, would probably have some bugs to iron out, the Army Ordnance service had issued an earlier manual on the carbine advising the soldier to take precaution not to shoot too fast, and that he should have readily available, a pocket knife which could be purchased from the Post Sutler. (Most of the knives were made from badly tempered iron, and sold for an exorbitant price.)[5]

The manual pointed out that . . . "Rapidity of fire may overheat chamber and barrel, causing cartridge cases to expand after firing. When this occurs, the

Because of corrosive copper shells or "verdigris" on the cartridge case, many shells would not extract. Cheap knives were used to extract the shells, but many broke under pressure leaving the carbine useless. "Verdigris" developed when copper cases came into contact with leather belt loops and were exposed to tanning chemicals that treated the leather. Carbine is Custer period, .45-55 Caliber.

Author's Collection

extractor may rip through base of cartridge due to wedging of case. If in garrison, the carbine should be turned over to Ordnance for repair. If in the field, a damaged case can often be pried out with a knife.[6]

The manual also advised the soldier that whenever a shell became jammed in the chamber, its head torn away, a spare ball should be rammed down the barrel to fill the shell, so that on opening the breech-block the ball and shell could be easily pushed out with the ramrod. The manual further advised that care should be exercised 'not to overheat' barrel or chamber and after firing five rounds the soldier was to 'allow to cool' or if time were pressing to 'blow out the barrel." This sort of advice, ranging from elementary to extreme measures, definitely indicates the enigma which confronted the Ordnance Service in their efforts to overcome the problem of jamming.[7]

Too many frontier cavalry officers paid little attention to the minor complaints of the common soldier and the objections they submitted in the field or in training. Most grievances were seldom investigated. Therefore, when the occurrence of a few jammed carbines came about in an early skirmish, the blame was placed upon the soldier and not upon the

weapon or cartridge. The word 'ramrod' was used on many occasions in the Ordnance Manual. However, in many of Custer's companies, only a few wooden and cut-down steel Infantry ramrods were available. This indicates that not much thought had been given to the possibility of some carbines jamming when needed most.

In examining the facts, the Springfield trapdoor, .45/55 carbine, was ballistically a great improvement over the old .50/70 caliber pumpkin roller. In 1873, some 1,942 carbines were manufactured, and in 1874, 10,874 were distributed to the cavalry service with serial numbers up to 35,000. A drop in production of carbines came in 1875, when only 7,211 were issued with serial numbers over 60,000. Any number of so-called 'Custer carbines' can be safely regarded as such, under the 35,000 serial number.[8]

When the 7th Regiment began receiving their new Springfield carbines in June and September, 1874[9] all officers were notified by Lt. Col. Custer to make certain that the men kept their new weapons well oiled and the carbine barrels spotless. Those already seasoned troopers wrapped flannel or woolen cloth saturated with light whale oil around the carbine's breech and hammer in order to keep the ever present alkali dust from caking on the metal.

Now that we have covered some of the general aspects that the Ordnance department warned the troops about, let's look into the finer points and possible causes of jammed carbines:

- With rapid fire continuing during the Little Big Horn engagement, the charcoal-saltpeter-sulphur made black powder cartridges cause high barrel temperatures to expand the mild steel. This caused the melting of the tallow and bee's wax lubricant from the deep, wide cannelures of the bullet which had been deposited in the grooves of the rifling, to deposit itself in the chamber. This mixed with burnt powder residue, caused the jamming of the copper casing.

- Unburned grains of black powder shaken into the chamber by rough handling were likewise soldering agents.

- During Cavalry operations in the field, the men did not have time to clean their weapons; thus, the piece fouled regularly.

- Another possible reason might have been the accumulation of 'verdigris' on the cartridge case. Verdigris makes brass and copper become brittle and then the cases split upon firing. Accuracy becomes erratic. The trapdoor action could also cause casehead separation on opening. The cause of this is explained by the fact that cartridges came into contact with leather belt loops and after a period of time were exposed to the chemicals used in tanning the leather causing a chemical reaction. This green sludge, that accumulated on the copper surface of cartridges may have been another contributing factor to jammed carbines.

As early as 1867, frontier cavalry men had perfected their own leather 'looped' cartridge belts, distributing the weight of shells, and making it easier for the soldier to get at his shells quickly. Cartridge boxes were a nuisance, as the shells often fell out while the trooper bounced in his saddle. These looped cartridge belts were called 'fair weather belts' and later were referred to as the 'prairie belt.'

- When the trooper rode into battle, his carbine was always loaded and at the ready. Slung across his shoulder was a wide carbine belt. At the end of this belt hung his weapon. But as the trooper bounced in his saddle during a hard gallop, the breech block was always liable to be thrown open, thus, ejecting the seated shell. This, of course prevented any certainty of his keeping the piece loaded while galloping into action.

- If the above situation was a continuance, the hinged pin to the breech block would wear thin, making it difficult to return the breech block in a normal manner. In returning the block, the trooper soon found that it would fall with a lateral motion, making it difficult to seat the block snug against the head of the shell.

- Since the .45/55 shells were made of a copper casing, the ejector spring often failed to do its work, and the cartridge would be partially pulled out of the chamber, due to the softness of the shell casing.[10]

After the Little Big Horn fight, the reputation of the .45/55 Springfield carbine suffered tremendously. As one officer put in a letter to the Editor of the *Army, Navy Journal,* Oct. 14, 1876;

"Sir;
   "The experiences of men engaged in the recent Indian campaign (referring to the Little Big Horn battle), has practically tested the merits of the weapon in the hands of the troops, far better than the scientific boards that occasionally convene at the Government armory and arsenals could have done. The theories of pressure, velocity, penetration, trajectory, windage, etc., are subjects that seem to have fully occupied the attention of the ordnance office to the utter conclusion of the more important matter, namely, the practical working of the weapon in actual field service. Among the distinguished officers who have urgently applied for a better carbine may be mentioned, General Mackenzie, who desired that his regiment might be supplied with the Winchester rifle in place of the Springfield carbine . . . , the sooner the Government makes a change, the better for its frontier soldiers, whose lives are at the mercy of a fickle steel spring."

The Indian situation was, however, the main topic on the government's agenda and the Springfield's investigation would have to be put off until another time. So serious was the Army's desire to punish the Indians who nearly wiped out Custer's command, that they proposed a bold winter campaign against the hostiles in the heart of Sioux territory. Col. Nelson A. Miles, commanding officer of the 5th Infantry Regiment, would lead his foot soldiers in the dead of winter. All through November December and January, Col. Miles maneuvered his foot soldiers overrunning and destroying the Indian encampments. The .45/70 Springfield rifles functioned without any serious problems. If soft copper cases caused any jamming, they were of no issue. The bitter cold was the answer to rifles not overheating, even during the rapidity of firing. Thus, the .45/70 trapdoor displayed its reliability as a rifle once again, however, the many reports against its disputed functions would still have to be investigated.

After careful examination of the returns of Cavalry and Infantry regiments for several years, Ordnance arrived at the conclusion that the average "service life" of cavalry carbines was five years. As the Model 1873s were called in for overhauling or storage, the carbine underwent a number of minor modifications and changes, each of insufficient importance to warrant any model designation changes. Some of the basic minor changes were;

1 . . . Rear sight allowing for windage adjustments.
2 . . . Breech-block arch filled to strengthen (pertains to models up to Serial Number 80,000).
3 . . . Breech-block widen and case harden.

These changes were progressive year to year and the improved parts were changed on the Model 1873 carbines either by company artificers, or at ordnance repair shops, as the arms were turned in for overhauling. Practically every Model 1873 carbine will be found to contain the later modifications. The Model 1877 was designated with the following changes;

1 . . . Trap added in butt covering a well to accommodate a 3 piece steel cleaning rod.
2 . . . Rear sight with "buck horn" type eyepiece on slide and different windage adjustments—Jan. 1879.
3 . . . Stacking Swivel was omitted and the band was replaced with the lower band from rifle.—Dec. 1879.
4 . . . In this model, there are four slightly different rear sights.[11]

No other remedy seemed to alleviate the Springfield's problem of faulty shell extraction, until a harder alloy was used later in cartridge manufacture. Seldom did it occur after the advent of the brass shell casing. In spite of the "trapdoors" faults, the Army continued to manufacture it in quantity. As late at 1894, two years after the "Krag-Jorgensen" .30 caliber rifles were officially adopted, some Regular Army units were still armed with them, and many troopers swore by the performance of the old "Springfield Trapdoor."

The War Horse

While General Sully was organizing his command at Fort Dodge (southwestern Kansas) in opposition to southern Indians in that territory, Captain Myles W. Keogh was in need of a second horse for the expedition. It was not unusual for officers to purchase "second" mounts from selected stock, due to the stepped-up marches of the cavalry.

Keogh was Inspector-General on Sully's staff in early September, 1868, and while the expedition was in preparation, Comanche was selected as Keogh's field mount. Paddy, Keogh's other horse, would be ridden during the long hard marches, and Comanche would be ridden during the thick of battle.

Comanche was almost five years old, weighing just under 925 pounds and standing fifteen hands high (four inches to one hand). The general termin-

ology used today would probably classify Comanche as a bay—a mixture of yellow and red coloration with a predominance of red, accompanying a black mane and tail. Although "claybank" has been used in describing Comanche's color in earlier books, it is now an obsolete term.

Anthony A. Amaral's *Comanche* chooses June of 1868 as when Keogh had purchased the horse, conflicting with General Godfrey's writings that Comanche was selected in September of that year. It would be hard to accept the latter statement, since Keogh was to use Comanche in an Indian engagement, with hardly enough time to train the horse within the same month.

During the Comanche Indian engagement near the Cimarron River on September 13, 1868, Keogh's

mount was hit in the right quarter by an arrow. Somehow, during the conflict, the shaft of the arrow was broken off and only noticed by a farrier in a temporary camp much later. The wounded horse, no doubt, obtained his name from this encounter because of the "Comanche" arrow.

Comanche received a second wound in June, 1870, during another clash with the Indians. The wound, in his right knee, was superficial but kept him lame for almost a month. Another injury in the right shoulder against the moonshiners in Kentucky, January 28, 1873, only scored a slight injury to the horse, and recovery was very quick.

Comanche, the nearest approach to the distinction of a lone survivor of the so-called "Custer Massacre," was the only living possession of the 7th Cavalry to be led away from the battlefield by cavalry units which stumbled upon the Custer dead early on the morning of June 27, 1876 (two days after the battle). While Gibbon's command was busily engaged in identifying the marking the dead on Custer Hill, Comanche appeared in the midst of the field neighing softly. The sight of the poor animal limping slowly toward the burial detail, with the saddle beneath his belly, the bit dangling from a broken cheek strap and throat-latch keeping the headstall from slipping off, must certainly have provided a most formidable sight.

Almost too weak to walk any further, he was approached by the officers and examined. Three wounds (neck, groin, and lung) sustained in battle were severe. It is almost conclusive that Keogh went down with Comanche, for a wound was found in the right shoulder of the horse and emerged on the left, exactly where Keogh's knee would have been. When Captain Keogh's body was found, his left leg and knee were badly shattered by a bullet. It is interesting to note that Keogh had changed from Paddy, his first field mount, to Comanche, a fresh mount, just before the battle.

Testifying at the Reno Board of Inquiry, Benteen and Girard told of finding another horse, wounded. This horse was laying on its side in a pool of mud and water on the bank of the stream where Custer and his little party of gallant men are believed to have attempted to cross in his attack on the Indian village.

Major Benteen stated that he shot the horse to put him out of his misery. Thus we can ascertain that Comanche was probably one of several horses found alive on the battlefield that day. As it is not certain what happened to the others, they presumably were shot.

Why Comanche was spared will forever remain a mystery. Yet it is true that any number of the 7th would have recognized Captain Keogh's horse, since he had owned him for eight years. Perhaps his life was spared out of respect for Keogh.

After the dead soldiers had been buried, Comanche was slowly led back in the midst of the wounded men, toward the steamer *Far West* anchored at the junction of the Little Big Horn and Big Horn Rivers. Several times, Comanche was unable to move during his fifteen mile march to the steamer, so a hasty conveyance was erected to move the veteran horse to the river. It is not known what type of conveyance was used, but Comanche could have been dragged with a tarpaulin or large canvas.

Aboard the steamer, a stall was erected near the paddle wheel while a soft bedding of fresh-cut grass was prepared. Under the watchful eyes of Veterinarian Stein, Comanche was attended to during the trip back to Bismarck, D.T. The 950 mile trip was made in the record time of fifty-four hours.

For almost a year, Comanche recuperated from his severe wounds, suspended in a sling with little space between the floor and his hooves. After the "sole survivor" had completely regained his strength, he had the free run of the post and roamed at will. Favorite hangouts were the Officer's Mess and the Enlisted Men's Club with a bucket of beer from a casual admirer every now and then. Every time the 7th found cause for another parade or ceremonial, Comanche was certain to lead his old Troop I, draped in mourning with a black net, an empty saddle with the symbolic empty boots reversed in the stirrups. The old war horse had served with his regiment since 1868, with only one other horse in the 7th Cavalry of equal rank.

Comanche may have officially been relieved of duty, but he still continued with his old Troop I on many marches and skirmishes. If any battle presented itself, Comanche was hurried to the rear and picketed with the other horses.

From Fort Abraham Lincoln, Comanche made many moves from one fort to another: Fort Totten, Fort Meade, and then to his final pasture at Fort Riley. Along the way, Comanche's reputation grew and many stories of the old war horse, or "Second Commanding Officer" as he was widely nicknamed, spread from post to post.

After a fourteen year association with Farrier Gustav Korn (Karn) who was designated as Comanche's caretaker, this trusting relationship came to an end when Korn was killed at the Battle of Wounded Knee, South Dakota, on December 29, 1890. From that moment on, Comanche seemed to have little or no interest in life. After a continued decline, on November 6, 1891, an attack of colic ended the life of the "Second Commanding Officer" of the 7th U.S. Cavalry. Comanche was close to twenty-nine years old.

Officers at Fort Riley decided that Comanche should be preserved and mounted as a last tribute to the "Old War Horse." Immediately, a telegram was sent to Professor Lewis Dyche, a naturalist at Lawrence, Kansas. They requested him to come to Fort Riley. After the professor arrived, he was approached by the officers with the matter of preserving the skin and mounting it. When the

officers learned that the amount of $450 was beyond their own pockets, they then agreed that the professor could mount the horse and have the privilege of exhibiting it for two years or so at the World's Fair in Chicago. When the $450 bill was paid, the horse would be returned to Fort Riley. Should the money not be raised after the fair was over, Comanche would then become the property of the University of Kansas Museum of Natural History. No attempts were made to pay the bill and the university became the permanent home for Comanche. While the hide was being mounted, the remains of the famous 'War Horse' received a military burial, with all honors, at Fort Riley, Kansas.

Comanche still carries on the spirit of the old 7th Cavalry as he stands today in the Dyche Museum at the University of Kansas. Here he remains as a silent memorial to the 7th Cavalry's most bitter defeat...at the Little Big Horn.

Source:
Amaral, Anthony A. *Comanche.*
Grey, Dr. John S. "Medical Service on the Little Big Horn." *Westerners Brand Book,* Chicago Corral, Vol. XXIV, January, 1968.
Luce, E.S. "Keogh, Comanche, and Custer." *The Cavalry Journal,* Vol. XXXV, July, 1926.
Harper's Weekly, May 25, 1878.
Graham, W.A. *Reno Court of Inquiry.*

Custer's Eye-Witness at the Little Big Horn

On September 8, 1876, the *Pioneer Press and Tribune* published an almost unbelievable interview with an old trapper, D.H. Ridgeley, who spent many months in the Yellowstone country. In between trapping and trying to elude small Indian war parties, he was finally captured late in March, 1876, and brought to Sitting Bull's camp where he was kept a prisoner until the Custer fight. The old trapper was not tortured, but was given to an old squaw as a slave. Other than that, his meals were regular and animal skins provided him warmth. In the Indian camp, Ridgeley noticed a number of white men, probably French Canadian because of the Red River carts coming and going at all hours of the day. When Ridgeley was not working under a watchful eye of the old woman, he was confined in a tepee.

On June 25, 1876—the day of the battle—the Indians stood ready for the attack, many of them clambered on the hillsides overhanging Custer's line of march down the Rosebud. The Indian camp was divided by a bluff or ridge, the front of which ran well down toward the Rosebud in the direction of the available fords on the river. The Indians had crossed the river to camp by this ford, and Custer had followed their trail down to the water's edge. From this point of observation there were only about twenty-five tepees visible to Custer. However, there were seventy-five double tepees behind the bluff, where they could not be seen by the white soldiers. Custer attacked the smaller village and was immediately met by a force of 1,500 to 2,000 Indians in regular order of battle, every movement being made

in military precision. From where the old trapper was confined, he had a complete view of the battle ground a mile and a half away.

Custer began to return the Indians' fire in a ravine near the ford, and fully one-half of the command seemed to be unhorsed. Then the soldiers retreated toward a hill in the rear and were shot down on the way with astonishing rapidity—the commanding officer falling from his horse in the middle of the engagement. After the resounding defeat of Custer's force, many Indians returned to camp with their plunder, delirious with joy over their success. With them were six soldiers, wounded but still alive. After being tortured these men were tied to stakes and burned to death; the bodies dropping to the ground a blackened, roasted and hideous mass. While the Indian camp now turned its attention to the troopers south of the river, the squaws with their children armed themselves with knives and battle-axes and proceeded to the Custer field, robbing the dead and bashing in skulls wherever there was any movement of bodies.

That night, after the victories scored by the Indians on the field, many braves returned to camp to drink whiskey and admire their new weapons and clothing that had been stripped from the dead. During this time, the squaws guarded Ridgeley and two other companions, which came as a surprise to the old trapper. During that night of pandemonium, the guards became very drowsy, and at the first chance, Ridgeley and his companions fled the camp. Finding several ponies they quickly made tracks back toward civilization, only to find the countryside literally crawling with Indian war parties. Any thought of traveling was certainly suicide, so they found enough cover in a section of wood to conceal themselves for four days. Finding it safe to travel again, they continued on at late evening keeping well out of sight of straggling Indians. On the fifth or sixth night, Ridgeley's pony stumbled, throwing him to the ground and breaking his arm in two places.

It is not known how long it took the three men to find Fort Abe Lincoln, some three hundred and twenty five miles away from the Indian encampment. From Fort Lincoln, the men were transferred by wagon to Fort Abercrombie safely, where one of the

men became afflicted with erysipelas and died several days later. Ridgeley, somewhat shaken by his ordeal, returned to his hometown of Minneapolis and his surviving companion rejoined his family, never to be heard of again. Ridgeley was once again among friends, one of whom was Hall McCleave of the firm Warner and McCleave, undertakers and furniture dealers. After listening to Ridgeley's incredible story, McCleave insisted that the old trapper retell his story to the local newspaper editor and allow it to be printed, leaving out none of the atrocities he had witnessed.

The story went to press on September 8, 1876. Overnight Ridgeley was made into an American legend. New York papers which picked up the story offered a purse as a testimonial of bravery and audacity of that alleged white man who escaped from Sitting Bull and gave a history of the fight through a Minneapolis newspaper.

Source:
Guns Magazine Feb. 1971, E.L. Reedstrom:
Pioneer Press and Tribune, Minneapolis, Minn., Sept. 8, 1876
Bugles, Banners and War Bonnets, E.L. Reedstrom, Caxton (1978).

Trapper D.H. Ridgeley, one year after his capture (1877). Sketch is by author from a faded photo.

Author's Collection

Definition of Military Terms

About—To change front; infantry turn to the left; so do artillery, but cavalry either right or left.

Accoutrements—The trappings of a soldier exclusive of his arms and dress.

Action—Active hostilities; an "affair" is a fight of less importance.

Adjutant—A staff officer in a regiment, ranking as First Lieutenant, appointed by the Colonel to aid him in performing his regimental or garrison duties. The Adjutant-general of a State has charge of all matters pertaining to the militia of that State. The "Adjutant-General" of the United States is the principal staff officer of the army, and assists the General of the Army.

Advice-boat—A vessel employed to carry dispatches.

Advance—That part of an army in front of the remainder.

Aid, or Aid-de-camp—An officer chosen by a General to convey orders to subordinates, aid him in his correspondence and assist in military movements.

Aiguilletee—A braid or cord on a military uniform, extending from one shoulder across the breast; a point or tag at the end of a fringe or lace.

Aim—Directing any weapon toward an enemy, as a gun, pistol, or sword.

Alarm-gun—A gun fired for the purpose of creating an alarm, or rousing soldiers to arms.

Alarm-post—The place where soldiers gather when an alarm is made.

Align—To form soldiers or cannon in line for parade or battle.

Allonge—A thrust with a sword, made by stepping forward and extending the arm.

Ambulance—A vehicle on wheels for conveying wounded soldiers from the battle-field to hospitals or elsewhere.

Ambush, or Ambuscade—The place in which troops are hidden preparatory to making a sudden and unexpected attack upon an enemy.

Ammunition—Material for charging firearms—balls, powder, bomb-shells, etc.

Appointments—The accoutrements of military officers, their sashes, belts, plumes, etc.

Approaches—Works carried on toward besieged works.

Arm—To provide with weapons; arms—the weapons employed in warfare, small arms—muskets, rifles, and revolvers, side-arms—swords and bayonets, a stand of arms—a complete set for each soldier; a particular branch of the army.

Armor—Any clothing, especially of metal, worn in warfare to protect the body.

Armstrong gun—A breech loading cannon, having a rifle-bore, and made of wrought iron, named after its inventor.

Army—An organized body of soldiers commanded by a General.

Arquebuse—An old-fashioned gun like a musket, very heavy, and fired from a rest.

Arsenal—A place of deposit for arms.

Articles of War—National rules governing the army.

Artillery—Usually applied to cannons, mortars and howitzers with their carriages and equipments, ammunition, balls, bomb-shells, etc.

Artillerist—A soldier attached to the artillery branch of the military service.

Assault—A furious effort to carry any fortified place.

Assembly—The signal to form in line by companies.

Attack—An onset on the enemy, either to seize his position or break his ranks.

Avant-guard—The advanced portion of an army; that force in the front.

Ball—A spherical shot for use in cannon, muskets, rifles or pistols; applied to an indefinite quantity of musket balls.

Band—The musicians of an army.

Barbican—An outer fortification defending the entrance to a city or castle.

Barbette—A hill, or mound, on which cannon are arranged so as to shoot over the wall of a fort or city, instead of through an embrasure, or opening; a barbette gun, or a barbette battery, is that thus mounted.

Barrack—A house for the use of soldiers in a fort.

Barricade—A temporary or hasty fortification, constructed of earth, trees, wagons or other material that will serve to obstruct the advance of an army, or defend those inside of the barricade.

Barrier—A sort of fence to prevent an enemy using a certain passage.

Bar-shot—Two cannon balls, or half-balls, united by a strong bar between them; fired from a cannon for the purpose of destroying masts and rigging on board of vessels.

Bastard-gun—A cannon of unusual make or proportions, whether long or short.

Bastion—That part of the interior of a fortification which projects toward the outside, consisting of the "faces" and the "flanks." The "curtain" is that part between and connecting two bastions.

Batardeau—A wall built across a fortification, or military ditch, arranged with a gate by which the amount of water in the ditch may be regulated.

Batis—Large branches of trees, having one end sharpened, laid in rows with the points outward, in front of a fortification, to prevent the approach of an enemy. The large ends are fastened to the ground.

Battalion-Battalia—The disposition of troops in the order of battle; a battalion is a force of infantry, formed of from two to ten companies; in England it means about 800 men, under a Lieutenant-Colonel.

Battering-ram—A machine used to beat down the walls of fortified places.

Battery—Any place where cannon or mortars are stationed for attacking an enemy or fortification, also a collection of cannon at one point.

Battery-wagon—A wagon used for transporting the tools and equipments of a battery from place to place.

Battle—An organized contest between two opposing armies; called, also, a combat, fight or engagement, a skirmish is a conflict of arms of a briefer, less organized character. In a "drawn battle," neither side is the victor; a "pitched battle" is one systematically entered into when both

sides are well prepared; to "give battle" is to attack.

Battle-array—An army prepared for battle.

Battle-axe—Formally an axe used as a weapon of attack.

Battlement—That part of a castle or fortification on which soldiers may stand and shoot at the enemy from behind defenses.

Bayonet—A short, sharp steel weapon attached to the muzzle of a musket; used for charging upon the enemy.

Besiege—See Siege.

Bivouac—A camp without tents, but around fires.

Block-house—A house made of strong timber or logs, and used as a military defense; having no windows; but only small apertures through which guns may be fired from inside.

Body—Any number of men under one commander.

Bomb—A hollow iron ball, or "shell," filled with powder or other explosive material, with a fuse attached, which is fired from a mortar or howitzer, and explodes in its descent, scattering death and destruction all around it.

Bombard—To attack with bombs.

Bombardment—The act of attacking a ship, town, or fort, with bombs.

Bomb-proof—able to withstand a bombardment.

Bonnet—Part of a parapet in a fortification sufficiently elevated to screen its other part during an attack.

Bore—The hollow part of cavity of a gun.

Breastwork—A temporary defense, as high as the breast of a man, hastily formed of earth or other material.

Breach—An opening in the walls of a fortified place, made by artillery.

Breech—The hinder part of a cannon or other gun.

Breech-loader—A gun that receives its charge of ammunition at the breech instead of its muzzle.

Breech-pin, or breech-screw—A stout iron plug screwed into the breech of a gun.

Brevet—The Brevet is a commission given an officer a nominal rank higher than that for which he has a salary. A great number of these honorary titles were bestowed during and after the Civil War.

Brigade—Two or more regiments of soldiers, either infantry, cavalry, artillery, or mixed, commanded by a Brigadier General; a "division" is composed of two or more brigades, and is commanded by a Major General; and an "army corps" comprises two or more divisions, and forms the largest body of troops in the organization of the army. The "Brigade-Inspector" inspects companies of soldiers before they are mustered into the service.

Brigadier-general—An army officer in command of a brigade, whose rank is lower than that of a Major-General, but above that of a Colonel. A "Brigade-Major" is an officer who may be attached to a brigade to assist the General.

Broad-sword—A sword with a broad blade and sharp edge.

Brush—A slight encounter; a skirmish.

Buckler—An ancient shield, often four feet long, used to protect the whole body.

Bullet—A small ball for muskets, rifles or pistols, usually made of lead.

Bullet-proof—Incapable of being pierced with bullets.

Bulwark—A mound of earth; an outwork, capable of resisting cannon-balls, and resembling a more elaborate fortification in its formation.

Busby—A high military cap, made of bearskin.

Cadet—A young man in the Military Academy at West Point, or in the Naval Academy at Annapolis; a student of naval or military science.

Caisson—A chest containing ammunition; in artillery, the wagon carrying the ammunition chest and military stores; also a chest of explosive material to be blown up under some of the enemy's works.

Calibre—The diameter of the bore or hollow of any gun.

Camp—The ground selected for the erection of tents and other shelter for soldiers or laborers; a collection of tents, huts, etc. arranged in an orderly manner, and also the whole body of persons occupying the camp; to "encamp" is to prepare a camp.

Campaign—A period occupied by a body of troops, either in action, marches or in camp.

Campaigner—An old soldier—a veteran.

Canister - shot—Small balls put into a canister and fired from a cannon.

Cannon—Guns of heavy calibre, comprising several varieties of form, for several purposes, and made of various metals.

Cannonading—Battering forts, towns or ships with cannon shot.

Cannoneers—Soldiers who handle and use artillery.

Capitulation—Surrender of an enemy upon stipulated terms.

Captain—The commander of a military company, usually of about 100 men. A "Captain-General" is the commander-in-chief of the army, or (like the Governor of a State) of the militia.

Carbine—A fire-arm smaller than a musket or rifle, and larger than a horse-pistol, used by mounted troops.

Carronade—A short cannon used to throw a heavy shot with moderate force, in order to break, rather than pierce, any obstruction presented, like a ship's hull.

Cartel—A agreement between two contending countries for the exchange of prisoners.

Cartouch—A roll of paper holding a charge of powder and ball for a fire-arm; resembling the modern cartridge; a "blank cartridge" is one in which nothing but powder is used; a "cartridge-box" is the case in which soldiers carry a supply of prepared cartridges.

Cartridge—See Cartouch.

Casemate—A bomb-proof chamber in a fort, from which a cannon may be fired through an aperture in the side; or it may be used as a powder magazine, or soldiers' quarters.

Case-shot—Small balls encased in canisters or iron cases, and fired from cannon. See Canister.

Casque—Defensive armor to protect the head and neck.

Cavalry—That portion of an army which habitually fights on horseback; not to be confounded with mounted infantry.

Chapeau Bras—A military hat that can be flattened and so carried under the arm.

Charge—(1) The quantity of powder used to load a musket, etc. (2) the advance of infantry upon the enemy with bayonets fixed upon the muzzles of their muskets; or a rapid attack of cavalry.

Cheval-de-frise, or **Chevaux-de-frise**—A piece of timber traversed with wooden spikes, pointed with iron, five or six feet long, used to defend a passage, stop a breach or make a retrenchment to stop an enemy. (Webster.)

Circumvallation, line of—An earthwork, with a parapet and trench, built around a place which it is intended to beseige.

Colonel—The chief commander of a regiment of soldiers; the next in rank below a Brigadier-General.

Colors—The silken flag of a regiment, or any military or naval ensign. "Camp-colors" are small flags (eighteen inches square), used to mark points in the evolutions of troops, the color line, etc; sometimes called "field-colors."

Color-guard—A detail of eight corporals, to whom is entrusted the protection of the colors of a regiment.

Combat—A battle; fight, or warlike engagement between opposing troops.

Commissary—An officer appointed to provide food for the army; called, also, a "commissary of subsistence."

Commissariat—The provision department of the army, at the head of which is a Commissary-General.

Company—A division of troops, comprising from fifty to 100 men, commanded by a Captain, Lieutenant, Sergeant, and Corporal.

Convoy—Any number of troops appointed to perform guard service in transferring men, money, ammunition, provisions, etc. from place to place in time of war.

Corporal—A non-commissioned officer of the lowest grade in a company, whose duty it is to place and relieve sentinels, etc.

Corps, army—The largest organization of troops in the United States army, consisting of two or more divisions, under the command of a Major-General. (See Division.) A simple "corps" is a body of troops under one commander.

Countersign—A changeable and secret military pass-word, exchanged, between guards and entrusted to those employed on duty in camp or garrison, in order to distinguish friends from enemies.

Court-martial—A tribunal composed of military officers for the trial of offenders against military laws, orders, etc.

Cuirassiers—Soldiers, usually in the cavalry service, who wear "cuirasses," or breastplates of metal, for protection.

Cul-de-sac—A position where a body of troops is so hedged in by enemies that the only way out is by an advance in front.

Curtain—That part of a fortification where contiguous bastions are connected with ramparts and parapets.

Dead-line—A line in a camp or military prison beyond which no prisoner may pass without being shot by a sentinel.

Defense—Any sort of fortification or work that serves to protect troops or places against the assaults of enemies, or ward off danger.

Defile—A narrow passage or road in which troops can march only a few abreast, or by flank; to "defilade" is to raise the outer works of a fortification in order to protect the interior from the assaults of enemies occupying an elevated position outside.

Deploy—To display or spread a body of troops in forming a line of battle; also, the act of taking intervals as skirmishes (Webster.)

Depot—A place were military stores or provisions are kept.

Detail, or **Detachment**—A body of troops detached from the main army to perform specific duty.

Discipline—The rules and regulations instructing and governing the army.

Dislodge—To force an enemy from his defense.

Dismantle—To demolish the outworks of a town or fortification.

Ditch—A trench dug to prevent an enemy from approaching a town or fortress; called also, a "moat" or "fosse," and it may be filled with water or not. The earth taken from the trench may also be used for forming a parapet or dense on its inner side.

Dragoons—Soldiers who are armed and trained to fight either on foot or on horseback.

Echelon—Military tactics, in which larger or small bodies of soldiers, divisions of battalions or brigades, follow each other on different lines, presenting the form of steps, and thus protect the front and one or both flanks of the army at once.

Elevation—In using a cannon, it means the angle included between the plane of the horizon and the line of the hollow of a gun.

Embrasure—The opening in the wall of a fortification occupied by the muzzle of a cannon fortification point outward.

Enceinte—The interior wall of a fortification that surrounds a place.

Encounter—A combat, fight, engagement, hostile collision, or skirmish.

Enemy—An opponent in war, national, sectional, or person.

Enfilading—Firing shot along the whole length of an enemy's line.

Engineers—A department of the army engaged in devising and constructing defensive and offensive works, keeping them in repair and sometimes in planning attacks upon, and defenses of fortifications.

Enlist—To join the army as a common soldier.

Epaulement—A species of embankment or breastwork, made of wickerwork, or bags filled with earth, bundle of sticks, etc., or earth heaped up, used to afford a cover from the fire of an enemy to the side or flank of any army.

Epaulette—An ornamental badge, worn on the shoulder by officers of the army and navy, having peculiarities of form or size to indicate the rank of the wearer.

Eprouvette—A machine for testing the strength of gunpowder. (Brande.) A small mortar.

Equipage—Military furniture, comprising whatever is necessary for efficient service by any body of troops in arranging or rearranging their position in the field.

Establishment—The permanent military force of a nation; implying the quota of officers and men in an army, regiment, troop or company.

Evolution—The prescribed or uniform movements made by a body of troops in arranging or rearranging their position in the field.

Exempts—Citizens who from their sex, age, infirmities, or occupations, are not liable to be called upon to perform military duty.

Expedition—An armed excursion of troops against an enemy, or in an enemy's country for some specific and valuable military purpose.

Facing—Movements of soldier when

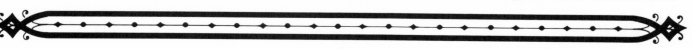

turning on their heels to the right or left in their places in line.

False attack—A movement in the nature of an advance calculated to divert the attention of the enemy from the point at which the attack is to be made.

Fascines—Twigs of trees or bushes tied up in long, round bundles, used to support earth in forming embankments or parapets in field defenses, filling ditches, etc.

Feint—A mock attack upon any troops or place designed to conceal the true assault.

Field—Any open space of ground where a battle is fought; also applied to the action of the army while in the field.

Field-colors—See Colors.

Field-day—A day set apart for instructing troops in field evolutions, the exercise of arms, etc.

Field-gun-Field-piece—A small cannon used on a battle-field.

Field-marshal—A military officer of high rank in Germany and France, and the highest in England, except the Captain-General.

Field-officers—The Colonel, Lieutenant-Colonel and Major of a regiment.

Field-work—A temporary earthwork or other fortification thrown up by troops in the field, for defense when besieging a fortress, or when defending a besieged point.

Fight—See Combat.

File—Soldiers marching in line, one behind another and not in ranks.

File-leader—The first soldier in file-marching.

Fire-arms—All weapons in which powder and ball, or shot, are used.

Flag—Colors, ensign or banner, having forms and hues indicating a difference of nationality, party, or opinion; the standard around which soldiers rally in a contest, as representing their country. A yellow flag designates a hospital; a red flag signifies defiance; a white flag, a desire for peaceful communication - a flag of truce; a black flag, no mercy; a flag half-mast, as sign of mourning; a flag wrong side up, distress; a flag hauled down in a fight, surrender; hauled down a few feet and immediate raised again, respect for a superior.

Flank—The side of any body of troops, large or small; the extreme right or left of an army. In a fortification, the flank is any part of a work by which another part is defended by firing guns along the outside of a parapet.

Flanker—A military force sent out to guard the flank of an army along its line of march. To "outflank" is to get the better of an army or body of, troops by extending lines of soldiers beyond or around it.

Flash—The sudden burst of flame and light that accompanies the discharge of fire-arms.

Flugelman—A teacher of manual exercises who stands before soldiers, and whose motions they imitate simultaneously; a fugleman.

Flying-artillery—Artillery-men trained to perform their evolutions with great rapidity, leaping on moving horses or ammunition carriages with agility.

Flying-camp—A body of troops trained to change their position from place to place with alacrity.

Foil—A blunt sword, used in fencing, having a metal button on its point.

Foot-soldier—See Infantry.

Forage—Ordinary food for horses; to forage is to send out a party of soldiers to gather feed for horses, called a "foraging party;" a "foraging cap" is a military undress-cap for the head.

Force—Any body of troops assembled for military purposes.

Forlorn-hope—A desperate enterprise; to carry a town or fortification by storming its walls; a duty involving great peril.

Fort, Fortress, Fortification—A large or small space, surrounded by high embankments, or stone or wooden walls, of great thickness, and strongly prepared for offensive or defensive warfare, usually so built as to command some important approach to a city, town or inland stream, and of such form as to repel invaders at all points of its structure. From the walls protrude, at intervals, the muzzles of ponderous cannon, while inside a body of troops, with stores or provision and ammunition, are expected to hold the fort against the assaults of their enemies. Outside of a fort is usually found a ditch, rampart and parapet, or else palisades, stockades, and other means of defense. A "fortalice" is a small outwork of a fortification. "Fortification" is the art or science of strengthening (or fortifying) places for defense. "Field-fortifications" is the art of constructing all kinds of temporary works in the field. A "fortress" is a more permanent and larger structure than a fortification.

Front-face—An order requiring soldiers to turn their faces to the proper front of the force which they compose.

Front of Operations—The front formed by an army as it moves on its line of operation. (Halleck.)

Furlough—Leave granted to a soldier to be absent from the army for a longer or shorter period.

Fuse—A tube fixed in a bomb-shell or hand-grenade, filled with combustible materials, which burn and explode the shell at the proper time.

Gabion—A cylinder made of wicker, resembling a tall basket without a bottom, filled with earth, and used in connection with others like it for sheltering soldiers in the field from the enemy's fire; also used in throwing up an intrenchment called a "gabionnade."

Gallery—Any passage in a fortification that is covered overhead as well as having sides.

Garrison—A body of troops quartered in a fort or fortified town, to defend it, or to keep citizens in subjection to the laws; also the place where they are quartered.

General of the Army—An officer of the highest rank, commanding all the armies of the United States.

Generalissimo—The chief commander of an army or other military force, especially where the army is in two divisions under separate commanders.

General Officers—All officers above the rank of Colonel. (See General of the Army, Lieutenant-general, Adjutant-general, Major-general, and Brigadier-general.)

Glacis—That sloping embankment in a fortress which serves as a parapet to the covered way.

Grape-shot—See Canister and Case-shot.

Grenade, or Hand-grenade—A small, explosive iron bomb-shell, thrown from the hand upon the enemy; used in defending a fortification. "Rampart Grenades" are of various sizes, and are rolled over the parapet upon the attacking force out of a trough.

Guard—A detachment of soldiers stationed to protect a position or a body of other troops against a surprise

from the enemy; also to guard Generals, prisoners of war, public property, etc. "On Guard," serving as a guard. "Running the Guard," passing the guard or sentinel without leave. "Advance-guard," a military force of infantry or cavalry marching before a moving army or division, to prevent surprise, or to give notice of danger. "Rear-guard," a similar guard, to follow a moving army for the same purpose. "Guard-mounting," the ceremony of placing on guard. "Grand-guard, " one of the posts of the second line belonging to a system of advance-posts of an army. (Mahan.) "Life-guard," soldiers selected to guard the persons of kings, queens, princes, etc. "Off the Guard," in a careless condition. "Van-guard," same as advance-guard.

Guidons—Small silk standards for cavalry, or to direct the movements of infantry. See Colors.

Gunpowder—A mixture of sulphur, salt-petre and charcoal—an important "sinew of war."

Harass—To perplex and hinder military movements, sieges, etc., by frequent attacks.

Haversack—The bag in which a soldier carries his provisions when marching.

Headquarters—The place occupied by the commanding officer and his staff as a residence.

Hilt—The handle of a sword.

Holsters—Leather cases for pistols, attached to a horsemen's saddle.

Hospital—Any place where the sick and wounded are attended to.

Hostilities—The condition of war between two nations.

Howitzer—A short, light cannon, for firing hollow-shot, canister-shot, etc.

Infantry—Soldiers who march on foot, carrying muskets or rifles, with bayonets.

Inroad—An irregular and sudden invasion.

Inspector-general—A staff-officer whose duty it is to inspect the troops at a stated time, and report as to their discipline, efficiency, instruction, and whatever else pertains to the army organization.

Intrenchment—See Ditch. It also means any sort of work intended to fortify a post against attack.

Invasion—The entrance of troops into a hostile country, for conquest or plunder.

Invest—In enclose, by seizing all avenues of approach to a town, so as to intercept aid or assistance from without, and prevent the escape of those within.

Knapsack—The leather or canvas bag carried by an infantry soldier on his back containing his clothing and other necessaries.

Lieutenant-colonel—The second officer in command of a regiment.

Lieutenant—The second officer in command of a company; he is the lowest officer who receives a commission.

Line of Battle—Troops arrayed in readiness for active combat.

Litter—A sort of bed in which wounded officers and men are carried off the battle-field.

Lodgment—Gaining possession of an enemy's position and holding it.

Lunette—A small field-work, resembling the bastion of a fortification.

Magazine—That part of a fortification where powder is stored; a storehouse for army provisions, arms, etc.

Major—The third officer in command of a regiment, next in rank above a captain, next below a Lieutenant-colonel, and the lowest grade of field-officer.

Major-general—An officer who commands a division of the army.

Martial Law—An arbitrary law emanating from the principal military authorities, without reference to any immediate legislative or constitutional sanction. It is founded on paramount necessity, in times of rebellion, war, insurrection, etc. and when instituted, extends to all the inhabitants of the prescribed district and all their actions.

Match—A substance used in war to convey fire to explosive or combustible material for the purpose of destroying it, exploding magazines, mines, etc. Two kinds are used—the "slow-match" and the "quick match"—so called on account of their different peculiarities in point of time for effecting the desired object.

Mine—An excavation made under an enemy's fortification, in which powder is placed for the purpose of blowing up the works and their occupants; resorted to in sieges.

"Counter-mine" is one made by the besieged under the fortification of the besieging party.

Mortar—A very short cannon, of large bore, and having a chamber; used for throwing bombs, stones, etc., into an enemy's camp.

Muster—A gathering of troops for parade, exercise, inspection, roll-call, etc. To "muster into service" is to inspect soldiers and place their names on the army pay-roll; to "muster out" is to formally dismiss soldiers from the service and strike their names from the army lists. To "pass muster" is to pass a proper examination without censure. A "muster-book" is the record of several military forces; a "muster-roll is a similar record of separate companies, troops or regiments.

Mutiny—Open and violent opposition to lawful authority, or any refractory conduct among soldiers.

Needle-gun—A breech-loading fire-arm, the detonating powder in which is exploded by a slender pin or needle that passed in at the breech.

Non-commissioned Officers—All officers below the grade of a company Lieutenant.

Neutral—A person or nation that take no part in the contests of others.

Orders—The lawful commands of an officer to his subordinate officers or men.

Ordnance—A term applied generally to all artillery, including cannon, howitzers and mortars.

Outposts—Troops stationed at points outside of a camp, to prevent surprises by an enemy; also the places where they are stationed.

Outrank—Having a higher degree of authority than another.

Outwork—An intrenchment or other defense beyond or outside of a fortification.

Palisades—Sharp-pointed, strong wooden stakes, set in the ground close together like a fence, around a fortification.

Parallels—Wide and covered trenches made by besieging troops between their various batteries and approaches, affording safe communication and passage from one to another.

Parapet—An elevation of earth, a wall, or rampart, in a fortification for the protection of soldiers from the enemy's fire; breast-high; hence a breastwork.

Park—A space of ground set apart in an encampment for the accumulation of animals, wagons, pontoons and other war material. Thus there is a "park of artillery," the space occupied by cannon; a "park of wagons," etc.

Parley—A conference with the enemy, usually conducted under a flag of truce.

Parole—The word of honor given by a prisoner of war that, if set at liberty, he will not take up arms again until exchanged, or that he will return to his captors at a certain time; a "parole" is also a word, like countersign (which see), given out in orders for the purpose of distinguishing friends from foes in the dark.

Party—A small detachment of soldiers engaged in any duty; a "fatigue-party" is one employed in manual labor about the camp.

Patrol—A vigilance party, consisting of a few soldiers under control of a non-commissioned officer, moving from post to post, along roads or through streets, to maintain safety, order, attention to duty, etc.

Pay-master—An officer whose business it is to pay the soldiers and camp men their wages; the "pay-roll" is the list of men and the wages due to each.

Pickets—Guards stationed in front of an army, and between it and the outposts; when attacked, the outposts fall back on the pickets for support.

Pillage—Booty captured from an enemy's camp, town or country.

Pioneers—A party of soldiers armed with axes, saws and other tools, who go before an advancing army to clear the way, repair roads or bridges and work on intrenchments.

Platoon—Half of a company of soldiers.

Pontoons—Light frames or boats, of wood or other material, placed in streams for supporting temporary bridges during the march of an army.

Port-fire—A mixture of combustible and explosive materials encased in cloth or paper; formerly used as a match for firing cannons, but now superseded by a patent primer.

Position—Ground occupied by an army encamped or in battle.

Priming—Powder or other combustible used to convey fire to the charge in a gun.

Private—A common soldier.

Projectile—A cannon-ball, bomb-shell, or other substance, projected by the force of powder or other explosive.

Provost-marshal—A military police officer, whose duty it is to arrest and retain deserters, prevent soldiers from pillaging, to indict criminals, and to see that sentences are executed upon offenders.

Put to the Sword—Slain with swords, as in ancient warfare.

Pyrotechny—The art of making fireworks for military signals or popular amusement.

Quadrangle—A fort having four sides and four corners.

Quadrant—An instrument used by gunners for regulating the elevation and pointing of cannon, mortars, etc.

Quarters—The station or encampment occupied by troops; place of lodging for officers or men. "Quarter," the encampment on one of the principal passages round a place besieged, to prevent relief and intercept convoys. (Webster.) To "give quarter" is to show mercy to a vanquished foe. To "beat to quarters" is a signal for prompt readiness for duty.

Quartermaster—The officer whose business it is to provide quarters, provision, clothing, fuel, storage, stationery, and transportation for the army, superintending all supplies. The chief officer in this department of the service is the "Quartermaster General," assisted by a "Quartermaster Sergeant."

Rally—To renew order and discipline among disordered or scattered soldiers.

Rampart—An earth embankment, or wall, surrounding a fortified place, to resist the enemy's shot, protect the barracks, etc. The strong works projecting outside the rampart or main wall are called bulwarks.

Range—Properly, the horizontal distance to which a projectile can be carried by the force of a gun; sometimes from the mouth of the gun to where the shot lodges, as at "short range" or "long range."

Rank—A line of soldiers standing or marching side by side; also the grade of an officer in authority.

Rank and File—That part of an army composed of non-commissioned officers and common soldiers.

Ration—The daily fixed allowance of food, drink and forage for each soldier.

Rear—The hindmost part of an army.

Rear-guard—A detachment of troops assigned to the rear of an army to protect it, prevent straggling, etc.

Reconnaissance, Reconnoitre—A preliminary survey of an enemy's country, the character of his operations, the approaches to his works, etc., for the purpose of ascertaining his position and strength. A "reconnaissance in force" is a demonstration of attack for the same purpose.

Recruit—A new and undisciplined soldier; one recently enlisted.

Redoubt—A small polygonal work in a fortification; an outwork within another outwork.

Regiment—A body of troops comprising ten or twelve companies, under the command of a Colonel.

Reserve—Troops not brought into action in a battle until towards its close or until actual necessity requires their presence on the field.

Retreat—The movement of retiring before an enemy, or of going back to a place recently occupied.

Retrenchment—An intrenchment thrown up to prolong the defense of another outside of it, when the latter is likely to be carried by the enemy.

Reveille—The morning beat of the drum to awake soldiers in camp.

Ricochet—The skipping or rebounding of shot and shells after striking the ground, when fired from a gun.

Roster—The list of officers in any one army organization, containing their names, rank, corps, date of commission and other details, as the roster of a regiment.

Round—A general discharge of firearms or cannon, each piece being fired only once. Also, the walk of a guard or officer around the ramparts of a fort, to see if the sentinels are vigilant, or if all is safe. A "round of cartridge" is one cartridge to each soldier.

Roundel—A bastion of a circular form.

Rout—The confusion and dispersion of an enemy when badly defeated or panic-stricken.

Saber—A sword with a broad and heavy blade, having a curve toward its point; a weapon used by cavalry.

Saber-tasche—A small pendant pocket attached to the sword-belt of a cavalry officer.

Sack—To plunder or pillage a town or city.

Safe-conduct—A convoy or guard to protect a person in an enemy's country, while going from place to place.

Safe-guard—A protection given by the General of an army to exempt an enemy's person or property from molestation or plunder.

Sally, or **Sortie**—The sudden issuing forth of a strong body of besieged troops upon the works of the besiegers, in order to destroy them.

Salute—To honor any day, person, or nation by a discharge of fire-arms; also, the ceremony of presenting arms by a soldier on the approach of an officer; also, touching or lifting the cap by a subordinate officer on meeting his superior in rank. A "salvo'" is a volley of fire-arms not intended as a salute.

Sand-bags—Sacks filled with earth, used to stop breaches in an intrenchment made by cannonballs, shells, etc.

Scaling—Climbing walls for hostile purposes by means of ladders, etc.

Scouts—Persons employed in gaining information as to the movement and condition of an enemy; also, horsemen sent in advance, or on the right or left of an army, to discover the whereabouts of an enemy.

Sentry, or **Sentinel**—A private soldier placed on guard, to watch the enemy, prevent a surprise, and perform any special duty connected with his post.

Sergeant—A non-commissioned officer in a regiment, ranking just below a Lieutenant and next above a Corporal, whose duty is to instruct recruits in discipline, to form soldiers into ranks, etc.

Sergeant-Major—a non-commissioned officer in a regiment whose business it is to assist the Adjutant in his duties. (See Adjutant.)

Service—A general term for the army and its prescribed duties as a branch of the national defense; also the professional duty of any officer or soldier.

Shells—See Bomb and Grenade.

Siege—Surrounding or investing any fortified town or fortress with an army and attacking it with batteries, mines, and assaults until it capitulates or the besiegers are driven off.

Skirmish—An unorganized combat between detachments in the neighborhood or two contending armies.

Spherical-cone Shot—Thin shells filled with musket balls and fired from a howitzer.

Storm—A violent assault of besiegers upon a fortified place by climbing its walls, breaking down its gates, etc.

Stratagem—A General's device to cover his designs during a campaign and to device the enemy.

Strategy—The science of conducting great military movements; also, the hostile movements of armies when beyond the reach of each other's cannon.

Stretcher—A litter, or frame, on which sick or wounded men are carried.

Surprise—An unexpected attack from an enemy.

Tamp—To pack earth or other materials around a mine so as to prevent an explosion in a wrong direction.

Tattoo—A drum beat at night, warning soldiers to retire to rest, if in camp, or to retreat if on the battle field.

Traverse—Parapets of earth raised to cover troops from the enfilading fire of an enemy.

Trench—See Ditch.

Troop—A company of cavalry.

Troops—A general term for a collection of soldiers.

Trophy—Anything captured from an enemy.

Tumbrel—A two wheeled vehicle accompanying troops or artillery, for conveying tools, cartridges, etc.

Vedettes—Mounted sentries at outposts.

Vent—The opening in fire arms where fire is communicated to the charge.

Volley—A simultaneous discharge of numerous fire arms at the funeral of a soldier or in a combat.

Wings—The right or left division of an army or battalion.

Works—Any of the military fortifications or intrenchments described in this lexicon.

Source:
Author's private collection of historical military terms.

CHAPTER VIII

THE AMERICAN COWBOY

Unlike the Indian who first settled the American continent, and the trapper that explored it, the cowboy and cattleman stayed in one location and plied his trade. The first of the breed were the Spanish Vaqueros—descendants of the Spanish Conquistadores of the South and the adventurers who were after Montezuma's gold. The army and the missionaries who had tried to convert the natives drifted north as far as Laramie, leaving a trail of adobe huts and roads. Others moved west up the coast of California and some moved to the east near San Antonio, Texas. All through the western lands, towns with Spanish names sprung up: Munchahambra, San Diego, Sante Fe, El Paso, Los Angeles.

The loyal Spanish begged their mother country for help. Embroiled in wars with other powers at the time, the Crown sent domestic animals—cattle, pigs, horses, sheep, and chickens—for the Spaniards to raise and feed themselves and others. Domestic animals were restricted to a very few that had been raised by certain tribes of the Indians.

So the Spanish, a resourceful people, founded a new industry. The name 'Vaquero' meant stock raiser, and the division between cattle owners and cattle raisers was blurred then. The success of the Spanish venture attracted others to Texas and surrounding areas, and people from the east began to move there in sizable numbers.

Before statehood would be accomplished, the Mexicans wanted a crack at the territory. Concerned about the numbers of English-speaking emigrants,

Mexico tried again and again to regain the allegiance of the Hispanic inhabitants of Texas.

The Texans—and they thought of themselves as Texans—kept asserting their independence. Davy Crockett went to Washington several times to plead the case for the Lone Star State, but was rebuffed by the Eastern politicians. The protection and assistance of the U.S. was not forthcoming.

In 1836, Santa Anna, the Mexican President-Dictator, moved into San Antonio with a huge army to put down the revolt by Texans. Outnumbering the Texans by thirty to one, Santa Anna slaughtered the Texans at the Alamo in San Antonio. The main body of the Texas Army under General Sam Houston, routed the Mexican Dictator, took him prisoner, and forced his signature on a treaty acknowledging the independence of Texas. Mexico City removed Santa Anna from power for the first of three times. The Texas Army marked a first—women and children joined the men of Texas in fighting the Mexican Army, and a number of famous fighters joined the fray. The memory of the brave men under Travis, Bowie, and Crockett, who had been cut down defending the Alamo, became a rallying cry for the Texans who fought together under a single-starred flag: Remember the Alamo. In 1845, Texas elected to join the then twenty-seven state union, becoming the biggest state by far, as it encompassed more territory than Illinois, Indiana, Iowa, Michigan, and Wisconsin combined.

The Texans, combining the original Spanish with the children of settlers from the U.S., practiced cattle raising with a vengeance. Hides, horn, tallow, and corned beef moved East and brought back dollars for reinvestment. Along with the dollars came outlanders, British and French money, Americans now a few generations on this side of the water with money earned in the gold fields and beaver traps, invested in cattle and land. The longhorn cattle began to be replaced by other breeds, including the Angus and the shorthorn. Cattle was king in Texas.

Cattlemen—the owners of the big Texas spreads—were fewer in numbers than the folk hero: the Cowboy. Because it takes several acres of the sparse Texas scrub to support a single cow and calf, the spreads had to be large. The art of raising cattle was to be able to collect the animals at regular intervals for branding, counting, calving, and driving to market.

Enter the cowboy. He was—and is—a tough, wiry fellow who rides his horse, jeep, or helicopter and keeps his herds in some kind of good order. In the mid-1800s, the horse was his transportation and his home for many months of the year as was his bedroll and herding equipment.

Cowboys ride. They did in the 1800s and they do today. Coming to an understanding with a horse is extremely important to the cowboy whose life and livelihood depends on kinship with a four-footed appendage to himself. Most cowboys in the early days could not afford more than two horses, and often at least one of them was a wild horse, captured by roping and broken to the saddle. The first time a cowboy rides a horse, certain patterns are established that are difficult to change. So, if the horse and rider are to be *simpatico,* it just has to be done right. In a short time, the horse can begin to sense what is expected by the feel of the shift of weight in the saddle.

For "breaking" a horse, the cowboy uses neither bridle nor bit, rather a halter called a hackamore. The soft halter permits the horse to run instead of rear or buck. Once a horse begins to buck—as he usually will if he has a bit placed in his mouth before he trusts his rider—it is extremely hard to break the animal of the habit. Once the horse is ridden with a hackamore, the saddle is placed on his back and he is ridden again, with the saddle cinched. After a horse

is "broken" to the saddle, the process of training the horse to drive cattle begins.

The process of breaking and training does not differ much today from the process used in the 1800s. The necessary ingredient is trust—the animal must trust the rider and vice versa. But during the 1800s, the trail was longer and terrors more immediate. Outlaws, wild animals, uncharted trails with no standardized maps all made the trust between man and horse imperative.

A controversial piece of equipment was a heavy bit placed in the animal's mouth. Yet, cowboys were very careful to use the heavy bit wisely if at all. If a gulch opened immediately ahead of the rider and immediate action was necessary, the bit would stop the horse on a dime without jerking the reins.

1880-1890s. Oklahoma cowboy is all decked out and ready for a long fall trail ride. He totes a .44-40 caliber colt pistol along with a .38-40 Winchester saddle carbine.

Courtesy Joe M. Gish Collection, Texas

Excessive use of the bit would have made a skittish horse, something no cowboy wanted.

What was it like to be a cowboy? He spent hours astride a horse, carefully working a herd of cattle during round-up times and cattle drives. He worked hours alone on the range when cows were calving and having problems. He would try for hours to get hay or food of some kind to the animals who were unable to move snow aside and crop the grass underneath. It was terribly hard work at pay low enough to prevent the cowpoke from ever putting much away. There was fear of wild animals destroying the herd, or of outlaws, or of missing a trail and not finding essential water. There was also the clear sky with the Big Dipper shining at night, and the sound of a killdeer calling its mate and the smell of sage and desert flowers. No walls, no neckties, and no stiff collars.

While the biggest ranches were in Texas during the mid-1800s, other range areas in the West were also used for cattle raising, and cowboys usually knew the entire area. Starting in the spring, after calving, cowboys were responsible for moving the herds to areas with enough grass to support the herd until fall, and round-up time. Until 1934, cattlemen could graze their animals on open range—Federal land—without permits. In the early part of the 1800s, there was plenty of open range, and the cattle could move over hundreds of acres without any constriction. Then, 1862, the Homestead Act gave 160 acres to any man who would live on it and farm. Homesteaders built fences around their land, and denied the cattlemen access to the area and to water that might be on the land. As the Homesteaders began to polka-dot the landscape, getting the cattle to new pasture got difficult.

During the open range era, one of the most important times of the cowboy's year was round-up. At this time, the cattle was gathered and new calves were branded, with a specially shaped mark burned into the animal's hide. This brand was well-known among the various ranchers, and served as a way of identifying ownership of the animals.

Getting the brand on the animal was understandably tricky. The animal was roped and thrown to the ground, albeit as gently as possibly, and marked. Roping the cattle took great skill with the lariat and rapport between man and horse. A wrong move from the horse when the lariat was around the cow's neck was a disaster; if the animal began to circle the horse and rider and the rope wrapped around the cowboy, a sudden lurch could cut him in half. A ton of frightened heifer was difficult to predict and harder to control.

Eventually the brands were applied and the cattle would move to market, usually driven in herds of several brands, to a railroad siding in Kansas. Herds would normally move ten to fifteen miles a day. Cattle cannot survive more than a few days without water, so the drive was carefully planned to accommodate water supply.

Henry Buckolen, cowboy and rancher from Montana. He is dressed in a "Sunday Meeting Business Suit" with "shot gun chaps" and sporting a .44-40 caliber, 7½ inch barrel Colt revolver. Photo was taken by W.R. Finch who was in the business in Billings, Montana from 1879 to 1885.

Courtesy Joe M. Gish Collection, Texas

This dependence on water helped to dictate the make-up of the drive personnel. The trail boss was the absolute dictator and maker of decisions during the months of moving cattle from Texas, Colorado, Arizona and New Mexico to the Kansas railroad. He depended greatly on his scouts, who rode ahead and verified that water was indeed where it was reported. Scouts also kept a sharp eye out for possible rustlers; water holes were a likely spot for these desperados.

Another important member of the drive was the cook, with his chuckwagon equipped with pots, pans, dry beef, potatoes, flour for flapjacks and biscuits, and coffee. The cook set up a camp of sorts, prepared meals and listened to a barrage of complaints about the weight of the food in the stomach. Coffee smelled wonderful after a hard day in the saddle—even if it would dissolve a spoon carelessly left in the liquid.

The bulk of the drive was run by the cowboy, riding now at the edge of the herd, then among the cattle, endlessly separating and combining the herd and calming the animals. At night, cowboys kept watch over the animals and each other, circling the herd and humming or whistling a tune with long-forgotten words. After his watch was over, the cowboy stretched out under his bedroll with his saddle for a pillow and his rifle for his bedfellow. Sleep was shallow—the sound of change within the herd galvanized the cowboy to action. The sound of a coyote, the snap of a twig—these were instantly evaluated by the semi-sleeping cowboy. His life and livelihood depended on being right.

A typical scene around the campfire; a boiling pot of "Rio Coffee" bubbles in a pot over the fire. Here stories from the ol' timbers blend into a mixture of truth and fantasy. Yet, the new greenhorns listen with much eagerness.

Author's Collection

As the 1800s wore on, the Homestead Act and its complicating patchwork of 160 acre farms in the middle of rangeland was joined with other circumstances. The 1880s brought a weather shift to the Southwest, and great storms with blankets of snow changed the wintertime character of the west. Cattle are poorly equipped for survival in snow cover, and many did not survive this twist of wind and weather. Many of the biggest ranches failed; the biggest spreads were subdivided and sold. Cowboys found their work more demanding and probably more prosaic. After the open range was lost, the ranches began to cultivate pasture land, add ponds and watering holes—in short, they began to fit the land to the cattle instead of moving the cattle to suitable land.

Unlike most of the institutions of the old west, the cowboy looks much like he did in the 1800s. Wide-brimmed hats still form their silhouette against the sky. There is still a bandanna knotted around the neck, and cuban-heeled boots with pointed toes still cause the pitched-forward rolling gait. The cowboy today probably has a degree from an agricultural university and drives a four-wheel drive truck as often as he rides a horse. He may even pilot a helicopter on a round-up. He usually tags a calf's ear instead of burning on a brand.

There is still space and sky . . . and neckties aren't mandatory.

Arizona cowboys had much to deal with. If the Apache arrows didn't catch up with them, the prickly heat and wild Havalinas did. Rattlers were over six feet in length and as thick in the middle as a man's forearm.

Author's Collection

The Stetson Hat

John Batterson Stetson (1830–1906), a sickly man at the age of thirty-three, made his first experimental hat while on an expedition to Pike's Peak in 1863, when he realized the need of a sturdy wide-brimmed hat to be worn in almost all weathers. The hat was fashioned with home-made tools and a hatchet. Felt material, in the old days, was made by scraping the fur from dried skins of animals, chewing it up and spitting the liquid through the teeth. Stetson followed this method when he made his first hat.

This all came about while watching men who frequented the mountain and plains make their own hats by hand. It was very simple. A hole was dug in

the ground large enough for a man's head. A piece of wet rawhide was stretched over the hole and staked down. Several handfuls of grass was placed in the middle of the wet skin and gently pushed down into the hole. This took a little time for the man to shape the crown from the inside. The brim was also tamped down and cut to whatever width the man desired. The rawhide was dried out and later smoked and heated over a campfire. This was to insure a waterproof hat.

These hats did not last very long. After a period of time, the brim looked like a corrugated board cracking and coming apart in chunks. However, the hat served its purpose. Stetson had the idea of adding fur on the outside of the hat much like the tall beaver hats back East that were in demand. And, after experimenting with several hats, he came up with one that satisfied him. On his way back East, the hat became much of a joke. Everyone laughed and made fun of it. While in St. Louis, he sold the hat to a bull-whacker who offered him five dollars for it. When he returned to Philadelphia, he began to modify his hat and soon found enough money to manufacture the Stetson hat. His first product was called "Boss of the Plains."

After sending samples out West, the hat soon became very popular. It was a natural-colored felt with a high crown and wide brim. Noticing that his hat did not quite catch on along the Rio Grande he discovered that the men insisted on wearing the high crown saucer-shaped Mexican sombrero. He began manufacturing these also. Stetson hats literally covered heads of kings, commoners, cowboys, movie stars, and even the U.S Marines, for a little over a hundred years. In 1906, at the age of seventy-six, John B. Stetson died peacefully in his sleep. His name passed into the language of Western contributors because of the American cowboy who favored the Stetson hat above all others.[1]

The "Montana Peak" . . . around the late 1890s.

Southwestern or Texas style. The brim was curled, but the crown was not creased at all (circa 1870–1900s).

The hat usually came like this—right off the "hat-block." The purchaser formed it according to his own taste. Some only creased the top crown, leaving the wide brim as is.

Both city slickers and stockmen purchased this style which was very popular around the 1900s. Only a few cowboys wore this style. They much preferred a wide brim hat instead of the short one.

Work Shirts

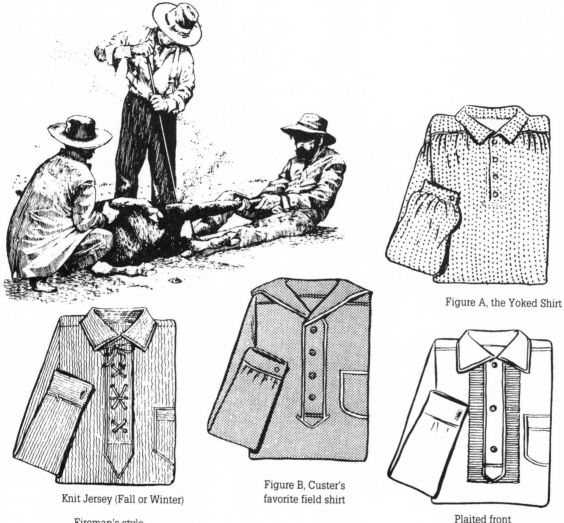

Figure A, the Yoked Shirt

Knit Jersey (Fall or Winter)

Figure B, Custer's favorite field shirt

Plaited front
for dress or work

Fireman's style

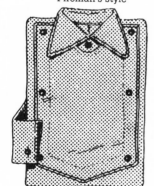

Most work shirts in the 1880s were the pullover type with a small foldover soft collar and a row of three or four buttons from the collar to about four inches from the belt line. The sleeves were straight and loosely hung with close fitting cuffs. If a man's arm was shorter than the sleeve length, he would use an adjustable arm garter made of elastic. Shirts were either wool or cotton, the colors subdued, and red was rarely seen. Favorites were colorful stripes, checks and solid patterns. Material varied from heavy knit Jersey to blue flannel, and from cassimere to percale, which is closely woven cotton fabric usually with a print on one side. A few shirts were manufactured without pockets, but the majority had one pocket on the left side. Price .75 to .90 each. Figure A, the yoked shirt of the 1850s and 60s came in a loud striped hickory, checked calico or gingham. The sleeves were full and loose at the wrist. Figure B, the popular Sailor shirt pullover was made fashionable during the Indian campaigns by Custer. Usually a dark blue color. Style from 1870s through the 1890s. Priced about .50 each.

Most shirts, designed to be worn with Levis, buckskins, or Army issue trousers were pullover types. Collars were usually soft fold-over styles, and three or four buttons formed a placket down the front of the shirt to a few inches above the belt line. Sleeves were straight and loose with a tight cuff buttoned around the wrist to keep the sleeve in place. Sleeves were usually made long, as shrinkage took place with laundering. When the garment was new, the longer sleeves were gathered up with an arm garter made of elastic.

Shirts were usually made from cotton or wool fabric and colors were somewhat subdued. Stripes, checks, and solid colors were the most popular: the red-and-black check now thought of as a western shirt was not seen in the real west. Fabrics could be a heavy knit jersey or a closely woven thin cotton called percale, usually printed on one side.

Most shirts had one pocket on the left side. Some shirts, such as the illustration A featured a gathered yoke across the top, usually made from checked calico or gingham or a bright striped pattern. These models cost about seventy-five cents to ninety cents each. Figure B is the popular sailor shirt worn by General Custer during his sojourn in the West. These were usually a solid dark blue with a decorative braid or piping. Price was about fifty cents.

These styles were popular between 1870 and 1890.

Riding Cuffs

Black leather "spots" and stitching with leather straps and buckles. Made in Malta, Montana.

From the
J.M. Gish Collection

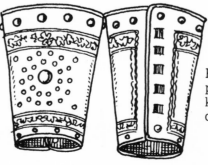

These basket-weave cuffs were used in the early "101 Ranch" Wild West Show, around 1890–1900.

From the
J.M. Gish Collection

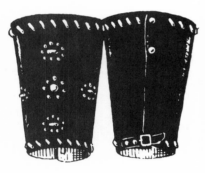

Cuffs with stars were often adopted for pride and identification by Texas cowboys.

From the
J.M. Gish Collection

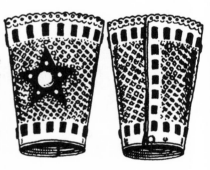

William S. Hart, re-knowned cowboy star of the early 1920s, introduced cuffs in his films.

From MGM movie prop auction—the kind used by movie cowboys of the 1920s.

From the
J.M. Gish Collection

Leather cuffs appeared as part of cowboy garb during the late 1800s. They were made from plain leather and worn to protect the wrists from rope or rein burns, barbed wire, thorns, mesquite, cactus—and the other ills of the western prairies. The cuffs were attached with leather straps and buckles, and usually replaced gloves entirely.

Later, cuffs became embellished with raised metal studs called "spots," layers of varied-colored leather and other decorations.

Cuffs became part of the movie cowboy's gear after they were worn by early star William S. Hart. Several cuffs that are now part of the J.M. Gish collection include cuffs made from black leather with spots and stitching, basket-weave cuffs with stars, and other designs.

The Cowboy's Riveted Britches

By 1877, Levi Strauss's riveted pants were available in indigo blue denim as well as the white-tan cotton duck that he had introduced in the California gold fields in 1850. The durable trousers with rivet-reinforced pockets and cinch straps had become a standard with the cowboy. He held up the pants with suspenders, attached to the provided buttons (two in back and four in front) until belt loops were added in 1922. The cotton fabrics shrank—to fit, the ads and salesmen told the wearers—and the extra inch or so at the waist was gathered into the cinch strap and buckle sewn into the back of the britches. Brown duck pants lost popularity, and ceased to be manufactured at sometime around 1896.

Source:
Levi's. Ed Cray, Houghton Mifflin Co., 1978

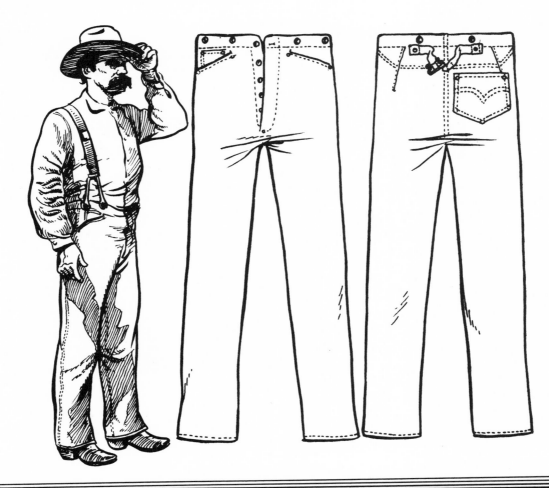

Chaps

Mexican vaqueros wore apron-like garments that they called Armas, tough leather flaps that fastened over the front of the saddle and were laid over his lap like a blanket after mounting the saddle. While these protected the rider from thorns and other woes, they were cumbersome and required affixing every time the rider mounted or dismounted. Also, the Armas were only effective when the cowboy was on his horse—and there were thorns in abundance when he was off the horse, too.

Texans substituted the Armitas—an apron that tied to the waist and around the knees. The leather fell below the knees slightly. These appeared around 1860. By 1870, a garment that covered both front and back of the legs, with fringes down the side appeared. Called Shotgun Chaps—pronounced "shaps"—the garment buckled around the waist and provided added pockets.

Chaps—derived from "chaparejos"—then evolved to include the batwing design which was wider and knotted with rawhide (appearing about 1900) for ease in removal. This garment originated at the foot of the Colorado Rockies. Grizzlies, Angora, or Woolies were made from hides with fur sides out, and were warmer in northern countries. These were seldom worn in the southwestern areas and were not acceptable at all in brush country.

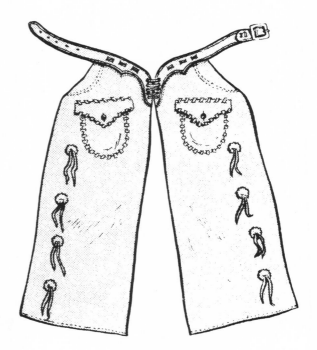

B. Batwing chaps

C. Grizzlies

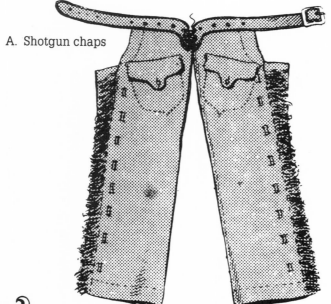

A. Shotgun chaps

Boots

Cowboys needed special footwear to help them when roping cattle or to assist in keeping tabs on a rearing, wheeling horse. These boots, with their high heels and pointed toes gave the cowboy the stance he needed—as well as a particular rolling walk that was characteristic of the profession. Boots were expensive; they cost about seven dollars for a general, store-bought pair, and up to fifteen dollars from a good bootmaker.

Source:
The Look of the Old West, Foster and Harris, Viking Press, 1955
They Saddled the West, Rice and Vernam, Cornel Maritime Press, Inc., 1975
What People Wore, D. Gorsline, Viking Press, 1952
The Cowboys, Time Life Series

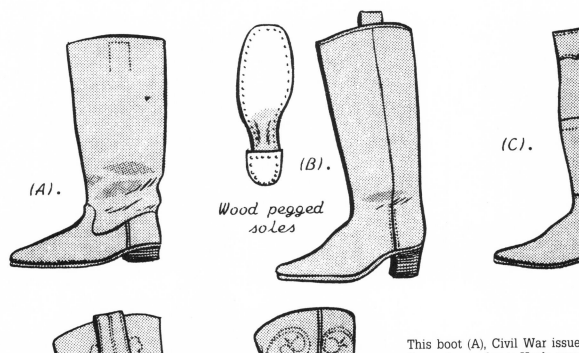

(A).

(B).

Wood pegged soles

(C).

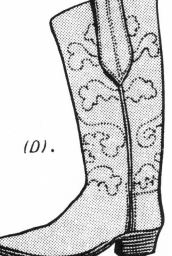
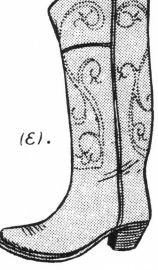

(D).

(E).

This boot (A), Civil War issue, was used by the early cowboys. Heels were flat and toes were round. This gave way to the cavalry boot (B) with a reinforced arch, higher heels and wood pegged sole. This boot appeared between 1860 and 1870. Toes became more pointed and "mule ears" appeared in (C), to assist in pulling the boot on. These appurtenances made their appearance in 1870-80, growing to the size shown in (D). Fancy tooling also found its way onto the boots. by the mid-1880s boots were quite fancy (E) with softer leather providing a snugger fit.

"Gut Hooks"

Spurs are chosen by the professional cowboy to do as little damage to the horse as possible, while maintaining control of the animal. Thus, spurs usually have larger rowls—the revolving points attached to the shank of the spur. The bigger the rowl, the less discomfort is caused. It is the small rowl with few points that cause pain to the animal.

Many different spurs were used over the years, including the early "OK" spur available around 1900. It was a practical spur for every day use.

The Chihuahua spur was used on the South-western border, and featured silver squares inlaid on the side of the heel bank.

During the 1892 and early 1900s, fancy spurs were introduced, with carvings and inlays along the heel banks.

The Model 1874 Army spur was all brass with a smooth finish. Small rowels, about dime size, were sometimes fitted.

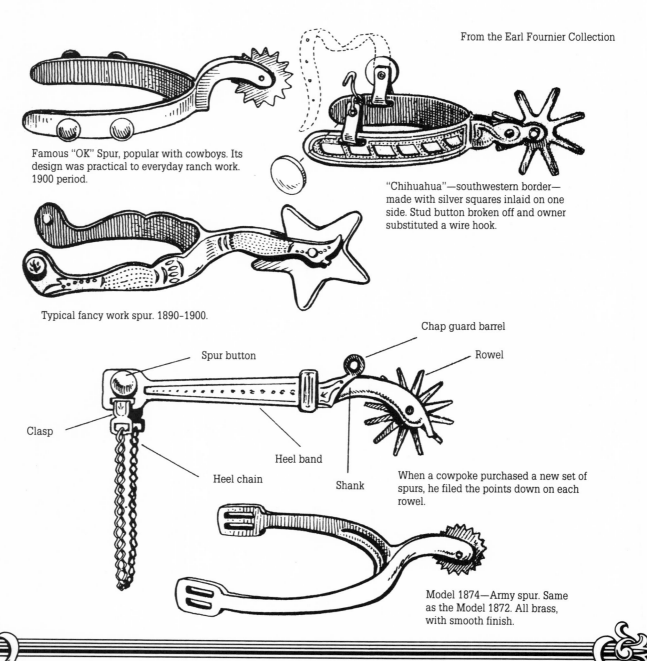

From the Earl Fournier Collection

Famous "OK" Spur, popular with cowboys. Its design was practical to everyday ranch work. 1900 period.

"Chihuahua"—southwestern border—made with silver squares inlaid on one side. Stud button broken off and owner substituted a wire hook.

Typical fancy work spur. 1890-1900.

Chap guard barrel

Rowel

Spur button

Clasp

Heel band

Heel chain

Shank

When a cowpoke purchased a new set of spurs, he filed the points down on each rowel.

Model 1874—Army spur. Same as the Model 1872. All brass, with smooth finish.

The Duster

The long, linen coat worn as protection from the clouds of dusts on cattle drives had its origin during the Civil War, when the all-purpose garment was worn by field surgeons, Army scouts, contracted haulers of materials—and almost anyone who traveled by stage coach a lot. The early designs featured a single row of buttons—usually six—down the front with a small turnover collar. A vented back permitted horsemen to mount the saddle with ease, while the duster rested over the horse's rib cage. An adjustable belt at the back permitted the duster to be fitted according to the wearer's needs.

After the Civil War, and about the time of the first of the great cattle drives, the duster was modified to include a split lapel at the front, to permit the flap to be closed for more protection. This duster almost touched the ground—it came to only a few inches above the rider's boot tops.

A double-breasted duster appeared around 1900, and was designed for the rider. This model was available in either linen or canvas.

Later models were provided for riders of new-fangled touring cars. These garments had either a double split collar or single falling collar, and slits under the pockets were added to enable the wearer to reach pants pockets as well.

Source:
Matthew Brady and His Works, Time/Life, Merserve Collection
Following the Frontier, F. Jay Haynes, A.A. Knopf
Sears and Roebuck Catalog, 1897

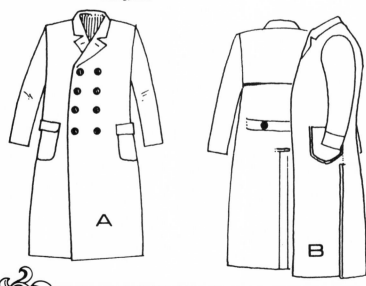

A. The double-breasted duster is a later model manufactured prior to 1900 and was made solely for the mounted man. The material was either linen or a lightweight canvas.

B and C. Both came after the 1900s. Style B shows a slit under the pocket on both the left and right sides. This duster was manufactured almost exclusively for the driver and passenger of the motorized touring car. Either a double split collar or a single falling collar was available with this design.

The Yellow Slicker

Riding a horse in the rain could be a miserable affair, sitting in a saddle full of water while more poured down the back of the hapless cowboy's neck. Cowboys worked in bad weather as well as good, and the introduction of a waterproofed coat, long enough to cover the saddle, helped alleviate the effects of Heaven's little tricks.

It appeared very early in the 1880s, and at that time cost $2.65–$3.00. Made from canvas or duck and coated with linseed oil, the "Fishskin" or "Tower" saddle coat, when the back vent was unbuttoned, fit comfortably over wearer and saddle. By buttoning the vent closed, the coat kept the wearer dry when walking.

The garment was ankle length, and available in chest sizes from 36 to 44. It was offered by several manufacturers, primarily for cowboys and cattlemen.

Early Western Saddles

Western saddles required 200 years of improvements, mostly by trial and error. Several types were developed during the 1800s and early 1900s, and specific types had their own following.

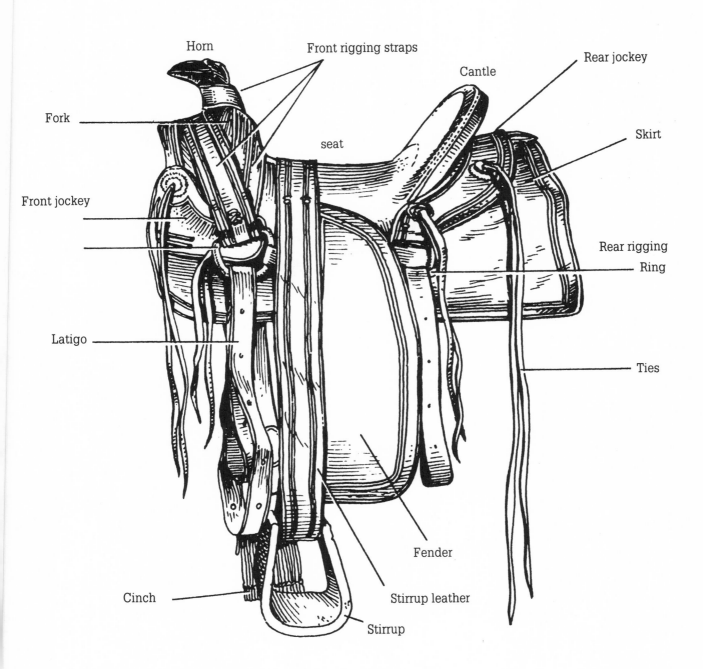

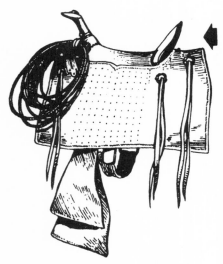

A. They called it the Mother Hubbard saddle, and it featured holes on the side skirts for ventilation. It was a typical trail driver's saddle right up to 1890, but was first seen around 1830. The long side skirts and the relative plainness gave rise to its name, compared to the fancy leatherwork and metal designs which developed over the years. Stirrups were hollowed wood, later covered with Tapaderas—leather casings.

B. "Mothers" skirts disappeared on the next version, called the Texas Saddle, which appeared around 1850. The leather covered wooden horn grew thicker and heavier to better hold the ropes needed to control cattle during round-up. Fenders made from leather were added to protect the rider from the sweating horse, and the saddle was double cinched.

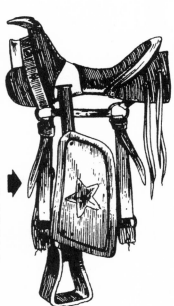

C. Saddles grew lighter, and the Cheyenne Saddle, appearing about 1875 featured a double cinch for heavy roping. The wooden frame was all leather covered, and the weight dropped to about 40 pounds.

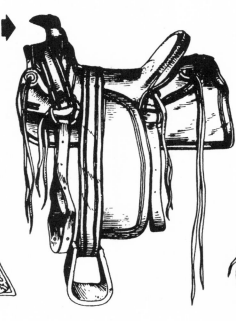

D. A metal horn was a distinctive feature of the California Saddle, appearing at the turn of the century. This fancy tooled saddle had a square skirt, and dished cantles added to the rider's comfort. The metal horn helped this saddle lose another 10 pounds without losing function.

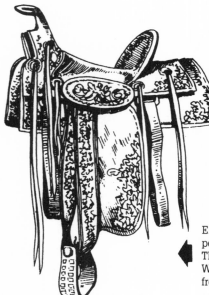

E. Between 1910 and 1920, the Oregon Saddle appeared, with its lower horn and lowered cantles. The swelled fork type was manufactured until World War I. In 1920, these saddles were banned from rodeos.

Western Bits

As cattle drives became more of an institution in the early years of this country, the cowboy found the Mexican type horse-bit far more successful in manipulating his horse on a trail drive than the Army bits or regular civilian riding bits. Controlling a horse not quite broken and a little skittish around moving cattle, took much more effort and the chance of some broken bones if the rider was ever thrown.

The basics of the Mexican bits seemed a bit harsh in a horses's mouth compared to what the cowboys were already using; these bits could tear at the animal's mouth, often causing severe damage. But, if a cowman operated his reins in a humane way, both rider and horse got along together very well.

In describing a horse's bit, we find the metal part of a bridle which goes into the horse's mouth and to which the headstall and reins are attached. The center bar of the bit which connects the two side plates or "cheeks" is known as the "mouth" or "mouthpiece." When this center bar is linked together in the middle, this is called a "snaffle bit." When the bar is curved upwards, this curve is called a "port." With the Mexican and Spanish bits, we find a small brass roller (corrugated) inside this port, called

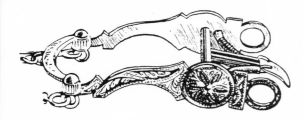

The "Spade Bit" was very painful to the animal in the hands of an unskilled cowboy. It had a flat metal projection on the top of the port which bent upwards pressing against the horse's tongue and with anything but a gentle touch of the reins, came in contact with the roof of the mouth, the horse's most sensitive spot.

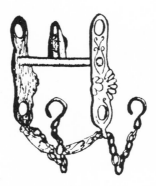

The "Half-breed" had a narrow wicket-shaped hump in the middle of the mouth-bar, or a rounded "A" where a roller or "cricket" was fixed so the horse could amuse himself with it. Another term for this roller was "taster."

The "Ring Bit" circled the horse's lower jaw; the ring pressed a sensitive nerve. The curb beneath the jaw also helped to control the animal. This bit was considered the cruelist device ever to be put into a horse's mouth. It was capable of breaking his jaw.

The "Snaffle Bit" was a center bar made in two pieces and connected with interlocking eyes, also called a "broken bit" or "limber bit." The chain bit was similar to the snaffle bit, but it was never widely adopted.

The "Curb Bit" or grazing bit was the simplest and most humane bit, as it had a low port. This was probably the most popular bit in cow country.

The "Bar Bit" like most bits, had a ring at each end to which the reins were attached. These bits were more suitable for driving teams than for cow ponies. This bit was not severe enough to stop an animal in his tracks.

a "roller" or "barrel roller." The horse likes to spin this copper roller or "taster" with his tongue.

As the years rolled by, the variety of bits was narrowed down to six basic designs: bar, snaffle, spade, ring, half breed, and curb bit. All designs fell into one of these categories, or were combination thereof.

It was fairly easy to tell where a cowboy hailed from just by examining his horse's bit. The Texans, east of the Rockies, favored the curb bit. West of the Rockies, where the Mexican influence was strong, the spade bit was preferred.

Barbed Wire

Barbed wire changed the face of the West forever and triggered bloody range wars. Early settlers had planted hedges to keep animals within specific areas. The most popular plant was the Osage Orange, whose heavy thorns successfully kept domestic animals at home and wild ones away. Seeing the thorns on the Osage Orange, and knowing that such trees wouldn't grow in the arid areas, Joseph Glidden of DeKalb, Illinois invented the next best thing—wire fencing with thorns. First manufactured commercially in 1873, Glidden's barbed wire fence angered the cattlemen and cowboys, but provided the means to divide the areas given to homesteaders under the Homestead Act.

There were several forms of barbed wire, from the locally fabricated "Thorny Fence" of 1868 to the Waukegan Wire, first introduced in 1890 and still being manufactured today.

Source:
Barbed Wire—Whose Invention, A.G. Warren, American Steel and Wire, 1926
The Wire that Fenced the West, H.D. and F. T. McCallum, University of Oklahoma Press, 1979

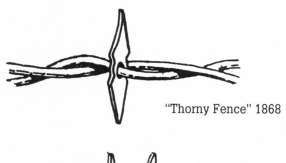

"Thorny Fence" 1868

"Blink Flat" 1881. Used extensively by the XIT outfit.

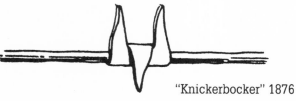

"Knickerbocker" 1876

"Decker Spread" 1884

"Ross's" Four Point 1879

"Waukegan Wire" 1890. Still being manufactured.

The Chuck Wagon

All of the Western movies featured a cook called "Cookie," a tough but understanding paragon who was usually much maligned for the quality of his cuisine. He held sway in the chuck wagon, a king of open-air kitchen, that, in real life was designed in 1866 by cattle baron Charles Goodnight-or so it is believed. The early wagons were based on old army wagons, with shelves and drawers added to the rear. The wagon was usually selected for its strong axles and rear wheels, where most of the extra weight rested. A tail gate was usually added, especially when ordinary farm wagons began to be used extensively.

The tail gate served as a table, and the drawers and shelves carried corn meal, flour, green coffee, potatoes, salt and soda, bacon, beans, a sourdough barrel, a bottle of calomel, and often a private stash of Cookie's favorite all-purpose remedy, probably rum or whiskey.

Under the tail gate or chuck box was the "boot," where cooking pots and utensils were stored. A barrel at one side of the wagon, held at least a two day supply of water. Counterbalancing the water barrel was a heavy tool box.

The wagon bed itself carried bedrolls, war bags, corral ropes, guns, ammunition, lanterns, kerosene, slickers, sections of canvas, and occasionally a sick cowboy or lame calf.

The chuck wagon was the meeting place for the hands during a roundup or other event, and the cook was an important member of the group. Food was cooked over brush or buffalo chips, and gathering the

fuel was one way of getting on Cookie's good side.

During the late 1800s, several companies began to manufacture the chuck wagons. The Studebaker Company produced one model offered for $75–$200, and other similar wagons were widely produced.

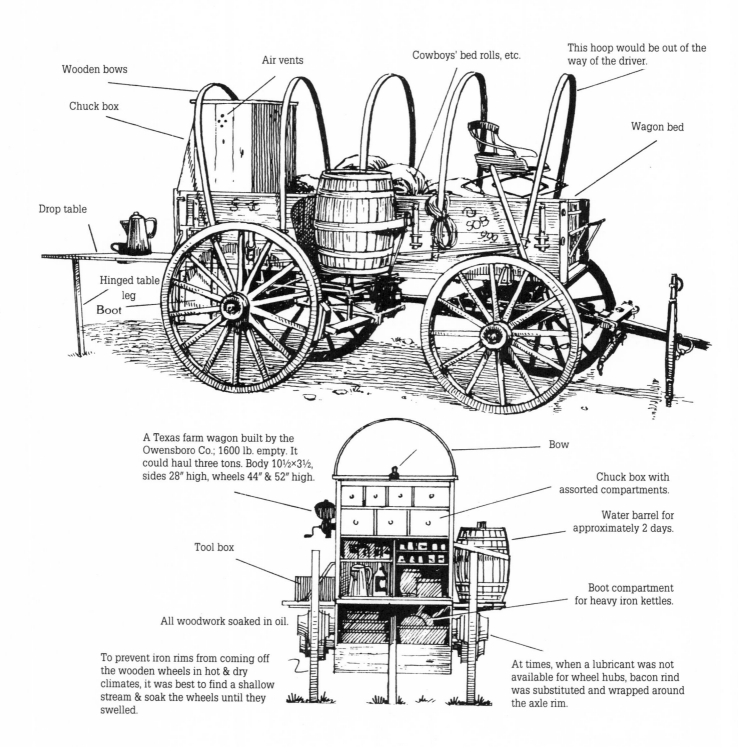

Wooden bows

Air vents

Cowboys' bed rolls, etc.

This hoop would be out of the way of the driver.

Chuck box

Wagon bed

Drop table

Hinged table leg

Boot

A Texas farm wagon built by the Owensboro Co.; 1600 lb. empty. It could haul three tons. Body 10½×3½, sides 28″ high, wheels 44″ & 52″ high.

Bow

Chuck box with assorted compartments.

Water barrel for approximately 2 days.

Tool box

Boot compartment for heavy iron kettles.

All woodwork soaked in oil.

To prevent iron rims from coming off the wooden wheels in hot & dry climates, it was best to find a shallow stream & soak the wheels until they swelled.

At times, when a lubricant was not available for wheel hubs, bacon rind was substituted and wrapped around the axle rim.

How to Throw a Rope

This is a complete description showing how this peculiar tool was used. It was so indispensable on the Great Trail Drives and on ranches during a roundup, that without it the cowboy was rendered useless. Here are many curious and interesting facts concerning the lasso.

A lasso was about forty feet long—seldom exceeding fifty feet—and out of that must be deducted the amount taken to make the noose and the part which is retained in the hand. Thus it was seen that the average overhead cast was about twenty-five or thirty feet, and the "roper" who could throw anywhere near fifty feet with accuracy was a rarity. In California they sometimes used a rope as long as sixty-five feet, but they seemed to have a habit of throwing an enormous loop, much larger than was really necessary. In actual work it was found that a man's hand was not large enough to properly hold much more than forty feet of rope when coiled ready to throw.

The lasso was a creation of a certain environment and need. Its place was on the broad prairies and grazing lands, and its chief utility lay in the stock business. It was "useless in a wooded country by reason of the obstruction afforded by branches and

bushes." The lasso seemed to be a weapon of the chase, peculiar to North America and the outcome of practical need.

The finest lassos were of rawhide, cut into thin strips and braided by hand, six-ply, into a rope of ⅜ inch to ½ inch in diameter. They were quite expensive, a good forty foot rope selling for seven dollars. On this account, in later years a fine, hard-twisted grass rope was used, but the rawhide rope was the best in a wind, as it was heavier and when filled with oil it was not affected by wet weather. A braided rope also had more of a tendency to kink than a twisted rope. Cowboys had a mixture of lard and beeswax with which they dressed their hemp or linen ropes to keep out dampness and to prevent them from getting too dry.

There were three general methods of throwing a rope, with many minor variations of individual habit. The rope was held in practically the same way in every case. First, in the plain, straight cast, the noose was swung around above the head from right to left by a rotating wrist movement. Some "ropers" threw a small loop, hard and fast, almost on a level. Others threw a larger, lazier kind, which nevertheless "arrived." The small loop thrown hard was a favorite, as it seemed the best all-round style, most effective against the wind or other adverse conditions.

The aim was somewhat to the right of the object to be roped (say a foot-and-a-half on a twenty-five foot throw), the exact instant of release being governed by the weight of the rope, wind, velocity of swing, etc. Judgement came instinctively with practice. The rest of the rope was held coiled in the other hand and released as fast as desired, two or three coils being retained.

To "snub" the rope (wind it around the pommel after casting) in the instant of time allowed, was a trick quite as difficult as throwing properly. The Mexicans, with their large-diameter pommels, only had to take one turn; the American pommels, being smaller, required two. The pommel often smoked from friction created and was frequently deeply grooved and almost burned by the rope.

The important part played by a trained cowpony

was obvious. He was taught to settle back on his haunches the instant the rope tightened, and in many other ways to materially assist his master.

The second method of throwing was exactly the reverse. The noose was swung from the left to the right above the head before release. This was called the "California Throw," and possibly gave a little greater range. At any rate, one or two of the longest throwers known presently at rodeos use it. Any "roper" can throw either way.

The third cast is the "Corral Drag," which, as its name implies, was for use within a corral or confined quarters. It consisted of trailing out the loop on the ground behind one and snapping it forward by an underhand motion.

It was possible to control the noose of a lasso by the remainder of the rope, but it was a dexterity which few acquired even after years of practice.

The spinning of the rope required great practice to acquire general accuracy, and was also useful in catching animals by the feet. It gave a certain

amount of control of the noose after it had left the hand (by manipulating the remainder of the rope), which those who did not practice did not attain. From this foundation of throwing a rope, many elaborate and interesting feats are possible.

In spinning the rope, many cowboys have been accused of sticking or securing the "hondu" or slip noose to keep it from sliding; but in reality it is perfectly free to move along the rope. In fact, one can readily start spinning a noose two feet in diameter and increase it steadily to eight or ten feet across.

In picking out and roping any particular leg of an animal while in motion, it would be difficult to analyze the method. The thrower whirled the noose while watching the foot rise and fall, and when the instinctive feeling comes of the right time, he let go.

The Mexican generally used a larger "eye" or more open "hondu" for the slip noose than the American did. The latter used the rope a good deal in branding calves, and required a small "hondu" to allow the noose to close quite snugly on their slender legs.

The Longhorn

The earliest Longhorn cattle arrived in America around 1540 with Francisco Vasquez de Coronado when he made his first exploration of what is now the southern part of the United States. These were the first cattle to enter the country.

Two distinct features made these animals stand out like a sore thumb. Their average horn spread was about four feet; horns over seven feet were uncommon. At full maturity some animals died from starvation as their horns grew and twisted on a downward angle, making it hard to feed off the ground. They were also called "rainbow cattle" because of their wide variety of colors. There were black, white, blue, mulberry, speckled, ring-streaked and spotted combinations along with bays and reds, white faces and black faces. No other animal known produced the color variation these Longhorns displayed. The Spanish cattle were the long, sharp-horned breed that had been raised by the Moors of North Africa and the Andalusians for thousands of years. They were a fierce, crafty breed that could fend for themselves

and survive everywhere. They were swift, cunning, and very dangerous. As Coronado journeyed northward, he left the crippled and exhausted stock along the way. After a number of years these stragglers multiplied to several hundreds. As wild cattle, they crossed the Rio Grande and spread through the Southwest. They did not roam as far as the horse, but only to the Red River which now separates Texas and Oklahoma.

By the middle of the nineteenth century, the great herds of American Buffalo were being slaughtered by hunters and hide hunters, leaving a vast ocean of rich grassland. Into this colossal pasture moved the cattle, and there multiplied by the millions. In 1860, an estimated six million Longhorns roamed the Texas plains alone. The first cattle drive of Longhorns arrived in New Orleans in 1842, and eight years later more were driven to California. In 1859, these "mustang cattle" (meaning strays), were driven across Indian Territory to Colorado. And, in 1867, a drove of "cimarrones" (the wild ones) ambled up the rugged trail from Lockhart, Texas, to Abilene, Kansas, beginning the great cattle drives which for the next seventeen years would bring 4,000,000 Longhorns up the trail to stock northern ranches and fill the slaughter houses for eastern markets.

As the cattle industry began to boom, ranchers saw that by breeding the rugged Longhorn with Hereford, Polled Angus and other types of cattle from the East, there was no longer a need for Longhorns, a high-hipped, long-legged animal. The need was more meat, so the wild Longhorn began to disappear. A preserve has been set aside by the government to save the remaining small number of the breed left in the Wichita Mountains Wildlife Refuge, Cache, Oklahoma.

Source:
The Longhorns (1941), J. Frank Dobie.

The Hereford

Buffalo herds were plentiful, but the eastern half of the United States was slow to accept the characteristic flavor of buffalo meat. Other animals were brought to the West, forming the great herds that provided meat and leather. One of the main animals was—and is—the Hereford, first bred in Herefordshire, England. The first of these stocky animals, with their glossy mahogany coats and white faces and underbelly were imported about 1817. A record of importation was kept by Henry Clay, the great orator, and his partner Lewis Sanders, in Kentucky in about 1817. Another recorded notice of these animals was that of the gift of Herefords from Admiral Coffin of the Royal British Navy to the Massachusetts Society for the Promotion of Agriculture. This gift was dated 1825.

The first real breeding herd appears to have been that of William H. Sotham and Erastus Corning of Albany, New York, in 1840.

Herefords became widely accepted in the West after that time as it was strictly a beef animal. Both bull and cow have the characteristic red and white coats, and curved horns, pointing downward. The animals are quite compact, with a short, broad face and wideset eyes, helpful when grazing over large distances where coyotes and other animals may be interested in their whereabouts.

The Brahman

Called "Brahman" or "Zebu," these cattle from India have intermixed with nearly half of the cattle in the world, improving both kinds of cattle and making them more adaptable to the grass ranges of the western states. The *Bos indicus* were first imported into the States by James Bolton Davis of South Carolina in 1849, followed by an important importation by the Pierce Estate of Wharton County, Texas in 1906. More of the Brahmans were brought through Mexico in 1924, to John T. Martin's ranches near San Antonio, Texas. Other importations followed, and the distinctive animals became a part of the western scene.

Brahmans offered a variety of characteristics to the American cattleman. The animals, with their humpbacks, short, up-curved horns and heavy foreheads appeared in several colors, including gray or red with white spots and similar colors and combinations, plus brown.

Since those early days in the west, Brahmans have become a specific American breed that differs from the Indian ancestors. They have been specially crossbred for extra weight and good beef characteristics.

Stampede

It is surprising what little things might start a stampede that would perhaps cost many lives and the loss of hundreds of cattle before it could be controlled.

Several cowboys are coming up the Texas trail keeping an eye on a standing herd of 4,000 cattle. One of the boys opens his tobacco pouch to get a chew. A gust of wind blows a shred or two of fine cut out of his fingers. The shred of tobacco floats away and lodges in a steer's eye. In a moment the eye begins to smart, and the steer goes wild. In its painful antics it annoys the others, and in ten seconds the whole herd is surging and dashing about, out of control. Then the stampede. It takes two days before the cowboys can bring the herd quietly together again. Two of the outfit's best trail boys are trampled to death, a score or more injured, and 400 cattle lost.

Hail storms were greatly dreaded by cowboys on the trail, especially when thunder-heads rolled in at night when the cattle were resting. If a hailstone happened to strike a steer in the eye, a stampede was certain to follow. It would spring to its feet and in thrashing around, tramp on the tails of others. They would jump up in pain. The herd is alarmed and before anything could be done, the whole lot were off like a flash. The bark of a coyote in a still night was sufficient to stampede a herd. Many seasoned cowboys, riding herd at night, would hum or sing in a soft tone. This would comfort the herd and reassure them of a peaceful night.

In a cattle stampede, the herd on the run across country could travel at a twenty-mile-an-hour gait, and there was no way of guessing which direction they would take. It was during a stampede that the

208

cowboys worked the hardest. One of the biggest jobs was to keep the flying herd together. They urged their mustangs dead against the advancing column of frantic cattle at the constant risk of their lives, trying to work the cattle gradually into a circle. The cowboys would all ride to the right around the stampeding herd, and if they could get the cattle to run in a circle, the first important step in controlling the herd was accomplished.

The cowboy was sometimes obliged to ride around a herd for a distance of over 200 miles before he could get them under control, and then it was only twenty-five miles from where it started. In all that time, not one of the men took a moment's rest or a bite to eat. But . . . when the time came when the cowboy was relieved of his duties, he would make a bee-line for the chuck wagon for a plate of hot beans, cornbread and quarter inch sliced bacon. After several cups of Rio Coffee, he finally crawled into his bedroll.

CHAPTER IX

The Bertillion System

This was the first method to prove helpful in identifying criminals in almost all countries by measuring certain boney parts of the body. The system was founded on three basic principles:

1. That precise measurements of certain parts of the body can be easily taken;

2. That these measurements remain constant after maturity,

3. That no two humans have the same dimensions in all the parts measured.

The measurements include length and width of the head, length and width of the right ear, length of left

Illustration of a later period (1900) identification file card on "Butch" Cassidy, alias George Parker.

Courtesy Pinkerton Inc.

FORM 55-3-'01-10M-AE.

P. N. D. A. .... No.

NAME......George Parker.   No. 469 R

ALIAS......"Butch" Cassidy; George Cassidy; Ingerfield.

NATIVITY...United States. COLOR......White

OCCUPATION...........:......Cowboy; rustler

CRIMINAL OCCUPATION..........Bank robber, highwayman, cattle and horse thief

AGE......37 yrs (1902). HEIGHT.....5 ft. 9 in

WEIGHT....165 lbs.... BUILD...... Medium

COMPLEXION ....Light

COLOR OF HAIR..........................Flaxen

EYES..........Blue. NOSE.....................

STYLE OF BEARD .....Mustache; sandy, if any

REMARKS:—Two cut scars back of head, small scar under left eye, small brown mole calf of leg. "Butch" Cassidy is known as a criminal principally in Wyoming, Utah, Idaho, Colorado and Nevada and has served time in Wyoming State penitentiary at Laramie for grand larceny, but was pardoned January 19th, 1896. Wanted for robbery First National Bank, Winnemucca, Nevada, September 19th, 1900 See Information No. 421.

middle and little fingers, and length of left forearm and foot. Measurements were classified in terms of small, medium and large sizes. Index cards were also divided into three groups, according to these measurements. Along with this, his record of prison time, convictions, and any other bits of information were recorded on these cards. A "descriptive portrait" was another of sectional photography introduced by Bertillion to revise the prevailing haphazard system of photographing suspects. Front and profile views were taken, as well as views of any distinguishing marks and characteristics.

Alphonse Bertillon's developed system became much used by police agencies from 1879 to the turn of the century.[1] His revolutionary system, including the "Portrait Parle," or "Descriptive" section photography, was used in Paris from 1882 and was officially adopted for all France in 1888. It was widely used in Europe and North America until the method of fingerprinting, a newer form of identification was introduced.

Source:
Indentification Anthropometrique. Alphonse Bertillon. (Paris, 1893)
Alphonse Bertillon. Henry Rhodes. (New York, 1956)

Early police mug shots after the Bertillon System, circa 1897–98.

Author's Collection

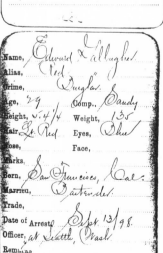

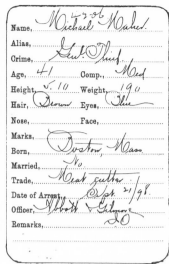

Fingerprinting

The first known scientific observation relating to fingerprints was recorded in the 1680s by a professor of anatomy and an English physician at the University of Bologna. In 1823, another professor of anatomy at the University of Breslau, published a paper on the diversified ridge patterns of the fingers, noting that they followed nine general pattern types. However, there still wasn't any indication that the ridges on the fingers could be adapted to individual identification.

In 1880 Dr. Henry Faulds of the Tsukiji Hospital in Tokyo, Japan, wrote a letter to an English magazine *Nature*, explaining his research of fingerprint identification. In this published work he observed and studied the great diversity among individual fingerprint patterns and the fact that they remained unchanged throughout one's lifetime. He suggested that these prints, found at various crime scenes, could possibly identify the offender.

The magazine *Nature* seemed to open locked doors involving the subject matter of fingerprints. Not long after the first article, a second followed written by a British officer stationed in Bengal, India. His letter revealed that for twenty years, fingerprints had been taken to identify government pensioners, as well as

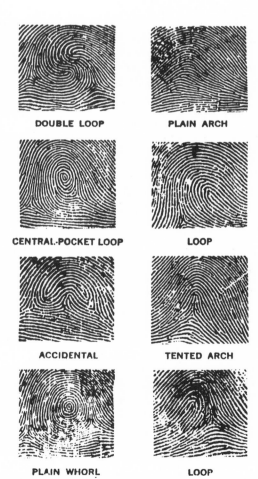

DOUBLE LOOP   PLAIN ARCH

CENTRAL-POCKET LOOP   LOOP

ACCIDENTAL   TENTED ARCH

PLAIN WHORL   LOOP

prisoners confined in prison. This was the first logical method of classification that made it practicable in filing and recording fingerprint records by law enforcement agencies.

The first feasible use of fingerprints for criminal identifications was made by New York State authorities who began to fingerprint prisoners in 1903.[2] Other police agencies soon adopted fingerprinting, replacing their rogues' galleries, which were based on photographs, description, and measurements of each convict.[3]

Fingerprint cards of criminals were, and still are, maintained separately, providing law enforcement agencies all through the country with an easier, and faster means of locating wanted criminals.

The Law Badge

Peace officers wore various types of badges; some were five pointed stars while others were six pointed. A circle around the points or a half circle above was all that was needed to show official rank. If a badge could not be displayed, a simple ribbon was used with an imprint of the official office. Sometimes a hat band might be used in place of a badge showing an imprint of office.

As early as 1868, companies manufacturing badges sent their salesmen out into different cities and towns, with catalogs showing different styles of badges either in nickel-plating or German silver. Suitcase samples were exhibited with gold inlay, silver, steel, copper, or brass, with prices from one dollar up. Regular stock items were much cheaper with the exception of the engraving, an additional price. Salesmen from different companies lugged sample cases with them displaying blank badges, a number set, tools, and a letter punch, with a chart of available letters to pick from.

Western border towns favored the Mexican silver pesos fashioned into badges by local jewelers with a five pointed star within the circle.

A man who wore a "Tin Star" was an expression used to tag a small town peace officer. There were many 'tin stars' cut out from the bottom of a tin can . . . till a regular badge could be struck.

1878 through 1900

1889

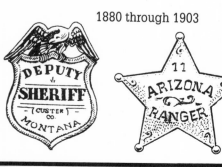

1880 through 1903

1912 through 1917

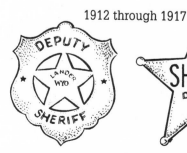

Poker

The origin of poker has been ascribed to Il Frusco, an Italian game of the fifteenth century, from which the game of Primiera (called in Spain Primero, and La Prime in France) where it was elaborated into L'Amigu or Le Mesle. In England, the game was played under the name of Post and Pair, of which the modern game Brag is only a variation. R.F. Foster proves that though poker is probably a descendant of Primero and perhaps of the ancient Persian game called As Ras, it is not a development of the English Brag. It was introduced from France into the colony of Louisiana, and the name merely an English mispronunciation of Pogue, a game described as early as 1718 in the *Academic Universelle dex Jeux*, and still played in Germany under the name Pochen.

The earliest mention of the game in America is in G.B Zieber's *Exposure of the Arts and Miseries of Gambling* (1843). It is probable that poker was generally played on the Mississippi steamboats as early as 1830. Twenty cards were used; the 'full-check poker' with fifty-two cards was invented later. 'Draw poker' was introduced about 1860.

Poker was played for money stakes; markers or chips were used to indicate value. These were either divided equally among the players, or more usually, one player acted as banker and sold chips to the other players, redeeming them at the end of the game. There were several varieties of the game, but Draw Poker, played by two to six or even seven persons with a pack of fifty-two cards, was the most popular. The player who won the cut for deal shuffled the pack, which was then cut by the player at his right.

Typical early day gambling.

Art by E.L. Reedstrom

He then dealt five cards, one by one, to each player. If a card was faced during the deal, the player had to accept it; if two were exposed a new deal ensued. Before the deal was complete the player at the dealer's left, who was said to hold the age, and is called "the age," placed (or put up) on the table in front of him half the stake for which he wished to play. This was called blind. The player at the age's left then looked at his hand and announced whether he would play. If his hand seemed too weak he threw his cards away face down and dropped out of the game. If he elected to play he put up his ante, which was twice the amount of the blind. The other players, including the dealer, then either came in (i.e. elected to play), each putting up his ante, or, deeming their hands worthless, dropped out. The age, who had the last say, then either dropped out, forfeiting his half-stake already put up, or came in and made good his ante (i.e. put up his unpaid half of the blind).

Each player in his turn had the privilege of increasing the stake to any amount not exceeding the limit,[4] which was always agreed upon before the game began. Thus, if the limit was one, and the age had put up .25 as his blind, any player could state when his turn came, "I play, and make it $5.00 more to draw cards," while at the same time placing the ante plus $5.00. Thereupon all the other players, each in turn, had to 'see' the raise (i.e., pay the additional sum) or drop out of the game, forfeiting what they had already paid into the pool. The age being the last to complete was in the best position to raise, as a player who has already completed is less likely to sacrifice his stake and withdraw from the game. On the other hand, each player had the right, in his turn after paying the extra stake called for, or raising further. This could continue until the players who had not dropped out had paid an equal sum into the pool and no one cared to raise further. Each player then threw away as many of his five cards as he chose and received new ones from the dealer.

In this supplementary deal no player could accept a face card, but received another in its place after all the other players had been served. The number of

This hand plus a trusty revolver won the pot. It is called Screw Jaw Davis' Blaze.

An unbeatable hand, yet many were caught cheating, losing both the pot and their lives. The only time a pair of sixes beat aces was when the sixes were six-guns.

This is called a skip straight. During the early days in Wickenburg, Arizona, this combination beat a flush.

new cards taken by each one was carefully noted by the other players, as it gave a valuable clue to the probable value of his hand. The following list shows the value of hands, beginning with the lowest, and is the list used by poker players today.

1. *One Pair* (accompanied by three cards of different denominations). If two players each hold a pair, the higher wins; if similar pairs (i.e., a pair of kings each) then the next highest card wins.
2. *Two Pairs*.
3. *Triplets* or *Three of a Kind* (i.e., three kings, accompanied by two other cards not forming a pair).
4. *Straight*. A sequence of five cards, not all of the same suit. Sometimes, but very rarely, these straights are not admitted. An ace may either begin or end a straight. For example: ace, king, queen, knave and ten is the highest straight; five, four, three, deuce and ace is the lowest. An ace cannot be in the middle. For example, three, deuce, ace, king, queen is not a straight.
5. *Flush*. Five cards of the same suit, not in sequence. If two flushes are held, that containing the highest card wins; if the highest cards are similar, the next highest wins, etc.
6. *Full* or *Full House*. Three of a kind with a pair; i.e. three sixes and a pair of fours. If more than one player holds a full house, the highest triplet wins.
7. *Fours*, or *Four of a Kind*; i.e., four queens, which beat four knaves and under.
8. *Straight Flush*. A sequence of five cards all of the same suit; i.e., knave, ten, nine, eight, seven of hearts.
9. *Royal Flush*. The highest possible straight flush; i.e., ace, king, queen, knave and ten of spades.

If no player holds at least one pair, then the hand containing the highest card wins.

After each player had received the new cards

"Wild Bill" Hickok drew this hand just before Jack McCall shot him in the back of the head. It has since been called "Dead Man's Hand."

From this hand, the 666 Ranch in Texas received its name.

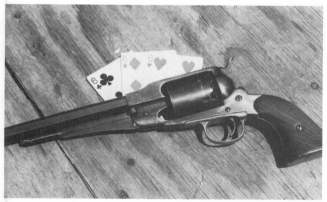

A Royal Flush is never drawn three times in one evening, but in Ashfork, Arizona, two drifters won the pot twice. They never got the chance to spend their winnings.

called for, the betting was opened by the player sitting at the age's left, should he consider his hand worth it; otherwise he threw down his cards and was out of the game. The next player (whom we will call C) made the first bet, which could be of any amount up to the limit, but was usually a small one, with a view to later developments. The next player, D, either dropped out, trailed, i.e., put up the amount bet by C (also called seeing and calling), or raised C's bet. In other words, he put in the amount bet by C plus as much more (within the limit) as he cared to risk. This raise on D's part meant either that he thought he held a better hand than C, or that he was trying to frighten C out. The last maneuver illustrated the principle of the bluff—the most salient characteristic of the game of poker.

If C, with two small pairs in his hand, bet half a crown, and D, with a hand of no value whatever, covered, or saw, C's bet and raised it to a sovereign, it was very likely that C would throw down his cards rather than risk a sovereign on his own by-no-means-strong hand. In this case, C had been bluffed by D, who, without even having to show his cards, won the pool, although his hand was far inferior to C's.

The ability to bluff successfully depended upon self-command, keen observation, judgment and knowledge of character, so as to only attempt the bluff when the bluffer was sure that there were no very strong hands out against him. Otherwise he would surely be called in his turn, and, having nothing of value, would lose the pool and suffer the ignominy of throwing away his money for nothing.

Two players with strong hands would often raise each other's bets repeatedly, until one of them called the other, upon which the hands were shown and the stronger won. The complete hands of the caller and the called had to be shown. The common practice of throwing away unshown—for purposes of conceal-ment—a losing hand after it had been called is illegal. A player who was not called was not obliged to show his hand, so that the company was often in doubt whether or not the winner had bluffed. When two hands were of exactly equal value, the pool was divided.

The game was often varied by the player "going blind," i.e., raising the ante before the deal. Another variation was "straddling the blind." This was done by the player sitting next to the age, who put up twice the amount of the blind with the words, "I straddle." This had the effect of doubling the stake, as every player then paid twice the amount of the straddle (instead of the blind) in order to play. The straddle could be straddled again in its turn if the aggregate amount did not pass the limit. The straddle did not carry with it the privilege of betting last, but merely raised the amount of the stake.

The regular Draw Poker game was usually varied by occasional jackpots, which were played once in so many deals, or when all had refused to play, or when the player dealt who held the buck, a marker placed in the pool with every jackpot. In a jackpot each player put up an equal stake and received a hand. The pot was then opened by a player who held a hand of the value of a pair of knaves (jacks) or better. If no player held an opening hand, the deal passed and each player added a small sum to the pot or pool. When the pot was opened, the opener did so by putting up any sum he chose, within the limit, and his companions paid in the same amount or dropped.

They also possessed the right to raise the opener. The new cards called for were then dealt and the opener started the betting, the play proceeding as in the regular game. If Progressive Jack Pots were played, the minimum value of the opening hand was raised one degree every deal in which the pot was not opened. Thus the opening hand must—in the first deal—be at least a pair of knaves; but if the pot was not opened, the minimum for the second deal was a pair of queens, and for the third a pair of kings, etc. Jackpots were introduced about 1870.

Straight Poker, or Bluff, was played without draw-ing extra cards. It was the only variety of the game played with a full deck, although fifty-two cards are now used instead of twenty, as formerly. The first dealer was provided with a marker called a 'buck.' Before dealing, having put up the antes of all the players, he passed the buck to the next dealer, who

must, in turn, ante for all when he dealt. The rules for betting, raising, etc., were the same as at Draw Poker. The hands, of course, averaged smaller.

Stud Poker is played like Draw Poker, except that there was no draw and, in dealing, the first card was dealt face down, the rest exposed. Each player in turn looked at his turned card and made his bet or raise. A common variation of Stud Poker stops the deal after two cards, one face up and the other face down, were dealt, and with betting on those two cards. A third card was then dealt and betting again to place. The process was repeated after the fourth and fifth cards had been dealt, the value of the different hands changing with each card added. A player failing to 'stand' any raise retired from that pot.

Whiskey Poker is also played without a draw. An extra hand, called the widow, was dealt to the table face down. The first bettor then examined his hand and had the option of taking up the widow and placing his own hand on the table face up in its place, or of passing and allowing the following players in turn the choice. After an exposed hand had been laid on the table in place of the widow, the next player might either take up one card from the new widow, replacing it with one from his own hand, or he might exchange hie entire hand for the widow, or he might 'knock' on the table. If he knocks, every other player in turn might exchange one card or his whole hand, and the betting then began, or there might be an agreement that the best hand won from all the rest, or that the poorest hand paid a chip to the pool.

Poker Terms

Big Dog—Ace high and nine low; not usually played. If played, it beats a Little Dog.

Blaze—Five court cards; not usually played. If played, it beats any two pairs.

Bobtail—Four cards of a flush or straight, the fifth card not filling.

Bone—The smallest counter or chip.

Buck—A marker, to who when a jackpot is to be played, i.e. when it is the holder's deal.

Burnt Card—Card on the bottom of the pack turned up to prevent being seen.

Chips—Counters.

Cold Feet—Any excuse of a winner for leaving the game before the time agreed upon.

Deadwood—The discard pile.

Deck—Pack.

Fatten—Adding chips and a jackpot after a failure to open.

Freeze Out—A game in which a player, having lost a certain agreed capital, must stop playing.

Inside Straight—Intermediate straight, i.e. deuce, three, five, six.

Kilter—Hand with no pair and no card above the nine, seldom played.

Kitty—A fund, to pay for cards or refreshments, made by taking a chip from each jackpot, or paid by a winner holding a valuable hand.

Little Dog—Deuce low and seven high, not usually played. When played it beats a straight.

Milking—Shuffling by taking a card from the top and one from the bottom of the pack with the same movement.

Mishgris—Poker with the joker added; the joker may be called any card the holder chooses.

Monkey Flush—Three cards of a flush.

Natural Jacks—Jackpots played because there has been no ante in the previous deal.

Openers—A hand on which a jackpot may be opened.

Pat Hand—A hand to which no card is drawn.

Pool—The chips in the middle of the table.

Show-down—Laying the hands face-up on the table after a call.

Show—Part of a pool to which a player is entitled who has bet as long as his capital lasted but is not able to stand further raises. If his hand is the best he wins whatever was in the pool at the time when he put the last of his capital into it.

Shy—Not having put up the jackpot ante.

Splitting—Having opened a jackpot with one pair and holding four other cards of one suit, throwing away one of the pair on the chance of making a flush.

Sweeten—Chipping to a jackpot after a failure to open.

Triplets—Three of a kind.

Under the Gun—The first player to bet.

Whangdoodle—Compulsory round of jackpots, usually agreed upon to follow a very large hand.

Widow—An extra hand dealt to the table, as in Whiskey Poker. See *Practical Poker* by R.F. Foster (1904, the most authoritative work).

A very important attribute of a successful poker player is sound judgment in discarding. This is based on the following mathematical table of approximate chances:

Poker Odds

To improve any hand in the draw, the chances are:

Having in Hand:	To make the Hand below:	The Chance is:
1 pair	To get two pairs (3-card draw)	1 in 4½
1 pair	To get three of a kind (3- card draw)	1 in 9
1 pair	To improve either way average value	1 in 3
1 pair and 1 odd card	To improve either way by drawing two cards	1 in 7
2 pairs	To get a full hand drawing one card	1 in 12
3's	To get a full hand drawing two cards	1 in 15½
3's	To get four of kind drawing two cards	1 in 23½
3's	To improve either way drawing two cards	1 in 9
3's and 1 odd card	To get a full hand by drawing one card	1 in 15 1/3
3's and 1 odd card	To improve either way by drawing one card	1 in 11¾
4 straight	To fill when open at one end only or in middle as 3, 4, 6, 7 or A, 2, 3, 4	1 in 11¾
4 straight	To fill when open at both ends at 3, 4, 5, 6	1 in 6
4 flush	To fill the flush drawing one card	1 in 5
4-straight flush	To fill the straight flush drawing one card	1 in 23½
3-card flush	To make a flush drawing two cards	1 in 24

Of course, these chances are somewhat improved by the fact that, in actual play, pairs and threes are, on account of careless shuffling, likely to lie together.

Faro

Faro (or Pharo), was the Frontiers' most popular card game. It required a large board with thirteen imprinted face cards. Reading from right to left in consecutive order, from the ace to the six card (top row), facing the board, the number seven card alone on the left, the bottom row starting with the eight card, reading from left to right—up to the king. This complete layout is in the "Spade" suit. Every dealer had a "case," a small folding box in which the deck of cards was placed face-up. Across the top of the case was the "cage"—thirteen wires, on each of which four single buttons were strung, forming an abacus. A tally of every card played was kept on this abacus—for example, one wire with its four buttons

represented the four kings and four aces. The cage was carefully kept to determine the odds and protect both player and dealer. The dealer usually kept the case himself, but in more elaborate establishments a second dealer was hired as casekeeper.

Bettors could back a card of any rank by laying their chips on a reproduction of the card fixed to the top of the board. Suits were non-important. After all bets were placed, a dealer dealt two cards from a box. Those backing the card dealt first lost; bets placed on the second card won. Bets on the other cards were either left for the next play or withdrawn by the players. If a pair was dealt, the bank took half of the money that had been staked on the paired card.

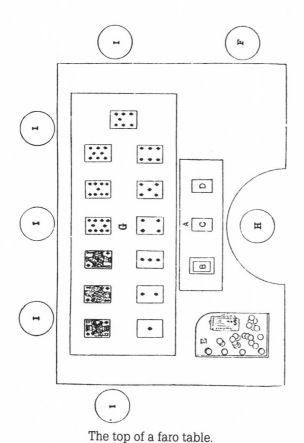

The top of a faro table.

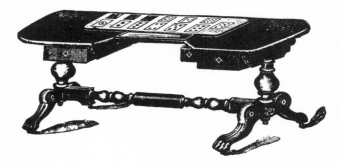

The 1860 Model Case-Keeper kept track of dealt cards and the gamblers could quickly see how many cards of any rank had been played.

An 1868 Hart's pasteboard package.

Faro table.

Faro Terms

Brace Game—A crooked Faro bank.

Break Even—A system of betting by which each card was played to win and lose an even number of times.

Both Ends Against the Middle—A method of trimming cards for dealing a brace game of Faro. A dealer who used such a pack was said to be "playing both ends against the middle."

Bucking the Tiger—Playing Faro.

Chips—The counters at Faro. At Poker they were properly called Checks.

Calling the Turn—To guess correctly the order in which the first three cards in the box would appear.

Case Card—The last card of each denomination.

Case-Keeper—A device for keeping a record of the cards as they were drawn. Also, the man who operated the device.

Cat—When two cards of the same denomination were in the last turn, it was called a cat; also cat-hop an cat-harpen.

Coppering a Bet—Betting a card to lose. To do so, the player placed a small copper disk provided by the dealer upon his stake.

Deal—Twenty-five turns.

Heeled Bets—Wagers which played one card to win and another to lose.

Heeler or Heel—A player who consistently made heeled bets.

In Hock—The last card in the box was said to be in hock. Originally it was known as the hockelty card, and in the early days of Faro, when it counted for the bank, a player who had bet on it was said to have been caught in hock. Also, a gambler who had been trimmed by another sharper was said to be in hock to his conqueror; as late as the middle 1880s, in the underworld, a man was in hock when he was in jail. The phrase is now principally used in reference to pawnshop pledges, but it seems to have acquired that meaning in recent years.

Keeping Cases—Manipulating the case-keeper.

Keeping Tabs—Making this record.

Last Turn—The last three cards in the box.

Leg—A professional gambler; probably a corruption of blackleg. In earlier times sharpers were also known as Greeks.

Lookout—The dealer's principal assistant, who paid and collected bets and kept a watchful eye on the players.

Losing Out—Betting on a card which loses four times in one deal.

Making a Pass—Putting the two parts of a pack of cards back as they were before the cut.

Marker—An article, sometimes a small piece of ivory provided by the bank, used by a player whose credit was good. He announced the value of the marker as he made his bet, and was supposed to settle after each deal.

Open Bets—Wagers which played cards to win.

Paroli—Parlay came from this word by way of parolet, parlieu and parlee. It meant exactly the same at Faro as it does in race track gambling.

Passed in His Checks—He cashed in. Originally this expression was "passed in his chips."

Pigeon—From about 1600 to recent times the victim of a professional gambler was called a pigeon.

Piker—One who made piking--very small--bets.

Piking—Making small bets all over the layout.

Playing On Velvet—Betting money previously won from the bank.

Playing On A Shoe-String—Starting with a small sum and running it into a large amount by consistently lucky bets.

Sleeper—A bet placed on a dead card. In many houses it belonged to the first man who grabbed it.

Snaking A Game—Stealing, marking and returning a dealer's cards, a trick often practice in the days when the pack was dealt face downward from the dealer's hand.

Snap—A temporary Faro game. A ten dollar snap was a temporary game with a ten dollar capital.

Stringing Along—Betting all odd or even numbered cards to play one way.

Stool Pigeon—Originally this word meant a pigeon used to decoy others into a trap. A few years before the turn of the nineteenth century it came into general use among American gamblers to designate a capper or a hustler for a Faro bank, and was still so used as late as 1915. An early mention of the word in this connection may be found in the New York Herald of July 31, 1835. The Herald reprinted a letter from a citizen of Baltimore to the Chief Judge of the Baltimore County Court, and quoted the citizen as saying that the gamblers of the Maryland metropolis preyed upon "such strangers as they can decoy in, by means of what they call stool-pigeons." The use of stool-pigeon as a synonym for police spy is apparently of comparatively recent origin; as late as the middle 1880s such an informer was known in the underworld simply as a pigeon.

Stuck—A player who went broke trying to call the turn was stuck.

Square Deal—Twenty-five turns in which the dealer used a pack with squared edges. With these cards the chances of a crooked deal were minimized.

Square Game—Faro bank which used squared cards exclusively.

Tabs—Printed sheets on which the players noted the cards as they won or lost.

Tiger—Faro. During the early 1830s a first-rate professional gambler carried his Faro outfit in a fine mahogany box on which was painted a picture of the Royal Bengal Tiger. A representation of the animal was also carved on the ivory chips and painted on the oilcloth layout. The gamblers adopted the tiger as the presiding deity of the game, and Faro soon became known throughout the country simply as "the tiger." Many large gambling houses had oil paintings of tigers hung above their Faro tables.

Velvet—The bank's money.

Winning Out—Betting on a card which won four times in one deal.

Whipsawed—Losing two different bets on the same turn.

The Holdouts

A card hold-out was attached to a man's arm (center forearm) and beneath his coat sleeve. It was easy to press a release and have a high card spring into the hand. Gamblers always had a hide-out weapon such as a dagger and an over & under Remington derringer, .41 caliber.

Courtesy *Guns & Ammo Magazine*

The term 'holdout,' in gambling, refers to an additional card (one or more) held out, or held up the sleeve or beneath a table. The name is also given to a mechanical contrivance constructed to enable the cardsharper to 'holdout,' or conceal one or more cards, until such time as he finds that they will be useful to him by turning the balance of fortune in his favor at a critical point in a game.

One of the simplest methods for a 'holdout' was to secretly position a card in the palm of the hand. Under cover of stretching, the card would be placed under the coat collar as the player sat with his back to the wall. When this card was needed, a second yawn, with an accompanying stretch from "fatigue" would bring it again into his hand. This was the first real 'holdout,' the back of a coat collar. Another very early 'holdout' was performed by putting choice cards under the knee-joint. When the player required the card, he would hitch his knee closer to the table and take the cards into his hand.[5]

The 'cuff-pocket holdout' was another early sharper's invention. As the name indicates, it was a pocket inside the coat sleeve with an opening situated on the under side of the seam joining sleeve and cuff. While playing a game of poker, the sharper would contrive to get three of a kind at the top of the deck while shuffling. Then he would insert his little finger between these three cards and the rest, while holding the pack in the left hand. Then, with his left hand in front of him, he would reach across it with the right, apparently to lay down his cigar or his chips. In this position, the opening of the pocket came level with the front of the pack, the latter being covered by his right arm. This gave the sharper the opportunity to push the three selected cards into this pocket, where they would remain until he had dealt all cards and given off all the 'draft' except his own. Still holding the deck in his left hand with his right hand before him, he would again cross his right hand over, this time to take up and examine his own cards. He had taken the precaution of dealing well to the left, to give him an excuse for crossing his hands. He would then remove the cards from the 'cuff-pocket' to

the top of the deck and lay the whole down upon the table. Unsuspected by the others, he would throw away three indifferent cards from his hand and deliberately help himself to the three top cards of the deck. These would be the three aces he had previously concealed in the pocket.

As the purveyors of crooked card games joined the westward movement, they could always find suckers who had pockets lined with gold or saddle-blanket-size dollars, waiting to be fleeced. Sharpers were aided and abetted in their nefarious activities by eastern manufacturers who kept inventing simple and clear devices for 'holdout' cards and other tricks of the trade. The following illustrations reveal a number of these devices sold by the eastern manufacturers:

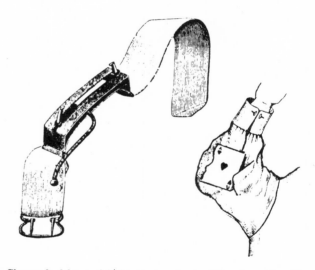

Sleeve holdout: this instrument consists of a pair of jaws, which being movable, will separate to allow a card to be held between them. The jaws are drawn towards each other by means of an elastic band slipped over them. Elastic was used in spring holdouts and could easily be replaced when worn out. The projecting lever at the side is for the purpose of separating the jaws when the cards are to be withdrawn. By pressing the bar from one side, it releases the cards and at the same time, throws up a little arm from the mechanism which thrusts the cards out. This is strapped on the underside of the forearm and inside a shirt.

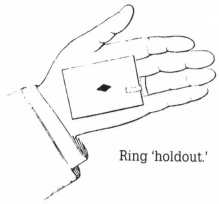

Ring 'holdout.'

The cards are held between a small piece of watchspring attached to a finger ring and the palm of the hand where the cards are held.

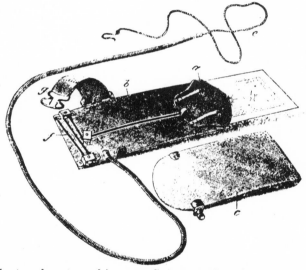

Coat and vest machines are fine examples of mechanical genius as applied to the art of cheating. At the end of a cord is fastened a hook for the purpose of attaching it to the 'tab' or loop at the back of the operator's boot. (The cord is a very good quality of fishing line.) The band with the buckle attached is intended to support the machine within the coat or vest. The edge of the right breast is unpicked and the machine is sewn into the gap. The flexible tube is passed down the left trouser leg until the hook at the end of the cord is ready to attach to the left boot. When the operator is seated at the table, he hooks the cord to the loop of his boot. By merely stretching his left leg, the cord is pulled, the seam of his coat opens (the operation is covered by his arm) and out comes the end of the slide. As the operator inserts the cards into the slide, he draws up his leg, and the cards disappear. When the cards are needed, another leg movement brings the cards into his hand.

The 'Jacob's Ladder'

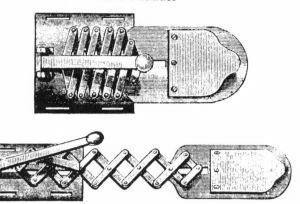

The baseplate carrying the working parts was curved so as to lie closely against the arm and hold the mechanism steady while in use. It also had to be strapped on the arm by two straps (see illustration). The 'lazy-thong' device was fixed to a baseplate at one end and the other was free to move and carry the clip for the cards. A lever was at an angle above the thongs and when pressure was applied to this, the connecting rod would force out the joint to which it was attached. The clip would spring forth beyond the coat cuff. In this position, the card could be inserted or removed.

The Bug was a little instrument which was easily carried in a vest pocket and used at a moment's notice. Nothing but a straight flat piece of watchspring, bent somewhat, was inserted into the handle of a very small shoemaker's awl. The point of the awl was struck into the underside or side of the table, in such a manner that the spring lies flat against the underside or side of the table unseen. When the cards are dealt out, the sharpy stands the cards on edge, face cards toward him, holding them with both hands. The card or cards he wishes to "hold out" are brought in front of the others and slowly slipped under or beside the table into the bug.

Match box shiner

Ring shiner

Palm shiner

Marked Cards in the Early 1840s

The secrets of advantage play included the use of dice spotting jigs, where the selected holes were drilled deeper to receive the load, and card trimmers. Here, contrived crooked decks were made by cutting cards in different widths and shapes. Trimming also extended playing life of frayed cards. The corner rounder cut neat corners on trimmed/worn cards.

Courtesy
Guns & Ammo Magazine

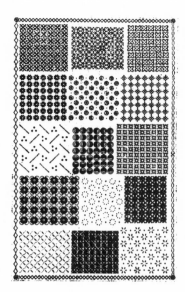

Marked cards of the early 1840s.

Author's Collection

POPULAR STANDARD BRAND READERS

Well liked and different.　　Very popular.　　A fast reader.

15F102　Wheel　　15F132　Acorn　　15F110　Emblem

Easy to read.　　Unusual, well liked.　　Hard to detect. Easy to read.

15F100　Cupid　　15F60　　15F41　Nautic

New fast readers.　　An old favorite.　　Good for Black Jack.

15F288　Broadway　　15F30　Tally-Ho　　15F27　Panel

All cards listed on this page are Standard Brands made by the leading manufacturers. Supplied in either red or blue marked for size only. When suit is desired add 25c extra for each deck.

Price Per Deck....$1.25　　Six Decks.....$6.75　　Per Doz.....$12.50

Methods of cheating at poker were numerous. The sharper who specialized in poker and other short card games used the marked and the stripped cards which had proven such a boon to the dishonest faro dealer, and in much the same way: to stack and milk the pack, to deal from the bottom, and to cold deck the sucker or secretly exchange his own pack for one actually in the game. Bottom dealing was one of the first ways in which the gambler sought to supplement his natural skill at poker. It is said to have been perfected by a sharper named Wilson in the early 1830s. When properly done by a professional in full view of several other players, it can hardly be detected. Bottom dealing was—and still is—practiced.

Marked cards used by the sharpers were prepared beforehand, and were known as 'paper' or were marked during the game with the finger nail or a needle point embedded in a ring. This process was called 'blazing,' and cards so marked were 'scratch paper.' Marking cards in a game was dangerous, but

Marked cards as displayed in an Eastern catalog displaying electrical devices, sporting goods and club room furniture. Gambling tables and devices of all kinds were displayed, but not advertised as such.

suitable for faro, where only the dealer handled the pack. By 1855, both 'paper' and 'scratch paper' had been largely supplanted by a variety known as 'stamped cards,' on which the markings were concealed in the printed design on the back. These were first manufactured around 1830.

More Potpourri

- Buffalo Bill Cody killed 4,280 buffalos in eighteen months, which is an official record for the largest amount of game killed in the same time period by any man.[6]
- The bite of the Tarantula, a large black spider, is not as dangerous as the rattlesnake. It can be painful, but hardly ever fatal. Its bite is treated like a rattlesnake bite. These ugly creatures of the desert were great favorites with cowboys of the early days and many tales were told about them jumping or springing at least six feet. Corner them first and tease them a little before they get mad and jump at you. Cowboys would place two spiders in a bowl—and sums of money would be bet on which one would kill the other. Winning spiders, or champions, would be taken from ranch to ranch for future fights. This was a sport the American cowboy invented to either bring in a few extra pesos or indulge in his habitual gambling sprees.

- A man can last eleven days without water—eight days without scotch in it.[7]
- Cattle: The reference to "wet cattle" indicated cows in milk with their calves. They were less likely to run away.
- Cowboy rodeos were informal affairs that were held in collaboration with parties and dances at which time cowboys put an exhibitions of their skills. The first public rodeo on record was held in Prescott, Arizona, in 1888. Since then, rodeos have become very commercial and are more like circuses than exhibitions of cowboy skills.[8]
- Cowboys referred to whiskey as "nose paint."
- A "horse puller" in the West was depicted as a cowboy who traveled with livestock on a train. They were also called "Bull Nurses."
- An average cowboy's wage was thirty-five dollars to forty dollars a month and room and board. Top hands got sixty dollars a month, and a good cook was paid more.

- A good "cookie" knew that when you start a batch for "Sourdough"—and it begins to orange—make it quickly and bake it. If she's gone green, best feed it to the buzzards.

- "Wet Mare"—when a colt accepts another horse to feed from in place of its mother (This when the real mother dies—and another horse is substituted).

- "Tepees on Wheels" was a general term used by plains Indians when referring to covered wagons.

- A lady's spittoon was usually a thing of fashion and beauty. Made of china, it measured from six inches to eight inches. Across the sides were always painted with flowers and possibly carried the owner's initials. In the early days, and even later, women often chewed or snuffed tobacco in their bedrooms.

- The last Indian battle actually took place on April 10, 1930, when a small band of Apache Indians attacked a ranch near Nacorichio, Sonora, Mexico, killing three people. These Apaches, apparently part of a small renegade band which remained in the Sierra Madre Moun-tains, did not want to give up their freedom. Witnesses say the band was led by a white man believed to be Charlie McComas. He had been kidnapped by Apaches in 1882, and was never rehabilitated after the raid. A posse destroyed the band. These were the last "Wild Apaches" in America.

- In the early 1850s, lawmen were often referred to as "Regulators."

- The average distance ridden daily by a Pony Express rider was, according to Alexander Majors, thirty-three and a third miles per day. Three horses were ridden on this "run." Stations were about ten to twelve miles apart.

- The famous "Twenty-one gun salute" was derived by adding up one plus seven plus seven plus six equals twenty-one, the four numbers in the year 1776, our Revolutionary year.

- The U.S. Army adopted olive drab for winter service uniforms in 1902.

- The California Gold Rush was one of the greatest stampedes in history. People flocked to the golden state from all over the world and by every means available. From records kept at Fort

Wagons going west were so overburdened that in a short time, the animals were worn out.

Laramie, Wyoming, it has been estimated that some eight thousand wagons, eighty thousand draft animals and thirty thousand people passed through that post on the way West in 1849.

- Army statistics show that the best shots are found among gray-eyed men who are invariably more proficient than dark-eyed men.
- Breathing into the rifle after firing is always a good plan as it tends to soften the deposit in the bore; another good idea is to wet the bullet before loading. This takes the place of oiling.
- The ammunition which should be used in the latest pattern rifles is 500 grain bullet and 70 grains of powder.
- It is said to be a good practice to keep both eyes open in aiming. A person keeping both eyes open, while aiming with one is not so long in getting the range. He is able to shoot better in much less time than a person closing one eye. Ira Payne, and many other famous shots always keep both eyes open.[9]

- A warming shot should always be fired before shooting at the target.
- Cleaning a gun often is nonsense. In the army the practice is to fire at least sixty shots without cleaning. In the regular army it is the practice to give a recruit considerable aiming drill, and then allow him to shoot on a short range, moving him back as his efficiency increases.[10]
- A "bad actor" was an undependable person, a drunk, a fighter who made a general nuisance of himself. Gunmen were also considered to be "bad actors."
- Hartshorn was used to bathe a yellow jacket sting. It would sooth and reduce the swelling.
- Laudanum (opium) was mixed with whiskey (in various preparations) and used as a pain killer.
- Boil the bark of an aspen tree for medical uses; it was used as a tea to relieve stress, tension and headaches.
- Vigilantes had a sure cure for "lynch fever" on the plains. A rope with a hangman's knot was tied to

In June of each year, the National Pony Express Association re-creates the horseback mail run of the 1860s. The members carry the mail in an old-style mochilla from St. Joseph, Missouri, to Sacramento, California, in ten days flat. Over 600 riders participate in this annual observance of Majors, Russell, and Wadell's original mail-carrying service. Here, *Guns & Ammo*'s Black Powder Editor, Phil Spangenberger, has just gotten the mail mochilla, and is galloping toward his relay point in Sacramento, California, during 1981's West to East run. Phil is attired in authentic mid-19th century clothing, riding a period slick-fork saddle and is armed with one of Colt's "reissue" 1851 Navies. These .36 caliber percussion six-shooters were favorites with the original Pony Express riders.

Courtesy *Guns & Ammo Magazine*

place to dry. The "rush" or the soft cotton-like fluff, which tops the stem, was plucked and used similar to goose-down for pillows and bedticking. The flat leaves, when dried, were woven into floor mats or for seating chairs.

- Pioneer gardens, no matter how large or small, were constantly plagued with rabbits. When young tasty shoots began to sprout, they were easily consumed by the rabbits, leaving nothing to show for the pioneer woman's toil. When the trappers and mountain men came down from their trap-lines and hidden canyons in the summer with their pelts, they solved this dilemma by swapping "ferret" droppings to the settlers. These were to be scattered about the garden. This scent in turn troubles the hungry rabbits and they would cease visiting the garden area for fear of their deadly enemy, the ferret. The odor has much to get accustomed to, but certainly if one can, it does the trick.

- You're safe from a skunk as long as you are standing in front of him? Believe it, and you'll be in for a surprise. He can aim his protruding spray

the end of a wagon tongue, and the tongue was lashed in an upright position. The reason for this was because of the lack of trees on the prairie. The condemned man generally heard these last words, "Point him to heaven — and give him a head start."

- In the late fall, pioneers harvested the tall marsh plant *(Typha latifolia)* or the "cattail," including their long flat leaves, and stored these in a warm

The Red River Cart, the common vehicle of Western Canada, was constructed without nails, joints made by dowelling, mortise-and-tenon, etc. Its five feet wheel rims were wrapped in rawhide so they wouldn't be heard by near-by camps.

Author's Collection

gun in almost any direction except over his head. He has two glandular magazines filled with ammo, and he can fire one or both simultaneously. After his first shot, which is usually a magnum, he's still loaded with six more rounds. Usually he stamps his feet before firing, but not always. Watch his tail! If it's erect but still curls at the tip, he's not yet ready to pull the trigger. But when that curl straightens—if you've hung around that long—don't bother running; it's too late. Incidentally, that ammo he uses is valuable stuff. When refined and the odor removed, it becomes the base for very expensive perfume. One spray of it will cling to a gal as long as the original will to a poor sportsman who doesn't take skunks seriously.

- There are only a few mammals that truly hibernate. They include the groundhog, chipmunk, ground squirrel, and a few bats. All other mammals that partake of a winter rest, such as bears, badgers, racoons, and skunks are only partial hibernators.

  A partial hibernator lowers its body temperature only about 8° or 10° F. It saves energy this way while still being able to wake up quickly if disturbed. The groundhog, a true hibernator, lowers its temperature from 98° F. (normal temperature of mammals) to about 40° F, the temperature of its ground home. It also goes further in slowing its body processes by slowing its heartbeats from 150 per minute to five or ten, and reducing the flow of blood to the part of its body behind the rib cage.

- A groundhog hibernates in periods of ten days. After that period, it is awake for about twelve hours and warms up to a normal 98° F. Then it lowers its temperature to 40° F and goes back to sleep for another period of about ten days. This cycle is repeated until its food—fresh green grass—appears in the spring.[11]

- An old remedy for a sore throat was:
  > 6 oz. of honey
  > 2 tablespoons (1 ounce) of glycerine
  > the juice of one lemon

Mix and store in jar. Do not take anything hot for a sore throat. Apple cider was sometimes used in place of lemon juice.

- Amazingly enough, through old letters and documents we find how eggs were transported aboard a wagon, and at the "end of trail," not a one was broken out of ten dozen.

  Several large barrels were lashed to the wagon side, and filled with either corn or oats for the stock. In between layers, eggs were positioned with oats or corn all around them, cushioning each egg. With each 'bump' on the trail, the eggs were in no danger of breaking. When the animals needed more feed, breakfast in the morning with eggs was certain.

- The wind-swept prairie in the West were treacherous with a woman's long flowing dress. On military posts, the women ("camp followers" or mostly officers wives), were harassed with this problem. Skirts swept over a woman's head in a hard breeze, exposing ankles and under garments, much to their embarrassment. It wasn't until Lt. Colonel George Armstrong Custer's wife, the gracious Elizabeth (Libby) Bacon Custer took matters in hand and recruited all women on post to sew "buck-shot" in the hem of their skirts, thus solving a daily problem.

- At the railhead, range hands used long wooden poles to force steers up a chute into stock cars, about eighteen head to a carload. The work was endless and tedious, and from this they acquired the lasting nickname "cowpoke."

- There were many good reasons why the early westerners wore their hair long. Their business was mostly out of doors, often during inclement weather and through many changes of climate. From experience, they learned that the greatest protection to the eyes and ears was long hair. Hunters, scouts, trail guides, and old prospectors knew this well, and those who had rejected it often suffered the miseries of sore eyes, pains in the head and loud ringing in the ears. Exposure without the protection of long hair also could

result in severe sunburn on the neck and ears, as well as loss of hearing in either ear after being exposed to the cold ground while sleeping. Of course, perfect hearing and keen eyesight were of the greatest importance to a scout, hunter or herdsman.

It was believed by many that the wearing of long hair not only preserved but strengthened their eyesight and made their hearing more acute. Farfetched as it may seem, the hair also acted as a measure of time. The hair, at various lengths, told the wearer how long he had been out on the plains or in the mountains. Certain white men whose interests called upon them to live and trade among the Indians let their hair grow long to gain favor with the tribes they lived with, and to help them associate comfortably. Long hair was the natural fashion of an outdoors man, and anyone who thought differently or ventured any sly remarks about it was challenged to fight with any choice of weapons he preferred.

Source:
Life and Adventures of the Genuine Cowboy
Bronco John H. Sullivan: Private printing, author's collection.

- During an Indian uprising, many soldiers and settlers were the prey of renegade Indians who often left their victims dead, mutilated and missing a portion of the hair from the top of their heads. Various designs became used in cutting scalps away. Upon close examination of a scalping, the experienced scout or plainsman could tell which band of marauding Indians was responsible.

  Each tribe had its own method of taking scalps, somewhat like a visitor leaving his calling card. One man's or woman's scalp might have a diamond-shaped cut, and another might have an oval-shaped cut. There were quite a few styles, including square, oblong, rectangular, circular, and triangular.

  There are two schools of thought on the origin of scalping. Apparently Indians either collected scalps as war trophies or they adopted the practice from the Europeans. During the American Revolution, the military as well as the white settlers offered bounties on Indian scalps and, in retaliation, the woodland tribes took scalps as trophies. Then, as the white man progressed westward across the American continent, he found the custom of scalping followed by almost all of the Indian tribes that he contacted.

Source:
The Origin of the North American Indians. John McIntosh. Sheldon & Lamport Publ. (1855).
33 Years Among Our Wild Indians. Col. I.J. Dodge, Archer House.

- Army scouts, trackers, and plainsmen often exhibited an original Indian scalp under their belts as positive evidence that they had confronted a warrior in hand-to-hand combat. Along with the grisly trophy usually came a story, lengthy and hair-raising enough to send a chill up the back of any listener. When the U.S. Army declared bounties for Indians scalps, many unusual tufts of hair began to show up, some causing serious questions as to their origin. In some cases it was found that the Army had purchased a swatch of dog hair or a coarse tuft of a horse's tail. In order to alleviate this problem, trusted Indians were hired to closely inspect the scalp. It was considered positive evidence that the scalp was that of an Indian if the hair was infested with nits, a nit being the egg of a louse or other parasitic insect. Many a "dog scalp" had been passed off in trade or for money to thrill-seeking eastern dudes accompanied by a chilling narration. "On the other hand," went a quote from a well-known Army scout, "if the scalp has fleas, we know for sure it's from a dog."

Source:
Handbook of the American Indian: Vol. 2.
Bugles, Banners and War Bonnets, E.L. Reedstrom, Caxton Printers, 1977

- The Compass Plant grows in our central and southern states. The name refers to the north-

Indian renegades.

south direction in which the young leaves tend to align. Another common name is Polar Plant. Pioneers credit this plant in saving many families from traveling in the wrong direction during the great white migration westward. The leaves of the Compass Plant are arranged in pairs and point due north and south, like that of a compass. It is a stately plant with stout stems, six to eight feet high, with lance-shaped, deeply divided leaves, twelve inches long, and terminal spreading clusters of bright, yellow flowers.

• A great deal of medical treatment in the nineteenth century was based on homemade concoc-

tions composed of roots, herbs and bits of leaves which were supposed to have great healing powers. The majority of these recipes were centuries old, passing from one generation to another. Many a pioneer mother had her file of cures, as today's modern housewives have their cookbooks.

Families in new settlements borrowed many remedies from Indians, near whom they lived, and it was not unusual for a native medicine man to mix up a brew of lilac leaves to sooth a white child's poison ivy. In return for his services he might receive the family prescription of squirrel

brains and crushed ginseng leaves. This, he was assured, was an excellent remedy for bruises. In the unsettled regions where only the hardiest of our pioneers dared to venture, medical treatment was even more simple and primitive. Here there were no real antiseptics for infections, and a man's injuries either went unattended or he received treatment that was often hardly better than useless.

A salve made of pokeberry leaves, flour, honey, and eggs was the usual application for burns, while the smoke of burning honeycomb was used to draw the poison out of wounds caused by rusty metals. Onion and turnip were used for boils. If a man was bitten by a poisonous snake, the regular remedy was to slash the wound and apply such things to it as oak bark tea or tobacco juice. Too often, these hardy men merely relied on drinking whiskey to forget their pain.

- Sharpshooter Annie Oakley's real name was Phoebe Mozee.
- The word 'Doughboy' came about in 1846 when our soldiers marched in to the southwestern desert during the war with Mexico. Their uniforms were caked with dust and sweat and they looked like they were splattered with adobe mix. They joked about dust everywhere and heavy enough to bake bread with. Thus, the word doughboy.
- The only portrait of an American Indian ever to appear on a unit of U.S. paper currency was that which was pictured on a five dollar 'saddle blanket' size note (silver certificate issued prior to 1928). The name of the native American was Chief One-Papa, a not-so-famous, but very typical and colorful example of the red man of the plains.

END NOTES

CHAPTER I: THE INDIAN

1. It was not uncommon to fashion snowshoes for horses.

CHAPTER II: FRINGE PEOPLE

1. Beaver pelts are rich with oil during the winter. They are heavier with fur and the skin is thicker because of the coming winter. A beaver pelt is more valuable during the winter season's hunt.

2. *National Geographic*, October, 1965.

CHAPTER V: WESTERN WEAPONRY

1. The Spencer retailed for twenty-five dollars.

2. The 1860 Henry sold for thirty-seven dollars.

CHAPTER VII: THE MILITARY IN THE WEST

1. *Army Navy Journal*, January 12, 1862, p. 326.

2. A short time after the Gatlings were delivered to the Army, it was noted that when cranking at top speed to attempt the firing power of two hundred shots per minute, shots occasionally struck the front cross bar of the frame, throwing lead and parts of metal back into the crew.

3. It is also believed that Custer refused these weapons because he knew that they were drawn by condemned horses. Condemned horses were branded with a large letter "C."

4. *Army Navy Journal*, August 19, 1876, p. 25.

5. *The Trapdoor Springfield in the Service*, Col. P.M. Shockley, p. 13.

6. Ibid.

7. Ibid.

8. *45/70 Trapdoor Springfields—Dixie Gun Works Collection*.

9. *Bugles, Banners, and War Bonnets*, E.L. Reedstrom (Caxton Printers), 1977, p. 282.

10. *Army Navy Journal*, November 4, 1876.

11. *45/70 Trapdoor Springfields—Dixie Gun Works Collection*.

CHAPTER VIII: THE AMERICAN COWBOY

1. Some other hat names are: Laloon, Army Service, High Roller, Congress, Carson, San An, South Carlsbad, Chapparal, Comanche.

CHAPTER IX: POTPOURRI

1. Many people confuse the Bertilllon System of Identification with the Fingerprint system. These two systems are entirely different.

2. In the spring of 1903, a pocket-size box containing the simple apparatus for recording fingerprints appeared, along with a copy of "Henry's" book of fingerprinting. Sir E.R. Henry, a commissioner of Scotland Yard, perfected and refined the first fingerprinting system.

3. Bertillon System after Alphonse Bertillon (1853–1914) French Anthropologist. A system for identification of persons by a description based on anthropometric measurements, notes or markings, color, impression of thumb lines, etc.

4. "Table stakes" meant playing strictly for cash. "Unlimited" explains itself, although even when this was the rule, a certain high limit was generally observed.

5. From France, called *coup de cuisse*.

6. *Harper's Weekly*, May 3, 1873.

7. From radio station WIND (Chicago), September 20, 1982.

8. *Real West*, March 1969.

9. *Volunteer Magazine*, September, 1889, p. 281.

10. Ibid.

11. W.H. Weisee, Cuvahoga Falls, Ohio.

SELECTED READINGS

"A Haunting New Vision of the Little Big Horn," *American Heritage Magazine,* June, 1970.

Adams, Andy. *The Log of a Cowboy.* Boston and New York: Houghton Mifflin, 1927.

Adams, Ramon F. *A Fitting Death for Billy the Kid.* Norman: University of Oklahoma Press, 1960.

———, *The Old-Time Cowhand.* New York: Macmillan Co., 1961.

Aken, David. *Pioneers of the Black Hills.* Fort Davis, Texas.

Alberts, Don. *Brandy Station of Manila Bay.* Boston, 1981.

Albright, Horace M. and Taylor, Frank J. *Oh, Ranger!* (Second Edition) Stanford University Press, 1928.

Allen, Durward L. *The Life of Prairies and Plains.* New York: McGraw Hill, 1967.

Alter, J. Cecil. *James Bridger, Trapper, Frontiersman, Scout and Guide.* Salt Lake City: Shepard Press, 1925.

Amaral, Anthony. *Comanche.* Los Angeles: Westernlore Press, 1961.

Ambrose, Stephen E. *Crazy Horse and Custer.* New York: Doubleday & Co., 1975.

Anderson, John A. *The Sioux of the Rosebud.* Norman: University of Oklahoma Press, 1971.

Andrews, Ralph W. *Picture Gallery Pioneers.* New York: Bonanza, 1964.

Andrist, Ralph K. *The Long Death.* New York: Macmillan, 1966.

Andrist, Ralph K. and Mitchell, C. Bradford. *Steamboats of the Mississippi.* American Heritage, 1962.

Annual Report 1904 Indian Affairs. Department of the Interior. Government Printing Office, 1905.

Appel, David. *Comanche.* Cleveland: World Publishing Co., 1951.

Armstrong, Hon. P.A. *The Piasa, or the Devil Among the Indians.* Morris, IL: E.B. Fletcher, 1887.

Army and Navy Journal. Published weekly in New York, 1865–1898.

Army Registers (Official). U.S. Printing Office, 1815–1891.

Assay, Karol. *Gray Head and Long Hair: The Benteen-Custer Relationship.* Paris, TX, 1983.

Atherton, Lewis. *The Cattle Kings.* Indiana: Indiana University Press, 1961.

Back, Joe. *Horses, Hitches and Rocky Trails.* Denver: Sage Books, 1959.

Bad Heart Bull, Amos. *A Pictographic History of the Oglala Sioux.* Lincoln: University of Nebraska Press, 1968.

Bailey, John W. *Pacifying the Plains.* Westport, CT: Greenwood, 1979.

Bakeless, John Edwin. *Lewis & Clark, Partners in Discovery.* New York: William Morrow and Co., 1947.

Baker, Ernest E. *The Heart of the Last Frontier.* Oregon Booklovers, 1915.

Baldwin, Alice Blackwood. *Memoirs of Maj. Gen. Frank D. Baldwin.* Los Angeles, 1929.

Baldwin, Leland D. *The Keelboat Age on Western Waters.* Pennsylvania: University of Pittsburg Press, 1941.

Banning, Capt. William. *Six Horses.* Century Co., 1940.

Barness, Larry. *Gold Camp.* New York, 1962.

Barton, Fred. *Charles M. Russel.* Published privately.

Basham, Ceil D. *Verse or Worse from Arizona.* Private Printing, 1963.

Bates, Alan L. *The Western Rivers, Steamboat Cyclopedium.* Hustle Press, 1968.

Bates, Charles F. *Custer's Indian Battles.* Bronxville, NY, 1936.

———, "The Red Man and the Black Hills," *The Magazine Outlook,* July 27, 1927.

Beach, Rex E. "The Great Sioux Festival," *Appleton's Booklovers Magazines,* September, 1905.

Beal, Merrill D. *The Story of Man in Yellowstone.* Caldwell: The Caxton Printers, Ltd., 1949.

Beckwourth, James P. *The Smiling Pioneer.* Private Printing, 1932.

Beebe, Lucius and Clegg, Charles. *U.S. West: The Saga of Wells Fargo.* New York: E.F. Dutton, 1949.

Berry, Don. *A Majority of Scoundrels.* New York: Harper & Brothers, 1961.

Berthrong, Donald J. *The Southern Cheyennes.* Norman: University of Oklahoma Press, 1981.

Billings, John S. *Report on Barracks and Hospitals with Descriptions of Military Posts.* Reprinted by Old Army Press, 1974.

———, *Report on Hygiene of the United States Army with Descriptions of Military Posts.* Reprinted by Old Army Press, 1974.

Billington, Ray Allen. *The Far Western Frontier.* New York: Harper and Row, 1956.

——— . *Western Expansion.* New York: Macmillan, 1962.

——— . *Soldier and Brave.* National Park Service Publication, 1963.

Blacks in the Western Movement. Washington, DC: Smithsonian Institution Press, 1975.

Blaine, James G. *Twenty Years of Congress,* 1861–1881. Norwich, CT, 1884.

Bledsoe, A.J. *Indian Wars of the Northwest.* Oakland, 1956.

Block, Eugene B. *Great Stagecoach Robbers of the West.* New York, 1962.

Boatright, Mody B. *Folk Laughter on the Frontier.* New York: Macmillan and Co., 1949.

Boniface, Lt. J.J. *The Cavalry Horse and His Pack.* (Reprint) Minneapolis, 1977.

Bonney, Orrin H. and Lorraine. *Battle Drums and Geysers.* Chicago: Swallow Press, 1970.

Bookwalter, Thomas E. *Honor Tarnished.* West Carrollton, Ohio: Littlehorn Press, 1979.

Botkin, B.A. (ed.), *A Treasury of Western Folklore.* New York: Crown Publishers, Inc., 1951.

Bourke, John G. *On the Border with Crook.* New York: Charles Scribner's Sons, 1891.

——— . *An Apache Campaign in the Sierra Madre.* New York: Charles Scribner's Sons, 1958.

——— . *On the Border with General Crook.* Palo Alto, CA: Columbus, 1950.

——— . "General Crook in the Indian Country," *Century Magazine,* March, 1891.

Boyes, W. *No Custer Survivors, or the Unveiling of Frank Finkel.* Rockville, 1977.

Bradley, Lt. James. *March of the Montana Column.* Norman: University of Oklahoma Press, 1961.

Bradon, William B. *The Last Americans.* New York: McGraw Hill, 1974.

Brady, Cyrus Townsend. *Indian Fights and Fighters, 1866–1876.* New York: McClure, Phillips, & Co., 1904. Also published New York: Doubleday, Page & Co., 1904.

——— . *Britton of the Seventh.* New York, 1914.

——— . *Northwestern Fights and Fighters.* Lincoln: University of Nebraska Press, 1979.

——— . *The Patriots.* New York, 1906.

Branch, Edward Douglas. *Westward, The Romance of the American Frontier.* Cooper Square, 1969.

Breihan, Carl W. *Badmen of the Frontier Days.* New York: McBride Co., 1957.

——— . *Great Lawmen of the West.* New York: Bonanza.

Breihan, Carl W. with Rosamond, Charles A. *The Bandit Belle.* Seattle: Superior Publications, 1957.

Brent, Lynton Wright. *The Bird Cage.* Philadelphia, 1945.

Brill, Charles. *Conquest of the Southern Plains.* Oklahoma City, 1938.

Brininstool, E.C. *Fighting Red Cloud's Warriors.* Columbus: The Hunter-Trader-Trapper Co., 1926.

——— . *Fighting Indian Warriors.* Harrisburg, 1953. Also printed in New York, 1958.

——— . *Trail Dust of a Maverick.* Los Angeles, 1921.

——— . *Troopers with Custer.* Harrisburg: Stackpole & Co., 1952.

Brooks, Elbridge, S. *The Master of the Strong Hearts.* New York, 1898.

Brown, Barron. *Comanche.* Kansas City: Burton Publishing Co., 1935.

Brown, Dee. *Bury My Heart at Wounded Knee.* New York: Holt, Rinehart, 1971.

——— . *The Westerners.* New York, 1974.

Brown, Jesse, and Willard, A.M. *The Black Hills Trails.* Rapid City: Ayer Co. Publications, 1975 (reprint).

Brown, Mark H. *The Plainsmen of the Yellowstone.* Lincoln: University of Nebraska Press (Bison), 1969.

Brown, Mark H., and Felton, W.R. *Before Barbed Wire.* Bramhall House, 1956.

Brown, Norman D. (ed.), *One of Cleburne's Command.* Austin, 1980.

Brown, William S. *Annals of Modoc.* Oakland, 1951.

Brownlee, Claudia J. *Colonel Joe, the Last of the Rough Riders.* New York, 1977.

Buecker, Thomas R. (ed.), "A Surgeon at the Little Bighorn," *Montana Magazine of Western History,* Autumn, 1982.

Buel, James W. *Heroes of the Plains.* Philadelphia: West Philadelphia Publishing Co., 1891.

Burbank, E.A. (as told to Ernest Royce) *Burbank among the Indians.* Caldwell: The Caxton Printers, 1944.

Burch, J.P. *A True Story of Charles W. Quantrell and His Guerrilla Band.* Vega, TX, 1923.

Burke, John. *Buffalo Bill: The Noblest Whiteskin.* New York: Putnam, 1973.

Burlend, Rebecca and Burlend, Edward. *A True Picture of Emigration.* New Jersey: Citadel Press, 1968.

Burlingame, Roger. *March of the Iron Men.* New York: Scribner's Sons, 1938.

Burns, Walter Nobel. *The Saga of Billy the Kid.* New York: Doubleday, 1952.

———. *Tombstone.* New York: Doubleday, 1929.

Burrough, John Rolfe. *Steamboat in the Rockies.* Ft. Collins: Old Army Press, 1974.

Callaway, Lew L. *Montana's Righteous Hangmen.* Norman: University of Oklahoma Press, 1982.

Canfield, Chauncey L. *The Diary of a Forty-Niner.* New York: Morgan Sheppard Co., 1906.

Cannon, Miles. *Toward the Setting Sun.* Portland, 1953.

Capps, Benjamin. *The Warren Wagontrain Raid.* New York, 1974.

Carey, A Meryn. *American Firearms Makers.* New York: Thomas Y. Crowell Co., 1953.

Carlisle, Bill. *Bill Carlisle, One Bandit.* Pasadena, 1946.

Carman, W.Y. *A History of Firearms from Earliest Times to 1914.* London, Routledge and Kegan Paul, Ltd., 1955.

Carriker, Robert C. and Eleanor R. *An Army Wife on the Frontier.* Salt Lake City, 1975.

Carrington, Margaret Irwin. *Absaraka, Home of the Crows.* New York: Lippincott, 1878.

Carroll, John M. (ed.), *Camp Talk.* Mattituck, New York: J.M. Carroll, Co., 1983.

———. *Cavalry Scraps.* Bryan, TX: Guidon Press, 1979.

———. *Custer in Periodicals.* Ft. Collins: Old Army Press, 1975.

———. *Custer in Texas.* New York: Sol Lewis Books, 1975.

———. *Eggenhofer: The Pulp Years.* Ft. Collins: Old Army Press, 1975.

———. *General Custer and the Battle of the Washita, The Federal View.* Bryan, TX: Guidon Press, 1978.

———. *Roll Call on the Little Big Horn.* Ft. Collins: Old Army Press, 1974.

———. *The Benteen-Goldin Letters on Custer and His Last Battle.* New York: Liveright, 1974.

———. *The Black Military Experience in the American West.* New York: Liveright, 1974.

———. *The Grand Duke Alexis in the United States of America.* New York: Interland Publishing, 1972.

———. *The Papers of the Order of Indian Wars.* Fort Collins: Old Army Press, 1975.

———. *The Two Battles of the Little Big Horn.* New York: Liveright, 1974.

———. *Another Libbie Custer Gallimaufry!* Bryan, Texas, 1978.

———. *A Very Real Salagundi: or Look What I Found This Summer.* Bryan, Texas. November, 1980.

———. *Broadside.* Bryan, Texas.

———. *Custer: From the Civil War to the Little Big Horn.* Bryan, Texas. February, 1981.

———. *Custer in Periodicals: Corrections and Additions.* New Brunswick. August, 1977.

———. *Custer in Periodicals: Corrections and Additions.* No. 2. Bryan, Texas. June, 1978.

———. *Custer in Periodicals: Corrections and Additions.* No. 3. Bryan, Texas. September, 1979.

———. *Custer in Periodicals: Corrections and Additions.* No. 4. Bryan, Texas. April, 1980.

———. *Custer in Periodicals: Corrections and Additions.* No. 5. Bryan, Texas. July, 1981.

_____. *Custer's Cavalry Occupation of Hempstead and Austin, Texas,* and *The History of Custer's Headquarters Building.* Glendale, 1983.

_____. *Custer's Horseshoe.* New Brunswick, NJ, 1977.

_____. *Fort Custer and a Bonus.* Bryan, Texas. June, 1983.

_____. *Four on Custer by Carroll.* New Brunswick, 1976.

_____. *The Frank L. Anders and the R.J. Cartwright Correspondence.* Vol. I-III. Bryan, Texas, 1982.

_____. *General Custer and New Rumley, Ohio.* Bryan, Texas. July, 1978.

_____. *A Graphologist Looks at Custer and Some of His Friends (And a Few Enemies).* Vol. I-III. Bryan, Texas, 1978.

_____. *In Memory of General Edward Settle Godfrey.* Bryan, Texas. September, 1978.

_____. *Letters!* Bryan, Texas, 1978.

_____. *A Libbie Custer Gallimaufry!* Bryan, Texas. January, 1978.

_____. *The Lieutenant Maguire Maps.* Bryan, Texas.

_____. *Major Marcus Reno.* New Brunswick, NJ. April, 1977.

_____. *Nomad: Custer in the Turf, Field, and Farm.* Bryan, Texas. June, 1978.

_____. *Order of Indian Wars, The Unpublished Papers of.* Vol. I-X. New Brunswick, NJ, 1978.

_____. *A Potpourri of Custeriana.* Bryan, Texas.

_____. *Readings from Hunter-Trader-Trapper Magazine.* Vol. I-II. Bryan, Texas, 1978.

_____. *A Seventh Cavalry Scrapbook.* No. 1-13. Bryan, Texas. March, 1978-December, 1979.

_____. *The Battle of the Rosebud Plus Three.* Bryan, Texas. October, 1978.

_____. *The D.F. Barry Correspondence at the Custer Battlefield.* Bryan, Texas. April, 1980.

_____. *The Fred Dustin and Earl K. Brigham Letters.* Book I-II. Bryan, Texas.

_____. *The Gibson and Edgerly Narratives.* Bryan, Texas, 1978.

_____. *The Indian Wars Campaign Medal: Its History and Recipients.* Bryan, Texas. April, 1979.

_____. *The Lieutenant E.A. Garlington Narrative.* Bryan, Texas. February, 1978.

_____. *The Medal of Honor: Its History and Recipients for the Indian Wars.* Bryan, Texas, 1979.

_____. *The Sand Creek Massacre.*

_____. *The Seventh Cavalry Winners of the Medal of Honor: The Indian Wars.* Bryan, Texas. June, 1978.

_____. *The Sitting Bull Fraud.* Bryan, Texas. October, 1978.

_____. *The Sunshine Magazine Articles.* Bryan, Texas. June, 1979.

_____. *Three Hits and a Miss.* Bryan, Texas. January, 1981.

_____. *To Set the Record Straight: The Real Story of Wounded Knee.* Bryan, Texas. October, 1980.

_____. *Transport of Sick and Wounded by Pack Animals, Surgeon General's Report No. 9.* Bryan, Texas. November, 1979.

_____. *The Writings of Selah Reeve Hobbie Tompkins, The Seventh Cavalry's Other Colonel.* Bryan, Texas. August, 1982.

_____. *Varnum—The Last of Custer's Lieutenants.* Bryan, Texas. June, 1980.

_____. *Von Schmidt: The Complete Illustrator.* Fort Collins, 1974.

_____. *With the Seventh Cavalry in 1876.* Bryan, Texas. August, 1980.

_____. *General George Armstrong Custer Historical Calendar, 1981 and 1982.*

Carson, Christopher. *Kit Carson's Own Story of His Life (or Kit Carson's Autobiography).* Chicago: R.R. Donnelly & Sons Co., 1935.

Carter, Robert Goldthwaite. *Four Brothers in Blue.* Austin, Texas, 1978.

_____. *The Old Sergeant's Story.* Reprint of 1926 Index. Bryan, Texas: J.M. Carroll & Co., 1982.

Cary, Lucian. *The Colt Gun Book.* New York: Arco Publishing Co., Inc., 1957.

Catlin, George. *Catlin's North American Indian Portfolio, Hunting Scenes, and Amusements of the Rocky Mountains and Prairies of America.* Chicago: Swallow Press, 1970.

Century Magazine. Vol. 41. 1890-91.

Chandler, Melbourne C. *Of Garry Owen in Glory*. Phoenix: Exposition, 1960.

Chapman, Arthur. *Out Where the West Begins*. Boston, 1917.

————. *The Pony Express*. New York: The A.L. Burt Co., 1932.

Chidsey, Donald Barr. *The California Gold Rush*. Crown, 1968.

Chittenden, Hiram Martin. *The American Fur Trade of the Far West*. Three Volumes. New York: F.P. Harper, 1902.

Clark, Donald Henderson. *The Autobiography of Frank Tarbeaux as told to Donald Henderson Clark*. New York, 1930.

"Clay Tobacco Pipes," *Annals of Wyoming*, October, 1961.

Cleland, Robert Glass. *This Reckless Breed of Men*. New York: Alfred A. Knopf, 1950.

Coates, Robert M. *The Outlaw Years*. New York, 1930.

Coblentz, Stanton A. *Villains and Vigilantes*. New York, 1936.

Coe, Urling C. *Frontier Doctor*. New York, 1936.

Connelley, William E. *Wild Bill and His Era*. New York: Press of the Pioneers, 1933.

Connor, Seymour V. and Faulk, Odie B. *North America Divided: The Mexican War, 1846–1848*. New York: Oxford University Press, 1971.

Cook, Charles W., Folsom, David E., and Peterson, William. *The Valley of the Upper Yellowstone*. Norman: University of Oklahoma Press, 1965.

Cook, James H. *Fifty Years on the Frontier*. Norman: University of Oklahoma Press, 1957.

Cox, James. *My Native Land*. St. Louis, 1895.

Crawford, L.F. *Rekindling Camp Fires*. Bismarck, 1926.

Crane, John and Kieley, James F. *West Point: The Key to America*. New York: McGraw Hill, 1947.

Croy, Homer. *Trigger Marshal: The Story of Chris Madsen*. New York: Duell, Sloan & Peirce, 1958.

Cullimore, Clarence. *Old Adobes of Forgotten Fort Tejon*. Bakersfield, 1949.

Cunningham, Eugene. *Triggernometry, A Gallery of Gunfighters*. Caldwell: The Caxton Printers, Ltd., 1982.

Cushman, Dan. *The Great North Trail*. New York, 1966.

Custer, Elizabeth B. *Boots and Saddles: or, Life in Dakota with General Custer*. New York: Harper & Bros., 1885.

————. *Tenting on the Plains: General Custer in Kansas and Texas*. New York: Webster & Co., 1887.

————. *Following the Guidon*. New York: Harper & Bros., 1890.

————. *The Kid*. Monroe, Michigan: Monroe Library, 1978.

Custer, G.A. *My Life on the Plains*. New York: Sheldon and Co., 1874.

————. *My Life on the Plains, or Personal Experiences with the Indians*. Chicago: Lakeside, 1952.

————. *A Report of the Expedition to the Black Hills Under the Command of Bvt. Major Gen. George Custer*. 43rd Congress, Second Session.

Custer, Milo. *Custer Genealogies*. Bloomington, IL, 1944.

Dale, Edward Everett. *The Range Cattle Industry*. Norman: University of Oklahoma Press, 1930.

Dale, Harrison C. *The Ashley-Smith Explorations and the Discovery of a Central Route to the Pacific*. Cleveland: Arthur Clark Co., 1918.

Dallas, David. *Comanche Lives Again*. Manhattan, KS: Centennial Publications, 1954.

Dane, G. Ezra and Dane, Beatrice J. *Ghost Town*. New York: Alfred A. Knopf, 1941.

Danker, Donald F. (ed.), *Man of the Plains*. Lincoln: University of Nebraska, 1961.

Davidson, Levette J. and Blake, Forrester (ed.), *Rocky Mountain Tales*. Norman: University of Oklahoma Press, 1947.

Davidson, Marshall B. *Life in America*. Boston: Houghton Mifflin, 1974.

Davis, Britton. *The Truth About Geronimo*. New Haven: Yale University Press, 1929.

Davis, Richard Harding. *The West From a Car Window*. New York, 1894.

De Barthe, Joe. *Life and Adventures of Frank Grouard.* St. Joseph, MO: Combe Printing Co., 1894.

Debo, Angie. *A History of the Indians of the United States.* Norman: University of Oklahoma Press, 1970.

De Lorenzo, Lois M. *Gold Fever and the Art of Panning and Sluicing.* ATR Enterprises, 1970.

De Trobriand, Philippe. *Army Life in Dakota.* Lakeside, Chicago, 1941.

DeVoto, Bernard. *Across the Wide Missouri.* Cambridge: Houghton Mifflin Co., 1947.

Dick, Everett. *Tales of the Frontier.* Lincoln: University of Nebraska Press (Bison), 1963.

Dillon, Richard. *North American Indian Wars.* New York: Western Tanager, 1981.

Dillon, Richard H. (ed.) *The Gila Trail.* 2nd ed. Norman: University of Oklahoma Press, 1960.

Dimsdale, Thomas J. *The Vigilantes of Montana.* 2nd ed. Norman: University of Oklahoma Press, 1953.

Dippie, Brian H. *Nomad: George A. Custer in Turf, Field and Farm.* Austin: University of Texas Press, 1980.

Dippie, Brian and Carroll, John M. *Bards of the Little Big Horn.* Bryan, TX: John Carroll, 1978.

Dobie, J. Frank. *Apache Gold and Yaqui Silver.* Boston: Little, Brown, and Co., 1939.

Donaldson, Thomas. *The George Catlin Indian Gallery with Memoirs and Statistics.* Washington, 1887.

Donnelle, A.J. *Cyclorama of Custer's Last Battle.* New York: Argonaut Press, 1966.

Doubleday, Russell. *Cattle Ranch to College.* New York, 1936.

Dowd, James Patrick. *Custer Lives.* Fairfield: Ye Galleon, 1982.

Downey, Fairfax. *Indian Fighting Army.* New York: Chas. Scribners. 1941.

———. *Indian Wars of the U.S. Army (1776-1865).* New York: Doubleday, 1963.

Drago, Harry Sinclair. *Road to Empire.* New York: Dodd Meade, 1968.

———. *Great American Cattle Trails.* New York: Dodd Meade, 1965.

Driggs, Howard R. *Westward America.* New York: Putnam's, 1942.

DuBois, Charles G. *Kick the Dead Lion.* Billings: Reporter Printing and Supply Co., 1954.

Duffas, R.L. *The Santa Fe Trail.* New York: Longmans, Green & Co., 1930.

DuFour, Charles L. *Ten Flags in the Wind.* New York: Harper & Row, 1967.

Du Mont, John S. *Custer Battle Guns.* Fort Collins: Old Army Press, 1974.

———. *Firearms in Custer Battle.* Harrisburg: Stackpole Co., 1953.

Dunlay, Thomas W. *Wolves for the Blue Soldiers.* Lincoln: University of Nebraska Press, 1982.

Dunlop, Richard. *Great Trails of the West.* Nashville: Abingdon Press, 1971.

Dunn, J.P., Jr. *Massacres of the Mountains.* New York: Harper & Brothers, 1886.

Dustin, Fred. *Echoes from the Little Big Horn Fight.* Saginaw, MI: Upton Press, 1988 (reprint of 1939 edition).

———. *The Custer Tragedy.* Ann Arbor, MI: Upton Press, 1965 (reprinted 1988 in two volumes).

Dykestra, Robert. *The Cattle Towns.* New York: Alfred A. Knopf, 1968.

Eastman, Edwin. *Seven and Nine Years Among the Comanches and Apaches.* Jersey City, 1874.

Eastman, Elaine Goodale. *Sister to the Sioux.* Lincoln: University of Nebraska Press, 1978.

Easton, Robert. *Max Brand, the Big Westerner.* Norman: University of Oklahoma Press, 1970.

Ege, Robert J. *After the Little Big Horn.* MT: Crow Agency, 1977.

———. *Curse Not His Curls.* LBH Battle.

———. *Settling the Dust.* Chinook, MT: Chinook Opinion, 1968 (also printed by Werner Publications, 1981).

———. *Strike Them Hard.* Bellevue, NB: Old Army Press, 1970.

Eggenhofer, Nick. *Wagons, Mules and Men.* New York: Hastings House, 1961.

El Comancho. *The Old Timer's Tale.* Chicago, 1929.

Ellsworth, Clarence. "Bows and Arrows," Southwest Museum Leaflet #24, Highland Park, Los Angeles, CA, 1950.

Elman, Robert. *Badman of the West.* Ridge Press/Bound Books, 1974.

English Westerner's Brand Book. *George Armstrong Custer.* England, 1958.

Erlanson, Charles B. *Battle of the Butte.* Sheridan, 1963.

Fahey, John. *The Flathead Indians.* Norman: University of Oklahoma Press, 1974.

Faulk, Odie B. *The Geronimo Campaign.* New York: Oxford University Press, 1969.

Favour, Alpheus. *Old Bill Williams, Mountain Man.* Chapel Hill: University of North Carolina Press, 1936.

Fehrenbach, T.R. *Comanches.* New York: Alfred A. Knopf, 1974.

Fenn, Forrest. *The Beat of the Drum and the Whoop of the Dance.* Santa Fe: Feun Publishing Co., 1983.

Ferris, Fred G. (ed.) *Prospector, Cowhand, and Sodbuster.* The National Survey of Historic Sites and Buildings. U.S. National Park Service, 1967.

————. (ed.) *Soldier and Brave.* The National Survey of Historic Sites and Buildings. National Park Service, Department of the Interior, 1971.

Finerty, John F. *Warpath and Bivouax.* Chicago, 1890.

Finley, James B. *Pioneer Life in the West.* Cincinnati, 1853.

Fiske, Frank B. *The Taming of the Sioux.* Bismarck, 1917.

Fladerman's Guide to Antique American Firearms. 3rd ed. Northfield, IL: DBJ Books.

Floyd, Dale. *Action with Indians.* Fort Collins: Old Army Press, 1979.

Foreman, Grant. *Indian Removal.* Norman: University of Oklahoma Press, 1972.

Fort Laramie. Brochure of the National Park Service. Washington, D.C.: Government Printing, 1942.

Fowler, Harlan D. *Camels to California.* CA: Stanford University Press, 1972.

Frackelton, Will and Seely, Herman Gastrell. *Sagebrush Dentist.* Chicago, 1941.

Frank, Maurice. *Photographer On An Army Mule.* Norman: University of Oklahoma Press, 1965.

Friswold, Carroll. *The Grattan Massacre, 1854.* CA: Glendale Press, 1983.

Frost, Lawrence A. *Custer Slept Here.* Monroe, MI: Monroe Library, 1974.

————. *With Custer in '74.* Provo, UT: Brigham Young University Press, 1979.

————. *Some Observations of the Yellowstone Expedition of 1873.* Vol. 6 of the Hidden Springs of Custeriana Series. Glendale: Arthur Clark, 1981.

————. *The Custer Album.* Seattle: Superior Publishing, 1964.

Ganoe, W.A. *History of the U.S. Army.* Ashton, MD: Eric Lundberg, 1964.

Gard, Wayne. *Rawhide Texas.* Norman: University of Oklahoma Press, 1965.

————. *The Chisholm Trail.* Norman: University of Oklahoma Press, 1954.

Gardner, Dorothy. *The Great Betrayal.* Garden City, 1949.

Garst, Shannon. *Custer, Fighter of the Plains.* New York, 1960.

Garstin, Crosbie. *Vagabond Verses.* London, 1917.

Geological Survey Bulletin 822-A, Washington, D.C., 1930.

Getlein, Frank. *The Lure of the Great West.* Country Beautiful, 1973.

Ghent, W.J. *The Road to Oregon.* New York: Tudor Publishing Co., 1934.

Glass, Maj. E.L.N. *The History of the Tenth Cavalry 1822-1921.* Ft. Collins: Old Army Press, 1972.

Glasscock, C.B. *The Big Bonanza.* Indianapolis, 1931.

————. *The War of the Copperkings.* New York, 1935.

Goble, Paul and Goble, Dorothy. *Red Hawk's Account of Custer's Last Battle.* New York: Pantheon Books, 1969.

Godfrey, Lt. E.S. *Field Diary of Lt. Edward Settle Godfrey.* Portland: Champoeg Press, 1957.

————. "Custer's Last Stand," *Century Magazine,* 1892.

Goetzmnn, William H. *Army Exploration in the American West, 1803-63.* New Haven, CT: Yale University Press, 1959.

Goodman, David M. *A Western Panorama, 1849-75.* Glendale, 1966.

Graham, W.A. *The Custer Myth.* Stackpole, 1957.

Grant, U.S. *Personal Memoirs of U.S. Grant, Volumes I and II.* New York, 1885.

Gray Wolf, Peter. *Gray Wolf Stories, Indian Mystery Tales of Coyote Animals and Men.* Caldwell, ID: The Caxton Printers, Ltd., 1943.

Greene, Jerome A. *Slim Buttes, 1876.* Norman: University of Oklahoma Press, 1982.

Greever, William S. *The Bonanza West.* Norman: University of Oklahoma Press, 1963.

Gregg, Josiah. *Commerce of the Prairies.* New York: H.G. Langley, 1844.

Grinnell, George Bird. *Fighting Cheyennes.* New York: Charles Scribners, 1915.

————. *Jack in the Rockies.* New York, 1904.

————. *Jack the Young Canoeman.* New York, 1906.

————. *Jack the Young Cowboy.* New York, 1913.

————. *Jack the Young Explorer.* New York, 1908.

————. *Jack the Young Ranchman.* New York, 1899.

————. *Jack the Young Trapper.* New York, 1907.

Griswold, Wesley S. *A Work of Giants.* New York: McGraw-Hill, 1962.

Gulick, Bill. *Chief Joseph Country, Land of the Nez Perce.* Caldwell, ID: The Caxton Printers, Ltd., 1981.

Hafen, Ann W. *Power River Campaigns and Sawyers Expeditions of 1865.* Glendale, CA: Upton Press, 1961.

Hafen, LeRoy R. *The Overland Mail, 1849–1869.* Cleveland: The Arthur H. Clark Co., 1926.

Haines, William Wister. *The Winter War.* Boston, 1961.

Haley, J. Evetts. *Charles Goodnight, Cowman & Plainsman.* Boston: Houghton & Mifflin Co., 1936.

Haley, James L. *The Buffalo War: This History of the Red River Uprising of 1874.* Norman: University of Oklahoma Press, 1985.

Hamilton, W.T. *My Sixty Years on the Plains.* Columbus: Forest and Stream, 1905.

Hammer, Kenneth (ed.) *Custer in '76.* Provo, UT: Brigham Young University Press, 1976.

Hammer, Kenneth M. *The Glory March.* Mono #7. Monroe, MI: Monroe Library, 1980.

Hanson, Joseph Mills. *The Conquest of the Missouri.* Chicago: Murray Books, 1946.

Hardin, John Wesley. *The Life of John Wesley Hardin.* Norman: University of Oklahoma Press, 1961.

Hart, Col. Herbert M. *Tour of the Old Western Forts.* Boulder: Pruett, 1981.

————. *Tour Guide to Old Forts of Montana, Wyoming, North and South Dakota.* Boulder: Pruett, 1980.

————. *Forts of New Mexico, Arizona, Nevada, Utah and Colorado.* Superior Publishing, 1963.

————. *Forts of Oregon, Idaho, Washington & California.* Superior Publishing, 1963.

————. *Forts of Texas, Kansas, Nebraska & Oklahoma.* Superior Publishing, 1963.

Hart, Jeff. *Montana Native Plants and Early Peoples.* Helena, 1976.

Hart, William S. *A Lighter of Flames.* New York, 1923.

————. *My Life East & West.* New York, 1929.

Hart, William S. and Hart, Mary E. *And All Points West!* Binghampton, 1940.

Havighurst, Walter. *Wilderness for Sale.* New York: Hastings House, 1956.

————. *Annie Oakley of the Wild West.* New York: Macmillan Co., 1954.

Hawgood, John A. *America's Western Frontiers.* New York: Alfred A. Knopf, 1967.

Haynes, F. Jay. *Fifty Views.* Helena, 1981.

Hebard, Grace and Brininstool, E.A. *The Bozeman Trail.* Cleveland, 1922.

Hedren, Paul L. *First Scalp for Custer.* Glendale, CA: Arthur H. Clark, 1980.

————. *King on Custer.* Glendale, CA: Arthur H. Clark, 1983.

Heikell, Iris White. *The Wind-Breaker.* New York, 1980.

Heitman, Francis B. *Historical Register and Dictionary of the United States Army.* Washington, D.C.: Government Printing Office, 1903.

Henry, Will. *No Survivors.* New York, 1960.

Heski, Thomas M. *The Little Shadow Catchers.* Seattle: Superior Publishing Co., 1978.

Hibben, Paxton. "The Story of a Soldier's Life," *The Mentor,* September, 1928.

Hilger, Sr. Mary Ione, O.S.B. *The First Sioux Nun.* Milwaukee, 1963.

Hine, Robert V. *The American West.* Boston: Little, Brown, 1973.

Hofstadter, Richard, Miller, William, and Aaron, Daniel. *The American Republic.* Englewood Cliffs, NJ: Prentice-Hall, 1970.

Holfing, Charles K. *Custer and the Little Big Horn.* Detroit, 1986.

Holbrook, Stewart H. *The Story of the American Railroad.* New York: Crown, 1947.

Holley, Frances Chamberlain. *Once Their Home or Our Legacy from the Dakotahs.* Chicago, 1892.

Hollon, W. Eugene. *The Southwest, Old and New.* New York: Alfred A. Knopf, 1961.

Holloway, W.L. *Wild Life on the Plains and Horrors of Indian Warfare.* St. Louis, 1891.

Holmes, Floyd J. *Indian Fights on the Texas Frontier.* Ft. Worth, 1927.

Holmes, Louis A. *Fort McPherson, Nebraska.* Lincoln, 1963.

Horan, James D. *The Great American West.* New York: Bonanza, 1959.

Horgan, Paul. *A Distant Trumpet.* New York, 1960.

Horn, W. Donald. *Skinned.* Short Hills, 1960.

————. *Witnesses for the Defense.* West Orange, NJ: Midland Press, 1981.

Hosmer, Allen J. *A Trip to the States.* MT: Montana State University, 1982.

House, Julius T. *John J. Neihardt, Man and Poet.* Wayne, 1920.

How, Elvon. L. *Rocky Mountain Empire.* New York, 1959.

Howard, Joseph Kinsey. *Strange Empire: A Narrative of the Northwest.* New York, 1952.

Howard, Robert W. *This is the West.* New American Library, 1957.

Hulbert, Arthur B. *Forty-Niners, A Chronicle of the California Trail.* Boston: Little, Brown and Co., 1949.

Humphrey, Seth K. *The Indian Dispossessed.* Boston, 1906.

Hunt, F. Frazier. *The Life of General Custer.* Monroe, MI: Monroe Library, 1979.

Hunter, Louis Clare and Hunter, B.J. *Steamboats on the Western Rivers.* Octagon, 1969.

Hunter, Robbins. *The Judge Rode a Sorrel Horse.* New York, 1950.

Huntington, Bill. *They were Good Men and Salty Cusses.* Billings, 1952.

Huntley, Chet. *The Generous Years.* New York, 1968.

Hutchins, James. *Boots and Saddles at the Little Big Horn.* Fort Collins: Old Army Press, 1958.

————. *Man Made Mobile: Early Saddles of Western North America.* Washington, 1980.

Hutchins, J.S. *The Cavalry Campaign Outfit at the LBH.* Military Collector's History, Vol. VII, No. 4. Winter, 1956.

Hyde, George E. *Red Cloud's Folk.* Norman: University of Oklahoma Press, 1937.

————. *Spotted Tail's Folk.* Norman: University of Oklahoma Press, 1961.

Innis, Ben. *Bloody Knife, Custer's Favorite Scout.* Fort Collins: Old Army Press, 1973.

Jackson, Donald. *Custer's Gold.* New Haven: Yale University Press, 1966.

Jackson, Joseph Henry. *Bad Company.* New York: Harcourt, Brace, 1949.

James, General Thomas. *Three Years among the Indians.* Waterloo, IL, 1846.

Jenkins, Olaf P. (ed.) *The Mother Lode Company.* San Francisco: State of California, Division of Mines, 1948.

Jocelyn, Stephen Perry. *Mostly Alkali.* Caldwell, ID: The Caxton Printers, Ltd., 1953.

Johnson, Barry C. *Custer, Reno, Merrill and the Lauffer Case.* London, 1972.

Johnson, Barry C. (ed.) *Ho, For the Great West!* London, 1980.

————. *Merritt and the Indian Wars.* London, 1972.

Johnson, Barry C. and Taunton, Francis B. *Benteen's Ordeal and Custer's Field.* London, 1983.

Johnson, Charles H.L. *Famous Scouts.* Boston, 1911.

Johnson, Dorothy M. *Famous Lawmen of the Old West.* New York, 1963.

Johnson, E. Pauline. *Legends of Vancouver.* Toronto, 1922.

Johnson, Roy D. *The Custer March.* Edited by John M. Carroll. Bryan, TX. May, 1981.

Johnson, Roy P. *Sitting Bull: Hero or Monster?* Bismarck, 1962.

Johnson, W. Fletcher. *Life of Sitting Bull and History of Indian War of 1890–91.* Edgewood Publishing Co., 1891.

Jones, Evan. *Citadel in the Wilderness.* New York, 1966.

Jones, Everett L. and Durham, Philip. *The Negro Cowboys.* New York, 1965.

Josephy, Alvin M. Jr. *The Patriot Chiefs.* New York: The Viking Press, 1961.

Judd, A.N. *Campaigning Against the Sioux.* New York: Sol Lewis, 1973 (reprint).

Judson, Katherine B. *Montana—Land of the Shining Mountains.* Chicago, 1918.

Karolevitz, Robert F. *Doctors of the Old West.* Washington: Superior Publishing, 1967.

Karsner, David. *Silver Dollar.* New York: Civici-Friede, 1932.

Kaufman, Fred. *Custer Passed Our Way.* Aberdeen, SD: North Plains Press, 1971.

Kein, Robert C. *Sheridan's Troopers on the Borders.* Philadelphia, 1889.

Keleher, William A. *Violence in Lincoln County 1869-1881.* Albuquerque, 1957.

Kelsey, D.M. *History of Our Wild West.* Chicago, 1901.

_____ . *Pioneer Heroes and Daring Deeds.* Philadelphia: Scammell & Co., 1883.

Kidd, James H. *Historical Sketch of General Custer.* Monroe, MI: Monroe Library, 1978.

_____ . *Personal Recollections of a Cavalryman.* Grand Rapids, MI: Black Letter Press, 1969.

King, W. Kent. *Tombstones for Blue Coats.* Vol. 1-5. Marion Station, 1981.

Kirsch, Robert and Murphy, William S. *West of the West.* New York: E.P. Dutton, 1967.

Klose, Nelson. *A Concise Study Guide to the American Frontier.* Lincoln, 1964.

Knight, Oliver. *Life and Manners in the Frontier Army.* Norman: University of Oklahoma Press, 1978.

Koenig, Arthur. *Authentic History of the Indian Campaign which Culminated in Custer's Last Battle.* St. Louis.

Kolb, Ellsworth. *Through the Grand Canyon From Wyoming to Mexico.* New York, 1946.

Koller, Larry. *The Fireside Book of Guns.* New York: Simon and Schuster, 1959.

Koury, Michael J. *Arms for Texas.* Fort Collins: Old Army Press, 1973.

_____ . *Custer Centennial Observance 1976.* Fort Collins: Old Army Press, 1978.

_____ . *Diaries of the Little Big Horn.* Fort Collins: Old Army Press, 1968.

_____ *Military Posts of Montana.* Bellevue, NB: Old Army Press, 1970.

Kownslar, Allan O. *The Texans: Their Land and History.* American Heritage, 1972.

Krause, Herbert and Olsen, Gary D. *Prelude to Glory, 1874 Expedition to Black Hills.* Sioux Falls, 1976.

Kroeker, Marvin E. *Great Plains Command: William B. Hazen in the Frontier West.* Norman: University of Oklahoma Press, 1976.

Kuhlman, Charles. *Custer and the Gall Saga.* Billings, MT: Private Publishing, 1940.

_____ . *Did Custer Disobey Orders at the Battle of the Little Big Horn?* Harrisburg: Stackpole, 1957.

_____ . *Legend into History.* Harrisburg, 1951.

Lake, Stuart N. *Wyatt Earp, Frontier Marshal.* New York: Bantam Books. 1959.

Langford, N.P. *Vigilante Days and Ways.* Vols. 1 & 2. Boston, 1890.

Larson, Dorothy W. *As Shadows on the Hills.* Billings, 1978.

Lass, William E. *A History of Steamboating on the Upper Missouri.* Lincoln, 1962.

Latham, Frank. *The Transcontinental Railroad.* Watts, 1973.

Laut, Agnes C. *Pilgrims of Santa Fe.* New York, 1931.

Lavender, David S. *Bent's Fort.* Garden City, NY: Doubleday, 1954.

Lawrence, Elizabeth A. *Rodeo, An Anthropologist Looks at the Wild and the Tame.* Knoxville: University of Tennessee Press, 1983.

_____ . *His Very Silence Speaks—Comanche, the Horse Who Survived Custer's Last Stand.* Detroit: Wayne State University, 1989.

Lawson, W.B. *Jesse James, The Outlaw.* New York: Smith and Smith, 1901.

Leckie, William H. *The Buffalo Soldiers.* Norman: University of Oklahoma Press, 1967.

Lee, Jack H. *Powder River, Let Er Buck.* Boston, 1930.

Leech, Margaret. *Reveille in Washington 1860-1865.* New York, 1941.

Lewis, Alfred Henry. *Wolfville Days.* New York, 1902.

Libby, O.C. (ed.) *The Arikara Narrative of the Campaign Against the Hostile Dakotas, June, 1876.* Bismarck, 1920.

Liddic, Bruce R. (ed.) *I Buried Custer.* College Station, TX: Creative Publishing, 1979.

Linderman, Frank B. *American, The Story of a Great Indian.* New York, 1930.

———. *Plenty-Coups.* Bellevue, NB: University of Nebraska Press, 1962.

———. *Pretty-Shield.* Bellevue, NB: University of Nebraska Press, 1974.

Logan, John A. *The Volunteer Soldiers of America.* Chicago: R.S. Peale & Co. Publications, 1887.

Longstreet, Stephen. *War Cries on Horseback.* Garden City, NY: Doubleday, 1970.

Lord, Walter. *A Time to Stand.* New York: Harper & Row, 1961.

Lowe, Percival G. *Five Years a Dragoon ('49 to '54).* Kansas City, 1906.

Luce, Earl. *Paha Spa: Land of Gods.* New York, 1967.

Ludlow, William. *Report of a Reconnaissance of the Black Hills of Dakota made in the Summer of 1874.* Government Printing Office, 1875.

Luther, Tal. *Custer High Spots.* Fort Collins: Old Army Press, 1972.

McCaleb, Walter F. *The Conquest of the West.* New York, 1947.

McChristian, Douglas C. *An Army of Marksmen.* Fort Collins: Old Army Press, 1981.

McClernand, Edward J. with Carroll Friswold. *With the Indian and Buffalo in Montana 1870-78.* Glendale, CA: Upton Press, 1969.

McConkey, Harriet E. *Dakota War Hoop.* Chicago: Lakeside, 1965.

McCoy, Tim. *Tim McCoy Remembers the West.* New York, 1977.

McCracken, Harold (ed.) *Frederic Remington's Own West.* New York, 1960.

McCrieght, M.I. *Firewater and Forked Tongues.* Pasadena, 1947.

McDaniel, Ruel. *The Saga of Judge Roy Bean, The Law West of the Pecos.* Kingsport, 1936.

McLaughlin, James. *My Friend the Indian.* Boston, 1910.

McReynolds, Edwin C. *Missouri, A History of the Crossroads State.* Norman: University of Oklahoma Press, 1962.

MacDonald, A.B. *Hands Up.* Indianapolis, 1927.

Mails, Thomas E. *The Mystic Warriors of the Plains.* New York: Doubleday, 1972.

Maine, Schuster. *Lone Eagle—The White Sioux.* Albuquerque: University of New Mexico Press, 1956.

Manion, John S. *General Terry's Last Statement to Custer.* Monroe, MI: Monroe Library, 1983.

Manion, John S. et al. *Addressing the Custer Story.* Essays presented at the Little Big Horn Association Meeting, 1980.

Marcosson, Isaac F. *Anaconda.* New York, 1957.

Marquis, Thomas B. *A Warrior Who Fought Custer.* Minneapolis: Midwest Co., 1931.

———. *Cheyenne and Sioux: The Reminiscences of Four Indians and a White Soldier.* Stockton, 1973.

———. *Custer, Cavalry and Crows.* Fort Collins: Old Army Press, 1975.

———. *Custer on the Little Big Horn.* Lodi, 1978.

———. *Keep the Last Bullet for Yourself.* New York, 1976.

———. *Memoirs of a White Crow Indian.* New York, 1928.

———. *Rain-in-the-Face and Curly, the Crow.* Hardin, MT, 1934.

———. *She Watched Custer's Last Battle.* Hardin, MT, 1933.

———. *Sitting Bull and Gall, the Warrior.* Hardin, MT, 1934.

———. *Sketch Book of the Custer Battle.* Hardin, MT, 1933.

———. *Two Days after the Custer Battle.* Hardin, MT, 1935.

———. *Which Indian Killed Custer?* Hardin, MT, 1933.

———. *The Cheyennes of Montana.* Algonac, 1978.

Martin, Charles. *A Sketch of Sam Bass the Bandit.* Norman: University of Oklahoma Press, 1956.

Meeker, Ezra. *Ventures and Adventures of Ezra Meeker or Sixty Years of Frontier Life.* Seattle, 1909.

Meketa, Ray (ed.) *Marching with General Crook.* Douglas, 1983.

Meketa, Charles and Meketa, Jacqueline. *One Blanket and Ten Days Rations.* Globe, AZ: Southwest Parks & Monuments Association, 1980.

Melton, A.B. *Custer's Last Fight.* Mobeetie, TX, 1963.

Mercer, Asa Shinn. *The Banditti of the Plains.* Norman: University of Oklahoma Press, 1954.

Meredith, Roy. *Mr. Lincoln's General, U.S. Grant.* New York, 1959.

Merington, Marguerite E. *The Custer Story.* New York: Devin-Adair Co., 1950.

Miles, Gen. Nelson A. *Personal Recollections and Observations of General Nelson A. Miles.* Chicago/New York: Werner Co., 1896.

Miles, Nelson A. *Serving the Republic.* New York, 1911.

Miller, Don and Cohen, Stan. *Military and Trading Posts of Montana.* Missoula, 1978.

Miller, Max. *It Must Be the Climate.* New York, 1941.

Miller, Francis Trevelyan (ed.) *The Photographic History of the Civil War in Ten Volumes.* New York, 1911.

Milligan, Edward A. *Dakota Twilight: The Standing Rock Sioux 1874–1890.* New York, 1976.

Mills, Anson. *My Story.* Washington, D.C.: Press of Byron S. Adams, 1918.

Mills, Charles K. *Charles C. DeRudio.* Mattituck, 1983.

_____ . *Rosters of the 7th Cavalry During the Campaigns.* New York, 1984.

Milner, Joe E. and Milner, Earle R. *California Joe.* Caldwell, ID: The Caxton Printers, Ltd., 1935.

M.N.O. "Resume of the Fremont Expeditions," *Century Magazine,* March, 1891.

Monaghan, James. *Civil Wars on the Western Border.* Boston: Little, Brown, 1955.

Monaghan, James (ed.). *The Book of the American West.* New York: Bonanza, 1963.

Monaghan, Jay. *Last of the Bad Men.* Indianapolis, 1946.

_____ . *Custer, The Life of General George Armstrong Custer.* Boston: Little, Brown, & Co., 1959.

Moody, Ralph. *Stagecoach West.* Crowell, 1967.

Morehouse, Lee. "The Vanishing Race," *The Metropolitan Magazine,* June, 1906.

Morgan, Dale L. *Jedediah Smith and the Opening of the West.* Nebraska: University of Nebraska Press, 1964.

Morison, Samuel Eliot. *The Oxford History of the American People.* New York: Oxford University Press, 1965.

Mulford, Ami Frank. *Fighting Indians! In the Seventh United States Cavalry, Custer's Favorite Regiment.* Corning, NY: Paul Lindsley, 1878.

Muller, William G. *Twenty Fourth Infantry, Past and Present.* Fort Collins: Old Army Press, 1972.

Murray, Robert A. *Johnson County, 175 Years at the Foot of the Big Horn Mountains.* Buffalo, 1981.

_____ . *Military Posts in the Powder River Country of Wyoming, 1865–1894.* Lincoln: University of Nebraska Press, 1968.

_____ . *Military Posts of Wyoming.* Fort Collins: Old Army Press, 1974.

_____ . *The Army Moves West.* Fort Collins: Old Army Press, 1981.

_____ . *The Army on the Powder River.* Bellevue, NB: Old Army Press, 1969.

Myers, John. *Doc Holliday.* Boston/Toronto: Little, Brown & Co., 1955.

Myers, Sandra L. *Cavalry Wife, The Diary of Eveline M. Alexander, 1866–1867.* College Station: Texas A & M, 1977.

Nadeau, Remi A. *Fort Laramie and the Sioux Indians.* Englewood Cliffs, NJ: Prentice-Hall, 1967.

Naef, Weston J. and Wood, James N. *Era of Exploration.* New York: Metropolitan Museum of Art, 1975.

Nakivell, John H. *History of the Twenty-Fifth Regiment, United States Infantry, 1869–1926.* Fort Collins: Old Army Press, 1972.

Neihardt, John G. *Eagle Voice, An Authentic Tale of the Sioux Indians.* London, 1953.

Nelson, Bruce. *Land of the Dakotahs.* Minneapolis: University of Minnesota, 1946.

Nicols, Alice. *Bleeding Kansas.* New York, 1954.

Noyes, Alva J. *In the Land of the Chinook.* Helena, MT: State Publishing Co., 1917.

Nye, Elwood L. *Marching with Custer.* Glendale: Arthur H. Clark, 1964.

Nye, Wilbur Sturdevant. *Plains Indian Raiders.* Norman: University of Oklahoma Press, 1968.

_____. *Carbine and Lance.* Norman: University of Oklahoma Press, 1957.

O'Connor, Richard. *Bat Masterson.* Garden City, NY: Doubleday & Co., 1957.

Odell, Thomas E. *Mato Paha.* Spearfish, 1942.

Oglesby, Richard. *Manuel Lisa and the Opening of the Missouri Fur Trade.* Norman: University of Oklahoma Press, 1963.

O'Neal, Bill. *Encyclopedia of Western Gunfighters.* Norman: University of Oklahoma Press, 1979.

O'Neill, Charles. *Wild Train.* New York, 1956.

Orpen, Adela E. *Memories of the Old Emigrant Days in Kansas 1862–1865.* New York, 1928.

Ostrander, Alson B. *An Army Boy of the Sixties.* Yonkers-on-the-Hudson: Pioneer Life Series, 1924.

Paden, Irene D. *The Wake of the Prairie Schooner.* New York: Macmillan, 1943.

Paine, Albert Bigelow. *Captain Bill McDonal, Texas Ranger.* New York, 1909.

Palladina, O.B., S.J. *Indian and White in the Northwest.* Lancaster, 1922.

Parker, Watson. *Gold in the Black Hills.* Norman: University of Oklahoma Press, 1966.

Parkman, Francis. *The Oregon Trail.* New York: Grosset & Dunlap. 1927.

Parrish, Philip H. *Wagons West, 1843–1943.* Portland, 1943.

Parsons, John E. and Du Mont, John S. *Firearms in the Custer Battle.* Harrisburg, PA: Stackpole Co., 1953.

Paul, Rodman W. *Mining Frontiers in the Far West.* New Mexico: University of New Mexico Press, 1963.

Paxson, Frederic L. *History of the American Frontier: 1763–1893.* Boston: Houghton-Mifflin, 1924.

Peattle, Roderick (ed.) *The Black Hills.* New York, 1952.

Peterson, Harold L. *A History of Firearms.* New York: Charles Scribner's Sons, 1961.

Peterson, William John. *Steamboating on the Upper Mississippi.* Iowa State Historical Society, 1968.

Phillips, Roger F. and Klancher, D.J. *Arms and Accoutrements of the Mounted Police 1873–1973.* Bloomfield, Ontario, Canada: Museum Restoration Service, 1982.

Pohanka, Brian. *A Summer on the Plains, 1870.* New York, 1983.

Point, Nicholas. *Wilderness Kingdom.* New York: Holt, Rinehart & Winston, 1967.

Pound, Louise. *Nebraska Folklore.* Nebraska: University of Nebraska Press, 1959.

Prassel, Frank Richard. *The Western Peace Office.* Norman: University of Oklahoma Press, 1972.

Prebble, John. *The Buffalo Soldiers.* New York, 1959.

Preece, Harold. *Living Pioneers.* World Publishing Co., 1952.

Prucha, Francis P. *Army Life on the Western Frontier.* Norman: University of Oklahoma Press, 1953.

Randolph, Edmond. *Hell among the Yearlings.* New York, 1955.

Rascoe, Burton. *Belle Starr, The Bandit Queen.* New York: Random House, 1941.

Rawlings, Gerald. *The Pathfinders.* New York: Macmillan, 1964.

Raynolds, Bvt. Brig. Gen. W.F. *Report on the Exploration of the Yellowstone River.* Washington, D.C., 1868.

Reed, Bill. *The Last Bugle Call.* West Virginia: McClain Printing Co., 1977.

Reed, Marjorie. *The Colorful Butterfield Overland Stage.* Best-West Publications, 1966.

Reedstrom, Ernest Lisle. "Accoutrements in 1876," *Little Big Horn Associates.* Winter, 1969.

_____. "A Follow-Up on Harrison's 'Another Eye-Witness Account on D.H. Ridgeley, Trapper in the Sioux Country'," *Little Big Horn Associates.* Fall, 1969.

_____. "Black Powder," *Guns and Ammo,* 1974.

_____. *Bugles, Banners and War Bonnets.* Caldwell, ID: The Caxton Printers, Ltd., 1978. Second Printing: Bonanza, 1986.

_____. "California Joe," Research Review, *Little Big Horn Associates,* Summer, 1970.

_____. "California Joe," *True Frontier,* April, 1972.

_____. "Comeback of the Cavalry," *Western Horseman,* 1972.

_____. "Cowboy's Gear," *Far West Magazine,* 1980.

_____. "Custer: After the War," Research Review, *Little Big Horn Associates,* December, 1979.

_____. "Fort Ben Harrison," *Guns Magazine,* May, 1972.

_____. "General Miles' Secret Weapon," *True West,* August, 1988.

_____. "Guide to the Guns of the Gunfighters," *Guns and Ammo,* Annual, 1975.

_____. "Hancock Expedition (1867)," *Little Big Horn Associates.*

_____. "Hawken Rifles," *Guns Magazine,* Part 1: May, 1970; Part 2: June, 1970.

_____. "Jammed Carbines on the Little Big Horn," *Guns Magazine,* August, 1980.

_____. "John Dillinger—Bad Shooter, Bad Driver, Bad Guy!" *Guns Magazine,* September, 1979.

_____. "Military Accoutrements," *Guns Magazine,* Part 1: October, 1971; Part 2: December, 1971.

_____. "The Red Cravat," *Little Big Horn Associates,* Fall, 1969.

_____. "The 7th Prairie Dandies," Research Review, *Little Big Horn Associates,* Fall, 1970.

_____. "The 17 Day Hero," *Guns Magazine,* February, 1971.

_____. "Tales of Buffalo and the Frontier," *Guns Magazine,* August, 1973.

_____. "Those Short-Legged Soldier Boys," *Military Collectors Journal,* September, 1983.

_____. "The War Horse," Research Review, *Little Big Horn Associates,* Winter, 1970.

_____. *Historic Dress of the Old West.* Poole, Dorset, England: Blandford Press, 1987.

Remburg, John and Remburg, George. *Charley Reynolds.* Kansas City: H.M. Sender, 1931.

Remington, Frederic. "Horses of the Plains and a Scout with the Buffalo Soldiers," *The Century Magazine,* 1888–1889.

Reusswig, William. *Picture Report of the Custer Fight.* New York: Hastings House, 1967.

Richardson, Rupert Norval. *Texas: The Lone Star State.* Englewood Cliffs, NJ: Prentice-Hall, 1970.

Rickey, Don. *Forty Miles a Day on Beans and Hay.* Norman: University of Oklahoma Press, 1963.

Ridge, Martin and Billington, Ray Allen. *America's Frontier Story.* New York: Holt, Rinehart & Winston, 1969.

Riegel, Robert E. *The Story of the Western Railroads.* New York: Macmillan Co., 1926.

Riegel, Robert E. and Athearn, Robert G. *America Moves West.* New York: Holt, Rinehart & Winston, 1971.

Rister, Carl Coke. *Border Command: General Phil Sheridan in the West.* Norman: University of Oklahoma Press, 1944.

Roe, Frank Gilbert. *The North American Buffalo.* Toronto, Canada: University of Toronto Press, 1951.

Rosa, Joseph G. *The Gunfighter, Man or Myth?* Norman: University of Oklahoma Press, 1969.

Rowan, Richard W. *The Pinkertons: The Detective Dynasty that made History.* Boston: Little, Brown, & Co., 1931.

Russell, Carl P. *Firearms, Traps, and Tools of the Mountain Men.* New York: Alfred Knopf, 1967.

_____. *Guns on the Early Frontiers.* Berkeley and Los Angeles: University of California Press, 1957.

Russell, Don. *The Lives and Legends of Buffalo Bill.* Norman: University of Oklahoma Press, 1960.

_____. *Custer's Last.* Amon Carter Museum, 1968.

Ruth, Kent. *Great Day in the West.* Norman: University of Oklahoma Press, 1963.

Sabin, Edwin L. *On the Plains with Custer.* Philadelphia: J.B. Lippincott, 1913.

Samuel, Ray et al. *Tales of the Mississippi.* New York: Hastings House, 1955.

Sasuly, Richard. *Bookies and Bettors.* New York: Holt, Rinehart & Winston, 1982.

Schmitt, Martin F. and Brown, Dee. *The Settler's West.* New York, 1955.

Schneider, George A. *The Freeman Journal.* California: Presidio Press, 1977.

Seton, Ernest Thompson. *Lives of the Game Animals.* 4 volumes. Boston: Charles T. Branford Co., 1953.

Seymour, Flora. *The Story of the Red Man.* Books for Libraries, 1970.

Sharpe, Philip B. *The Rifle in America.* New York: Funk & Wagnals Company, 1947.

Smith, Grant H. *History of the Comstock Lode.* Reno: Nevada State Bureau of Mines, 1943.

Smith, Helena Huntington. *The War on Powder River.* New York: McGraw-Hill, 1966.

Sonnichsen, C.L. *The Mescalero Apaches.* Norman: University of Oklahoma Press, 1958.

————. *Roy Bean: Law West of the Pecos.* New York: Macmillan Co., 1943.

Spencer, Robert F. and Jennings, Jesse D. *The Native Americans.* New York: Harper & Row, 1965.

Sprague, Marshall. *Money Mountain: The Story of Cripple Creek Gold.* Boston: Little, Brown, & Co., 1853.

Still, Bayrd. *The West: Contemporary Records of America's Expansion Across the Continent, 1607–1890.* Capricorn Books, 1961.

————. *Urban America: A History with Documents.* Boston: Little, Brown, & Co., 1974.

Stuart, Robert. *The Discovery of the Oregon Trail. Robert Stuart's Narratives of His Overland Trip Eastward from Astoria in 1812–13.* Philip Ashton Rollins, Editor. New York: Charles Scribner's Sons, 1935.

Sumner, E.V. "Besieged by the Utes," *Century Magazine,* October, 1891.

Swartwoot, Annie Fern. *Life and Times of Annie Oakley 'Missie'.* Blandchester, Ohio: Brown Publishing, 1947.

Taylor, Edith W. *Money on the Hoof.* Fort Collins: Old Army Press, 1974.

Thwaites, Reuben Gold (ed.) *The Original Journals of Lewis and Clark.* New York: Dodd, Mead, 1904.

Tibbles, Thomas Henry. *Buckskin and Blanket Days.* Nebraska: University of Nebraska Press, 1957.

Tilden, Freeman. *Following the Frontier with F. Jay Haynes, Pioneer Photographer of the Old West.* New York: Alfred Knopf, 1964.

Turner, John Peter. *The North-West Mounted Police from 1873–1893.* 2 Volumes. Canada: Edmond Cloutier, Kings Printer & Controller, 1950.

Trails West. Washington, D.C.: National Geographic Society, 1979.

Twelfth Bienniel Report of the Board of Trustees of the State Historical Society of Idaho for the Years 1929–30, Boise, ID, 1930.

Urwin, Gregory. *The United States Cavalry: An Illustrated History.* (Illustrated by Ernest Lisle Reedstrom) Poole, Dorset, England: Blandford Press, 1983.

Utley, Robert M. *Frontiersmen in Blue.* New York: Macmillan, 1967.

————. *High Noon in Lincoln.* Albuquerque: University of New Mexico Press.

Van Name, Willard G. *American Wild Life.* New York: William H. Wise & Co., Inc., 1961.

Vestal, Stanley. *Warpath and Council Fire.* New York: Random House, 1948.

Waggoner, Madeline Sadler. *The Long Haul West.* New York: Putnam, 1958.

Wagner, Jack R. *Gold Mines of California.* Norwell-North Books, 1970.

Wahl, Paul and Toppel, Don. *The Gatling.* New York: Arco Publishing, 1965.

Walker, Henry Pickering. *The Wagonmasters.* Norman: University of Oklahoma Press, 1966.

"Warbonnets," *American Indian Magazine,* 1971.

Ward, Fay E. *The Cowboy at Work.* New York: Hastings House, 1976.

Washburn, Wilcomb. *The Indian in America.* New York: Harper & Row, 1975.

Waters, Frank. *The Earp Brothers of Tombstone.* New York: Clarkson N. Porter, Inc., 1960.

Watkins, T.H. *Gold and Silver in the West.* New York: American West Publishing Co., 1971.

Webb, Todd. *The Gold Rush Trail and the Road to Oregon.* New York: Doubleday, 1963.

Webb, Walter Prescott. *The Great Plains.* New York: Grosset & Dunlap. 1957.

Weems, John Edward. *To Conquer a Peace: The War Between the United States and Mexico.* New York: Doubleday, 1974.

————. *Dream of Empire.* New York: Simon & Schuster, 1971.

Wellman, Paul I. *Glory, God and Gold.* New York: Doubleday, 1954.

_____. *The Indian Wars of the West.* New York: Doubleday, 1954. Previously published as *Death on Horseback,* 1947, combining *Death on the Prairie,* 1934, and *Death in the Desert,* 1935.

Welsch, Roger L. *Sod Walls.* Purcells, Inc., 1968.

Wild Animals of North America. Washington, D.C.: National Geographic Society, 1960.

Winther, Oscar. *The Transportation Frontier: Trans-Mississippi West, 1865–1890.* New Mexico: University of New Mexico Press, 1964.

Winther, Oscar Osburn. *The Old Oregon Country: A History of Frontier Trade, Transportation and Travel.* Stanford, CA: Stanford University Press, 1945.

Woestemeyer, Ina Faye and Gambrill, J. Montgomery. *The Westward Movement.* Appleton-Century, 1939.

Woods, Daniel B. *Sixteen Months at the Gold Diggings.* New York: Harper & Brothers, 1852.

Young, Otis E., Jr. *Western Mining.* Norman: University of Oklahoma Press, 1970.

Young, Stanley P. and Jackson, H.H.T. *The Clever Coyote.* Harrisburg, PA: Stackpole Co., 1951.

INDEX